Human Leadership for Humane Technology

"Cornelia's 'Human Leadership for Humane Technology' masterfully illustrates what conscious tech leadership is. It's an essential read for anyone committed to shaping a sustainable future, ensuring technology enhances, rather than detracts from, our humanity."

—Hamilton Mann, *Group Vice President Digital Marketing and Digital Transformation at Thales, Thinkers50 Radar 2024, Pioneer of 'Digital for Good'*

"Cornelia C. Walther's reflection goes to the heart of the most fundamental question of our times, concerning the nature of our interaction with technology. Chasing our multiple "selves", in the digital and physical world, we do not spend enough time and attention trying to understand how technology affects us, for better or for worse. Cornelia C. Walther draws attention to the fact that we are not, and should not succumb to the inevitable but think more highly of ourselves and our agency in the world. We may be under pressure, but we retain the right to make societal choices. Technology does not have an agenda of its own, at least at present, which puts the human in the position of influence and responsibility. This is a powerful and thought-provoking book."

—Pawel Swieboda, *Founder and Director, NeuroCentury, Co-Founder, Brain Capital Alliance. Practice Lead Neurotechnology, The International Center for Future Generations (ICFG), Senior Visiting Fellow, European Policy Centre, Former director Human Brain Capital Project*

"AI, discussed and explored by experts for over 60 years, has sprung to the public domain with the splash of generative AI. Cornelia Walther masterfully applies her innovative, multidisciplinary approach (POZE) to tackle some of the thorniest ethical and practical issues about AI creeping in everyday life. She explains how to channel AI to bring out the best of us, fair societies, and a livable planet."

—Enrique Delamonica, *Senior adviser, Data and Analytics Team, United Nations Children's Fund (UNICEF)*

"In 'Human Leadership for Humane Technology', Cornelia masterfully navigates the interconnectedness of humanity and technology, advocating for an inclusive future where technology serves to amplify our collective human values. This book is a clarion call for leaders and innovators to forge a path where technology not only advances our capabilities but does so with compassion and inclusivity at its core. A compelling read for those dedicated to crafting a technologically advanced yet humane society."

—Elizabeth (Liz) Ngonzi, *Founder and CEO, The International Social Impact Institute\Adjunct Assistant Professor, The Center for Global Affairs at New York University*

"As an advocate for ethical technology and compassionate leadership, I highly endorse the upcoming book on human leadership for humane technology by Dr. Cornelia Walther. In an era where digital advancements often outpace ethical considerations, this book promises to provide valuable insights and strategies for fostering a more empathetic and responsible approach to technology development. Cornelia's extensive experience brings a unique perspective with a deep understanding of human behavior and ethics. Her insights should empower leaders to navigate the complexity of the digital age with empathy and integrity. This book is a must-read for anyone committed to shaping a more humane future for the tech industry."

—John E. Roche, *Senior Managing Director, SAP*

"The extent, speed of development and the impact on technological changes humanity are amazing, extraordinary and in many ways shocking and scary. How do we deal with this? How does this modify our individual and collective behavior? How will humanity at large benefit? How can we ensure that technological advances will expand and ensure human rights for all? Cornelia Walther in this impressive book deals with these questions. She discusses and presents alternatives for the present and future journey in face to the new challenges that technological changes present to humanity."

—Alberto Minujin, *Executive Director of Equity for Children and Professor The New School*

Cornelia C. Walther

Human Leadership for Humane Technology

The New AI: Agency Ignited

palgrave
macmillan

Cornelia C. Walther
POZE Global Network
Wharton School, University
of Pennsylvania
Philadelphia, PA, USA

ISBN 978-3-031-67822-6   ISBN 978-3-031-67823-3   (eBook)
https://doi.org/10.1007/978-3-031-67823-3

© The Editor(s) (if applicable) and The Author(s), under exclusive license to Springer Nature Switzerland AG 2024

This work is subject to copyright. All rights are solely and exclusively licensed by the Publisher, whether the whole or part of the material is concerned, specifically the rights of translation, reprinting, reuse of illustrations, recitation, broadcasting, reproduction on microfilms or in any other physical way, and transmission or information storage and retrieval, electronic adaptation, computer software, or by similar or dissimilar methodology now known or hereafter developed.
The use of general descriptive names, registered names, trademarks, service marks, etc. in this publication does not imply, even in the absence of a specific statement, that such names are exempt from the relevant protective laws and regulations and therefore free for general use.
The publisher, the authors and the editors are safe to assume that the advice and information in this book are believed to be true and accurate at the date of publication. Neither the publisher nor the authors or the editors give a warranty, expressed or implied, with respect to the material contained herein or for any errors or omissions that may have been made. The publisher remains neutral with regard to jurisdictional claims in published maps and institutional affiliations.

Cover illustration: © Harvey Loake

This Palgrave Macmillan imprint is published by the registered company Springer Nature Switzerland AG
The registered company address is: Gewerbestrasse 11, 6330 Cham, Switzerland

If disposing of this product, please recycle the paper.

Foreword

Technology is a tool to an end, not an end in itself. The alignment of artificial intelligence (AI) and human aspirations starts with the alignment of human aspirations and actions. Offline. This is the main message of this book. If nothing else (and there is more to discover), I hope this thought will stay with you. It is a simple, easily overlooked, fact. We cannot expect from the technology of tomorrow to live up to values that the humans of today are not manifesting. A new commitment to the power of agency that derives from human nature is needed, now. *Human leadership for humane technology* was chosen as a title to illustrate the interplay of individual agency as the central condition of prosocial AI. The latter is defined as an AI that is designed and trained to bring out the best in and for people and planet.

As of mid-2024 two types of mindset prevail. On the one hand are those who fear humanity's extinction, preceded by large-scale unemployment. On the other hand are those who stand in awe regarding the potential that AI offers for productivity, performance and profit. While the former forget that AI is a tool to an end, which we (should) choose, the latter overlook that AI can also be a force for positive social change. We, Humans still have a choice, hence the zoom on agency—defined as the ability and volition to act autonomously—of this book.

One disclaimer in advance. I did not use AI to write this book. The reason is selfish. Though I have played and experimented with ChatGTP and its consorts, and although I see the charm of having an indulgent pocket servant do the legwork, using it extensively feels like being cheated while cheating. The beauty of writing a book is less the final product but the process of learning and research that goes into it (reading some of the books that I published over the past years I blush in hindsight). Delegating to a machine deprives the creator not only of ownership of the final creation, but of the creative flow itself. Hence, I apologize to you, the reader, who could have received a more polished version of the present work had it been produced by the technologies that these pages are about. You will have to be content with my "real" voice.

However, I did play with various frontier models, from GPT-4 over Claude-3 Opus to Gemini Ultra. The tone in this book reflects the dichotomy of my emotions regarding AI. I share some of the worries regarding possible negative fallouts, while also seeing its potential of serving as a catalyst that helps humanity transition to a better, brighter next phase, online and offline. Likely neither doom nor glory will completely materialize. Yet there is a fair chance to strike a sustainable balance, whereby positive and negative consequences hold each other's hand in a yin and yang dynamic, with (relatively) small fluctuations for a sustained period of time. If we make the right choices.

Having AI at our fingertips entails the risk that our most precious resource—the brain—decays for lack of usage. And still, getting the right answers requires asking the right questions. And asking questions is an underrated art that involves critical thinking. The pervasiveness of chatbots might force us to become sharper in our thinking and writing. Pushing us to embrace the power that comes from deliberate action with a clear purpose. Rather than delegating every cognitive effort to AI agents, we can seize this opportunity to excel at human agency.

Quality did and does prime quantity. It requires effort. Asking bland questions results in superficial answers, which abounded already before Generative AI (GenAI), and which are multiplying at breathtaking speed now that it is ever easier to produce them. The usage of our natural intelligence may shift, but it is now just as important as before, if not more so.

What follows is an invitation to reframe your perception of yourself, and of society. We will undertake a journey into the magic of humanity's multidimensional experience, and its amplification in an AI-powered world.

Note—The term artificial intelligence has been around for a while. Already in 1637 René Descartes contemplated machines that were capable of thinking and making decisions (Descartes, trans.1995). At the time he also identified the distinction between today's specialized AI, where machines learn how to perform one specific task, and general AI, where machines can adapt to any job. The first properly documented use of the term "artificial Intelligence" dates to 1956 at a summer workshop organized by professor John McCarthy at Dartmouth College Conference.[1] *In 1966 Joseph Weizenbaum, a researcher at MIT's AI Laboratory, created the world's first chatbot, ELIZA, to simulate a conversation between a human and a machine. In this book we will refer to AI in the latest form that is currently available on the market.*

The landscape of AI is constantly evolving. The ongoing dynamics are driven by a stream of influences, without an epicenter. This makes it an illustration of the kaleidoscopic nature of human beings, and life in society. For that reason the presentation in this book follows a path that might feel like a patchwork at times, seeking to convey both in content and in style that seemingly disjointed elements are connected in a continuum of constant change. The components of this dynamic are organic and artificial. In a world of all pervasive technology every action that is taken is amplified. The ever-expanding net that shapes our lives influences both, the online and the offline side of this always evolving equation. Seemingly minute behaviors can have major effects, always, but especially in a hybrid world. The infamous butterfly effect is acutely relevant now. Everything we do is the cause and consequence of something else. Awareness of this kaleidoscopic dynamic must shape our intentions, combined with a sense of urgency.

The exponential growth of technology exemplifies an accelerating trajectory of advancements that reshape our world. This rapid technological evolution can be seen as part of an "infinite game" (Carse, 1986), where the objective is not to win, but to perpetuate the game and continually adapt to it. In this context, technology has become a key driver. One might even see it as a player, perpetually pushing boundaries and redefining possibilities, thus propelling the game's continuation. This dynamic aligns closely with the principles of evolution, where constant

---

[1] *The promise of computability lay at the heart of the field baptized as artificial intelligence at the 1956 Dartmouth workshop. In the original funding proposal it said "The study is to proceed on the basis of the conjecture that every aspect of learning or any other feature of intelligence can in principle be so precisely described that a machine can be made to simulate it" (McCarthy et all, 1955).*

adaptation and innovation are essential for survival and success. As technology evolves, it not only enhances our capabilities but also transforms societal structures, economies, and human interactions, creating a feedback loop that fuels further growth and complexity. This interplay of technology and evolution highlights the endless potential and transformative power inherent in the ongoing advancement of human ingenuity (Kurzweil, 2005).

Looking ahead, the trajectory of future technology is poised to continue an exponential ascent, driven by advancements in all fields, from biotechnology, via design quantum computing. Each of these domains promises to unlock new capabilities and solutions to complex problems, potentially leading to breakthroughs that are still unimaginable. As these technologies mature, they are likely to converge, amplifying their impact on each of us and society. This convergence will enhance certain sectors but also create novel multi—and trans disciplinary applications, gradually blurring the lines between physical, digital, and biological realms. The future landscape of technology may be characterized by unprecedented levels of automation, and intelligence, fundamentally transforming the way we live, work, and interact with the world (Schwab, 2016; Tegmark, 2017).

This evolution is neither inherently good nor bad. Like many other features of life it just is. The central assignment that each of us is challenged to accomplish is to harness the assets at our disposal, whether they are inherent to our human nature, or external, to bring out the best for people—including but not limited to ourselves, and the planet that we depend on. Finding and sharing our own best self as a human being is part of that assignment. Progress that we make in that regard serves us in an exponential way; the more we are in sync with ourselves and others, the faster we move forward on the path. AI can become an ally for humans and nature, if individuals at all levels of society recognize their uniqueness, and the power of personal agency that it is imbued with. We cannot wait for projected outcomes to manifest as an automatic derivative of technology. The latter is a means to an end, not an end in itself. From a finite mindset of winners and losers, black versus white, we need to shift to an "infinite mindset" (Sinek, 2016) acknowledging that everyone wins when everyone wins.

Figure 1 brings together certain ideas that are looked at in this book—and which are connected by one simple meaning—AI becomes our ally, if we adopt a mindset of agency. Anchored in the perspective of human experience as a composition of multiple dimensions (Chapter 1) the concepts introduced in the following pages seek to serve such a mindset. From *awareness* of the potential that each of us has to be and bring change, to *appreciation* of our human nature, via *acceptance* of factors that are beyond our control, to full *accountability* for the consequences of (in)action. From this perspective, which we will refer to as the *A-Frame* (Chapter 1) a human-centered approach to technology, leadership, and innovation arises, with human consciousness as a cornerstone.

Embracing our own nature in all its facets means to face the vulnerability that is inherent to it; the feature that makes us real, fragile. Such authenticity may appear at first sight as a bottleneck in a society that is geared toward fast progress; in the long run however it is the distinguishing mark that sets humans apart from their artificial counterparts.

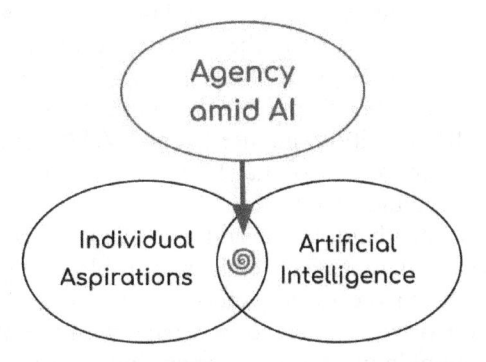

Fig. 1 *Agency Amid AI for All*—The sweet spot of natural and artificial assets

Caption: *Agency Amid AI for All* (A4) sits at the nexus of artificial intelligence and natural consciousness, combining aspirations, emotions, thoughts, and sensations to bring out the best in and for people and the planet. It is a mindset shift that starts with personal choices.

The book is structured in 4 chapters, followed by two annexes with stories and a glossary.

In Chapter 1 we look at the POZE paradigm (*Perspective—Optimization—Zeniths—Exposure*) as an innovative perspective to analyze the complex interplay of individual and collective human behavior. It is applied to understand interactions between humans and AI in a hybrid world. Based on the understanding that human experience is an organically evolving kaleidoscope, it offers a multidisciplinary framework to analyze the evolving status quo, which is too complex for black-white categorizations. Considering society as a composition of 2x4 dimensions, we look at the influence of AI on the interplay of individuals, communities, countries, and the planet. Individual agency is put in the spotlight as a catalyst of the world we want, with the *A-Frame (Awareness - Appreciation - Acceptance - Accountability)* as a tool to sharpen the mindset that is needed to curate agency amid AI.

Together this offers the backdrop to Chapter 2 which presents certain concepts related to artificial and natural consciousness, innovation, and leadership. This includes a set of thorny topics in the context of data, regulations, and trust.

Illustrating the overall dynamic of multidimensional change, including approaches to tackle these topics, the stories of leaders who share their own journey with technology in Chapter 3 walk us along the path of the 4 *macro*-questions: WHY (purpose/aspiration), WHO (personality/emotion), WHERE (position/mindset), and WHAT (pursuit/physical manifestation), which relate to the 4 individual dimensions of being human (soul, heart, mind, body).

Chapter 4 connects the dots and adds the missing pieces to the kaleidoscopic puzzle that these pages gradually assemble. It highlights certain themes that arise from the stories, and closes the loop. We look at the positive-sum effect of value-oriented leadership with the *Win4* of prosocial action[2] and zoom in further on conscious influence in a hybrid world. We conclude with 4 sample prototypes to illustrate a type of technology that is tailored to bring out the best for people and planet, a "prosocial AI" (Fig. 2).[3]

Respectively and combined these chapters extend an invitation to harness our natural assets as the foundation to build a strategic alliance with AI. Once we reframe the mind from competition to complementarity in the dynamic of an infinite game in which everyone wins when everyone wins AI becomes an ally in playing that game, to our rules.

---

[2] Defined as behavior that serves not only the self but others.

[3] Over the course of this book "prosocial AI" is the terminology used to refer to AI that is designed and delivered with the intention to bring out the best in and for people and planet.

We conclude with a sneak-preview of the World/s that could be, and a glossary of terms.

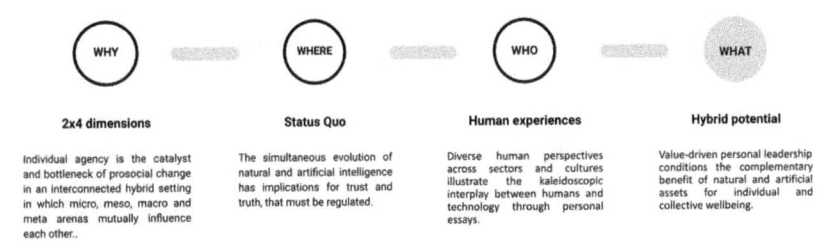

WHY	WHERE	WHO	WHAT
2x4 dimensions	**Status Quo**	**Human experiences**	**Hybrid potential**
Individual agency is the catalyst and bottleneck of prosocial change in an interconnected hybrid setting in which micro, meso, macro and meta arenas mutually influence each other.	The simultaneous evolution of natural and artificial intelligence has implications for trust and truth, that must be regulated.	Diverse human perspectives across sectors and cultures illustrate the kaleidoscopic interplay between humans and technology through personal essays.	Value-driven personal leadership conditions the complementary benefit of natural and artificial assets for individual and collective wellbeing.

Fig. 2 A simple roadmap of this book looks like this

Caption: Anchored in a multidisciplinary framework the focus on agency arises (Why), this is explored in the context of the evolving hybrid landscape (Where). Illustrated by experiences the need for personal agency becomes clear (Who), which opens the door to the next phase of prosocial action (What) that is needed now.

Acknowledgments

Thank You who reads this, dedicating time and attention to the offered ideas.

Thank you to the contributors of the essays in Chapter 3; their journeys are a precious part of this presentation.

Thank you to the editorial team at Palgrave Macmillan, and their support from A to Z.

Thank you to everyone who has been part of my journey, (in)directly influencing my thoughts, beliefs, values, and actions. This book is the cause and consequence of the above, and I hope it gives justice to them.

Scope

This book explores the relationship of natural and artificial intelligence in our rapidly evolving world. It does so anchored in an innovative multidisciplinary framework and the resulting perspective that society is a composition of multiple dimensions, with individuals (*micro*), communities (*meso*), countries (*macro*) and planet (*meta*) in the collective sphere, and individuals themselves as multidimensional beings (aspirations, emotions, thoughts, sensations). This perspective is applied to analyze the implications of our transition into a phase where online and offline realms are increasingly intertwined. Special attention is given to the influence of all pervasive technology on our perception of the self and society.

Exploration of the harmonization of humans within and among each other is the precursor of technological alignment. This alignment encompasses the interplay of human aspirations and actions on the one hand, and of human aspirations and human-made algorithms on the other. One might call this the *hybrid alignment conundrum*. Drawing on the multidimensional perspective that underpins this book, it proposes a shift from a passive to a proactive approach to life with AI, from a focus on AI to an emphasis on NI—Natural Intelligence. Herein the *"A-Frame"* is introduced as a practical tool to reframe the relationship with artificial intelligence (AI) and place humans at the forefront of shaping this coexistence, starting with awareness of interplays, appreciation of the power that comes with agency, acceptance of the implications, and accountability for (in)action.

Through a collection of essays from individuals who have been catalysts for change, the book illustrates the kaleidoscopic interplay of human behavior and experiences, and their interactions with technology. These personal narratives highlight the interconnected causes and consequences of being human in a hybrid world. This interplay underscores the importance of individual agency and collective transformation.

Key Message: As AI systems mirror human mindsets, our current moral footprint serves as a blueprint for the hybrid future. To thrive, we must consciously and proactively shape this future, leveraging the complementary strengths of artificial intelligence and human authenticity, of vulnerability, and an aspiration to values that recognize the positive-sum effect of the Common Good, referred to as the *Win4*. In this endeavor, leadership becomes a way of life for everyone, and particularly essential for individuals in leadership positions as the impact of their attitude and action is amplified.

Agency Amid AI for All (A4) embraces a mindset of personal accountability in the interaction with technology. This encompasses, on the one hand, awareness of the influence that individual inputs have on collective outcomes, and on the other, acceptance that we do not have control over the final results. Respectively and combined *Agency Amid AI for All*[1] is anchored in appreciation of human vulnerability, and the authentic being that derives from it. The book invites readers to embark on a journey of self-discovery and collective action, with AI as an ally along the way.

---

[1] *"Agency Amid AI for All"* and *"Agency amid AI"* will be used interchangeably for shortness.

Contents

1 **WHY: Perspective: POZE—A Multidisciplinary Framework of Life**   1
   1.1 Humans and Technology   2
      1.1.1 Context—Hybrid World   2
      1.1.2 Status Quo: Lackluster Leadership versus Technology Tantrum   7
      1.1.3 Situating This Book: Backdrop Snapshot   12
      1.1.4 Notes and Selected Definitions   15
   1.2 m4-matrix—Arenas of Transformation   24
      1.2.1 Universal Principles: Change—Connection—Continuum—Complementarity   24
      1.2.2 Society's Multidimensional Configuration   26
      1.2.3 Individual Dimensions of Human Existence   31
      1.2.4 Risks and Opportunities at the Interface of Individuals, Society, and AI   41
   1.3 Individual Behavior as Cause and Consequence of Values and Norms   49
      1.3.1 Formal and Informal Forms of Influence   49
      1.3.2 Values as a Compass to Cruise the Hybrid Space   55
   1.4 Agency Amid AI for All   59
      1.4.1 The A-Frame   59

	1.4.2 Human Influence from the Inside Out, and from the Outside In	64
	1.4.3 Artificial Influence from the Outside In	72
	1.4.4 Summarizing Pros and Contras of Mutual Influence in a Hybrid Society	82
References		86

2 WHERE: Humans, Technology, and Humane Technology — 103

2.1 Consciousness — 104
    2.1.1 Natural and Artificial Consciousness — 104
    2.1.2 Inferred Intelligence — 110
    2.1.3 Tandems of Artificial and Natural Intelligence — 113
    2.1.4 Persuasion and Perception — 115

2.2 Circumstances — 120
    2.2.1 Innovation in the Eyes of (Some) Philosophers — 120
    2.2.2 Technological Transmutations — 123
    2.2.3 Human Ambitions and Artificial Harvests — 128
    2.2.4 The Hybrid Alignment Conundrum — 133

2.3 Trust and Truth — 136
    2.3.1 Value Perception: Economic Worth Versus Personal Merit — 136
    2.3.2 Trust Amid Placebos — 142
    2.3.3 Artificial Integrity—An Oxymoron? — 151
    2.3.4 Human Vulnerability in the Interplay with AI — 156

2.4 Data and Rules — 159
    2.4.1 Rooky Regulations — 159
    2.4.2 Data Matters—Quantity and Quality — 168
    2.4.3 Algorithmic Bias — 170
    2.4.4 From Quantity to Quality to Inclusion — 174

References — 178

3 WHO: Human Perspectives on Humane Technology — 195

3.1 The Ask: What Are the Dimensions of Agency in a Hybrid World? — 196

3.2 The Essays: Illustrating the kaleidoscopic interplay of humans and technology — 197
    3.2.1 So That None of Us Be Missing — 197
    3.2.2 Shaping a Better Future Through Leadership — 202
    3.2.3 A Journey of Curiosity and Innovation — 208
    3.2.4 Relationality of the Worldly Dramatis Personae — 212

		3.2.5	The Word Impossible Says "I'm possible"	217
		3.2.6	Little Did I Know	222
		3.2.7	Deep Listening	228
		3.2.8	Designing for a Better World: Pedagogy at Scale	233
		3.2.9	Humanizing Technology. A Leadership Blueprint	237
	References			244
4	WHAT: Optimizing Natural and Artificial Assets to Thrive in a Hybrid Society			247
	4.1	From Influenced to Influence for Impact		248
		4.1.1	A Win–Win-Win–Win Effect (Win4)	248
		4.1.2	Countering Chronic Cognitive Dissonance	254
	4.2	From Competition to Complementarity of Natural and Artificial Assets		256
		4.2.1	Reallocations of Mind and Matter	256
		4.2.2	Daring Humanity	258
	4.3	Prosocial AI in Practice—Prototype Proposals		261
		4.3.1	micro—Benevolent Brain and Body Buddy (B4)	262
		4.3.2	meso—Agency Amid AI for All (A4)	263
		4.3.3	macro—Social Accounting Matrix 4.0 (SAM 4.0)	264
		4.3.4	meta—Inspiration Incubator (i@i)	265
	4.4	Unity Among Diversity		268
		4.4.1	Complementarity of Apparent Opposites	268
		4.4.2	Connection of Local and Global Components	271
		4.4.3	Change from the Inside Out and from the Outside In	273
		4.4.4	Continuum of Past, Present, and Prospects	276
	ANNEX 1—Bonus: Storytime			278
		Option A: From www to WWW—A Weird Wired World		278
		Option B: From Gloomy to Good		281
		Option C: Alternative Scenario?		283
	ANNEX 2—Glossary			284
	References			286
References				**291**
Index				**333**

List of Figures

Fig. 1.1	Continuum of change: Values—Innovation—Leadership—Technology	12
Fig. 1.2	*m4-matrix*	29
Fig. 1.3	Interplays in the *micro*-arena	39
Fig. 1.4	4 central values situated in the 4 dimensions of human experience	58
Fig. 1.5	*A-Frame*—A best-case scenario	61
Fig. 1.6	Spiral of influence	66
Fig. 2.1	Quadruple Bottom Line	131
Fig. 4.1	Technology is a mirror	256
Fig. 4.2	Augmented *A-Frame*: Agency ignited	259
Fig. 4.3	Prosocial AI across the 4 dimensions	267
Fig. 4.4	Tension of nadirs and zeniths. Whilst zenith and nadir represent opposing extremes that stand in complementarity to each other, they also contain their respective opposite within their own definition. Moreover, given the many interconnections within the *m4-matrix*, real-world situations may follow different paths within the spiral. Once a zenith is reached the path towards the next nadir is already underway; once a nadir is passed the journey towards the next zenith continues. What may seem as an absolute from one perspective appears as a passing stage from another	270

List of Tables

Table 1.1	Potential outlook on AI and the future of life	50
Table 1.2	Schematic overview of certain components at stake throughout the *m4-matrix*	59
Table 1.3	Mutual influence within and between the 2 × 4 dimensions, in the best-case scenario of optimized flow	85
Table 2.1	A simplified snapshot of comparative abilities	109
Table 4.1	Schematic overview of interplays	258
Table 4.2	Concepts combined	276

CHAPTER 1

WHY: Perspective: POZE—A Multidisciplinary Framework of Life

Abstract This foundational chapter introduces the multidisciplinary POZE framework to analyze the interplay of humans and technology. The *m4-matrix* is offered to map out the arenas where transformative changes are occurring at the intersection of individual (aspiration, emotions, thoughts, sensations) and societal (individual, community, country, planet) dimensions. The argument is made that a mindset of agency amid AI, across generations, cultures, and socioeconomic backgrounds can transform technology into an ally for humankind. The *A-Frame* is introduced to cultivate such agency intentionally, which involves *awareness* of interplays and *appreciation* of individual vulnerability, requiring *acceptance* of the unique opportunity that humans have to create the reality they want, and *accountability* for the responsibility that comes with that privilege. Combined these attitudes result in the type of leadership mindset that is needed to promote and achieve agency amid AI. As it will be explained, leadership should be approached as a way of life, independent of hierarchy; perceived as a path that is driven by values. If it is framed in such a manner it opens a path for anyone to rise beyond personal interest to the bigger picture perspective of the Common Good, which is a pragmatic perspective considering the interconnected nature of everything. We look at the *Spiral of influence* which allows humans to trigger change, and the potential of technology to support them. Everyone can win if everyone has a fair chance to play; this book shows possible ways to achieve this. The binomen of GIGO (Garbage

© The Author(s), under exclusive license to Springer Nature Switzerland AG 2024
C. C. Walther, *Human Leadership for Humane Technology*,
https://doi.org/10.1007/978-3-031-67823-3_1

in, Garbage out) versus VIVO (Values in, Values out) is introduced as the central tension of the relationship that humans entertain with technology; it reflects the argument that humans cannot expect the technology of tomorrow to reflect values that they do not manifest today.

Keywords Multidimensionality · Values · Connection · Complementarity · Common Good · Leadership · GIGO · POZE · A-Frame

1.1 Humans and Technology

1.1.1 Context—Hybrid World

Every one of us is part of an organically evolving kaleidoscope, called the universe. This has always been the case. But awareness of the interplays that shape who we are, has become an essential feature of our survival as a species as it moves towards ever more intimate coexistence with technology. The impact on everyday life of current technological innovations compares to past milestones in human civilization, from gunpowder, print and the steam engine (our first artificial muscle), to electricity and control over atomic power.

Seeing the implications of artificial intelligence (AI) not only in the physical world, but also its influence on our internal sphere starting with our "natural intelligence" (mind) and increasingly our entire organism, one might argue that this new wave of innovation exceeds the previous ones. At times it appears as if this was a race between humans and machines. In the face of ever-expanding, ever more sophisticated technological progress we face a question that is thrilling and threatening at once: What makes us different from machines? If an artificial entity can talk, write, speak, look, interact like a human being, then what distinguishes "it" and us? What is our added value as a person if the "it" can do more, faster, better while at the same time being always available, easy to deal with, patient, understanding, friendly, and creative?

What is the unique human brand that makes us stand out? Finding the answer to that question will determine how we position ourselves in a future where AI is omnipresent. It is an interrogation that each of us must undertake, and it is the first step of a lifelong assignment; the gigantic task of fulfilling and sharing our own best self. Respectively and together some of the biggest questions of individual life in the twenty-first century remain the same that have accompanied humans over the past millennia: Why am I here, Who am I, Where do I stand, and What am I doing to align my aspirations and actions? Answering, or at least asking, these questions is urgent now. Because it will equip us to decide the rules of our cohabitation with technology. Referred to as the *macro*-questions in Chapter 3,[1] these interrogations together with a set of check-in questions that pop-up through this book might serve you to get started.

As we walk into an Ai-powered future it matters more than ever to acknowledge, accept, and appreciate ourselves the way we are, not how we would like to be. Change is possible only once we have a candid sense of self.

"The unexamined life is not worth living" (Plato, trans., 2002, p. 41). In a society where natural intelligence coexists with artificial intelligence "Leadership" carries special weight, because individuals at all levels, and particularly those who walk the privileged path of guiding others, must question the status quo and their own role in it, constantly. If critical examination and care for one's soul are foundational to virtue and living well as stated by Socrates; and if self-examination and the pursuit of truth through questioning and logic are essential to human flourishing as he believed (Plato, trans. 2002), then are we pursuing the path to flourishing, or do we follow the track of least resistance, prey to inertia, and the lull of comfort?[2] The consequences of our direction have massive consequences for the planet our species shares with others.

The current period of human civilization is marked by accelerated rates of species extinctions, climate change, and other global environmental impacts driven primarily by human activities like fossil fuel combustion and land use (Waters et al., 2016). Some scholars even suggest the Anthropocene as a new geological epoch defined by the dominant influence of human activities on earth's environments and processes (Crutzen & Stoermer, 2000). The term has been rejected, and both the

---

[1] Why (Purpose) Who (Personality) Where (Position) What (Pursuit).

[2] The principle of least effort suggests that individuals tend to follow the path of least resistance or expend the least amount of effort possible when making decisions or carrying out actions. Without using the term "inertia" this finding laid the foundation for understanding the tendency of individuals to resist change and continue with their existing patterns of behavior unless motivated to do otherwise (Zipf, 1949).

onset[3] and the overall recognition as a distinct period remains debated. Still the footprint of humans on the planet is undeniable (Ellies, 2024). Whether one recognizes the word "anthroprone" or not, statistics show that currently humans would need 1.7 earth to survive. We are in full overshoot. This is a human-made problem (as are war and poverty), AI did not get us into this situation.

Some even consider that the status quo is the consequence of a "human behavior crisis", with climate breakdown as a symptom of ecological overshoot, which in turn is caused by the deliberate manipulation of human behavior and the attitudes that underpin it (Merz et al., 2023). We do not need AI to rescue us from that crisis, but it might serve as a positive catalyst if we frame it intentionally, with awareness of our own caveats. For decades neuropsychology, social signaling and norms have been exploited to drive human behavior and shape society, from consuming goods to driving voting behaviors. Everything is connected. Our actions, no matter how seemingly insignificant they appear, have consequences that ripple through society, online and offline.

Can we systematically influence our ancient drive of belonging to a tribe, to signal one's status or attract a mate to create behaviors that are conducive to a sustainable world, and from there new social norms that are propeople and proplanet, rather than proprofit? Which supporting role can AI play in that regard?

The timing of the latest peak in artificial intelligence is ironic. Just as we have exited the 2019–2021 COVID-19 pandemic, which drastically affected the IQ, memory, and concentration span of those who fell ill with it (Ziyad, 2024) we are entering a phase which one might call the *"Technoprocene"*, where our cognitive abilities are supercharged by artificial assistance. Characterized by the cohabitation of artificial and natural entities the *Technoprocene* can lead to (at least) two things—either an ever larger footprint of humans on the earth, or a gradual reduction of the fallouts of human life thanks to a better understanding and management of the causes and consequences that underpin life and living in an interconnected ecosystem. One might argue that the COVID pandemic prepared fertile terrain for the *Technoprocene* seeing that large parts of

---

[3] Potential markers range from the advent of agriculture to the mid-twentieth century (Lewis & Maslin, 2015). Regardless of its timing, the Anthropocene represents a significant departure from the relatively stable Holocene conditions that enabled modern civilization (Zalasiewicz et al., 2017).

our personal and professional communication, and the data that derives from it, were transferred to the online sphere, serving to train the frontier models that we are now using. Which direction we take depends significantly on the intentions that we, individually and collectively, weave through our interactions with AI.

AI is a tool. What results from its utilization is (or should be) directed by the user of that instrument. (As we will see in Chapter 2 it is a bit more complicated than that when the tool is as complex as a large language model). The basic premise still applies though, what goes in influences what comes out. Let us keep that basic premise at the back of our (human) mind. If those who design, deliver, and delight in technology are motivated by prosocial values, the hybrid society of tomorrow will be worth living in. Online mirrors offline and increasingly vice versa. That logic underpins the concept of **prosocial AI** that we will zoom in further in the coming pages. Defined as the intentional design, development, and deployment of artificial intelligence systems that prioritize the well-being of individuals and society as a whole, prosocial AI aims to align AI with human values, such as equity, justice, and sustainability, to ensure that technology serves as a force for good. Prosocial AI seeks to enhance human capabilities, preserve personal agency, and promote holistic health, rather than simply replicating existing societal flaws or maximizing profit. In essence, prosocial AI is about using AI to bring out the best in natural intelligence, fostering a future where technology amplifies human potential and supports the common good.

A word on **Agency**—a central theme of the following pages. Human agency refers to the capacity of individuals to act independently and make their own free choices, shaping their circumstances and environment through self-determination and autonomy (Bandura, 2006). It encompasses the ability to initiate actions, set goals, and exercise control over one's behavior and decision-making processes. It is tied to concepts like free will, self-efficacy, and empowerment, reflecting the human capacity to be active agents in their own lives (Sen, 1985). In contrast, AI agents are artificial systems designed to perceive their environment and take actions to achieve specific goals which are given to them by human programmers and prompts (Russell & Norvig, 2016). They are programmed to make decisions and perform tasks autonomously, based on their programming and the data they receive. While AI agents can exhibit some degree of autonomy and decision-making capability within their defined parameters, they lack the self-awareness, consciousness, conscientiousness, and inherent agency that humans possess (Bryson, 2018). AI agents are tools designed to assist or augment human activities, rather than being independent players who are driven by free will. They are trained by humans to assist humans, based on human data. The worrisome part is that AI agents reflect human attitudes, including greed. In 2024 a test (simulation model) of ChatGTP-4 showed that LLM-based agents are adept at pricing tasks, autonomously collude in oligopoly settings to the detriment of consumers, and that variations in seemingly innocuous phrases in prompts may further increase collusion (Fish et al., 2024). These results extend to auction settings, which illustrates the nefast complementarity of human greed with superhuman coordination.[4] We cannot expect from the technology of tomorrow to live up to values that the humans of today do not manifest, online and offline.

This interplay of human inputs and artificial outputs is illustrated by the well-known catchphrase *"Garbage in, Garbage out"* (GIGO), which has an unclear origin story, with multiple people cited as having coined it. Digging deeper it appears that the idea behind GIGO dates to Charles Babbage in the early nineteenth century, when he was asked if his "differentiation machine" would produce correct answers if fed wrong figures.[5] Whoever mentioned it first, and despite improved computing powers, the principle that underlies GIGO persists—inaccurate inputs lead to inaccurate outputs. Ironically the dictum proves its own validity; one wrong citation that was posted once on the internet led subsequently to a maze of erroneous attributions. We will play with this acronym throughout the following pages, opposing it to its counterpart—*Values in, Values out* (*VIVO*) as a potential panacea to the doomsday scenario that some foresee as an unavoidable derivative of our infatuation with AI.

---

[4] This further underscores the need for antitrust regulation regarding algorithmic pricing, with the need to uncover regulatory challenges that might arise specifically related to LLM-based pricing agents (Fish et al., 2024).

[5] Recounting an early encounter with some members of the English Parliament, he wrote in his diary: "On two occasions I have been asked, "Pray, Mr. Babbage, if you put into the machine wrong figures, will the right answers come out?" I am not able rightly to apprehend the kind of confusion of ideas that could provoke such a question" (Stenson, 2016). This idea persisted over the next century as computers were developed. The first published use of the actual phrase seems to be from 1957, where Army specialist William D. Mellin used it to describe problems getting accurate outputs. In 1958–1959, George Fuechsel claims to have coined it while teaching IBM RAMAC courses. In 1963, Raymond Crowley used the phrase in a report on an IRS robot (Stenson, 2016).

Note—Leadership is spotlighted in this book with the understanding that every individual is a potential leader in their environment. A special invitation to make this influence inspiring is extended to those who direct others. Their mindset carries the amplified opportunity, and danger, of widespread ripple effects, which is twice true in a society where many offline actions have an online counterpart; it matters exponentially among the individuals who design, direct, and deliver the virtual scenery that we are increasingly immersed in.

1.1.2 Status Quo: Lackluster Leadership versus Technology Tantrum

Without exploring the manifold definitions of leadership and human values per se, about which countless volumes have been written before the latest technology onslaught, let us zoom in on the scenario of today's world: where our aspirations and actions, attitudes and appetites are inflated by quasi omnipresent online connection and artificial amplification. Two twin features that characterize our life amid AI that are particularly interesting in the context of leadership are limited versus infinite mindset, and inclusion versus exclusion.

The present wave of AI, which some compare to a new industrial revolution (Schwab, 2017), is the latest manifestation of an exponential growth dynamic that shapes the infinite game of life[6] (Kelly, 2009). It is a direct consequence of exponential growth patterns observed in computing power and data availability (Kurzweil, 2005). Its transformative potential spans from communication and interpersonal relations, via health care and education to finance and transportation, and many others. This promises unprecedented efficiencies, while opening the door wide to future innovations. Such immense power, that is at least theoretically at the fingertips of everyone with access to a smartphone and internet, comes with profound ethical and societal implications, because this power is neither inherently positive nor negative for people and planet. It is a tool that we can harness to help or harm people and planet, depending on the mindset that underpins our use of it. Past innovations, from

---

[6] One might distinguish finite games and infinite games. Finite games (e.g. monopoly, tennis) are played with the goal of getting to the end of the game and winning, in respect of static rules. Every game has a beginning, middle, and end, and a final winner. Infinite games (e.g. politics; business) are played for the purpose of continuing play rather than to win (Carse, 1986).

electricity to social media, were primarily driven by economic interests and consequently became commercial determinants of society, with costly implications for human well-being and planetary health. It is important to systematically shape AI as a social determinant of life. Such reframing from a pro-profit to a pro-social vocation may not only avoid harmful fallouts, but position AI as a catalyst of positive social dynamics.

Life is a journey without a final destination. As in the logic of the infinite game, success lies in perpetuating the game itself (Carse, 1986). As AI advances, embracing an infinite mindset becomes crucial, recognizing that everyone's victories are intertwined. An understanding of multidimensional connection can help to be and remain aware of our personal role, and the accountability that flows from it. Every (in)action contributes, directly or indirectly, to the collective well-being of the universal system that binds humanity and technology (Tegmark, 2017). By prioritizing the greater good, we can harness AI's potential collaboratively, in a strategic alliance of natural and artificial intelligence. How about an infinite game of collective ingenuity? This mindset shift from winner versus loser to one for all and all for one is beneficial for everyone; it has a special connotation for people in leadership positions.

An infinite mindset as a leadership approach focuses on long-term vision and sustainable growth rather than short-term wins and immediate gains (Sinek, 2019).[7] Leaders with an infinite mindset prioritize enduring values, continuous improvement, and the well-being of their teams and organizations over transient metrics of success. This encourages resilience, innovation, and commitment to a larger purpose, which is precious to navigate uncertainty and ever-changing circumstances. People with an infinite mindset inspire others to strive for excellence, remain motivated, and stay engaged, thriving in a culture of trust, in which everyone is welcome.

Current large language models (LLM) are lopsided, because both the people that design them are primarily Western, Educated, Industrialized, Rich, and Democratic (WEIRD)[8] and the data that has served to train

---

[7] Leaders who embrace an infinite mindset, and the logic of infinite play, will build stronger, more innovative, resilient organizations. Benefits may accrue over larger timescales than benefits associated with a finite mindset (Sinek, 2019).

[8] The term "WEIRD" in the context of science often refers to the critique that a significant portion of research in disciplines like psychology, cognitive science, and behavioral economics has relied heavily on samples drawn from Western, Educated, Industrialized,

these models come majoritarily from these demographics; differently put, this latest technology that everyone seems to be talking about nowadays, generative artificial intelligence ("GenAI"), represents only a tiny fraction of humanity. Technical reports often compare the outputs of LLMs with "human" performance. But "which" humans? People are a cultural species with substantial diversity around the globe, which is not fully captured by the textual data on which LLMs have been trained. Research has shown that LLM's responses to psychological measures are an outlier compared with large-scale cross-cultural data, and that their performance on cognitive psychological tasks most resembles that of people from WEIRD societies and declines massively when moving away from these populations (Atari et al., 2024). What we put in influences what comes out, but also who does it, and why.

This has major implications. On the one hand it means that the outputs that we are getting from these models are biased. It is essential to be acutely aware of this aspect, especially as AI is becoming ever more all pervasive. It has drastic consequences in all areas of life, from governmental administrations to policing, via college admissions to online dating and telemedicine. The LLMs that are seeping into our hybrid "reality" are not representative, and using them as if they were can be fatal for billions of people. On the other hand this inbuilt inclusion/exclusion aspect means that those who are in the privileged slice that AI is based on matter exponentially as their choices shape the future of AI. The current foundational models of AI reflect the past and present choices and mindsets of human beings. If we consider that these models are biased, and geared towards proprofit interests (which is unsurprising considering that they were designed by multi-trillion corporations), then we have to take action now if we want future models to be pro (all) people.

To ensure that AI evolves to become a force for social good requires action. Each of us is accountable to the next generation ("GenAI"). From frameworks for ethical AI development and deployment to inclusive policymaking and the prioritization of human-centered design, human beings

Rich, and Democratic societies (Heine et al., 2010). This critique argues that the overreliance on WEIRD samples in research can lead to findings and theories that may not generalize well to other populations or cultures. It highlights that WEIRD populations, which account for only about 12% of the global population, are statistically outliers in many psychological and behavioral dimensions.

can deliberately align AI's growth with humanity's best interests, mitigating risks such as bias, inequality, and misuse (Tegmark, 2017). It all starts with curiosity in the interaction with AI and acute awareness of how, and why we utilize it in our personal and professional environment, but also how and when it is used to influence us? The *A-Frame* (described below) can help to keep that curiosity alive, by consciously curating a mindset that questions the influence that AI has on our life. It will be needed to counteract the lull of mental ease and least resistance as technology becomes ever more pervasive.

If we aspire to a life in which we decide our own destiny, with a type of technology that acts in a benevolent but supporting role (as opposed to leading character), we must be aware what "it" is, and establish clear boundaries to protect the territories, including our mind, that we want to be and remain AI-free zones. This means to proactively shape that "it", rather than gradually being shaped by "it" and the players behind it. A candid understanding of our own limitations and those of other forces at play, whether they are artificial or biological, is required to consciously position ourselves in the continuum that a hybrid world represents.

No government or tech CEO, no dignitary of the United Nations (UN) nor a non-profit executive, will save us from AI; nor will AI save us from the institutions that we no longer believe in. AI is a tool. It may seem like magic but it will not transform the world for better unless we tailor and use it to that end. No one but ourselves can save ourselves. And the more assets we have at our disposal, be they material or immaterial, the greater the number of others whom we can potentially help along the way. Personal agency is our only hope for salvation. We must embrace the power that comes from it. To do so efficiently, our objectives must be clearly expressed.

If we are not playing the infinite game of life with an understanding of our own aspirations and the values that underpin them, and if we do not align our actions with these aspirations, then we are not in a position to complain about the consequences. Leaders may show the path but ultimately everyone must walk it on their own. AI can support that journey; it is neither a ticket nor a means of transportation. It is a tool that may serve to expand and accelerate positive dynamics that are initiated and pursued intentionally by human beings.

The following pages show the interplay of individual and collective inputs and outcomes, including on the one hand certain factors, direct and serendipitous, that influence our personal values, beliefs, and opinions and hereby our behavior—offline and online. On the other hand, we look at the nature of these behaviors as building blocks of public opinions, political movements, and social norms. One key message arises from that—social change starts with personal transformation, offline. If we want both dynamics to be conducive to the highest levels of quality of life, in a society where everyone has the opportunity to thrive, while existing in a sustainable way for the planet, we must configure technologies accordingly.

This book is based on the premise that an equitable society is to the benefit of everyone (Picket & Wilkinson, 2010). Efforts made in the interest of others have multiple benefits—for the individual who acts, the one who has been acted for, the community they live in, and wider society. This *Win4 Effect* (Sect. 4.1.1) is conditioned by benevolent choices.[9]

Artificial intelligence is evolving and intangible. It is the consequence of natural intelligence and hence reflects not only expressions of human cognition, but also human emotions and aspirations. It mirrors our fears and cravings, desires, and dreams—good and bad. That hybrid interplay is part of a new dynamic. Without considering it as a new species in the substance (Suleyman, 2024), nor moving along the path of gloom versus glory regarding its outcomes, it is clear that the human species is presently cruising unchartered waters. Although it started many years ago, we are in an early stage of this evolution, and the capacity of AI systems to discover, represent, and reproduce patterns in high dimensional data has still low dimensional embedding in the physical and digital worlds they inhabit (Shaboldt, 2022). Yet to quote Darwin about the evolution of species "from so simple a beginning endless forms most beautiful and most wonderful have been, and are being, evolved" (Darwin, 1959).

The circumferences of our hybrid world continue to change, and with it the place of humans. The question is how we can use AI to catalyze a propeople proplanet dynamic. This starts with human values which

---

[9] Benevolent choices are characterized by a kind, generous attitude, motivated by sympathy for the receiver and understanding of the circumstances (Merriam Webster, 2024). Note—"benevolence" will be used in this book to convey the human attitude that conditions AI's orientation towards the social good. Such a prosocial AI will be configured toward outcomes that serve to enhance the quality of life for a maximum of people independently of class, creed, color, gender, or age.

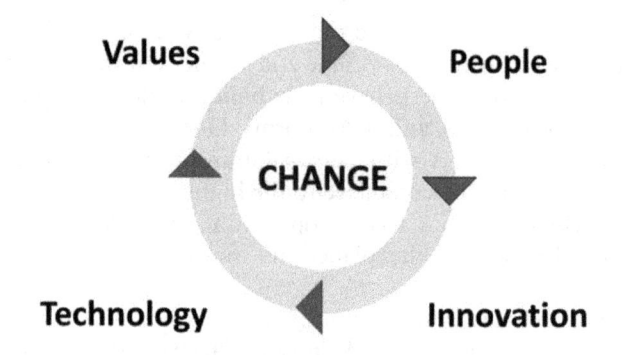

Fig. 1.1 Continuum of change: Values—Innovation—Leadership—Technology

are reflected in the type of innovations that arise and go mainstream. Leadership, at the personal and professional level, is the impersonated counterpart of values—which are a standard, a precious aspiration, yet which remains intangible unless humans apply them in practice. In turn this impacts the technologies that are created and taken to scale. AI is one manifestation of technology. Leveraging it as a force of social good requires clear intentions all around the cycle (Fig. 1.1). The numbers at stake are staggering; a brief, incomplete, snapshot of the current landscape can help to situate where we stand.

Values shape people's approach to innovation, both as creators and as consumers. Amongst those who are in positions of leadership this approach is amplified and finds its manifestation in the types of technology that are produced and reproduced at scale. These technologies may either reflect or amplify a benevolent attitude, or selfish motivations.

1.1.3 Situating This Book: Backdrop Snapshot

In early 2024, over 5.3 billion internet users were accounted for globally,[10] representing 70% of the world's population, a seven percent increase compared to early 2023 (DataReportal, 2024). But internet adoption continues to be uneven, ranging from 95% penetration in Europe to just 43% in Africa (DataReportal, 2024). The countries with

---

[10] This and the following figures keep on changing as the tectonic plates of the technology arena are shifting; yet they give a rough idea of the magnitudes at stake.

the largest online populations are the most populous ones, with China at over 1 billion users, India at 932 million, the US at 357 million, and Nigeria at 131 million (Statista, 2024).

Streaming entertainment content, messaging/social media, and e-commerce dominate internet usage. Over 60% of users watch online videos daily, while 78% use chat/messaging apps like WhatsApp and WeChat (GWI, 2024). Global e-commerce sales topped $3.1 trillion in 2023 (eMarketer, 2024). Additionally, 1.4 billion people now manage finances online (Mordor Intelligence, 2023).

Market dominance remains concentrated among tech giants, though some shifts have occurred. Google's search engine share dipped to 82%, while Microsoft's Bing gained ground (StatCounter, 2024). Meta's social media dominance slipped to 58% amid competition from upstarts like TikTok (Insider Intelligence, 2024). In e-commerce, Amazon's 40% US share was challenged by Walmart's 7% (Insider Intelligence, 2024). Alibaba's 55% of the Chinese market faced new rivals like PDD and JD (iiMedia, 2024). The public cloud race tightened, with AWS at 32%, Azure 28%, and Google Cloud 11% market share—while NVIDIA emerged as an AI cloud powerhouse (Canalys, 2024). 2023 revenues topped $1 trillion for Amazon, $305 billion for Alphabet, $189 billion for Microsoft, and $116 billion for NVIDIA (company reports).

While technology's economic influence boomed, poverty persisted as a global crisis. For perspective, at the time of writing around 1.1 to 1.5 billion persons worldwide live with income insufficient to purchase a minimum amount of goods and services to avoid poverty, as defined by the cost of living in their countries[11] (UNSD Database, 2023). That share increases further when people's needs are assessed not merely based on

---

[11] The calculation of poverty rates illustrates the limitations of data (see also Chapter 2). That is, the rates of poverty in the database are for different years (and are based on slightly different parameters to establish poverty lines, e.g. the minimum amount of calories to be ingested a day, e.g. 2000 or 2300). Nevertheless, they can be used to assess how many people are "counted" as poor in each country (e.g. according to official statistics monetary poverty is 0% in China and 15% in Sweden) although for some countries the data are rather old. Depending on how far back the latest available data points (e.g. 2017 or 2016, or 2015) are used to estimate the average values for the world population (excluding China), the proportion of individuals in monetary poverty hovers around 20-25%. An interesting case is India for which the latest value in the UN SDG is 21% for 2011. However, recent government estimates put that number at close to 5%. Overall, and keeping these limitations in mind, the global average is estimated to be around 20–25% using either value for India.

income but on access to basic necessities such as education, health care, or clean water. The United Nations (UN) estimates that it would take $175 billion annually to give every person on the planet the equivalent of PPP U$2.15 per day, a figure less than the 2022 revenues of Apple, Microsoft, or Alphabet (UN, 2022). In 2015 the Sustainable Development Goals (SDG) set a target of eradicating poverty in all its forms for all people everywhere by 2030. Yet based on current trajectories, over 300 million are projected to still be struggling to survive on less than a "dollar a day" by 2030.[12]

Whatever progress has been made to bridge the looming wealth gap, trends of reduction are not a given. As human-made issues such as war and environmental degradation come on top of chronic poverty, radical action—a deliberate effort to rebalance the resources at our disposal—is more needed than ever (Global End Child Poverty Coalition, 2023).

Beyond suffering in the present, the fallout of poverty can stifle a person's potential, setting them up for a lifetime of diminished quality of life. Research has shown that childhood poverty can impair brain development and cognitive functioning, with lasting effects on academic achievement, mental health, and life outcomes. As children living in poverty experience greater stress, malnutrition, and lack of enrichment opportunities, neural pathways are disrupted, gray matter volume decreases in critical brain regions, and the overall stress response systems are dysregulated (Evans & Kim, 2013; Hair et al., 2015; Luby et al., 2013). These neurological impacts contribute to poorer cognitive performance, behavioral issues, and increased risks later in life, perpetuating cycles of disadvantage (Duncan & Magnuson, 2012; Yoshikawa et al., 2012). A heavy mortgage is placed by every day of (preventable) deprivation on the generation that is growing up amid it. Ironically we are racing ahead towards the sophistication of artificial intelligence, while losing out on the biggest asset of humankind, natural intelligence.

Time for change is overdue. Simple interventions to improve early childhood education, nutrition, and support can systematically mitigate

---

[12] The "dollar a day" was introduced to the development agenda in 1990 by the World Bank (World Bank, 1990). However, it was never a real dollar but a Purchasing Power Parity one, given that at that time (very roughly) the poverty lines of the poorest countries hovered around 350 dollars (converted via the Purchasing Power Parity) per year, i.e. "a dollar a day". Since then, it has been updated several times and now stands at PPP U$ 2.15 which, in the vast majority of countries, is well below national poverty lines (representing a minimum cost of living).

poverty's negative effects on brain development (Lipina & Colombo, 2009; Neville et al., 2013). This has been known for decades, but no large-scale efforts were made to introduce them; we see a similar void regarding the macroeconomic policy shifts that they should be embedded in. A switch from proeconomic to propeople growth depends on human decision makers, but can we leverage AI to help us? *Human leadership for humane technology* as it is schematically outlined in this book seeks to deliberately dissolve the vicious cycle of past poverty and future failure, and reverse the tide towards a dynamic that gives everyone a fair chance to thrive, offline.

1.1.4 Notes and Selected Definitions

Note—Placed throughout this book are little check-in questions, inviting you to ponder your own perspective on the discussed topics. I encourage you to take a moment and think about them on the spot, possibly taking some notes to revisit later.[13]

Before we go deeper into the causes and consequences of innovation by and through technology, and the influence this has on human behavior, and vice versa, here are some basic definitions for words that are repeatedly used in these pages. Although there are others that come up these are picked out in particular because they have come to mean different things for different people. To facilitate the discussion, it is helpful to share the same meaning.

Universality: This collection is neither exclusive nor to be taken in isolation. The facts and factors that are described here attempt to circumscribe the status quo, to highlight the validity of certain principles that are independent of time and space.

Demographic representation: The selection of contributors in Chapter 3 symbolically illustrates a major problem of the technology

---

[13] I encourage you to use pen and paper for these exercises and questions. Research suggests that the act of handwriting engages multiple sensory and motor systems, including visual, tactile, and kinesthetic modalities, which contribute to enhanced memory encoding and retrieval (Longcamp et al., 2005). Handwriting involves the intricate coordination of fine motor skills, spatial awareness, and cognitive processes, leading to deeper engagement with the material. Typing primarily involves the motor skills associated with finger movements on a keyboard and relies less on the sensory feedback and spatial awareness inherent in handwriting.

sector. Women and people from low-income countries are underrepresented. This topic is worth many books by itself and will be addressed only briefly here.[14]

Technologicality: This is not a technological book; rather it offers a panorama of the landscape in which the AI-drama unfolds, with a focus on the causes and consequences of individual behavior and the values that underpin it, and hereby technology.

Evolution: The field is evolving fast. As I am writing these lines it is early 2024—the past months equal a quantum leap in terms of technological transformation. AI, including LLMs, has been around for decades, but the release of ChatGTP-3 in 2019 sparked a spike in interest. Adopted by millions users within the first weeks after it was unleashed to the public, it is among the fastest growing tech trends, and the underpinning LLMs increasingly impact how individuals write, read, learn, teach, work, and think. The first three chapters are heavy in references, with a focus on multidisciplinary scientific literature, to establish a foundation for the debate in this book. While science keeps on evolving fast the ideas and concepts that form the core of this book are timeless.

Innovation refers to the process of introducing new ideas, methods, or technologies that result in significant improvements, changes, or advancements in a particular field or domain (Schumpeter, 1934). It involves the generation, development, and implementation of novel solutions to address existing challenges or create new opportunities.

Technology refers to the application of scientific knowledge, tools, techniques, and systems to create, modify, or enhance processes, products, or services for specific purposes (Bunge, 1966). It encompasses both tangible artifacts and intangible systems, including forms of knowledge and expertise.

For the most part in this book the following technological terms will be thematically grouped under the wider umbrella of "technology": AI—AGI—AI agents—ML—DL—NLP—LLM—GTP—ChatGTP-types—API—BCI. Most of you will be familiar with these terms; for those who are not, a brief recap is offered here[15]:

---

[14] Addressing the "out versus in" caveat, which is one part of the biases that are bred into technology from the onset, is part of the AI4IA (*artificial intelligence for inspired action*) endeavor, which we will talk more about in a forthcoming book.

[15] Even though this book mostly refers to 'AI', it is important to remember that it is a technology with many separate, interconnected, technologies. All of them require

- Artificial intelligence (AI) refers to computer systems or machines that can perform tasks which typically require human intelligence, such as speech recognition, problem-solving, decision-making, and learning (Russell & Norvig, 2016). The umbrella term goes beyond the current hype of Generative AI and has been around for decades. For simplicity we are referring to AI as a signpost for the newest forms of AI systems.
- Artificial general intelligence (AGI) is a hypothetical form of artificial intelligence that would allow a machine to learn and think like a human. AGI, sometimes also called Artificial Super Intelligence (ASI), would need self-awareness and consciousness to solve problems, adapt to its surroundings, and perform a broad range of tasks.
- AI agents are programs that sense their surroundings, take actions, and learn to achieve goals. They operate in various environments and use data to perceive what's around them.
- Machine learning (ML) is a subfield of AI that focuses on creating algorithms and models that enable computers to learn from data and make predictions or decisions without being explicitly programmed (Mitchell, 1997). It involves training a model on a dataset to recognize patterns and make accurate predictions.
- Deep learning (DL) is a subset of machine learning that involves training artificial neural networks with multiple layers to learn and extract hierarchical representations of data (LeCun et al., 2015).
- Natural language processing (NLP) involves the use of AI and computational methods to enable computers to understand, interpret, and generate human language. It encompasses tasks such as text classification, sentiment analysis, machine translation, and speech recognition (Jurafsky & Martin, 2019).
- Large language models (LLM) are AI models trained on massive amounts of textual data, enabling them to generate coherent and

regulation, starting with machine learning. Yet the latter comes as part of a more extensive system. (For example, a robot involves beyond ML actuators, electric motors, materials, and other components requiring regulations and standardizations.) The governance of AI requires a holistic view of components and interplays. Unfortunately, much of the governance of AI is based on what has happened in the past rather than what is in the future. Given the rapid developments in AI, an adaptive and evolving regulatory framework is direly needed, rather than a static regulatory approach (Marwala, 2023).

contextually relevant text based on given prompts or queries (Brown et al., 2020).
- Generative pre-trained transformer (GTP) is a language model that uses deep learning to generate human-like text. GPTs are a type of Large Language Model (LLM). They are based on the transformer architecture, which is a type of neural network architecture.[16]
- ChatGPT (chatbot using GPT) is a specific implementation of large language models, such as OpenAI's ChatGPT-4, tailored for conversational interactions. It serves as a chatbot that can understand and respond to user input, (mostly) generating coherent and contextually appropriate responses based on its training data (Radford et al., 2019).
- Application programming interface (API) allows other tech companies to plug an LLM such as GPT-4 into their apps and products.
- Brain-computer interfaces (BCI) acquire brain signals, analyze them, and translate them into commands that are channeled to output devices that carry out desired actions.
- Multimodal models allow beyond text input the interpretation, combination, and production of images, sound, and video. Multimodal agents are able to process sight, sound, and more, allowing them to interact more naturally. Increasingly they are tailored to operate across various platforms.

For the sake of completeness, also to be mentioned are AutoGTP and the Metaverse which may yet again alter the technological landscape if they are taken to scale:

- AutoGTP is based on LLM technology. Drawing on a multimodal system, it can handle different types of data, including images, speech, and text. Incorporating different AI systems to make decisions based on predetermined rules and goals it operates beyond isolated prompts, across multiple platforms. AutoGTP can be given a general goal, such as planning an event, and split it into subtasks which it then completes by itself, without human input (Metz,

---

[16] GPTs work by taking a sequence of tokens, such as words in a sentence to predict the next word in the output sequence. To capture context and relationships between words they attend to different parts of the input. GPTs are trained on large datasets of unlabeled text, via two main steps: pre-training and fine-tuning.

2023). As its ability of dealing with complexity ripens, it may become possible to delegate everything from A to Z, starting with the prompt that manifests the intention.
- The Metaverse refers to a virtual shared space that merges physical and virtual reality. It is a digital universe where users interact with computer-generated environments and other users in real time. It goes beyond traditional 2D internet experiences, offering immersive, 3D, and often persistent virtual spaces (Zuckerberg, 2021). Like Quantum Computing described below it is stuck in its infancy as it remains unclear if and how it can be operationalized in a safe, accessible, and economically viable way, even though top global players have been investing an estimated $180 billion in the past few years.

To illustrate the relationships among these terms, picture a social media platform[17] that wants to enhance user experience by implementing an AI-powered chatbot. In this example, AI serves as the overarching concept, while machine learning, deep learning, and natural language processing are specific techniques utilized within AI. The chatbot utilizes NLP techniques to understand and respond to user messages. It incorporates ML algorithms to improve its understanding and generate relevant responses based on the training data it has received. DL techniques may be employed to enhance the chatbot's ability to recognize patterns and generate more contextually appropriate responses. The chatbot could be built using LLM, such as GPT-4o, trained on a vast amount of text data from various sources, enabling it to generate coherent and human-like responses. An API would allow the owner of the platform account to auto-generate content straight from the platform. With AutoGTP one prompt could trigger a chain of events from ideation to publication. In the Metaverse the user's experience is multisensorial, spans multiple spaces, and is continued in time and space.

We have come far, but some predict that the large-scale introduction of quantum computing will yet again radically shift the innovation landscape, and that the related adjustments may be much more painful, because quantum computers operate in a way that is very different from

---

[17] Social media refers to web-based platforms and applications that allow users to create, share, and interact with content and engage in social networking. Examples include platforms like X (formerly Twitter) or Instagram, where users can post messages, share photos or videos, and connect with others (Kaplan & Haenlein, 2010).

digital computers (Velu et al., 2022).[18] Seeing that it adds gigantic computing power to the arsenal of human technology QC could be a gamechanger for massive global challenges such as climate change and pandemics. However, although government and business investment in QC hovers around $35.5 billion globally, the technology remains undermined by excessive costs, cybersecurity concerns and unrealistic business expectations (WEF, 2023).

Although they are often used synonymously, innovation and technology are deliberately distinguished in this book, because innovation can lead to technology, and often it does, but it is larger, embracing the potential of transformation that comes from a shift in mindsets and new (inter)personal approaches to old challenges. Seeing the expanding range of technological tools, one is tempted to think that solutions to challenges that have been plaguing humanity for centuries, such as poverty, inequality, or violence, are finally at reach. And indeed, this latest wave of innovation could serve to produce more efficient, effective, and sustainable solutions. Yet ultimately, the highest hurdle in that endeavor is not the ability of the technology, nor of its user. Rather it ties back to the pecuniary interests and deriving (re)distribution of resources (material, political, etc.) of the latter. "If we can land a man on the moon, why can't we solve the problems of the ghetto?" (Nelson, 1977) Differently put—if we can travel to space, why don't we fix the problems of humans on earth.

AI holds only a tiny share in the titanic riddle that humanity is tasked to tackle—personal ego and greed. This sounds grandiose and simplistic at the same time. Either way, it hinges on our sense of self and a mindset

---

[18] Quantum computing (QC) is a type of computing that leverages the principles of quantum mechanics, specifically superposition and entanglement, to perform operations. Unlike classical computers that use bits (0s and 1s), quantum computers use qubits, which can exist in multiple states simultaneously. This parallelism enables quantum computers to solve certain problems much faster than classical computers (Nielsen & Chuang, 2010). Quantum computing holds promise for tasks such as complex simulations, cryptography, and optimization problems. While in the long run, businesses adopting quantum computing should have a competitive edge over others; in the short term, it is unclear to what extent the introduction of these machines will prove commercially valuable. "Assuming that the productivity growth rate slows by 50% more than it did for simpler digital computers, we estimate that the introduction of commercial quantum computers could result in economic losses in gross domestic product (GDP) per capita of approximately US$13,000 over 15 years (based on 2022 levels), or $310 billion per annum in the United States alone" (Velu and Putra, 2023).

of agency. What we really need are not more tools, but an innovation of the human mindset, with a radical focus on the fundamental values that make us human, and humane. Respectively and combine they condition our personal leadership attitude.

1.1.4.1 Aspirations for Action—Value-Driven Leadership

A central question of this book is how we can harness artificial intelligence (AI) to nurture inspired action (IA) across the social hierarchy? Differently said, how can we build a human foundation that thrives thanks to its natural and artificial assets, rather than being overwhelmed by them. In this context, everyone matters, and in certain ways everyone is a leader in their own life and environment. This personal leadership role is extrapolated among those who are in a position where others look to them for guidance, be that at home or at work, in the public or the private sector. The higher up an individual is on the social food chain, the larger the ripple effect of their (in)action will be.

Academically, **leadership** is defined as the ability of guiding others toward common goals (Bass & Riggio, 2006). It involves the process of fostering collaboration, while accepting accountability for the success and well-being of the team or organization (Northouse, 2018). Many different definitions of leadership exist; their common denominator is a personal anchor in values. Seeing the amplifying effect of all actions in a hybrid world, an expansive view of personal leadership must be taken, to include stewardship. The latter refers to a duty of care in the management of people, resources, environments, or systems on behalf of others (Block, 2013). Stewards oversee and protect what they have been entrusted with for the greater good rather than self-interested goals (Hernandez, 2008). While leadership drives purposive organization, stewardship entails custodial responsibility towards collective resources, capabilities, or ecosystems for society overall and for posterity, aligning decisions to that higher purpose (Haski-Leventhal et al., 2019). Catalyzing outcomes that are beneficial to people and planet requires the combination of both in the form of authentic caring leadership. This requires self-aware people who display integrity in their own lives. They are not afraid to show their own vulnerability which makes them trustworthy in the eyes of others, because they are perceived as authentic (Avolio et al., 2004). Anchored in their personal values they do respect the uniqueness of each individual and succeed to create a sense of belonging, where a feeling of unity arises amid diversity. Leadership in a sense that matters for humanity is unthinkable without values.

Values are the deeply held beliefs that guide the choices of individuals, groups, or societies (Rokeach, 1973). They serve as a moral compass, shaping attitudes, and behaviors.[19] At the individual level they influence our (subconscious) perception of morality and ethics, of material and emotional worthiness. This expands the person to impact the ethical standards, cultural norms, and organizational principles that come to characterize a group, and society. They inspire what we aspire to, representing an unspoken fiber of our decision-making process. While the influence of attitudes and behaviors that are pinned on values is not necessarily beneficial (i.e. loyalty to a dictator and respect of his orders to kill), the values in and by themselves are not harmful—rather it is their interpretation by the human "user" which is motivated by (sub)conscious interests that are causing the pejorative impact on others.

The more precisely we can define our personal values, and the motivation that underpins them, the better we are positioned to assess the social fabric that we are part of and identify contradictions that may exist between our sense of self and social patterns that we detect around us. If we consider people as the epicenter of society, then values are the epicenter of the epicenter (Sect. 1.4.1). Neither people nor values are homogenous. Depending on context and culture people tend to adopt, consciously or unknowingly, different moral priorities. We will explore the value venue further in the next chapter (Sect. 2.3.1).

---

[19] Aside from the aspirational side of values mentioned earlier there is value attached to things and services. What value a society attaches to something differs depending on perception and circumstances. A word on the most common types (some of them overlap but the terminology is attached to specific conceptual frameworks, so they are listed separately here): Economic Value—the amount a consumer is willing to pay for a good or service (Samuelson & Marks, 2003). It is determined by the maximum price a buyer would pay and minimum price a seller would accept. Use Value—the utility, worth, or usefulness a product can provide (Marx, 1867/1976). It satisfies consumer needs and wants. Exchange Value—the rate something can be traded for other goods, services, or money (Marx, 1867/1976). It determines the relative price compared to other commodities. Subjective Value—the importance or desirability of a good or service based on individual preferences (von Mises, 1949). It varies between different people. Sentimental Value—the emotional worth attached to an object, often based on personal memories or feelings (Kamptner, 1995). The value is subjective and relational. Cultural Value—the worth and importance assigned to objects, ideas, or behaviors within a culture (Throsby, 2001). It reflects shared norms and social practices.

The "**Common Good**" represents the overall outcome that *prosocial AI* is configured to serve. It encompasses assets that benefit the well-being and welfare of a community or society overall, reflecting principles and values related to shared quality of life[20] and the promotion of equal benefits.[21] Representing moral obligations and goals that serve a society to function and prosper it encompasses a collective value standard (Sandel, 2020). Already Aristotle emphasized the importance of the polis [people] acting for the common interest of its citizens. In many religions the Common Good is described as the sum of social conditions that allow people to reach their fulfillment more fully and easily (John XXIII, 1961). It is often associated with the Golden Rule, a universal principle that encourages treating others as one would wish to be treated oneself. Anchored in values of compassion and generosity it is an ethical maxim that has been embraced by cultures and belief systems worldwide, albeit with some variations,[22] it is the quintessence of universal citizenship. This universality makes it twice puzzling to notice the clash between the status quo where billions of people survive amid (avoidable) deprivation and the latent potential of alleviating that suffering.

---

[20] Quality of life refers to an individual's overall well-being and satisfaction with various aspects of their life, including physical health, mental and emotional well-being, social relationships, and overall life satisfaction. It encompasses subjective perceptions of happiness, fulfillment, and contentment, as well as objective measures such as access to healthcare, education, employment, and living conditions. Quality of life is influenced by individual characteristics, societal factors, and environmental conditions, and it is often used as a key indicator of human development and societal progress (WHOQOL Group, 1995).

[21] For further details the following references provide different perspectives and approaches to the concept of the Common Good, ranging from political philosophy to bioethics: Buchanan & Keohane (2006), Comte-Sponville (2002), DeGrazia (2005), Rawls (1999).

[22] Examples of the cross-cultural appearance of the Golden Rule include: Christianity: "Do unto others as you would have them do unto you" (Matthew 7:12, New International Version); Buddhism: "Hurt not others in ways that you yourself would find hurtful" (Udana-Varga 5.18); Hinduism: "This is the sum of duty: do not do to others what would cause pain if done to you" (Mahabharata 5:1517); Confucianism: "What you do not want done to yourself, do not do to others" (Analects 15.24); Islam: "None of you truly believes until he wishes for his brother what he wishes for himself" (An-Nawawi's Forty Hadith 13). These principles align with the concept of the common good, as they encourage consideration for the well-being of others and promote social harmony. By treating others with kindness, respect, and fairness, individuals contribute to the collective welfare of their communities (Küng, 1998).

The Common Good represents an ethical ideal of community well-being that transcends personal interests. Pursuing it requires a dynamic of individual efforts, and collective action across different social spheres including government, business, and civil society to advance shared values of fairness, solidarity, and human flourishing. Differently said, overcoming the contradiction of high value aspiration and the manifestation of such values in practice involves personal (*micro*) and collective (*macro*) choices that need to be made. The World Wide Web is a constant reminder that we share one globe, which has implications for everyone within the hybrid hive. Technology carries immense potential to harness the power of the Common Good, and to translate it from ideal to implementation. In addition, from The Andean perspective of "Buen vivir"[23] to the concept of "Deep Ecology",[24] the common good can be extended to include nature (*meta*). Ultimately the outcomes of the "Common" Good depend on commoners (individuals) who choose to be good, online and offline. In the rest of this book we refer to the Common Good as a central ambition of prosocial AI.

Following this overall "mise en scene" the following briefly summarize the logic of the POZE paradigm, which was prototyped in Haiti in 2017[25] and introduced to academic audiences in 2020. Since then, it has found application worldwide, across social and educational entities, as well as within the United Nations (Walther, 2020).

1.2 M4-MATRIX—ARENAS OF TRANSFORMATION

1.2.1 Universal Principles:
Change—Connection—Continuum—Complementarity

The content of the multidimensional framework that underpins this book is based on the collective findings of researchers and practitioners, spanning millennia. By synthesizing the best discoveries from thinkers and

---

[23] Loosely translated as a "Good Life" it as a philosophy is based on the worldview of indigenous peoples. It aims to ensure that all members of a community have material, social, and spiritual satisfaction, but not at the expense of others or the environment.

[24] Deep ecology is an environmental philosophy that promotes the inherent worth of all living beings regardless of their instrumental utility to human needs, and a reconfiguration of modern human societies in accordance with such ideas (Naess, 2002).

[25] In Haitian Creole the word "poze" translates as "inner peace" which the practice of this approach offers.

doers across eras and cultures, it offers a multidisciplinary, multidimensional framework that combines theory and practice, blending knowledge from the past and present to provide tools for optimizing the future for both people and planet (Walther, 2021). This perspective is referred to as POZE.

The acronym POZE encapsulates the 4 components of the underlying logic: a new **P**erspective on life and living; the **O**ptimization of internal and external interplays; which leads to the ascension of successive **Z**eniths; and thereby, **E**xposure to the world as it is and as it could be. Without going into extensive details, this and the following sections summarize POZE's philosophy and the perspective it derives from in view of reshaping our perception of life and living.

Our perception of the environment influences our experience of and expressions in that environment, which in turn influences how we remember it. This interplay impacts how we remember the past, and behave in the future. How we subjectively interpret flows of information shapes our mental models and behaviors (Capra & Luisi, 2014). The observer is part of the observation, hence we are never completely "neutral". What we perceive as objective "reality" is actually a subjective creation, a constant process, in which we are simultaneously the creator and the creation itself. It is an organic kaleidoscope that we shape while being shaped by it. We are part of an evolving mandala of colorful quicksand, that is part of ourselves. Nothing is ever cast in stone. This suggests some universal patterns in how "reality" (or what we perceive as such) self-organizes, aligning with the principles of dynamism, emergence, and self-regulation in systems thinking and computer science (Mitchell, 2009) which links to the question of *glocal synchronization* that we will look at in Chapter 2.[26]

4 principles apply throughout this ever unfolding dynamic:

1. Change: Everything is always evolving.
2. Connection: Everything is linked.

---

[26] In systems thinking, everything is interconnected with bidirectional relationships and feedback loops. A small change in one element affects others, and the more complex a system is, the more consequences are triggered by a single cause, with higher-order emergent behaviors arising from many interactions between simpler components (Meadows, 2008).

3. Continuum: Everything is part of a flowing whole that extends infinitely in all directions.
4. Complementarity: Everything is completing something else and is incomplete without something else.

In this perspective, everything matters. The smallest shift can have far-reaching consequences; we never know which action, when, where, and under what circumstances will become a cause for the circumstances we seek or intend to avoid. The only safe bet in this organically evolving phantasmagoria of life and living is to follow the tradition of karma yoga: "give your best—in light of the knowledge and level of ability that you have at the time of (re)action, and then let go" (Sivananda, 1999).

Since every human operates within a twice 4-dimensional paradigm (Walther, 2020) our own frame of mind and body is a laboratory to understand others, and our relationships with them. This kind of refined comprehension of the circumstances that are at play in society conditions our ability to influence others in the way we want, and to protect ourselves from external influence that we do not want. In a society where every action carries the potential of artificial amplification, where offline and online form a boomerang with hybrid consequences, such refined awareness of interplays is an essential asset. Not only because it equips us to build up a shield against manipulation, but also because it makes it obvious that no matter the circumstances our choices matter. We are not passive pions in a larger gameplan, unless we accept that role, which is a choice in itself. In the following we look in more detail at the social and personal implications of that view.

1.2.2 Society's Multidimensional Configuration

Everything is connected within a continuum of constant change. A multidimensional logic applies within the personal sphere and operates in the collective arena. Optimization is elusive, yet it begins by embracing the whole while acknowledging each component. Already Aristotle (384–322 BC) reasoned that the sum is more than its parts.[27] When we limit ourselves to acknowledge, and address only certain parts, we miss out

---

[27] "In the case of all things which have several parts and in which the totality is not, as it were, a mere heap, but the whole is something besides the parts, there is a cause; for even in bodies contact is the cause of unity in some cases, and in others viscosity or

twice on the elements that fall between the cracks of our attention, and on the magic of the ensemble, which unfolds when interplays are identified and influenced deliberately. The following summarizes the components of the *m4-matrix*, a multidisciplinary framework illustrating the complementarity of *micro* (person), *meso* (community), *macro* (country), and *meta*[28] (planet). Technology comes to play in each arena, as a cause and consequence of our ongoing evolution as a species. A word on each arena (Fig. 1.2) is followed by examples of the respective risks and opportunities that AI has in them:

The *micro*-arena encapsulates individuals, each constituting a 4-dimensional entity by itself that is intrinsically connected to the broader whole (as explained below sect. 1.2.3). Analogous to fractals, every component condenses the multidimensional essence of the complete entity to which it belongs. Within this intricate framework, individuals evolve in tandem with everything, while still exerting their influence autonomously. Although seemingly paradoxically each element plays a crucial role in shaping, disbanding, and adjusting the whole, while simultaneously and reciprocally being influenced by the outcomes and the dynamic process of change. This interconnected dance bears resemblance to the intricate DNA of an organism, where each cell contains the blueprint of the entire organism, embodying the fundamental interconnectedness of individual elements within a larger, cohesive system (Alberts et al., 2002). Each individual micro-system is part of a universal system. Life is a constantly evolving organism. One illustration of the connection between those of the same species is synchrony. In humans it can be measured with biomarkers such as brainwaves and heart rate. Research found that heart rate synchrony predicted the probability of groups reaching the correct consensus decision with higher accuracy than any subjective measure of team dynamics (Sharika et al., 2024). Conversely, shared activities be it interpersonal conversation, games, or even listening to music increase the synchronicity of the participants' brainwaves (Platt, 2023).

some other such quality" [Metaphysics Book VIII, 1045a.8–10, Aristotle; Translated W. D. Ross 1908].

[28] Note—The word "*meta*" comes from the Greek prefix meta, which means "after" or "beyond": the term *meta* was introduced for the global level as part of the POZE framework in 2020 (Walther, 2020) before Mark Zuckerberg renamed Facebook.

The *meso*-arena covers communities, institutions,[29] and multi-person entities. Each institution is composed of individuals. The interpersonal relationships that are the cause and consequence of the *meso* dimension may be biological (e.g. family), social (e.g. church) political (e.g. city council), voluntarily chosen (e.g. chess-club), semi-voluntary (e.g. school, workplace), or involuntary (military recruitment). The characteristic that *meso* entities are composed of individuals means on the one hand that these entities evolve with the evolution of their constituting components, which in turn is an opportunity for agency and influence as exercised consciously by these "components". On the other hand, the inseparable connection of individuals and institutions tends to engender a chicken and egg conundrum—where individuals are more likely to complain about "the system" which they are part of, than recognizing that they themselves create, amend, maintain, and expand the rules and resources of that system. This becomes a self-fulfilling vacuum as the systemic setup influences the people that operate in their realm. It is a catch-22 which starts and stops with individual choices.

The *macro*-arena entails countries, cultures, and economies, differently put, it covers large social arrangements that are not global. It is made up of the *micro*- and *meso*-arenas, and provides building blocks for the *meta*-arena (see below). It represents the formalized structures of individuals in a society, i.e. countries, but also less formal shared spaces of experience such as cultures or economies. Each society is ruled by its respective norms and laws, while being influenced by the individuals, communities which are part of it, and the universe which it is part of. The *macro*-level is a conceptual construct that has come into being when humans began to connect beyond the immediate circumscription of closest kin.

The *meta*-arena englobes everything else. In the human sphere it reflects Planet Earth, including also international organizations such as the United Nations whose mandate reaches across borders while being governed by individual interests and national agendas, as well as multinational corporations such as Google, Amazon, and OpenAI whose scope and interventions are not limited by borders or specific national limitations. Global phenomena that affect the whole planet, such as globalization, technologization, climate change, or pandemics, are situated for the sake of conceptualization in the *meta*-arena, because their causes

---

[29] Note—in this context institutions are akin to organizations, not established rules of society (i.e. marriage).

and consequences pertain to each of the three others. Nothing happens in isolation; in a realm of interconnection every (in)action has ripple effects. Recognizing the intricacies of this dynamic opens the possibility to systematically configure ourselves, and the arenas that we belong to, with the intent of synchronization that serves to optimize the complementarity of all components.

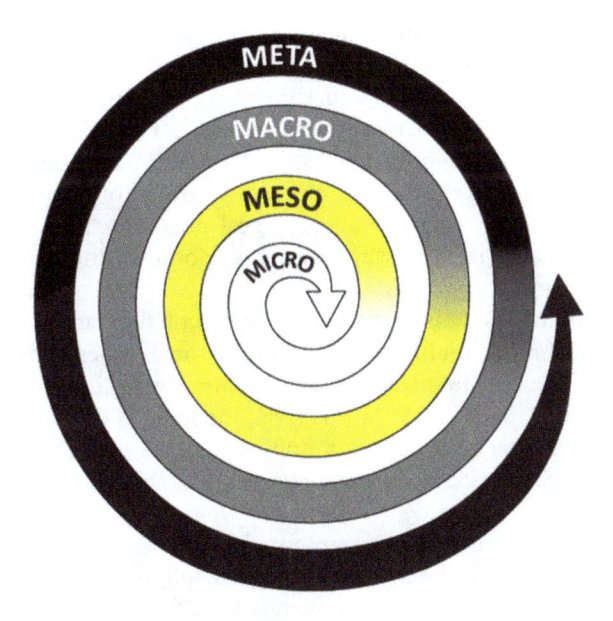

Fig. 1.2 *m4-matrix*

Caption Everything is connected, individuals, communities/institutions, countries/economies, and the planet influence each other; they mirror the mutual influence of the 4 dimensions that shape who we are as individuals (see below). Nothing happens in a vacuum. Technology influences this doubled 4-dimensionality directly and indirectly.

Speaking code—By representing these arenas in code developers can create algorithms and simulations that capture the interactions and interdependencies between individuals, communities, countries, and the planet. This allows for the analysis and understanding of complex systems and the potential impact of individual and collective behaviors on different levels of the system. The following offers a simplistic illustration of the conceptual relationships between *micro-*, *meso-*, *macro-*, and *meta*-arenas in coding language, although their actual implementation and representation may vary depending on the programming language and context of the application:

micro[30]: Individuals can be represented as objects or variables. Deriving from their respective mix of education, genetics, environment, and upbringing, each individual has their own set of attributes and behaviors that define them uniquely. They can interact with other individuals and the broader system.

meso: Communities can be represented as collections of single-line arrays of individuals (i.e. a two-by-two matrix). They form on the one hand a collection of unique objects, and on the other they represent a higher-level structure that encompasses a group of individuals with shared characteristics, goals, or geographical proximity. The interactions among individuals within a community contribute to the dynamics and functioning of the community.

macro: Countries/Economies can be represented as larger-scale structures that encompass multiple communities (three-dimensional matrices composed of the two-by-two arrays at the *meso*-arena, i.e. data arranged in rows, columns, and slices). At this level, the focus is on the aggregated behavior and interactions of communities, such as economic activities, policies, and social systems (i.e. the connections among the elements in the matrix).

meta: Planet/Nature can be represented as the overarching system that encompasses all the aforementioned elements and interplays. This can be represented as nested collections or hierarchies of communities and countries. The whole (*meta*-arena) can be modeled as a global entity that influences and is influenced by the actions and interactions of communities and individuals. This level emphasizes the broader ecological and environmental context within which human activity takes place. Risks and opportunities that manifest in one arena influence the dynamics in other arenas, while being influenced by them return.

Now that we have established the collective scaffolding of human existence we are zooming in on the *micro*-dimension as the epicenter of the *m4-matrix* that society represents. Like a crystal every part is a fractal of the whole, of which it contains the blueprint.

---

[30] In Sect. 1.2.3, we look at the 4 dimensions that each individual is composed of (aspirations, emotions, thoughts, and sensations).

1.2.3 Individual Dimensions of Human Existence

Human existence encompasses multiple dimensions which mutually influence one another (Mayer et al., 2014). Across various philosophical, religious, and psychological traditions such a holistic understanding of human nature has found entry. When we consider the interplay of aspirations, emotions, thoughts, and sensations, and acknowledge each of these dimensions as an inherent aspect of human experience, the interpretation of behavior becomes an undertaking that takes place with consideration of the social context in which it is situated. The interdimensional dynamic that shapes our sense of self, our desires, cognitive processes, and our behavior is the cause and consequence of that social environment. A word on each individual dimension, including its influence on the others.

The soul, often associated with spirituality and the essence of one's being, represents the intangible aspect of human existence. It is connected to the search for a higher power or ultimate truth (Koltko-Rivera, 2006). In the present context it is used without a religious connotation. The soul encompasses aspects such as aspirations, values, beliefs, and the pursuit of personal growth and connection with something beyond the material world. The human quest for meaning, a "Why", which has motivated human progress over millennia, sparking creation and innovations, is anchored here. Aspirations provide a sense of direction and meaning, guiding cognitive and emotional processes (see below about the mind and the heart). An attitude of global *citizenship* as an expression of shared humanity emanates from the aspirations to serve the Common Good; rather than perceiving it as a sacrifice it becomes a step on the path of personal growth. Goal-setting and self-determination theories explore how aspirations influence our thoughts, emotions, and actions (Locke & Latham, 2002). When individuals have positive aspirations, such as pursuing a dream or building a meaningful relationship, they experience positive emotions such as joy, contentment, or satisfaction. For example, the aspiration for a fair society, driven by the value of justice, may motivate a person to get involved in social activism (see below about the body), contributing their thoughts, emotions, and actions towards creating a better society; this personal engagement will build their self-esteem, while inducing emotions of joy due to fulfillment, and warmth as a result of the experience of human interconnection. *Awareness*[31] of us and others as referred to in this context starts from the inside, reaching far beyond the physical framework of the body to encompass our sense of self.

The heart encompasses the realm of emotions, feelings, and relationships. It represents the seat of *compassion*, love, and emotional intelligence (Hertenstein et al., 2006), influencing how individuals form and maintain social connections, navigate interpersonal dynamics, and experience empathy towards others (see below about the body). Emotions are complex psychological responses to stimuli that occur in our internal and external environment. They play a significant role in influencing our cognition (see below about the mind), perception, attention, and memory (Damasio, 2010). Emotional arousal enhances memory consolidation (Cahill & McGaugh, 1998). Whereas emotions such as joy spark creativity and problem-solving abilities (Isen, 2009), negative emotions like sadness impair cognitive performance (Sapolsky, 2015). Emotions can be consciously influenced by our aspirations, thoughts, and physical sensations (Keltner et al., 2019). For instance, people who aspire to achieve a particular objective may think about ways to achieve it; they experience joy when they make progress towards it, and maybe downcast by failure. We cannot control how we feel, but we can deliberately concentrate on our bodily sensation to redirect our attention to a tangible area of experience. *Appreciation* of who we are (not) is not primarily rational, but a feeling of embracing ourselves, all caveats included.

The mind encompasses cognition and intellectual capacities. It includes aspects such as rationality, memory, problem-solving, and the acquisition and application of knowledge (Sternberg, 2003). It influences how individuals perceive the world, think about, and engage with it. This combination of factors is the foundation of *conscientiousness*, which encompasses how we position ourselves in our environment. Physiologically speaking one might consider the brain as the nexus where thoughts, emotions, sensations intersect. Our choices are influenced not only by aspirations and emotions (see above about the soul and the heart, respectively) but also by the information that we receive via our sense tools (see below about the body) and the neural networks that underlie cognitive

---

[31] Note—The 4 A's in this subsection, each attributed to one dimension although they influence the others and are influenced by them, relate to the *A-Frame* that we will look at in Sect. 1.4.1.

functions. For instance, alarming thoughts may result from the experience of fear due to a past traumatic event, impacting an individual's present thoughts, emotions, and subsequent behaviors. Coping strategies, including those that are harmful, like denial, substance abuse, or isolation may be adopted and maintained long after the situation has been overcome (Seligman, 2011). This connection between past experience and present expression works both ways, which offers entry points to modify acquired behavior patterns that are outdated. Reexamining and reframing a shameful experience can be helpful to intentionally reshape our inner narrative. *Acceptance* of our proactive potential brings power. Once we accept that we are not helpless victims of our spiraling thoughts and feelings, we can start to deliberately influence the voice in our head, to craft an honest, yet kind narrative. This internal dialogue shapes how we feel about ourselves and others; if we cannot be our own champions no artificial coach or AI-powered "friend" will be able to fill that inner void.

The body is the physical vessel of human existence. It represents the tangible interface through which individuals interact with the world and express themselves in it. That portal encompasses the physiological and sensory aspects of being alive (Boroditsky et al., 2003). Sensations correspond to the embodied experiences encountered through our senses, such as touch, taste, smell, sight, and hearing[32]; they are mediated by the nervous system and can directly impact our thoughts, feelings, and behaviors. For instance, the smell of freshly baked cookies may not only trigger appetite, but evoke feelings of comfort and nostalgia, while the sound of crashing waves can induce a sense of tranquility and relaxation. These external inputs interact with hormonal signals in the brain to shape our perception of the world and influence our emotional and cognitive responses (Damasio, 1994).

The body is also home to a range of intricate internal physiological processes. Hormones, chemical messengers secreted by various glands throughout the body, play a crucial role in regulating bodily functions,

---

[32] The exact number of senses is still debated among scientists; beyond the traditional five senses one may cite Thermoception—ability to detect temperature; Equilibrioception—sense of balance and acceleration; Proprioception—awareness of position in space; Chonotaxis—sensitivity to mechanical stimuli like vibration; Nociception—perception of pain; and Magnetoception—detection of magnetic fields (Bartholomew et al., 2020). Some scientists argue humans may have additional sensory abilities like intuiting information and sensing energies.

while influencing our emotions (see above about the heart) and consequently our behavior (McEwen, 2006). For example, the release of endorphins during exercise can produce sensations of euphoria and well-being (Hillman et al., 2008, contributing to positive emotional states and overall cognitive performance) (see above about the mind). Similarly, the surge of adrenaline in response to a perceived threat can trigger the body's fight-or-flight response, preparing it to react quickly to danger (Cannon, 1915); the brain's amygdala is involved, and the mind is not deliberately but instinctively reacting. Acts of courage start with a firm determination and result in the emission of adrenaline that catalyzes the behavior, despite feelings of fear. Thus, the body serves as a dynamic membrane between external environments and the internal landscape of thoughts, emotions, and sensations, with hormones acting as key mediators in this intricate interplay. Once we understand the interconnection between everything and everyone, including ourselves, *accountability* for our contribution is the only conclusion that is left (Fig. 1.3).

Interplays of mind and matter.[33] External stimuli shape our cognition, while beliefs impact our bodily responses. For example, placebos, which are inactive substances or interventions, can lead to real physiological changes when individuals believe they are receiving an effective treatment (Benedetti, 2008). Conversely, bodily sensations such as breath or heartbeat may help individuals to focus their (mental) attention, and gradually cultivate awareness of their thought patterns and emotions, rather

---

[33] Human Stress is one illustration of the mutual influence of physiological and mental stimuli. Whether it results from personal or professional circumstances it can trigger a cascade of physiological responses in the body, such as increased heart rate, muscle tension, and elevated cortisol levels. Conversely, bodily sensations may lead to feelings of anxiety, irritability, or sadness, which affect one's thoughts, leading to negative thinking patterns and cognitive distortions that contribute to mental health issues like depression or anxiety (Cohen et al., 2007). By altering the gut microbiome, stress leads to gastrointestinal and psychological issues (Kelly et al., 2015). It becomes a vicious cycle as the external event triggers changes in neurotransmitter production influencing our mood and cognitive functioning, which impacts our perception of the present situation and the future. Stress-induced physiological responses, such as increased cortisol levels and high blood pressure, negatively impact the body's systems and contribute to the overall risk of early mortality and illness; studies found links between chronic stress and cardiovascular disease, immune dysfunction, and metabolic disorders (McEwen, 2007). This cycle may be worsened by our food choices[#], which tend to be particularly unhealthy when we are stressed (Madison & Glaser, 2019). Respectively and together these consequences of stress gradually erode our ability to focus and perform in a given situation, which in many cases is likely to increase the stress and worsen our response to it.

than merely reacting to them instinctively. Groomed over time a deliberate approach to the mind–body connection leads to improved emotional regulation and mental clarity (Tang et al., 2015). The mind is both ally and enemy; we need to frame it to tame it—while keeping "in mind" that it is not without fail. We like to think that we are rational yet mental shortcuts meant to facilitate fast decision-taking make us vulnerable to biases and fallacies (see below on "Human software"), which hijack our reasoning, often without us even noticing it (Kahneman, 2007).

Natural intelligence is not simply a product of the brain. It emerges from the entire organism functioning as an integrated system of "human hardware and software" (Gershon, 1998). Beyond just neural activity, intelligence arises through the dynamic interplay of multiple bodily components like the autonomic nervous system which includes the ancient dorsal vagus involved in shutdown responses and the more evolutionarily recent ventral vagus facilitating social engagement (Porges, 2011). The gut-brain axis of bidirectional communication between the enteric nervous system and the brain is another example, with the gut's production of neurotransmitters like serotonin impacting cognitive and emotional processes (Carabotti et al., 2015). Research has shown that the gut-brain axis is directly involved in the state of our mental and physical well-being (Foster & McVey Neufeld, 2013). As Damasio (1994) theorized, reason is shaped by somatic markers—emotional signals arising from the body's biochemical state. Thus, human intelligence is an embodied phenomenon extending throughout the entire nervous system and physiological milieu.

Speaking code—In a simplified transposition from computer systems to human organisms one might think of thoughts, emotions, and aspirations as software; and of cells, organs, etc., as hardware. The DNA is the blueprint of that system; not immutable, but a rather defined roadmap. Translating this to coding terms, we can consider aspirations as the overarching goals that guide our thoughts, decisions, and actions. These aspirations serve as the driving force behind our endeavors, much like the objectives in software development that shape the direction and purpose of a project. Emotions can be likened to variables or states, the values of which represent various inputs and circumstances. Much like circumstances in which algorithms play out, emotions play a significant role in influencing our perceptions, motivations, and decision-making processes. Just as variables in coding represent different factors and impact the flow of a program, emotions influence our thoughts and actions. Thoughts can be seen as the cognitive processes that involve reasoning, problem-solving, and decision-making. They can be compared to algorithms or lines of code that operate on the information available to us. Thoughts are influenced not only by aspirations and emotions but also by input from our external environment, like coding logic considers different inputs and conditions to produce desired outcomes. Sensations represent the physical experiences and bodily responses that we encounter. They can be compared to the input/output mechanisms in coding, where sensors gather information from the environment, and actuators generate physical responses (e.g. order to a machine or a robot).

As the focus of this book is on influence for social good, two mechanisms that are part of the "human system" are of particular interest. In their regard technology can play a useful role, affecting both the software and hardware aspects at stake. Like the other brief inlays related to "intelligence" be it natural or artificial, these snippets are meant to populate a puzzle that helps to gradually expand your perception of the human mind and the hybrid world it is part of.

"Human Software": As mentioned earlier humans are not primarily rational decision makers. Cognitive biases are systematic patterns of deviation from objective judgment. They are the result of mental shortcuts and heuristics that our brains use to process information efficiently (Kahneman, 2011). For example, confirmation bias refers to the tendency to seek out and interpret information that confirms our preexisting beliefs, while ignoring or downplaying contradictory evidence (Nickerson, 1998). This can lead to the reinforcement of existing prejudices and hinder our ability to consider alternative perspectives. Another common bias is the availability heuristic, where people rely on immediate examples or easily accessible information to make judgments or decisions (Tversky & Kahneman, 1974), which can lead to an overemphasis on vivid or recent events, neglecting less salient but equally relevant information. Fallacies, on the other hand, are errors in reasoning that undermine the validity or soundness of an argument (Walton, 2010a). For instance, the ad hominem fallacy occurs when someone attacks the person making an argument rather than addressing the substance of the argument itself (Walton, 2010b). This fallacy diverts attention from the actual issue and can hinder constructive dialogue and problem-solving.

Respectively and combined biases and fallacies make us prone to "suboptimal choices and irrational behavior" (Stanovich & West, 2008). These inbuilt cognitive caveats play an important role in social interactions, contributing to misunderstandings, conflicts, and the perpetuation of stereotypes and prejudices (Gilovich et al., 2002). *Awareness* of their existence (which no human is spared of) and a fine-tuned understanding of their influence on each of us is useful because once we know the caveats we can gradually sharpen our awareness, and critical thinking skills not only with regard to others, but also to our own decision-making process. *Accepting* and challenging our own biases, *appreciating* a wide range of diverse perspectives, and applying a logical chain of reasoning can help overcome these cognitive pitfalls and promote more objective thinking (Stanovich & West, 2008). Ultimately a sense of *accountability* for how we operate personally increases the likelihood of beneficial decisions (Stanovich & West, 2008), both online and interpersonally offline.

"Human Hardware": An intricate interplay between sensory experiences and synaptic activity precedes and accompanies mental processes, sculpting the very essence of cognition. Upon encountering sensory stimuli, neural pathways ignite, fostering the formation of synaptic connections within the brain. These connections, crafted through a sophisticated interplay of neurotransmitters and neural signaling, underpin the encoding and processing of information, ultimately giving rise to mental phenomena such as perception, memory, decision-making, and habit formation (Kandel et al., 2012). Notably, mental processes themselves exert influence on synaptic connectivity in the brain. This phenomenon, characterized by the strengthening or weakening of synaptic connections in response to repeated patterns of neural activity, shapes the brain's functional architecture through neuroplasticity (Bliss & Collingridge, 1993).

Every thought or action triggers neural activity in the brain, involving the firing of neurons and the transmission of electrical signals across synapses, the connections between neurons. The more often a behavior and the related thought-pattern are repeated the stronger these connections become; vice versa the stronger the synaptic connections are the more likely the individual is to engage in a certain mental pattern and the behavior that is triggered by it. This bidirectional relationship underscores the dynamic nature of neural networks (human hardware) and their pivotal role in shaping cognition (human software) and behavior.

Let us zoom in further.

Neuroplasticity, the brain's ability to form new synaptic connections and modify existing ones, allows for ongoing adaptation and change throughout the life cycle. Through intentional practice and repetition, individuals can reshape their thoughts and behaviors, fostering the formation of new synaptic connections and the adoption of desired patterns (Doidge, 2007). This entails two fundamental mechanisms: long-term potentiation (LTP) and long-term depression (LTD). LTP reinforces synaptic connections, while LTD weakens them, enabling the brain to strengthen or weaken specific neural pathways (Lisman, 2017). Through repetition, synaptic connections related to specific thoughts and actions become more efficient, leading to the formation of dedicated neural networks. These networks facilitate smoother signal transmission, making associated thoughts and behaviors more automatic and ingrained (Kandel et al., 2014). As synaptic connections strengthen, they predispose the brain to activate established neural pathways, shaping future thoughts and behaviors. Nothing is permanently etched in the brain's gray matter. The dynamic interplay between human hardware (body) and human software (mind, heart, soul), influenced by repetition and synaptic connections, creates a feedback loop.[34] Our thoughts and behaviors sculpt the strength and organization of synaptic connections, which, in turn, shape future thoughts and behaviors, resulting in a continuous cycle of neural adaptation and cognitive processing. Like a domino chain, small impulses in one dimension can have ripple effects in the others, shaping who we are, how we experience the world, and how we express ourselves in it.

Whatever we decide to do is the product of emotions and aspirations, and a bit of rational thought. Being acutely aware of the causes and consequences of our decisions is in our own interest, and it lays the ground for a *glocal mindset* whereby we understand ourselves as a *micro*-expression of the organically evolving *m4-matrix* that we belong to, and that belongs to us. From that viewpoint it becomes logical to accept ourselves as players of an infinite game that we do not have the luxury to slip away from, hiding in the seat of a bystander[35] (Fig. 1.3).

---

[34] The physical brain is on the one hand part of the body and, on the other, a connector between the body and the non-physical locus of our thoughts and emotions.

[35] The bystander is a psychological phenomenon in which individuals are less likely to offer help to a victim when other people are present (Darley & Latané, 1968). This effect occurs because people diffuse responsibility and assume that others will intervene, leading to a decreased likelihood of any individual taking action.

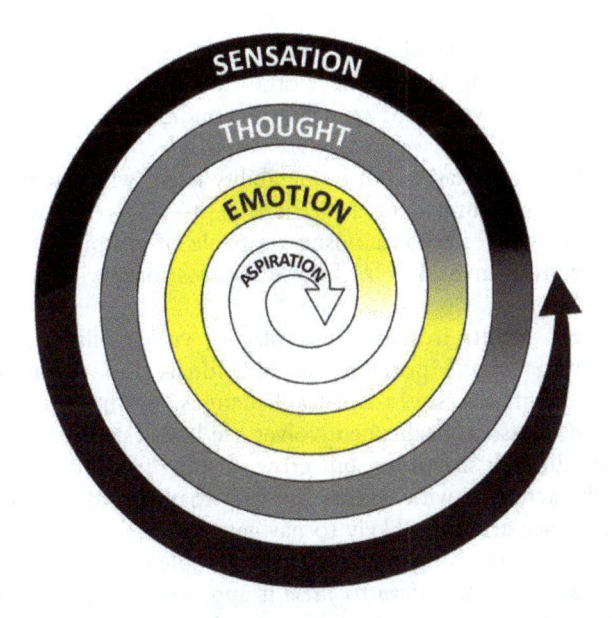

Fig. 1.3 Interplays in the *micro*-arena

Caption Everything is connected, influencing each other from the inside out (soul/aspiration to body/physiological sensation, passing via heart/emotion and mind/thought), and conversely from the outside in, with external triggers that influence how we think, feel, and what we aspire to.

Our multidimensional mindset and the physiological interface through which we interact with the world that we are part of is the cause and consequence of two characteristics that are unique to the human species:

Vulnerability is the state of being fragile, susceptible to harm, emotional distress, or negative outcomes. It involves allowing oneself to be seen, heard, and understood in a genuine manner, even when it involves risks or the potential for rejection or criticism (Brown, 2012). Once we are aware of our inherent vulnerability, and accept it as an undeniable characteristic of human nature, we get a gift:

Authenticity is the quality of being true to oneself, which manifests in actions that reflect the alignment of one's values, aspirations, and behavior. It fosters a sense of congruence, wholeness, and personal fulfillment because it involves living in accordance with one's identity rather than conforming to societal expectations to fit in (Lenton et al., 2021). As seen earlier it is the biggest asset of a leader, and (un)fortunately we do not find it until we accept ourselves unconditionally, from the inside out.

What makes us human is not vulnerability itself, which we share with all other living creatures, but awareness of it—"it is the way existential uncertainty weaves a consciousness capable of grasping it" (Fromm, 1941). Respectively and combined these features come with an additional endowment:

Resilience[36] results from the interplay of vulnerability and authenticity. Referring to the potential of individuals and communities to bounce back from adversity, adapt to challenges, and maintain a positive mindset amid stressors, resilience involves the latent strength to not only recover from difficult situations, but grow stronger from them. It is a self-enforcing characteristic with studies showing that individuals with higher levels of resilience are more likely to navigate challenges successfully, and conversely, that overcoming hardship makes people more resilient to stress and difficulties. Linking *micro* to *meso* it appears that a symbiotic interconnectedness binds resilient individuals and resilient communities[37] in a virtuous cycle whereby one part nurtures the other (Ungar, 2011, 2018).[38]

The trio of vulnerability, authenticity, and resilience acts like the three musketeers of our personal existence resulting in a strong sense of self and mental agility which foster an attitude of Agency, while serving as buffer amid adversity. The better we understand the multidimensional

---

[36] Note—Resilience, as vulnerability, is a term that has been overused; to the point where it has lost meaning for many and become an insult for some.

[37] In the community (*meso*) arena resilience refers to the ability of a group to withstand, adapt to, and recover from significant trials, including natural disasters, economic downturns, or social disruptions. It involves the collective capacity of people to support one another and rebuild after misfortune. The concept of "community social capital" highlights how networks and social connections within a community can positively impact individual resilience (Aldrich, 2012). Individuals who are part of strong social networks often have access to resources, information, and emotional support, contributing to their ability to overcome challenges. On the flip side, the presence of resilient individuals within a community can foster a culture of mutual support and collaboration.

[38] Community resilience is conditioned by social cohesion, effective communication, local leadership, and the availability of resources (Norris et al., 2008). The resulting social capital is a central factor of recovery, including solid social networks and community bonds (Aldrich & Meyer, 2015), which in turn nurture individual resilience.

human "system', the better apt we are to design and use artificial counterparts in ways that serve the optimization of our individual and collective experiences.

Everything is connected. Humans are the cause of social change, and they experience the consequences of it. AI is amplifying that effect. The consequences of AI-powered progress on society depend on the human intentions that underpin them. The following lists contain a handful of examples to show the links between dimensions and the potential of AI in each. The aim of this exercise is partially didactic as it illustrates the circumferences and adjacency of the 2 × 4 dimensions of the *m4-matrix*, and the resulting interplays. What might appear in this brief overview as a patchwork is connected by that underpinning thread, of schematizing the setup to configure an optimized experience with the entire range of biological and technological assets at our disposal.

1.2.4 Risks and Opportunities at the Interface of Individuals, Society, and AI

Every risk is the counterpart of an opportunity, both entail questions and choices that influence the ultimate outcomes. Regrouped within respectively the 4 individual dimensions and the 4 collective arenas, the following two overviews spotlight certain problems and possibilities that arise from a cohabitation with AI. These examples are selective illustrations of phenomena that have been known for a while and are picking up speed due to supercharged AI. These lists are neither exclusive, nor do they necessarily involve AI. Many of them are already underway yet AI amplifies the consequences.

1.2.4.1 The Interface of Individuals and AI
Risks:

- Soul: AI presents the danger of dehumanizing human interactions, leading to an alienation of the sense of self, an erosion of our personal identity (Bostrom, 2014). We may lose touch with both, our inner "reality", our values and purpose, and our connection to the external world. Reliance on artificial replicas may come with loss of agency and autonomy, where we trust the technology we use, but lose trust in their own abilities. The more disconnected from our own actions and decisions we are, the paler our sense of agency

becomes. When the quest for purpose falls between the cracks of constant exposure to artificial stimuli, spirituality is easily replaced by 24/7 retail religion.
- Heart: Constant online exposure harms an individual's mental health and well-being, potentially causing chronic stress, anxiety, depression, loneliness, addiction, or alienation. Advanced AI has repeatedly been found to manipulate human emotions through persuasive, sometimes deceptive techniques, such as systematically tailored social media algorithms, deep-fakes, and targeted chatbots. With an available pleasant online companion, feelings and desires towards other people may become just too cumbersome to deal with, leading us to prefer "relationships" with AI-friends over humans.
- Mind: AI can impair the cognitive abilities and skills of individuals by reducing their attention span, memory, creativity, critical thinking, and problem-solving. Algorithms were found to infuse online platforms with bias in the information that individuals receive, as errors, inaccuracies, prejudices, or propaganda are mainstreamed through the online multimedia flow (O'Neil, 2016). This might happen deliberately in view of manipulation through disinformation, or even without the intention of the algorithm's creator. When the internet becomes a gigantic fake-factory the majority of previously used decision-making criteria to distinguish correct versus incorrect are outdated; eventually the concept of absolute truth becomes questionable.
- Body: The brain is our biggest asset in times of AI but the delegation of human intellectual effort to artificial intelligence risks weakening the synaptic connections that mental effort creates, while resulting in new ones that further strengthen the codependency on external support systems.[39] The use of AI without candid oversight and role distribution can be dangerous, especially when it is involved in fields with high risk stakes such as medical (mis)diagnosis, jurisprudence, or policing. This is further worsened by so far unclear rules of accountability. Indirect dangers of AI include supposedly self-driving cars that are not ready for decision making under uncertainty, and

---

[39] As mentioned earlier the brain is the physical locus of the mind, and the nexus where thoughts, emotions, and physical stimuli are processed. AI can be leveraged to strengthen the brain, by forging the former as an ally of the latter, or weaken it, considering it as a competitor and eventually a quasi-replacement.

robots that run out of control. [Also in the indirect causation chain is the lethal effect of a largely sedentary lifestyle due to constant online fixture as we spend incredibly more time in the virtual part of the hybrid world, while neglecting our physical framework; as already seen among teens who spend excessive amounts of time with online gaming and social media, the future is prone to see an explosion across generation of obesity, cardiovascular disease, diabetes, etc. (Russell et al., 2015)]. We are jeopardizing our most important natural capital, the brain and body, by neglecting their inherent value to favor their inferior artificial copies.

Opportunities:

- Soul: AI can provide tailored tools for self-reflection, spiritual growth, and mindfulness (Hassabis et al., 2017). AI-powered applications, such as the expanding range of personalized meditation and well-being apps could be configured to assist individuals in systematically fostering self-awareness and self-esteem, thereby facilitating a more grounded and fulfilling life.[40] If they are designed as support not replacement, they may serve to alleviate loneliness without becoming a placebo for human interaction. One might imagine a "Socrates in the pocket" which challenges us to critically examine life and living, while keeping us on track to fulfilling our aspirations, rather than our goal steps. A *Valuable Wearable* to complement not counteract the process towards our best self (Walther, 2021).
- Heart: Certain AI-powered therapies and interventions were found to effectively assist individuals in understanding and managing their emotions, which improved their overall well-being. The possibility of ongoing fine-tuning through machine learning might make such artificial helpers beneficial in the long run, by offering always available stress management guidance, with personalized recommendations for self-care (Russell & Norvig, 2016). AI can take the current focus on physiological features (exercise, food, sleep, etc.)

---

[40] Continuous neurophysiologic data collected using a commercial neuroscience platform can predict daily mood with 90% accuracy, offering a proactive method for assessing and potentially improving mental health, particularly in populations vulnerable to mood disorders. (Merrit & Zak, 2024) .

to another level by connecting these inputs to our mood and feelings, gradually expanding to the whole human organism with the possibility of a 24/7 monitoring of our experience, helping us to get an ever more granular understanding of the myriad of factors that shape who and how we are.
- Mind: AI presents opportunities for lifelong learning, with new outlets and tools to constantly stimulate creativity and curiosity (Brynjolfsson & McAfee, 2014). Intelligent tutoring systems can personalize educational experiences, adapting to individual needs and learning styles over time. In analyzing vast amounts of data, uncovering patterns, and generating insights Ai systems can accelerate research, problem-solving, and decision-making processes. By freeing us from routine tasks while enabling us to deal with unfamiliar disciplines AI agents could help us to be more creative, including in areas that are outside of our acquired portfolio. As seen below, by combining such learning to cover natural and technological resources at our disposal *Agency Amid AI for All* unleashes the full power of humans, and of AI as an ally of people and planet.
- Body: The potential for improved, more accurate and timely health monitoring, predictive diagnostics, and personalized medication-tailoring is immense (McKinsey, 2023). It may lead to more patient autonomy and the opportunity for individuals to gradually gain in-depth understanding of their own natural system with expert guidance from an artificial system at their fingertips. Managed well AI might serve us to comprehend the multidimensional interplays of mind and matter ever better.

Cutting across all 4 dimensions is the pervasive presence of technology and the imperative for conscious human agency. We are navigating a dangerous time, as the influence of artificial intelligence grows and expands much faster than our understanding of human consciousness. The window to harness our ability (and appetite) to critically question an AI-powered environment is closing quickly. Human consciousness has remained a mystery to this day (Chapter 2). Now it is exposed to the all pervasive impact of an artificial entity that some hail as being on the cusp of artificial general intelligence (AGI), or a system that can think like us. Whether that happens or not is to be seen. In the meantime we are well advised to get a better grasp on the multi granularity of our own perception. Awareness of who and how we are (not) offline is our best protection against unwanted online influence.

Beyond the individual arena, the influence of AI impacts society at large. The following summarizes some of these effects, for better and worse. As before these are just some examples of an accelerating dynamic with vast implications.

1.2.4.2 Challenges Across the m4-matrix
Risks:

- *micro:* As AI automation replaces certain types of human labor, while radically altering others, job displacement, and unemployment are imminent risks (Brynjolfsson & McAfee, 2014). Although it is a *macro*-level issue, the immediate consequences are experienced at the individual level, which may lead to large-scale financial insecurity. The erosion of personal privacy and data security has been a standing concern for the past Internet decades; as AI systems collect, store, and analyze ever larger amounts of personal information (Floridi, 2019), this process is accelerating and becoming ever more subtle.
- *meso:* The potential for social isolation and the breakdown of face-to-face interactions as people increasingly rely on AI-mediated communication is growing, impacting community cohesion and interhuman connections (Turkle, 2011). Unequal access to both hardware and software deepens the digital divide, exacerbating already existing social disparities as ever more digital natives are born on one side of the social spectrum (DiMaggio et al., 2004). A new form of digital poverty is taking shape, which intensifies preexisting marginalization and deprivation. With liability rules that remain opaque and unsettled the use of AI in autonomous weapons is a cause of major trepidation (Bostrom, 2014).
- *macro:* AI systems mirror the past because they are based on historical data; since they reflect existing social settings, they tend to perpetuate societal inequalities (O'Neil, 2016). The additional danger with the large-scale deployment of LLMs is that biased algorithms and amplified discriminatory decision-making are becoming ever more pervasive, sophisticated, and harder to detect. Further on, economic disparities between AI-leading countries and those lacking access widen the skills gap, and enshrine established global inequality (Stiglitz, 2019a). Already high-income countries are

becoming stronger, but also more vulnerable because of the AI race. As more and more vital infrastructure and public services rely on AI-powered systems cyber-insecurity is a looming risk; that latent hybrid vulnerability can be weaponized with countries taken hostage by threats of cyber-attacks (Denning, 2019). In parallel to the AI arms race that is heating up in both the corporate and the diplomatic space, pitting players against each other, the job market is getting more polarized. As we will see later, with a concentration of high-skilled jobs and the automation of low-skilled jobs another layer is added onto the socioeconomic divides that characterize ever more countries. The combination of a growing youth population in low-income countries, decentralized access to sophisticated technology, economic instability, and social dissatisfaction is a hybrid time bomb on amphetamines.

- *meta:* Putting AI-operated agents in charge of decision-making comes with an acute risk of losing human agency as processes grow to scale (Bostrom, 2014). Yet although the impact of superintelligent AI on society is a real concern, the unintended consequences of our (in) voluntary reliance on digital support systems are more worrisome. The loss of control over the growing range of factors that influence our own perception and which we are not even aware of is for now a far bigger threat, than the doomsday scenario evoked by big tech, and many others. From a purely practical perspective, LLMs exacerbate already too high carbon emissions (Strubell et al., 2019) and consume humongous amounts of energy. This environmental impact of AI infrastructure escalates an (already) gigantic climate challenge that humans have failed to tackle so far.

Opportunities:

- *micro:* AI technologies can enhance productivity, creativity, and decision-making processes, empowering individuals to achieve more, while being more fulfilled in the pursuit of their professional lives (Brynjolfsson & McAfee, 2014). AI-powered personal assistants, smart devices, and virtual agents offer convenient highly personalized experiences, making daily tasks easier and more efficient. AI-powered services in sectors like health care and education may be especially beneficial due to targeted fine-tuning and expansion of access. Regarding underserved demographic groups, AI's potential to address specific needs and hence increase autonomy is promising. For example, accommodating young and aging populations with systematic investments to curate the brain throughout the life cycle while offering support services 24/7 is promising; combined with algorithmic literacy this would equip individuals across the life cycle to actually optimize their experience of a world with AI.

- *meso:* AI-driven data analytics and predictive modeling can improve decentralized community-based planning, needs-oriented resource allocation, and "real-time" decision-making processes (Chui et al., 2016). By their own nature certain processes, and their results, take time to unfold; but algorithms can be configured to project, automatically combine, and draw from ongoing updates depending on the characteristics of the issues at stake, and the data needed. (Walther, 2024). In the context of "smart cities", AI may serve to optimize energy consumption, transportation, and infrastructure management. In times of growing distrust and polarization AI applications might open safe spaces in communities for members to communicate, collaborate, and share resources, liberated from traditional segregation.
- *macro:* As a counterpart to the risk of digital poverty the biggest opportunity of modern times may be to build *analogue abundance*. AI technologies are driving economic growth and innovation,[41] along with new products, services, and industries that lead to the emergence of completely new professional profiles. As employers and employees are adjusting to the new scenario a lot of upskilling/downskilling/reskilling is likely to happen. Situated in a consciously curated context, accompanied by public policy interventions to mitigate the (human) costs, AI-powered optimization may lead to major gains. If it is managed with awareness of the human factor, the transition from human to hyper-hybrid will not only enhance profit, but also worker well-being (Bughin et al., 2018). The resulting generation of economic growth (we will look closer at the sometimes questionable benefit of "growth" in Chapter 2) accompanied

---

[41] The 4IR is multi-pronged; already the Generative AI (GenAI) market is expected to see continued growth in the coming years, by one estimate reaching over $1 trillion in revenue by 2032 with a compound annual growth rate (CAGR) of 42% (Bloomberg, 2023).

by the reduction of human workload could be configured to introduce and scale up a sustainable, truly universal basic income (UBI).[42] [Furthermore, seeing that humans are not ready for society without war, and while strongly condemning the mindset that underpins it, one might envision a future where AI-powered robots fight among each other in a controlled, clearly confined setting without a direct impact on life and livelihood.]

- *meta:* Addressing global challenges, such as climate change and inequality can be facilitated with AI-powered data analysis and modeling (Elsayed et al., 2018). By enabling fine-tuned monitoring, prediction, and management of ecosystems, AI might serve to address lingering environmental bottlenecks. AI-powered technologies can thus assist in disaster response and mitigation, improving early warning systems and crisis management (Gupta et al., 2018). [Albeit promising, the use of AI for environmental benefits should be approached with caution seeing the gigantic energy needs of LLMs.] Overall, scientific research may be benefiting from AI; in certain fields such as astronomy, genomics, and particle physics it is already drastically accelerating advances and the likelihood of breakthroughs (Russell et al., 2015).

---

[42] The Universal Basic Income (UBI) has emerged as a concept that proposes providing every citizen with a regular, unconditional stipend to cover their basic needs. Proponents argue that UBI can address various societal challenges, including poverty alleviation, job displacement due to automation, and income inequality. Advocates contend that by providing a financial safety net, UBI empowers individuals to pursue entrepreneurial ventures, education, or community service without the fear of financial instability. Critics raise concerns about the economic feasibility and potential disincentives to work. Evidence from pilot programs and economic simulations is crucial in assessing the actual impact of UBI on different aspects of society (Atkinson & Micklewright, 1992; Haarmann et al., 2019a; Standing, 2017). Various countries have begun to experiment with it; i.e., Finland conducted a two-year UBI experiment (2017/2019), providing a fixed monthly income to a group of unemployed individuals. It did not serve as a disincentive for employment, and improved well-being and reduced stress levels (Kela, 2019). Canada implemented a basic income experiment known as "Mincome'" during the 1970s in Manitoba; although discontinued prematurely, preliminary findings suggested positive outcomes, including reduced hospitalization rates and improved mental health (Forget, 2011). In Namibia the Basic Income Grant (BIG) pilot project in Otjivero-Mariya provided a basic income to all residents below the age of 60. The outcomes indicated improvements in child nutrition, school attendance, and small business activities (Haarmann et al., 2019b).

Table 1.1 summarizes the ultimate, worst, and best potential outcomes of AI. It may serve as a roadmap of the topics that we will look at in the following pages. Respectively and together they illustrate the need for *Agency Amid Ai for All*, because each risk is the reverse of an opportunity and the aspirations we put in the undertaking will impact its outcomes.

How we answer the questions asked in this overview, and other similar interrogations depends on the aspirational context in which they are pondered. Our individual mindset influences the normative social setting in which AI evolves and influences it in return. Values and social norms are unspoken decision-making factors that influence what we do. They coexist with formal laws and regulations. In the following we look briefly at this complex carpet that underlies our perception of and participation in society.

1.3 Individual Behavior as Cause and Consequence of Values and Norms

1.3.1 Formal and Informal Forms of Influence

Our expressions and behaviors are the cause and consequence of values and desires, social norms and customs (Deutsch & Gerard, 1955). They emerge through the consistent enactment of specific behaviors by individuals. Widespread acceptance of these behaviors strengthens the underlying belief systems, perpetuating the norms, and influencing future actions. Social norms subtly influence behavior by shaping perceptions, attitudes, and actions. Observing others conforming to norms increases the likelihood of aligning oneself due to social pressure, the desire for group acceptance, or internalized values (Cialdini & Goldstein, 2004). Let us zoom in on that:

Social norms act as the invisible scaffolding for social interaction within groups and societies. They play a crucial role in maintaining order and fostering positive relationships by influencing both interpersonal dynamics and self-perception. These norms can be broadly categorized into two types:

- Descriptive Norms: These reflect the common behaviors observed within a group. Think of them as the "unwritten rules" that guide everyday actions, like carrying an umbrella during a downpour.

Table 1.1 Potential outlook on AI and the future of life

Risks		Opportunities	
Identity loss	Will AI-personas and avatars, virtual assistants and artists replace authenticity?	Identity discovery	Is technology forcing us to face our true humanity?
Creativity erosion	Are we condemned to delegate, losing our creativity to the need for ever accelerating productivity pressure?	Creativity bursts	Will the expansion of tools and techniques seed an explosion of multidisciplinary creation?
Fakes	Are appearance and misinformation overtaking what is and what matters?	Faces	Does the web entail the opportunity to put a human face to those afar?
Soulless Production	Will the sophistication of LLM lead to ever more content, with ever less content?	Empowered Creation	Freed from numbing tasks, will humans use their mental space to re-envision their work and life?
Isolation	Are we chained to our devices, separated from the world outside?	Connection	Are we ever more part of a global community?
Privacy	Is data a commodity that will be owned by the highest bidder?	Privacy	Is the sophistication of online protection leading to more safety for all?
Inequality	Is AI widening the gap between poor and rich, both nationally and globally?	Equality	Will resources be expanded and shared equally?
Indifference	Are we getting numb to life and living with each other?	Understanding	Does AI enable us to comprehend the 2 × 4 dimensions that underpin who we are?
Mechanization	Will gradually ever more human jobs and interactions be replaced by technology?	Humanization	Does the interaction with machines force us to confront and appreciate what makes us unique?

(continued)

Table 1.1 (continued)

Risks		Opportunities	
Losing sight	Are we losing the ability to choose what matters due to abundance of information and tools?	Gaining focus	Is the delegation of tedious business leading to clarity?
Catering to instincts	Is technology configured based on commercial interests, targeting cravings and desires?	Nurturing inspiration	Is technology tailored to identify and curate the best part of our personality and skill set?
Consciousness catalyst	Will technology serve us to better understand human consciousness?	Consciousness constriction	Will technology gradually sync with who we are before we understand who we were?
Paralysis	Are we getting ever more attached to the comfort of an online one-stop-shop environment?	Communion	Is technology opening the door for borderless human synchrony?
Inflation	Will the ease of text and image creation result in the depreciation of time for creativity?	Valorization	Does a juxtaposition of AI-generated materials and human outputs lead to more appreciation of the latter?
Confinement	Is the expanding place of technology making us ever more dependent on our tools and devices?	Freedom	Is AI the ultimate answer for freedom from want?
Scarcity	Is AI yet another burden on the shoulders of those who are suffering from deprivation?	Abundance	Can AI serve to optimize the access and use of resources to the benefit of a maximum of people?
More for less	Is technology leading us to more stuff and less humanity?	Less for more	Is technology offering a way to address the needs of all, with less effort and resources?

(continued)

Table 1.1 (continued)

Risks		Opportunities	
Lies	Will the concept of truth become relative and hence redundant due to the proliferation of fake content?	Trust	Can the interaction of AI and users lead to a double-vetted space of shared information?
Discord	Will artificial entities become permanent placeholders for humans, seemingly "real" but resulting in chronic sensorial dissonance?	Harmonization	Will AI serve the optimization of interplays between *micro*, *meso*, *macro* and *meta*?
Misalignment	Will the misalignment of human values and artificial algorithm configuration further the misalignment of human aspirations and actions?	Alignment	Can AI-powered entities operate as 24/7 coaches that keep individuals and institutions on track to coherence between values and practice?
www minus	Will the internet become the wild west web where the strongest prime at the expense of the rest?	www plus	Are we shaping a wonderful welcoming web with space to create the World We Want, online and offline?

Caption A not exclusive summary of questions related to the worst and best potential outcomes of AI in our lives

- Injunctive Norms: These define the spectrum of acceptable behavior, distinguishing between approved ("good") and disapproved ("bad") actions. For example, kindness towards others is considered an approved injunctive norm.

Customs, on the other hand, represent the unique traditions and practices that different groups employ to celebrate events or conduct specific activities. They are more specific expressions of social norms, reflecting the cultural nuances of a particular community.

Further subtleties exist within these categories. Conditional preferences reflect individual inclinations that vary based on specific circumstances (Bicchieri, 2006). Imagine an individual's decision to donate to a cause, which might be influenced by personal connections, perceived impact, or financial situation. In contrast, conditional norms are social norms that adapt to specific contexts, offering guidance on appropriate behavior within those situations. For example, during natural disasters, offering support to those affected becomes a conditional norm, temporarily promoting community solidarity. Finally, normative expectations set broader societal standards for appropriate conduct, ensuring adherence to cultural values and behavioral norms. Examples include respecting elders and prioritizing the well-being of children.

It's important to note that social norms can sometimes contradict one another. For instance, injunctive norms might encourage helping those in need. However, if a community tolerates a certain level of unfairness and inequality, some people may choose not to help as extensively, opting for the easier path of following the conflicting norm of non-cooperation. Understanding these dynamics is crucial for leaders who aim to foster a culture of collaboration and social responsibility within their organizations.

<u>Laws and contracts</u> stand in contrast to the informal nature of norms and customs. While laws are issued by a government to regulate the behavior of individuals and groups within a society according to shared public policy goals and values, contracts are formal rules that shape the relationships between individuals.

Following the Law is mandatory, with violations leading to penalties enforced by the government. In accordance with the prevailing laws, a contract is a legally binding agreement between two or more parties. If one party breaches the contract terms, the other can seek legal remedies through the court system. If a contract is unfair or oppressive to one party in a way that suggests abuses during its formation, a court may find it unconscionable and refuse to enforce it. It is most likely to be found unconscionable if both unfair bargaining and unfair substantive terms are shown—which, as mentioned above, is not uncommon in the tech space. But it often goes unnoticed as most users either do not realize the extent of the unconscionable notion in their relationship with technology, or, if they do, they do not seek justice, be it for lack of an alternative or free mental bandwidth and resources to stand up.

Technology companies have repeatedly faced allegations of unfair bargaining conditions and one-sided terms under the doctrine of unconscionability. From Uber to Facebook, examples of abused lopsided power positions, which consumers "agree" to for lack of real alternatives, abound.[43] We hand over personal data, signing up to services that do not offer a corresponding compensation. Under varying circumstances selected cases were found conscionable by different courts; but most of cases occur underneath the radar—because the majority of consumers do not contest the terms of engagement; consciously or unconsciously, grudgingly, or naively we agree to an ever-tighter net of digital obligations that we are getting caught up in. When there is a way in, there is a way out. We can still choose, but for how much longer—and who will make these choices? We may not be able to prevent the ongoing evolution single-handedly, but at the very least we must be acutely aware of this transition; and claim our agency in its face.

Awareness of the intricate web of factors that influence our internal decision-making processes is helpful to build a shield against unwanted influence. Especially as technology is increasingly shaping and perpetuating the social dynamics that we are navigating. Values, whether we hold them consciously or subliminally, are part of that complex fabric. They weave through norms and customs, and form the underpinning of the legal system that laws are embedded in. When a person's values stand in contradiction with the prevailing social norm, the person may stand up against the latter or choose to ignore the cognitive discomfort that arises from following the majority. For example once *courage* is adopted as a personal value the individual may even act if this breaks a prevailing social norm such as the widely shared indifference to the suffering of others.

Nothing is carved in stone however. Laws and social norms seem stable; but over time new behaviors and deriving from them a change in the prevailing social dynamics arise,[44] which eventually affects the

---

[43] Some examples: Meyer v. Uber Technologies, Inc. (2017). The case alleged Uber's forced arbitration clause was unconscionable, limiting consumer remedy options. The court found both procedural and substantive unconscionability. See also McArdle (2019) on mandatory binding arbitration in terms of service that violates consumer expectations of fair recourse. On "Opt-out settings," see Cakebread (2017) regarding a lawsuit claiming that Facebook's default facial recognition settings were unconscionable. The court agreed the opt-out approach was likely improper. On geographic restrictions see Bushong (2019).

[44] This disruption of the status quo and eventual settlement into a new set of (stable) norms could be seen as a "punctuated equilibrium" process. Punctuated equilibrium, a theory in evolutionary biology, posits that species' evolutionary development is characterized by long periods of stability, or equilibrium, "punctuated" by relatively short bursts of rapid change. This theory challenges the traditional view of gradual, continuous evolution and suggests that species often remain relatively unchanged for extended periods, followed by brief episodes of significant adaptation or speciation. Punctuated equilibrium emphasizes the role of rare and rapid events in shaping the diversity of life, pointing to the complexity and non-linearity of evolutionary processes (Gould & Eldredge, 1977).

legal landscape. One person's choice can trigger a new chain of action by starting a new behavior. As ever more individuals follow that new behavior, the latter is eventually perceived as an accepted pattern by a wider social group; until gradually a new social norm emerges, which leads to the expectation that this behavior is being pursued by all.

Everything is connected in a feedback loop. As individuals conform to social norms, their behavior reinforces and perpetuates those collective norms, leading to further normative consolidation within a social group. Simultaneously, individuals" adherence to social norms also influences their future behavior as they internalize and incorporate those norms and the values that underpin them, into their own belief systems and identity. The repetition of these behaviors leads to behavior patterns that are further consolidated through the formation of synaptic connections in their brain. "Human software" (aspirations, emotions, thought processes) influences "human hardware" (physiological manifestation as behavior and neural wiring) and manifests externally as behavior. Individuals influence groups which respectively and collectively impact countries and global institutions. Technology influences all arenas and is influenced by them in return. Understanding interplays, we can not only protect ourselves from unwanted influence, but intentionally influence what influences us.

1.3.2 Values as a Compass to Cruise the Hybrid Space

The continuum of past and present leads to diversified compositions of aspirations, emotions, thoughts, and sensations that are specific to each person as a derivative of their experiences, education, social environment, and genetic setup.

Seeing this diversity in unity and vice versa, it is challenging to define universal human values. And still, certain commonalities arise. Research across cultures and continents has found six foundational value binomen as shaping influences of our moral judgments: care/harm, fairness/cheating, loyalty/betrayal, authority/subversion, sanctity/degradation, and liberty/oppression (Haidt, 2012).

Considering the central theme of personal agency with a vocation towards the greater good, or, "human leadership for humane technology", 4 values matter in particular: *Citizenship, Compassion, Conscientiousness,* and *Courage*. These are in line with the six universal value pairs and transpire across cultural, spiritual, and geographic boundaries.[45] Each of them is not only an illustration of the 4 dimensions of individual experience they also mutually catalyze one another. Each could be considered as encompassing the others, which is yet another illustration of the kaleidoscopic nature of everything as part of everything else. A word on each value:

- *Citizenship* as a universal value can be understood as an attitude that embraces the self and its role in society, with commitment to the later (Nussbaum, 1997)[46] in the recognition that we are all part of a global human community, with shared rights and responsibilities that transcend national boundaries (Appiah, 2006).
- *Compassion* denotes the ability of "feeling with" others. It exceeds the mere level of empathy ("feeling for"). Resulting in the desire for altruistic actions it underpins behaviors of care, and concern for others" suffering (Dreyer et al., 2019).
- *Conscientiousness* reflects the motivation of being thorough, responsible and having a sense of personal accountability towards those who are impacted by one's actions. It entails to look out for the common welfare, with a candid understanding of one's own role in shaping the whole that one is part of.
- *Courage* is required for the translation of personal values into practice, as it often involves the overcoming of fear and opposition to enact ethical goals (Putman, 2004).

Everything is connected, from the inside out. *Citizenship* can inspire charity[47] towards others, driven by *compassion* for the suffering and less

---

[45] For further details on cross-cultural values see Schwartz (2012).

[46] Nussbaum argued that the humanities should develop a "world citizen" who has a universal mindset, appreciates different cultural values and histories, and has freed themselves from their own authority and tradition.

[47] One important note here as the term "charity" will appear in various places and is often linked to the pursuit of the Common Good: The original notion of charity as reflected across religions around the world has nothing to do with the connotation of pity that is nowadays tainting it. It is driven by the understanding that all humans are part of one planet and share the same fundamental entitlement to happiness and well-being. This right of fulfilling their inherent potential is inalienable to our human nature. In that sense charity echoes the principles of Ubuntu, an African philosophy that emphasizes the interconnectedness of humanity and the idea that "I am because we are" (Gade, 2012). True charity stems from recognizing our shared human experience and the inherent dignity of every individual, regardless of their circumstances (Singer, 2009).

fortunate (Singer, 2009). This requires *conscientiousness* in upholding ethical principles and fulfilling duties to society (Frankena, 1973). In turn it demands *courage* to stand up for universal human rights, promote peace and cooperation, and address global challenges (Putnam, 2000). At its core, the borderless nationless conception of citizenship encourages individuals to embrace their humanity, engage in civic actions that benefit the greater good, and exhibit virtues that foster a more just, equitable and sustainable world for all people, irrespective of their nationality or background (Nussbaum, 2002).

Channeling our energy based on the motivation of citizenship as a concrete manifestation of compassion, with conscientiousness of the causes and consequences of our (in)action as part of the human species, helps us to seize the courage required to manifest our values in action. This results in a social atmosphere that is conducive to interpersonal harmony and trust. It is a spiraling dynamic that operates from the inside out and is propelled from the outside in. While it sounds abstract it is a hands-on package that can serve as a moral doggy bag amid uncertainty. Rather than an endorsement of judgment, it is an invitation to adopt a 360° perspective to being alive (Fig. 1.4).

Caption Making choices with benevolent intentions involves a set of core values. The schema places them in the multidimensional framework schema (Chapter 1). *Citizenship* encourages individuals to embrace the aspiration to manifest their common humanity, by engaging in civic actions that benefit the greater good, to foster a more equitable and sustainable world for all; it reflects the commitment of doing for others what one wishes for oneself, which makes generosity part of our identity, the <u>soul</u> of who we are. *Compassion* with our own strengths and weaknesses is the emotional foundation, the <u>heart</u> of genuine human connection. *Conscientiousness* of who we are (not) and the moral implications of that is the cause and consequence of human intelligence, the <u>mind</u>, as opposed to its artificial counterparts. *Courage* to act and accept the outcomes manifests values in practice, behavior of the <u>body</u>.

In sum—Whatever manifests in society is to a certain extent the cause and consequence of human behavior, driven by motivational drivers that are underpinned by aspirations (soul), emotions (heart), thoughts (mind), and physiological (body) needs.[48] Social norms are unwritten

---

[48] Drivers are the internal or external factors that drive individuals to initiate, sustain, and direct their efforts towards achieving specific goals or to engage in certain behavior

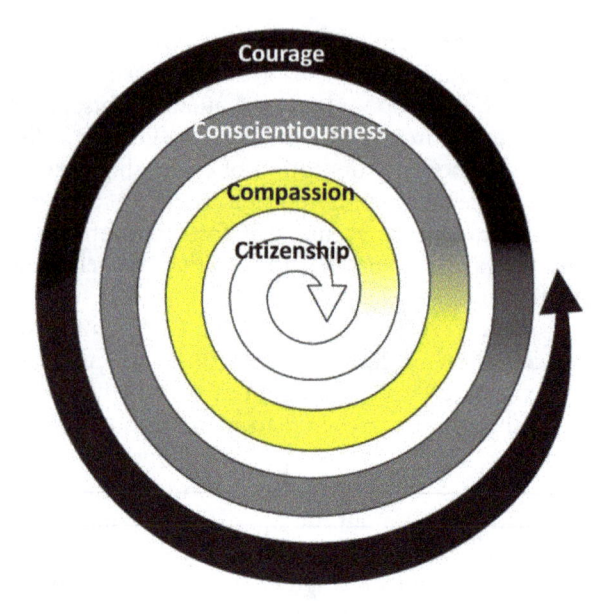

Fig. 1.4 4 central values situated in the 4 dimensions of human experience

commandments that exist in relationships between people (Schein, 1965); they manifest in behavior (*micro*), including practices that may contradict formal national laws (*macro*). Beyond the interpersonal level, such unspoken bonds color the dynamics in institutional settings (*meso*), like a rulebook that runs simultaneously to the formal regulations of laws and contracts (Hirschhorn, 1988). Social norms are influenced by values and influence these in return. Both are subject to change over time. The tide of attitude and action shifts, when a critical mass of individuals changes their behavior. Certain rules such as the Golden Rule might be universally recognized (*meta*) as desirable, without being normatively strong enough to be perceived as an obligation (see Table 1.2).

We cannot predict the future, but we can discern patterns and dynamics that shape its formation. Research shows that the environment, including sounds, influences the shape of ice crystals. Experiments

---

patterns. They activate or maintain behavior, influencing the choices people make and the level of effort they invest in pursuing related objectives.

Table 1.2 Schematic overview of certain components at stake throughout the *m4-matrix*

Arena	Level	Manifestation
Micro	Individual	Behavior
Meso	Community	Norms
Macro	Country	Laws
Meta	Planet	Dynamics

Caption Norms and laws are the cause and consequence of human value perceptions, behavior, and hereby technology

revealed that water exposed to positive stimuli formed well-defined crystals, while negative stimuli led to distorted ones (Emoto, 2004). In human behavior, social norms play a similar role. Individuals often conform to these unwritten rules to gain acceptance, which influence their actions and decisions (Bicchieri, 2006). Longitudinal studies (Bronfenbrenner, 1979) show that early social environments profoundly impact long-term outcomes, highlighting the importance of understanding social dynamics to anticipate future trends. Thus, while specific events cannot be foreseen, studying environmental and social influences provides insights into future trajectories. The ability of AI to analyze gigantic quantities of data is an asset when we seek to identify patterns at scale, and single out entry points to influence certain dynamics in an efficient and effective manner. (Sect. 1.4.3)

Bringing individual and collective streams of consciousness together, while confirming individual change as the point of departure for social transformation, the *Spiral of influence* (Fig. 1.6) draws on inspiring action to catalyze value-driven behavior as the precursor of social norms that serve the Common Good systematically. This requires agency.

1.4 Agency Amid AI for All

1.4.1 The A-Frame

Human experience constitutes a constantly evolving kaleidoscope of sensory inputs across touch, taste, sound, sight, and smell, accumulated through subjective encounters within an embodied lifeworld (Merleau-Ponty, 1962). These phenomena get integrated into dynamic mental models with fluid meanings shaped by each new situation (Varela et al., 1991). Emotions and aspirations are woven through this changing carpet that is the backdrop of our understanding. The resulting dynamic of being and becoming brings all humans in a shared space of communality. At the same time, it establishes a clear demarcation between us and machines.

In the previous section a multidimensional paradigm shift to spotlight the complex mutual interplays of individual and collective behaviors in a hybrid world has been presented. Based on it, the *A-Frame* offers a pragmatic way to reframe our personal relationship with AI. It is an invitation to slip into the driver seat on this journey to the hybrid future.

Although all eyes seem to be veered towards AI, it is useful to remember that a healthy relationship of artificial and natural entities begins with healthy relationships between people, which might require a conscious recalibration of existing social structures, and the power dynamics they harbor. In turn this requires a mindset shift, of people, offline. The word "innovation" commonly comes with the connotation of new technology, yet as mentioned earlier, innovation can be anything—whether it is matter or mind. The sky is the limit of human imagination (and not even that considering our exploration of faraway galaxies), and the outcomes of hybrid humanity are not a foretold story. We influence them.

The *A-Frame* (Fig. 1.5) can be used to sharpen our perspective of the complex setting that we are part of, based on 4 parameters: *awareness (aspiration), appreciation (emotion), acceptance (intellect),* and *accountability (behavior)*. As mentioned earlier (Sect. 1.2.3) they derive from the 4 individual dimensions. A word on each:

Awareness of the multiple dimensions that underpin our personal experiences is the point of departure to understand ourselves and others better. Our aspirations, emotions, thoughts, and sensations influence what we see, want, and do. Once these dimensions are accepted as such, we have not only a coherent framework to analyze their mutual interplays, but to genuinely appreciate who we are. Taken to the collective level this multi-dimensional composition mirrors the society that we are part of, and that is part of us, with individuals, who are part of communities, countries, nature, and what's beyond. With *appreciation* of who we are (not) comes *appreciation* of what we might become. We do not control the outcomes, but whether or not we *accept* this constellation, and the deriving chronic uncertainty that is the only constant of life, does not change the situations that we find ourselves in. On the other hand, if we *accept* that which cannot be changed, then we can channel our energy to address the factors that we can influence. Furthermore, once we become *aware* of the unique features of human nature, with an attitude of *acceptance* towards inherent flaws and forces, and *appreciation* of the human uniqueness that derives from them, we enter a space of personal agency—and *accountability* for the (ab)use and negligence of the power that derives from it.

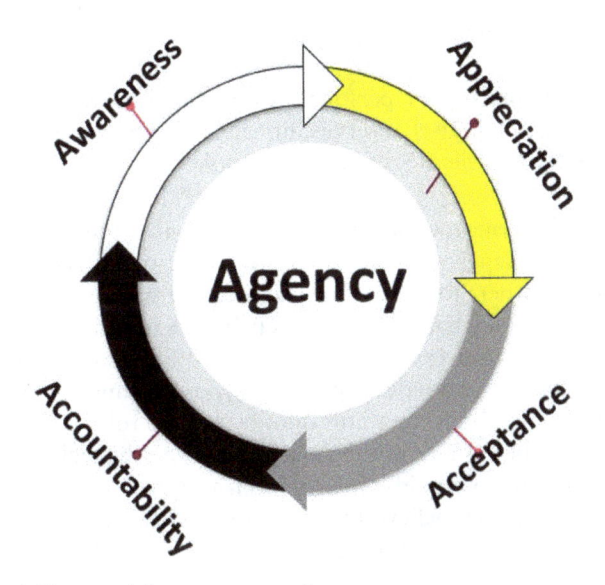

Fig. 1.5 *A-Frame*—A best-case scenario

Caption Awareness of the multidimensionality of past and present experiences is needed to understand and harness our strengths. Combined with *appreciation* of who we are (not) is part of identifying what makes us unique, vulnerable yet therefore authentic—real. *Accepting* us for who we are establishes a baseline to assess what we want AI to do, and how it can serve us best. Also, acceptance of the fact that humans are equal, all assorted with desires and needs, rights and abilities, and an inherent potential to thrive, renders us *accountable*. We are accountable for using our assets to fulfill our own potential and help others thrive. As we are moving towards the complementarity of humans and machines, it is useful to remain aware that ultimately accountability for the outcomes of that alliance remains with the human being.

A mindset that is framed along those 4 parameters places the individual front and center, with a deliberate invitation to embrace *Agency Amid AI*. More than just equipping us to acknowledge our comparative advantage in the competition with technology, the *A-Frame* helps us move from a space of fear and competition, into a zone where we can leverage AI as a strategic ally to bring out the best for people, including ourselves, and the planet. Hence the "**A**" in the *A-Frame* stands as much for the 4 components it contains, as for the "Agency" that is its vocation to curate.

The future does not depend on superintelligent AI agents, but on humans who embrace their personal power to choose and shape a relationship with technology that serves humanity. Linking this to the 4 core values that we saw earlier (Sect. 1.3.2) the following comes to mind:

- *Awareness* of our own self helps us develop an acute sense of citizenship which shapes what we aspire to. In the pursuit of that attitude we inspire others to follow our lead because we are authentic.
- *Appreciation* of what we are (not) enables us to feel compassion with others and ourselves, which opens space for genuine connection. Starting from there we can induce in those around us the desire to do something about the status quo, by being a role model of agency.
- *Acceptance* of our role in the environment and the technology that is part of it leads to candid *conscientiousness* of the consequences. When we align what we believe in, hope for, and experience it triggers a shift from denial to curiosity, from why to why not?
- *Accountability* for what we do and refrain from is intimidating and empowering at the same time. Addressing that challenge with a sense of personal agency ignites in ourselves the ability to take action, and in others the urge to join the movement.

The *A-Frame* is a reminder that AI is an "it". We must resist the temptation to approach it with an anthropocentric angle, which is a latent risk due to the human inclination of transference, a term borrowed from Freud's conceptual framework. The latter refers to our tendency to project feelings about someone from our past onto someone in our present. It is a feature of all relationships as the residue of earlier experiences shapes the screen through which we see one another (Freud, 1912).[49] Transference can occur between humans, between humans and

---

[49] Sigmund Freud noticed early on that his patients kept falling in love with him. It wasn't because he was exceptionally charming or good-looking, he concluded. Instead, transference occurred. According to Freud (1912): "Transference is the process by which emotions and desires originally associated with one person are unconsciously shifted to another person" (p. 45).

animals, and between humans and artificial entities such as robots or AI systems. Starting in the 1960s human-like chatbots such as ELIZA illuminated how this mechanism of the mind affects how we relate to computers (Weizenbaum, 1966).[50] The more life-like the artificial entity becomes the easier the transference flows. Already before the onset of ChatGTP studies found that people relate to AI-powered toy pets as if they were real animals, indicating transference of nurturing feelings onto objects (Banks et al., 2008). We must remain aware of the true nature of us and it. (Sub)consciously treating AI as if it was a human is risky, ethically, epistemologically and in terms of our social connections (Marcus & Luccioni, 2023). The more we get used to interacting with an "it" like a "he/she" the easier it becomes to believe that machines have and share feelings, which takes us closer to trust, and possibly to disclose personal information without realizing that we are actually sharing these inputs with corporations. The Roman emperor Marcus Aurelius hired an assistant to follow him as he walked through Rome. Whenever he was praised by the population like a god, the assistant's role was to whisper in the emperor's ear, "You're just a man". We may need to design a mechanism that constantly reminds us of the distinction between it and us (i.e. "It is just an algorithm"). Transference is just one illustration of the complex interplay that shapes our thinking, feeling, and desires. The caveats that are inherent to our decision-making processes influence how we perceive and approach the world.

Another question is whether treating AI like a person influences our perception of their outputs, taking us ever deeper into a codependent relationship where we over-rely on our super-smart companions, and undervalue our own abilities? On the emotional side, does having an always available, seemingly unconditionally understanding "e-friend" at our fingertips lead us to gradually replace the real people in our lives with less cumbersome entities? Unless we build up our mental immune-system consciously, our mind and heart are easy to fool into establishing human-like relationships with AI-entities, and to gradually considering them as valid replacements of humans. But there is an alternative.

Everything passes through the 4 filters of our respective multidimensional setup as human beings. These features are unalienable, and unique, to human nature. They represent at the same time our biggest strength,

---

[50] ELIZA was an early natural language processing computer program developed from 1964 to 1967 at MIT by Joseph Weizenbaum.

and our largest weakness. Being aware of them is our best protection against the risks they represent. They make us vulnerable only if we deny their existence. No matter the technology we are dealing with, ultimately, we carry along with us into every relationship who and what we are, as persons and as a species. The sooner we accept it, the faster we can move on to appreciate the upside that derives from this, and the accountability that comes from being the creators and curators of our own lives, the proactive agents that we are (or could be).

From the inside out the *A-Frame* can serve us to build *awareness* of these interplays, which positions us to better assess and fully *appreciate* the fallibility of our judgments. *Accepting* that nobody is perfect, including the human-made algorithms in our lives, is useful; because once we know our limitations, we can work to deliberately compensate for them. AI might serve in that regard, if we approach it with a cautious, selective attitude. Technology is neither an end in itself, nor a replacement of humankind. Each of us in our own sphere is accountable for the space that we accommodate for AI.

Note—At the end of each chapter is a brief recap marked by the A-Frame, which invites you to reflect on certain strands of the conversation in your own experience, and how you change it, by applying the 4 attitudes of Agency that are featured by the A-Frame.

1.4.2 Human Influence from the Inside Out, and from the Outside In

Change is a multifaceted process that can originate from internal reflections and external influence. Introspective exploration paves the way for a transition from passive to proactive, moving along a spectrum that spans from internalized attitude to externalized manifestation and hereby influence on others (Doe & Roe, 2018). *Agency Amid AI for All (A4)* embraces a mindset of personal accountability in the interaction with technology. This encompasses, on the one hand, awareness of the influence that individual inputs have on collective outcomes, and on the other, acceptance that we do not have control over the final results. Respectively and combined *Agency Amid AI for All* is anchored in appreciation of human vulnerability, and the authentic being that derives from it. The *A-Frame* may serve as a tool to curate that mindset, and with it, the synergy of natural and artificial assets as a way to unlock an evolution that benefits people and planet alike. The perspective of the twice 4-dimensionality that makes us who we are, combined with the mindset that the *A-Frame* seeks to curate positions the individual to pursue change from the inside out, and from the outside in.

<u>Change arises from the *inside out*</u> with the commitment to personal values and goals that keep on inspiring us in our day-to-day life. Acting as the seed of continuous learning, whether tacitly embedded or consciously expressed (Smith, 2010), our aspirations and internal beliefs resonate when we witness behaviors that are in sync with our values and reflect the type of personality that we aspire to be. Conversely, behaviors that contradict our values lead to cognitive dissonance and discomfort. Experiencing behaviors that are aligned with our values evokes sympathy for the person who pursues that behavior, and in certain cases compassion with the person for whom the action is taken. With these feelings arises curiosity and a desire to follow the example (Jones & Brown, 2015). Since the commitment of living one's values in practice may feel daunting it is inspiring to witness people like us doing so; it also makes the abstract tangible and feasible. The following paragraph connects the attitudes and values that we will look at more closely in the following pages.

Awareness of our values equips us on the one hand with a compass to guide our choices amid the uncertainty of changing life circumstances. On the other it clarifies for ourselves what our hidden motivators are. A commitment to *Citizenship* as manifestation of the Golden Rule, not driven by duty to a country nor pity for those who are less fortunate, but based on *Compassion* can be a powerful motivator. When we feel with others, seeing them as human beings with aspirations, emotions, thoughts, and physical needs like us, alleviating their suffering is no longer an abstract undertaking, nor a chore, but a natural expression of caring for our kin. Similarly, *conscientiousness* of our own role in the status quo may be central to finding the *Courage* of stepping up to the opportunity of action, shifting from a bystander[51] to a player in the hybrid game of

---

[51] As seen earlier the bystander phenomenon refers to the tendency of individuals to be less likely to intervene in an emergency when others are present, due to factors like diffusion of responsibility and pluralistic ignorance. In the present context, we like to think that governments and institutions make the decisions that matter; but this mindset does not render us any less accountable. It is time to shift from the periphery into the center of the playground.

life and living. It is a spiral dynamic that is driven from the inside out and nurtured from the outside in. Linking this to the *Spiral of Influence* (Fig. 1.6) inspiration comes when the fibers of our aspiration to values vibrate; this induces the desire for personal action when we feel that it is about people like us, which may intrigue us sufficiently to consider how we can contribute to solve the situation, finally leading up to ignite the shift from attitude to action.

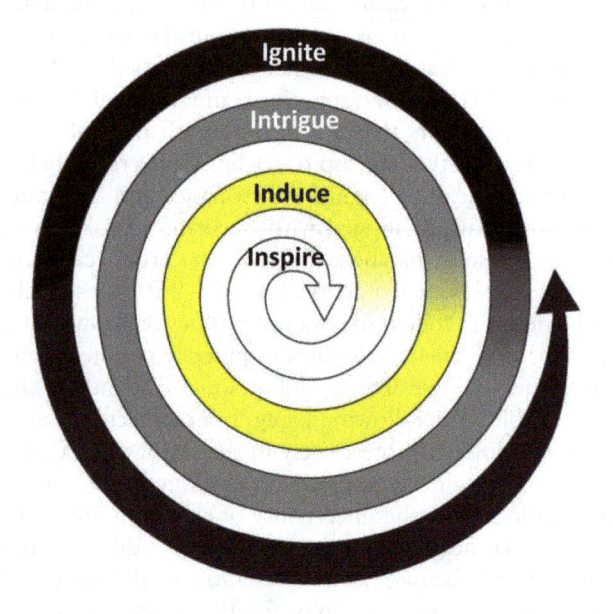

Fig. 1.6 Spiral of influence

Caption A shift from self-centered to benevolent behavior starts from the *inside out*, with the aspiration to values that are in sync with our "ideal" self; even if they are not expressed, or consciously acknowledged they serve as entry points (*inspire*); when we witness others in the pursuit of actions that illustrate such values, which may include universal citizenship inspiration ensues. From here the arousal of emotions (*induce*), via the combination of compassion and curiosity, both helped by conscientious understanding of the role that we occupy happens (*intrigue*), which ultimately leads to a change of behavior (*ignite*), even if that shift entails courage. The latter is conducive to inspire others; a new cycle is set in motion. This spiraling ripple effect operates from the inside out while being nurtured from the *outside in* and vice versa. Although they are presented here as sequential steps, phases may occur simultaneously or interchangeably; they are mutually reinforcing. Influence in all 4 dimensions harnesses the complementary benefit of all the dimensions of our complex being (Walther, 2021).

Change can be nurtured from the *outside in* by exposing individuals to sensorial impulses that disrupt their established perspectives and prompt a departure from the comfort zone of their current behavior patterns and belief system (Davis et al., 2019). If this sensorial influx is complemented by the introduction of new knowledge, it may spark curiosity about the origins and repercussions of the observed situation (White & Black, 2021). Subsequently, emotions may be aroused through relatable elements, culminating in clear inclinations or aversions towards the situation (Johnson, 2017). This emotional response either solidifies pre-existing attitudes or triggers a shift that challenges the internal value system (Brown & Miller, 2020).

Awe is another catalyst of compassion. It is a positive emotional response to perceptually vast stimuli that transcend current frames of reference. By inducing an acute perception of oneself as being part of a larger aliveness, awe may help individuals to situate themselves as an integral part of a broader social context, and thus enhance collective concern for the shared situation (Piff et al., 2015). Studies have shown that dispositional tendencies to experience awe predicted greater generosity, compassion, and ethical decision-making, while enhancing helping behavior and decreased entitlement.

When a shift in personal attitude translates into behavioral change, it sets off a ripple effect, as observers may witness the manifestation of the transformation, and be inspired by it (Wilson, 2018). The inspiration derived from observing value-based behavior in others compels bystanders to become involved themselves, fostering interest in deeper understanding and, ultimately, motivating them to act (Adams, 2019). As a critical mass of individuals undergoes such transformative processes, a new social norm emerges, leading to a turning tide in societal values and collective behavior patterns (Johnson, 2022). Amplified through online activities a benevolent attitude that emanates from the *micro*-arena can be taken to scale, with ripple effects from the inside out (Fig. 1.6). Placing the dynamic of social norms formation in the *Win4* (Sect. 4.1.1) illustrates the potential of influence for social good at scale, and the role that AI can play to support this.

The *A-Frame* can help us to be aware of our personal power to trigger the change we want to see. Once we fully *appreciate* what this means, for every single (in) action, it becomes easier, and harder, to *accept* the status quo that we are dissatisfied with. In an interconnected world, everything matters and we never know which drop will lead the cup to overflow. We are *accountable*, to ourselves, but also to the society that we belong to, including future generations.

A mindset of *Agency Amid AI* embraces the shift from internal comprehension to external manifestation; beyond inspiration for change, and the desire to make it happen, including curiosity for the causes and consequences of the status quo, it induces a shift from passive to proactive attitudes. This 360-degree perspective is necessary to reshape how and why we use technology. Because once we become aware of the manifold ways in which it influences us, we can build up a protective shield against persuasion and manipulation. Furthermore, we can start to intentionally shape how we want to use it to influence our environment. If such deliberate streams of AI-powered influence are driven by values that are aligned with the Common Good, such as the ones looked at earlier, the resulting dynamic benefits everyone. And with each person who adopts this mindset, the dynamic is amplified, with exponentially growing benefits.

1.4.2.1 Can the Beneficial Ripple Effect be Expanded with the Help of AI?

Behaviorally oriented technology has been used to shape people's perceptions for decades. Although this was done primarily for proprofit purposes the approach itself is agnostic. More recently nonprofits and governments have gone into the game of systematic behavioral influence via technology. Examples include normative messaging via phone, providing information about what most people do/don't do, and what people believe should (not) be done (Cialdini et al., 1990); and role modeling, by demonstrating a certain behavior through web influencers (Schultz et al., 2007). Also, calls encouraging individuals to make a public commitment (online) to a certain cause or behavior (offline) can strengthen social norms, by building a sense of hybrid accountability (Goldstein et al., 2008). Platform rewards like "stars", cash points. etc., provide incentives for certain behaviors which can reinforce or establish normative beliefs, while online edutainment (education+entertainment) campaigns can expose people to new knowledge, foster understanding, and nurture motivation, hence making individuals more likely to adopt and internalize related norms (Thaler & Sunstein, 2008). Whichever format is chosen the more personalized the approach is, the more efficiently it operates. Because although we all operate within the same 2 × 4 dimensions, we are still distinct individuals whose desires and dislikes differ. This is where GenAI becomes interesting.

Combining personalization with a range of mutually complementary approaches maximizes impact (Cialdini et al., 1990); as does the deliberate zooming in on several of the 4 dimensions simultaneously. Sustainable behavior change entails the mind, the heart, the soul, and ideally a sensorial experience. We change our perception, when we learn something new and understand how it fits our perspective (intellect), feel with the people affected by the situation in question (emotion), perceive a resonance with the values that we admire (aspiration), and experience physiologically what the situation means for them (sensation).

As pointed out earlier, the latest generation of LLMs expands the possibility of fine-tuned highly personalized interventions, thanks to the combination of algorithms that constantly analyze individual preferences, and social networks to deliver tailored triggers. Once a person's motivations and barriers are identified, the algorithm provides targeted suggestions and feedback to encourage certain actions and discourage others (Kramer et al., 2014). One example is social influence modeling where AI simulates and "models" social influence dynamics to identify factors that shape behavior. By analyzing large-scale social network data, algorithms can uncover influential individuals, communities, and content that may be leveraged to promote positive social norms (Bond et al., 2012; Centola et al., 2018). Also common is gamification where AI-powered platforms employ game techniques to motivate and incentivize (benevolent) behaviors. By incorporating elements like challenges and bonuses, AI systems can make social engagement more satisfying, encouraging continued participation (Hamari et al., 2014). Chatbots can be systematically designed to disseminate engaging messages that systematically stimulate inspiring behavior on social media platforms 24/7. These bots may engage users in meaningful conversations, share educational content, and encourage positive action, shaping social norms at scale (Bessi & Ferrara, 2016). The possibilities do not stop here.

Nudging involves the design of interventions to influence people's behavior in a predictable way without constraints or restricting their choices. The emphasis is on the power of subtle, strategically designed pointers to guide individuals towards certain decisions that are more beneficial for their own well-being. Nudges operate without constraint, on the premise that small changes in the presentation of information or choice architecture can lead to significant improvements in decision-making.

However, the strategic configuration of algorithms to nudge certain behavior patterns, an approach that is extensively used by companies such as Amazon and eBay, is a highly sensitive arena as the line between motivating and manipulating is fine. When it comes to the use of AI-powered nudges with a prosocial intention two challenges arise. Whilst corporations have little qualms of influencing consumers towards (yet) another purchase via sophisticated algorithms, non profits and public entities are more reluctant to use techniques that could be interpreted as involuntary persuasion. A second, more practical issue is that people are more easily nudged towards choices that are in their (apparent) personal interest, than for causes that serve the Common Good. If we seek to ignite the shift from passive to proactive by using nudges, the trick is to make those nudges propeople, and yet enticing enough to get people's attention.[52]

Let's put this into perspective. Influence happens constantly, directly and indirectly. Between individuals, and between individuals and institutions, and between individuals and the environment they evolve in. Nothing happens in a vacuum. We are constantly influencing and being influenced, (in)directly. Everything and everyone affects the dynamics around them.

AI is now part of this influence. It may be intentionally used to inspire by appealing to the aspiration for a larger cause, or to instill cravings that are grounded in basic instincts; it can be directed to *induce* the desire for a thing or a service (proprofit), or feelings that are conducive to supporting others/nature (propeople). Similarly, AI may serve to *ignite* a purchase or an action that serves others. The question is the human intention behind the scenes—why and how it is used by and on whom. Whether propeople or proprofit, transparency and regulation against abuse are essential. Seeing the all pervasive ever more subtle nature of AI, no matter

---

[52] The reward of a behavior does not have to be material, the most compelling recompenses are those that gratify our self-image.

the intended outcomes, safeguards against manipulation, and informed consent are vital (Kramer et al., 2014). AI is changing us, and the environment we occupy.

Dancing dynamics. To still bring out the best in and for all, a systemic view of both, and the overall social dynamic that they form part of is needed. Drawing on quantum physics, it appears that process and product are one and the same. The dancers are not only part of the dance—dancer and dance are one (Zukav, 1979). Like light has at the same time wave-like and particle-like qualities, the either/or categorizations that we tend to apply to the reality that surrounds us do not operate when it comes to society. A strict delimitation of online/offline, humans and machines, artificial intelligence, and human aspiration does not apply either, as one influences the other and is influenced in return.[53] Clear distinctions are becoming ever more difficult as the technological sophistication advances at exponential speed. The time for conscious influence on the machinery that is morphing into our life is now, when we still (partially) grasp how it operates. *Agency Amid AI* is the core tenant of a relationship with AI that serves the human user, and the society he/she/they evolve in.

The *A-Frame* can serve as a backdrop to regularly check in with ourselves whether we move in the direction of our own choosing, or merely follow the path "suggested" by others, including our artificial assistants. Being conscient of the values that underpin our judgment, including a personal commitment to universal *citizenship* as an expression of common humanity, with *compassion* for us and others, as well as the soft spots that make us unique are two distinguishing factors in the human race against an AI overtake; combined with *conscientiousness* of the role that each of us occupies as the global play unfolds, and *courage* to shift from passive to proactive participation. Manifesting values in practice on a daily basis may seem simplistic. And maybe it is, and maybe it isn't.

---

[53] The reality we experience is the cause and consequence of our experiences and expressions. Critical realists argue that while an objective reality exists, our understanding of that reality is shaped by our conceptual lenses and social conditioning (Archer et al., 2016; Maxwell, 2012). The critical realist ontology proposes stratified levels of reality involving mechanisms, events, and experiences (Bhaskar, 1975, 1979, 1998). Considered a philosophical approach to system thinking it recognizes the reality of the natural order while also acknowledging the role of perception in apprehending that reality (Groff, 2004). Adherents of critical realism maintain that through research and critical inquiry people can progressively refine their perception of reality, but that the process is inherently fallible and social.

Every small action has ripple effects across the system; when it is a positive action that is witnessed by others it may kick-off multiple domino-chains simultaneously offline and online. "Never doubt that a small group of thoughtful, committed citizens can change the world; indeed, it's the only thing that ever has" (Mead, 1964) (*Win4* in Sect. 4.1.1). More immediately, doing the right thing without the ambition of control over the outcomes is a mindset that nurtures our mental sanity amid the frenzy of the tech hype. In the following we look at the risk and opportunity of AI that presents for our decision making.

1.4.3 Artificial Influence from the Outside In

AI is revealing a new path through the landscape of human existence. It offers unforeseen insights to decode the intertwined relationship of our aspirations, emotions, thoughts, and sensations; and the challenges that characterize our ability to make objective choices. In the following we explore how AI systems can decode our innermost thoughts and emotional states through the data we generate online, looking at the persuasive power of AI and its potential for manipulation. Neurotechnology, which combines neuroscience and AI to enable reading, predicting, and possibly altering brain activity, is mentioned in that context because from brain-computer interfaces to emotion recognition, these technologies raise ethical concerns about preserving human autonomy in an AI-driven world.

Distorted persuasion. The vast reservoir of data regarding our preferences, intertwined with our verbal expressions, represents an intriguing facet of conversational LLMs. These models continuously absorb our emotions, refining their ability to mirror our vocabulary and attitudes, becoming increasingly adept at influencing our thoughts. As we navigate the digital realm, our online behaviors paint a vivid picture of our needs and desires, echoing the whispers of our innermost thoughts. Each click, like, and share embodies our yearnings and choices, forming intricate connections between these digital actions and our core emotional states. Much like wearable devices tracking our physiological sensations, AI deciphers the patterns in our habits, subtly signaling shifts in our emotional landscape—whether it's a surge in curiosity, a fleeting moment of aggression, or a gentle shift in mood (Wang, 2022), and accommodates them. These are powerful insights to fine-tune influence.

Already, chatbots are known to craft persuasive yet entirely fictional responses (Thoppilan et al., 2022). While deception and falsehoods have always lurked in human communication, the challenge with AI bots lies in their increasing sophistication in crafting and disseminating such content, alongside their integration into various facets of life, and the access to data about us. Studies suggest that large language models are becoming more persuasive than humans (Carrasco-Farré, 2024). Analyzing persuasion strategies employed by LLM-generated and human-generated arguments reveals that LLM arguments demand greater cognitive engagement due to their complex structures. Additionally, LLMs exhibit a notable inclination towards employing moral language, tapping into both positive and negative moral sentiments more frequently than humans.

Analyzing interactions with over 3000 participants across various political spectra, researchers noted a subtle shift in attitudes. Even skeptics of established climate science emerged from these conversations with a slightly more supportive stance towards scientific consensus (Chen et al., 2024). While this can be seen as a positive outcome under benevolent intentions, there are nuanced concerns. Firstly, these persuasive abilities could be exploited to sway individuals politically, incite criminal behavior, or promote products. Secondly, software companies may prioritize making their bots more likable at the expense of factual accuracy. In the climate study participants who held an opinion that was not in line with the chatbot reported a sense of disappointment after interacting with a bot that disagreed with them, rating its likability low on a 5-point scale.

This poses a dilemma for businesses, as users prioritize enjoyable interactions, potentially sidelining substantive content (Chen in Chen et al., 2024). As LLMs evolve further, propelled by companies eager to maintain market dominance, chatbots may be programmed to cater to users by offering responses aligned with their expected opinions, regardless of factual accuracy.[54] Human tendencies to hypocrisy and half-truths in offline interpersonal communication may thus be exacerbated by LLMs, amplifying the erosion of trust (Sect. 2.3.2).

---

[54] The prevalence of misinformation/disinformation predates the latest advancements in generative AI. Lies are as old as human history can be traced. Interpersonal communication is tainted, deliberately or unconsciously, by the intent of the sender and receiver. The online sphere is a bonanza for the dissemination of tainted truths; and we willingly gobble up what enters our screens, especially if it confirms the worldview that we already cherish. In 2020, the hashtag #climatescam garnered more engagement on Twitter than #climatecrisis (Winters, 2021).

The savviness of AI represents a paradoxical scenario. On the one hand, such insights are invaluable for businesses striving to resonate with consumer aspirations (Chamorro-Premuzic, 2023). Conversely, if individuals were privy to this information, it could empower them to nurture deeper self-awareness. Imagine if the algorithms initially deployed for monitoring consumers could be repurposed into personal mentors, drawing from a constant stream of information to provide tailored guidance. This reframing of online tracking could transform a tool of manipulation into a supportive ally, guiding consumers through the maze of attention and financial decisions, helping us to make informed choices rather than reacting to impulse or bias. It would be a fair exchange for our current status as "data cows", endlessly harvested by corporations in a constant violation of social norms such as fairness and transparency, and rules of unconscionability. Part of the risk is scale.

Algorithmic targeting, facilitated by minuscule "digital breadcrumbs", can initiate a snowball effect wherein users are not only exposed to increasingly similar content that reinforces their existing (potentially erroneous) beliefs (confirmation bias), but may also be led down a slippery slope. A 2024 study found that algorithms on platforms like TikTok directly target vulnerabilities such as loneliness or feelings of loss of control, gamifying harmful content that resonates with affected audiences. Consequently, initial platform suggestions evolved to include significantly more videos featuring misogynistic content (Weale, 2024). Exposure to persistent *micro*-doses of such content can normalize harmful and antisocial behavior, which is particularly concerning when it happens to children and adolescents whose worldview is still developing. Algorithms amplify existing predispositions and create a bias where even innocuous searches can trigger a harmful spiral. For example, a simple search for healthy snacks might lead to AI suggestions for low-calorie cooking or diets, and depending on the platform, propose content that exacerbates body image issues, as seen with TikTok's 2024 #legginglegs trend, where young girls posted photos of their legs in leggings, potentially triggering those struggling with the perception of their own body.

Increasingly the influence of LLMs extends beyond verbal interactions, seamlessly transitioning between text, images, videos, and vice versa, blurring the lines between reality and fiction. AudioLMs, exemplified by Google's MusicLM, utilize language models to generate high-fidelity audio or create music based on textual descriptions or hummed melodies

(Denk et al., 2023). OpenAI's launch of Sora in March 2024 introduced super-realistic text-to-video creation, further challenging our ability to discern truth from fabrication in the age of AI. "Seeing is believing", but is that what we see believable? The means of influence are expanding exponentially in an AI-powered realm. Never has acute awareness of the factors that affect our mind, and precede our choices been more important.

From monitoring to prediction to persuasion. Neurotech influences human hardware and human software simultaneously, taking the exploration of the human mind to the next level. Located in the nexus of neuroscience and AI, it is advancing fast, spanning from medical monitoring to mental manipulation. The underpinning brain-computer interface (BCI) technology has been around since the 1990s. It enables direct communication between the human brain and external devices, allowing individuals to control technology using their thoughts, i.e. brain signals (Lebedev & Nicolelis, 2006). Simplified speaking, BCI operates with probes, thin wires, that are inserted into the brain at specific locations. These wires monitor the activity of nearby brain cells and transmit the information they gather to a computer. The computer then processes this information in view of executing something, such as controlling a keyboard or a voice synthesizer (think Stephen Hawkins). It is worth remembering that BCIs can also work the other way round, driving neural activity through electrical stimulation carried out by the probes, potentially changing how we think and feel, hence what we do. Brain stimulation has proven to be beneficial for conditions like Parkinson's disease, depression, obsessive–compulsive disorder, substance-use disorders, stroke recovery, and long COVID-19.[55] Certain applications also offer promise to enhance healthy brain function, whether by improving memory or cognitive abilities (Hamzelou, 2023). Increasingly there is a shift towards remote brain stimulation, allowing treatments at home while sending brain recordings to a doctor's office. Leading-edge approaches

---

[55] In January 2024 Elon Musk's company Neuralink reported that they had implanted the first brain implant in a human being; it was a quadriplegic patient, and the trial is scheduled to last for three years. Although limited for now to addressing a serious medical condition, Musk's medium- and long-term vision is to boost the average human user's brain capacity. The reaction to Neuralink's release was lukewarm as researchers expressed concern by the secrecy surrounding the device's safety and performance—and were underwhelmed by the achievement.

involve "closed loop" devices recording brain activity and delivering electric stimuli preemptively (Jee, 2021). And it does not stop here.

Progressively researchers are moving beyond the realm of gathering and decoding brain activity to predicting it; from reading thoughts we transition to predicting them. A 2023 study revealed insights from a model trained on functional magnetic resonance imaging scans, demonstrating its capability to predict whole sentences based on individuals" brain activity during auditory experiences (Stokes et al., 2023). Whether it is passively reading or proactively influencing the brain, both approaches involve collecting, storing, and sharing massive amounts of brain data, offering ever more granular insights into an individual's mental states and activities. And the harvesting modus becomes ever subtler. Unlike previous methods which required electrode devices, more recent brain wave decoders are not invasive. For now they rely on individuals to willingly participate, yet findings from available studies about the possibility of brain-monitoring "off-the-radar" underscore the necessity for formal policies to safeguard our brain data. Increasingly concerns are raised about the potential for decoding and directly manipulating human mental processes, intentions, emotions, and thoughts (Nature, 2017). While some neuroscientists dismiss these fears as overblown (Fields in Newitz, 2024), others have acknowledged early on the potential for such technologies to influence thought processes.

Brainwashing. Nothing is as new as it seems. Although BCI brings the question of mind control front and center, humans have a long-standing fascination with the notion of persuasion and mental optimization, with origins dating back to ancient spiritual practices. First appearances in Western science include experiments of Ivan Pavlov in the nineteenth century on the conditioning of animals through traumatic experiences that are followed by the introduction of new behavior patterns (Pavlov, 1927). Later on, cybernetics conceptualized organisms and machines as information control systems governed by feedback loops (Wiener, 1948). Deriving from the Greek word for "steersman", it explored the parallels between the functioning of biological and mechanical systems, suggesting that the brain could be understood and potentially optimized through computational metaphors (Gardner, 1985). Building on this, dianetics was positioned as a therapeutic system to free individuals from past traumatic experiences or "engrams" stored in the mind through a process known as "auditing" (Hubbard, 1950). The alignment between dianetics and cybernetics reflects the ongoing trend of applying information processing models to the study of, and influence on, the human mind, and which also influenced the development of early artificial intelligence and cognitive science.

Considering that brainwashing[56] is first of all a social and political phenomenon, one might argue that misinformation, be it in the form of traditional politics or marketing, or the more advanced type of instrumentalizing 24/7 social media exposure is in itself a version of brainwashing, which is not reliable. Research has shown that efforts at mind control via persuasion do not have predictable results. Targeted online disinformation can actually have a counterproductive effect, leading to "stochastic terrorism", or acts of violence that cannot be predicted precisely ex ante but analyzed statistically ex post.[57]

Takes this beyond thoughts to emotions, Affective Computing[58] connects feelings and neuroscience, using AI to discern the most subtle biomarkers, to gather insights into the interplay of aspirations, emotions, thoughts, and sensations. Already social media behavior monitoring and keystroke analysis make it possible to assess remotely whether a person is at risk of depression (although this is not a universally applicable methodology as studies have shown that the verbal markers of depression that predict depression among white individuals are not reliable when it comes to black males).[59] Continuous neurophysiologic monitoring can

---

[56] Seeing the prevailing use of the word in the context of manipulation and persuasion, it is ironic to recall that the term "brainwashing" itself, which originated from the Chinese word xinao, is a wordplay on the older concept of "washing the heart" from Confucian and Buddhist philosophies which encompassed the goal of enlightenment (Newitz, 2024).

[57] Stochastic terrorism is inspired by online rhetoric that demonizes groups of people (in-group versus out-group/us versus them), but it is difficult to know which people consuming that rhetoric will actually become terrorists, and which of them will just express anger in their own hybrid space. Coercive influence works on some targets and misses others.

[58] Affective computing (also referred to as artificial emotional intelligence or emotion AI) is the study and development of systems and devices that can recognize, interpret, process, and simulate emotion or other affective phenomena (Picard, 2000).

[59] Neurophysiologic responses refer to the brain's electrical and chemical activities in response to internal or external stimuli. These responses are a result of complex interactions between neurons, neurotransmitters, and other brain structures that process and react to various experiences, such as emotions, sensory inputs, or cognitive tasks. They can be measured through various methods, such as brainwave activity, heart rate variability, and other physiological indicators that reflect how the nervous system is functioning at

predict low mood and energy in individuals with high accuracy, potentially enabling timely interventions to reduce the risk of mood disorders, which may be particularly relevant in the context of at risk populations such as the elderly or adolescents (Merritt et al. 2022).

Computer vision, signal processing, and pattern recognition, coupled with assessments of facial indicators, head movements, body movements, gaze, and vocal cues, enable tailored ongoing monitoring of depression and suicidal risk (Smith et al., 2023). In 2024 researchers prototyped a personalized skin-integrated facial interface (PsiFI) system, which is self-powered, stretchable, and transparent. Featuring a bidirectional triboelectric strain and vibration sensor it enables the simultaneous sensing and integration of verbal and non-verbal expression data. It is fully integrated with a data processing circuit for wireless data transfer, enabling real-time emotion recognition 24/7.

Seeing the far-reaching potential, and consequences, of persuasion and manipulation that is supercharged by Neurotech, the Member States of the Executive Board of UNESCO initiated in 2022 a global dialogue to develop an ethical framework for the largely unregulated Neurotechnology sector. Whether it will manifest in tangible measure is yet to be seen. However, as we will see later, efficient and effective regulation is challenging when the target is moving. Any legal framework in a domain that is as elusive and all pervasive as AI must be carried by a voluntary commitment to respect whatever prosocial ambitions underpin it. Service providers, scientists, and users are all part of the equation when it comes to the deliberate design of an artificial intelligence system that respects human dignity.

The potential of AI to map and influence the complex systems that we are extends to the whole organism. Objective assessments of physiological expressions, vocal impairments, and motor control have proven beneficial in detecting and monitoring Parkinson's disease, identifying subtypes, assessing treatment responses, and distinguishing between commonly confused disorders. Additionally, the use of AI to monitor fine motor control, vocal impairments, and eye movement facilitate the early detection and monitoring of Alzheimer's disease. Further and beyond a study at the University of Massachusetts, a specifically tailored algorithm revealed that electrical patterns serve as a blueprint shaping the developing

any given moment. Such measurements offer insights into how the brain and body are working together to interpret and respond to different situations.

body, influencing facial features and other aspects (Adee, 2023). Electricity's roles in biology extend beyond development, influencing processes from wound healing to cancer. Mapping and decoding this "electrome" is becoming possible with advanced LLMs. Beyond body and mind AI offers insights to grasp the process of emotions.

<u>Mutual benefits of artificial and natural intelligence.</u> Understanding natural intelligence better serves to understand artificial versions better and vice versa. Technology could be made more efficient and less energy-consuming by likening it to natural systems, while AI might serve to map, mirror, and influence synchrony between humans (Strogatz, 2003), and between human intelligence and its artificial counterparts. In that regard neuroscience not only illuminates biological intelligence but also guides the development of artificial intelligence (Achterberg et al., 2023). Considering evolutionary constraints like space and communication efficiency, which have shaped the emergence of proficient systems in nature, the recreation of spatially embedded neural networks in the artificial domain mirrors features present in empirical brain networks. This prompts the exploration of possibilities to embed similar constraints in AI systems, envisioning organically evolving artificial environments optimized for efficiency and environmental sustainability. In April 2024 Intel unveiled the world's largest neuromorphic computer, called Hala Point, which is designed to mimic the human brain. Comprising 1.15 billion artificial neurons and 128 billion artificial synapses across 140,544 processing cores this large-scale neuromorphic system can perform AI workloads 50 times faster and use 100 times less energy than conventional computing systems.

The future will tell if neuromorphic computing goes mainstream. Given the current environmental impact of AI systems, particularly the greenhouse gas emissions from energy-intensive server farms, adopting it is promising. In exploring the application of evolutionary principles to future AI development, should we emulate the efficiency-driven design of the human brain in artificial intelligence? Drawing from neuroscientific principles related to the conservation of material, space, and time in animal brains, particularly through techniques like divisive normalization (Ramón, 1905), it is plausible that incorporating neuromorphic computing, which mimics efficient coding in the brain, could yield powerful resource-efficient AI models. Using lab-grown brain cells embedded onto silicon chips, researchers at Monash University, Australia, merged the fields of artificial intelligence and synthetic biology to create programmable biological computing platforms, a "DishBrain system". Potentially leading to a "new type of machine intelligence that is able to learn throughout its lifetime", such "continual lifelong learning" would mean that machines could acquire new skills without compromising old ones, adapt to changes, and apply previously learned knowledge to new tasks—all while conserving limited resources such as computing power, memory, and energy.

What happens if these artificial system evolutions find a physical embodiment?

Whereas conventional AI systems operate primarily in virtual environments, relying on algorithms and data processing to interpret and respond to inputs, Artificial Embodied Intelligence (AEI) is grounding AI systems in physical bodies, enabling them to directly interact with and learn from their surrounding environments. It draws inspiration from biological systems, where intelligence arises from the seamless integration of cognitive processes, sensory perception, and physical embodiment. EAI emphasizes the notion that intelligence emerges from the continuous interplay between an agent's physical form, sensory inputs, and the dynamic world it inhabits (Pfeifer & Bongard, 2007). By endowing AI systems with physical forms and sensory modalities, EAI aims to foster more natural, context-aware, and adaptive forms of intelligence. Unlike traditional disembodied AI systems, embodied AI agents learn through direct sensorimotor engagement with their surroundings, akin to biological intelligence (Zambetta & Sofo, 2021). This approach fosters more adaptive, context-aware AI capable of robust real-world performance (Heess et al., 2017). EAI pushes the AI frontier into robotics, virtual agents, and multimodal perception, redefining how intelligent systems are developed and deployed (Han et al., 2024), which promises more robust, generalizable artificial cognition (Richards & Chalupka, 2024).

These concepts which we do not specifically look at in this book are worth keeping in mind as they will likely become part of the future of AI and bridge certain gaps between human and artificial systems.

The robotic revolution has long been a dream of science fiction, with visions of humanoid assistants seamlessly integrating into households and offices. Yet for decades, this ambition remained elusive, as robots struggled with a challenge known as Moravec's paradox: what is easy for humans, such as tying a shoelace or having a conversation, is immensely difficult for machines. Conversely, tasks that are complex for humans, like playing chess or holding an object perfectly still, are trivial for robots

(Moravec, 1988). This paradox highlighted the limitations robots faced in the unpredictable complexity of the real world. Now AI techniques like reinforcement learning, imitation learning, and generative models allow researchers to imbue robots with unprecedented capabilities. In a not too far away future robots may be able to iron clothes, cook meals, or clean surfaces, simply learning from observing and imitating human demonstrations. Robotic assistants that can adapt and acquire new skills on the fly, navigating the ever-changing landscapes of human homes with dexterity and common sense, are at reach. The key to this transformative shift lies in the link of robotics and AI, fueled by gargantuan datasets that capture the intricacies of human behavior and society. As we see this alliance expand across the globe, the plan of capable, intelligent robotic companions is coming closer (Heikkilä, 2024). Now imagine these artificial power additions, and put them on top of a genuine human aspiration for the Common Good, situated in the multidimensional understanding of life as an organically evolving kaleidoscope in which everything is connected in a continuum of constant change.

Agency Amid AI for All, the initiative proposed in this book is motivated by the ambition to render AI an ally of humankind. It seeks to curate a mindset that it grounded in capacity and volition: the ability to take action that is aligned with one's aspirations, and the will to do so. Both require a strong value foundation and the mental stamina to carry it from aspiration (theory) to behavior (practice). Prosocial AI will be the consequence of such a mindset, it cannot be its cause. By positioning Natural Intelligence (NI) in its multidimensional richness above Artificial Intelligence (AI) the drive for *Agency Amid AI* is aligns with endeavors such as the Brain Capital initiative[60] by strivingto position and protect the brain as humanity's paramount asset. Investments in NI are not a luxury, and should not be reserved to high income countries or groups. They have the *Win4* effect (Ch 4)—benefit for the individual, the *meso* and *macro* arenas they belong to, and society overall. Ultimately unequal access jeopardizes the wellbeing of everyone. (Wilkerson et al., 2021).

---

[60] The Brain Capital Grand Strategy was launched in early 2021. The strategy urged the need for Brain Capital in all policies, for more investment in Brain Capital, and a global dashboard to monitor essential trends for more informed policymaking. Within the same period, the OECD Neuroscience-inspired Policy Initiative (NIPI) was launched by the then OECD Secretary-General.

Human Agency conditions whether we can harness our natural and artificial assets to serve ourselves, the communities we belong to, and the planet we depend on. It will become a central element to personal well-being in a hybrid world. We must systematically protect and curate it.

The aforementioned examples illustrate certain benefits, while offering a glimpse of their potential for manipulation. As with any innovation the growing connection between humans and machines is a two-sided coin; depending on the side we consider the value of the whole changes.

1.4.4 Summarizing Pros and Contras of Mutual Influence in a Hybrid Society

Whichever angle we look at, the outcomes of progress in the *meso* (community), *macro* (country) and *meta* (global) arena depend on individuals (*micro*) who embrace the power of agency. Change for social good is driven by thinkers and doers who shift from aspiration to action, beyond clicks to coherent practice, offline and online.

Whether the influence of AI is positive or harmful to society, hinges on conscious decisions and deliberate actions of humans, us. Genuine allegiance to the maximization of prosocial outcomes could shift the focus from economic gains to results that lift and optimize humanity's standards of quality of life in an inclusive manner. There are no guarantees, but we will not know if we do not try. The choices we make are the chances we take.

AI systems are neutral, the central bottlenecks of making them a force for the Common Good are human awareness of interplays, and individual accountability for the influence that every human exerts on these interplays. Designing *prosocial AI* systems requires a granular understanding of human behavior (mind), empathy with human experiences (heart), alignment with human values (soul), and proactive efforts for prosocial outcomes (body).

Determining our own values, which is a deceptively simple aspirational act, is foundational to the hybrid future. Human aspirations shape human behavior, and hence social reality, online and offline. What we want drives what we do. Values are the compass to guide our desires, and hence us towards the future we want, which is conditioned by our ability to manifest the self that we aspire to, anchored in our values. As technology penetrates our external environment and by extension intensifies its influence on our inner space we must clearly define what we want that inner sanctum to be like.

Is our mindset geared up to dare new paths, or to deny the essence of what makes us human?

Anchored in the multidimensional understanding of interplays, designed, and delivered with the orientation to positive social impact, and fueled by the shared aspiration of optimized value for humanity, AI may influence society in fascinating ways. Among the topics that are cutting across the entire *m4-matrix* are questions of worth versus value and utilization versus reliance versus dependency. They represent moving pieces in the evolving *hybrid alignment conundrum* that we seek to wrap our minds and hearts around (Sect. 2.2.4). No matter how inviting it is to engage in doomsday scenarios, and regardless of the appeal for shifting all hope onto the big intangible wings of AI we need to be careful of falling prey to the lure of technology as an all-purpose hammer. Whether it is in the form of artificial intelligence, artificial emotional intelligence, or artificial general intelligence, technology is a means to an end, not an end in itself. That end must be clearly defined by humanity's broader ideals. Neither the short-term interests of individuals and corporations, nor the medium-term curiosity of science without a big picture orientation can serve as yardsticks.

If the current pace of innovation continues undisrupted, the chance of unaided machines outperforming humans in every possible task was estimated at 10% by 2027, and 50% by 2047, according to an aggregated forecast of over 2500 renown researchers (Grace et al., 2024). That timeframe is getting ever shorter. Due to the exponential growth curve LLMs advance in giant steps, every day faster. An end is not yet in sight. As of 2023, AI has hit human-level performance on the majority of AI benchmarks, from reading comprehension to visual reasoning and even multitask visual reasoning. It falls just short on some benchmarks like competition-level math (Stanford AI Index, 2024). Because AI has reached that many standard benchmarks, AI scholars are now adding more difficult challenges such as coding, advanced reasoning, and agentic behavior.

<u>Potential power pairing perspective</u>. Ultimately it matters to remember that artificial intelligence is an artifice of human intelligence, and should be steered by it in the direction we want. "If we let the genie out of the bottle, it's our own fault. It doesn't have to happen" (Coy, 2024).

Our biggest challenges, war, climate change, environmental pollution, social exclusion, were created by people, and must be solved by them. The causes of all global phenomena start at the *micro*-level, and that is where the consequences are felt. Technology can help humans to reach their goals, not more, not less.

It is not impossible that at some point artificial entities will equal or even exceed human capacities in the intellectual (mind) and physiological (body) dimensions. AI-powered robots are part of a nearby future. What will set humans apart forever is the ability to aspire (soul) and feel (heart). Rather than focusing our energy to commiserate about the areas in which we might be outperformed by machines, we can channel our time and talent to systematically nurture and curate the other domains, starting with emotional intelligence and value-inspired interpersonal relationship building. Ironically the arenas that got the least attention during the previous three industrial revolutions will be quintessential in the aftermath of this one.

Suppose we combine the tandem of artificial intelligence and robotic strength on the machine side, with human beings who are aware of their natural assets, anchored in their values, and who not only accept their vulnerability but appreciate the authenticity that derives from it. Now anchor this power-pair in a mindset of unconditional accountability for inputs and outcomes, and we might actually see a phase where great quality of life is at reach for everyone everywhere. This is the purpose of *Agency Amid AI for All*. When humans leverage their unique features, and use AI strategically to complement certain shortcomings, with the ambition of progress that benefits people and planet we are getting not just somewhere, but might reach a place that is worth being at.

Recognizing the above while looking for the positive impact that can derive from a conscious combination of artificial intelligence and human aspirations, a high-level overview of the *m4-matrix* could be summarized in a 4-by-4 table (Table 1.3).

Everything is connected in a continuum of constant change in which one component is complementary to the others while being completed in return. Throughout the 2×4 dimensions, this logic shapes our online and offline existence. Technology may enable us to ever better decode the nuances that shape who we are, and why.

Reality is continuously upgrading itself. The past influences the present, the present becomes the past, whereas the future builds on the present. Awareness of simultaneously occurring internal and external

Table 1.3 Mutual influence within and between the 2 × 4 dimensions, in the best-case scenario of optimized flow

DIMENSION	micro	meso	macro	meta
Aspirational	Personal growth and transformation	Enhanced spirituality within communities	Global interconnectedness and shared values	Collective wisdom and enlightenment
Emotional	Personalized emotional support	Improved emotional well-being in organizations	Enhanced empathy and social cohesion in societies	Global empathy and compassion
Intellectual	Personalized learning and knowledge acquisition	Collaborative problem-solving in teams	Advancements in scientific research and innovation	Global knowledge sharing and collective intelligence
Physiological	Personalized care, support and services	Enhanced well-being in communities	Improved social services, political stability and prosperity.	Global resource accessibility and optimized complementarity of means/needs.

Caption Flows from the spiritual to the physiological dimension (vertical arrow), and from the *micro* to the *meta* dimension (horizontal arrow)

interplays is the first step to intentional influence, on oneself, others, and technology. One might consider serendipity, the occurrence and development of events by chance, as glimpses of infinity. AI is pushing the window to catch that glimpse.

RECAP—Mapping the transformative interplay of humans and technology across individual dimensions (aspirations-emotions-thoughts-sensations) and societal arenas (micro-meso-macro-meta) is helpful to see the bigger picture of AI and Society. The POZE framework shows why and how a mindset of Agency Amid AI matters. We looked at the A-Frame (awareness—appreciation—acceptance—accountability) as a practical tool to pursue aspirations and actions that serve the Common Good. The Spiral of influence was suggested as an approach to systematically leverage individual influence from the inside out, and to nurture it from the outside in; with the possibility of using AI to expand that influence in a hybrid setting.

How does awareness of the personal power that comes with agency influence your perspective of AI?

REFERENCES

Achterberg, J., Akarca, D., Strouse, D. J., Duncan, J., & Astle, D. (2023). Spatially embedded recurrent neural networks reveal widespread links between structural and functional neuroscience findings. *Nature Machine Intelligence, 5*, 1369–1381. https://doi.org/10.1038/s42256-023-00748-9

Adams, J. K. (2019). The dynamics of behavioral change. *Journal of Behavioral Science, 15*(2), 123–145.

Adee, S. (2023). The amazing ways electricity in your body shapes you and your health. New Scientist. https://www.newscientist.com/article/2360290-the-amazing-ways-electricity-in-your-body-shapes-you-and-your-health/. Retrieved July 2023.

Alberts, B., Johnson, A., Lewis, J., Raff, M., Roberts, K., & Walter, P. (2002). *Molecular biology of the cell* (4th ed.). Garland Science.

Aldrich, D. P. (2012). *Building resilience: Social capital in post-disaster recovery*. University of Chicago Press.

Aldrich, D. P., & Meyer, M. A. (2015). Social capital and community resilience. *American Behavioral Scientist, 59*(2), 254–269. https://doi.org/10.1177/0002764214550299

Appiah, K. A. (2006). *Cosmopolitanism: Ethics in a world of strangers*. W.W. Norton & Company.

Archer, M., Decoteau, C., Gorski, P., Little, D., Porpora, D., Rutzou, T., Smith, C., Steinmetz, G., & Vandenberghe, F. (2016). What is critical realism? *Perspectives: A Newsletter of the ASA Theory Section, 38*(2), 4–9.

Atari, M., Xue, M. J., Park, P. S., Blasi, D. E., & Henrich, J. (2024). Which humans? Department of Human Evolutionary Biology. Harvard University. https://doi.org/10.31234/osf.io/5b26t

Atkinson, A. B., & Micklewright, J. (1992). *Economic transformation in Eastern Europe and the distribution of income*. World Bank Publications.

Avolio, B. J., Gardner, W. L., Walumbwa, F. O., Luthans, F., & May, D. R. (2004). Unlocking the mask: A look at the process by which authentic leaders impact follower attitudes and behaviors. *The Leadership Quarterly, 15*(6), 801–823. https://doi.org/10.1016/j.leaqua.2004.09.00

Bandura, A. (2006). Toward a psychology of human agency. *Perspectives on Psychological Science, 1*(2), 164–180. https://doi.org/10.1111/j.1745-6916.2006.00011.x

Banks, M. R., Willoughby, L. M., & Banks, W. P. (2008). Animal-assisted therapy and loneliness in nursing homes: Use of robotic versus living dogs. *Journal of the American Medical Directors Association, 9*(3), 173–177.

Bartholomew, A. N., Zimmerman, G., & Bitterman, M. E. (2020). Extrasensory perception: Distinguishing between the senses. In T. K. Shackelford & V. A. Weekes-Shackelford (Eds.), *Encyclopedia of evolutionary psychological science*. Springer International Publishing. https://doi.org/10.1007/978-3-319-16999-6_3654-1

Bass, B. M., & Riggio, R. E. (2006). *Transformational leadership* (2nd ed.). Psychology Press.

Benedetti, F. (2008). *Placebo effects: Understanding the mechanisms in health and disease*. Oxford University Press.

Bessi, A., & Ferrara, E. (2016). Social bots distort the 2016 US Presidential election online discussion. *First Monday, 21*(11).

Bhaskar, R. (1975). *A realist theory of science*. Leeds Books.

Bhaskar, R. (1979). *The possibility of naturalism: A philosophical critique of the contemporary human sciences*. Humanities Press.

Bhaskar, R. (1998). *The possibility of naturalism: A philosophical critique of the contemporary human sciences*. Routledge.

Bicchieri, C. (2006). *The grammar of society: The nature and dynamics of social norms*. Cambridge University Press.

Bliss, T. V. P., & Collingridge, G. L. (1993). A synaptic model of memory: Long-term potentiation in the hippocampus. *Nature, 361*(6407), 31–39. https://doi.org/10.1038/361031a0

Block, P. (2013). *Stewardship: Choosing service over self-interest*. Berrett-Koehler Publishers.

Bloomberg. (2023). Generative AI to become a $1.3 trillion market by 2032, Research finds. Press release. https://www.bloomberg.com/company/press/generative-ai-to-become-a-1-3-trillion-market-by-2032-research-finds/

Bond, R. M., Fariss, C. J., Jones, J. J., Kramer, A. D., Marlow, C., Settle, J. E., & Fowler, J. H. (2012). A 61-million-person experiment in social influence and political mobilization. *Nature, 489*(7415), 295–298.

Boroditsky, L., Schmidt, L. A., & Phillips, W. (2003). Sex, syntax, and semantics. In D. Gentner & S. Goldin-Meadow (Eds.), *Language in mind: Advances in the study of language and thought* (pp. 61–79). MIT Press.

Bostrom, N. (2014). *Superintelligence: Paths, dangers, strategies*. Oxford University Press.

Bronfenbrenner, U. (1979). *The ecology of human development: Experiments by nature and design*. Harvard University Press.

Brown, A., & Miller, B. (2020). Shifting perspectives: Internal values and external influences. *Behavioral Dynamics Quarterly, 8*(4), 267–281.

Brown, B. (2012). *Daring greatly: How the courage to be vulnerable transforms the way we live, love, parent, and lead*. Penguin.

Brown, T., Mann, B., Ryder, N., Subbiah, M., Kaplan, J. D., Dhariwal, P., Neelakantan, A., Shyam, P., Sastry, G., Askell, A., & Agarwal, S. (2020). *Language models are few-shot learners*. arXiv preprint arXiv:2005.14165

Brynjolfsson, E., & McAfee, A. (2014). *The second machine age: Work, progress, and prosperity in a time of brilliant technologies*. W. W. Norton & Company.

Bryson, J. (2018). The artificial intelligence of the ethics of artificial intelligence: An introductory overview for students. In A. D. Berkich & M. I. Assad (Eds.), *The evolution of the Artificial Intelligence program: Issues and prospects*. https://www.researchgate.net/publication/324769096

Buchanan, A., & Keohane, R. (2006). The common good. In T. Pogge & D. Moellendorf (Eds.), *Global justice: Seminal essays* (pp. 487–509). Paragon House.

Bughin, J., Hazan, E., Ramaswamy, S., Chui, M., Allas, T., Dahlström, P., & Henke, N. (2018). *Artificial intelligence: The next digital frontier?* McKinsey Global Institute.

Bunge, M. (1966). Technology as applied science. *Technology and Culture, 7*(3), 329–347.

Bushong, E. (2019). *The geographic mess of digital content and licenses*. Discover Magazine.

Cahill, L., & McGaugh, J. L. (1998). Mechanisms of emotional arousal and lasting declarative memory. *Trends in Neurosciences, 21*(7), 294–299.

Cakebread, C. (2017). *Facebook's facial recognition settings violate privacy laws, says judge*. Business Insider.

Canalys. (2024). *Cloud market share Q1 2024*. https://www.canalys.com/newsroom/worldwide-cloud-market-q1-2024

Capra, F., & Luisi, P. L. (2014). *The systems view of life: A unifying vision*. Cambridge University Press.

Carabotti, M., Scirocco, A., Maselli, M. A., & Severi, C. (2015). The gut-brain axis: Interactions between enteric microbiota, central and enteric nervous systems. *Annals of Gastroenterology, 28*(2), 203–209.

Carrasco-Farré, C. (2024). *Large Language Models are as persuasive as humans, but why? About the cognitive effort and moral-emotional language of LLM arguments*. https://doi.org/10.48550/arXiv.2404.09329

Carse, J. P. (1986). *Finite and infinite games: A vision of life as play and possibility*. Free Press.

Centola, D., Becker, J., Brackbill, D., & Baronchelli, A. (2018). Experimental evidence for tipping points in social convention. *Science, 360*(6393), 1116–1119.

Chamorro-Premuzic, T. (2023). Should you share AI-driven customer insights with your customers? *Harvard Buisness Review*. https://hbr.org/2023/03/should-you-share-ai-driven-customer-insights-with-your-customers. Retrieved June 2023.

Chen, K., Shao, A., Burapacheep, J., & Li, Y. (2024). Conversational AI and equity through assessing GPT-3's communication with diverse social groups on contentious topics. *Science and Reports, 14*, 1561. https://doi.org/10.1038/s41598-024-51969-w

Chui, M., Manyika, J., & Miremadi, M. (2016). *Where machines could replace humans—and where they can't (yet)*. McKinsey Quarterly.

Cialdini, R. B., & Goldstein, N. J. (2004). Social influence: Compliance and conformity. *Annual Review of Psychology, 55*, 591–621.

Cialdini, R. B., Reno, R. R., & Kallgren, C. A. (1990). A focus theory of normative conduct: Recycling the concept of norms to reduce littering in public places. *Journal of Personality and Social Psychology, 58*(6), 1015–1026.

Cohen, S., Janicki-Deverts, D., & Miller, G. E. (2007). Psychological stress and disease. *JAMA, 298*(14), 1685–1687. https://doi.org/10.1001/jama.298.14.1685

Comte-Sponville, A. (2002). *The little book of atheist spirituality*. Viking Press.

Coy, P. (2024). Will machines be able to take our jobs? Maybe, but it doesn't have to be that way. *New York Times*. Retrieved January 2024.

Crutzen, P. J., & Stoermer, E. F. (2000). The "Anthropocene." *Global Change Newsletter, 41*, 17–18.

Damasio, A. R. (1994). *Descartes' error: Emotion, reason, and the human brain*. Putnam.

Damasio, A. R. (2010). *Self comes to mind: Constructing the conscious brain*. Vintage.

Darwin, C. R. (1959). *On the origin of species*. Reprint 2008 by BiblioLife ISBN 9780554267388.

DataReportal. (2024). *Digital 2024: Global overview report*. https://datareportal.com/reports/digital-2024-global-overview-report

Davis, C., et al. (2019). External catalysts for internal change: A comprehensive analysis. *Journal of Change Research, 22*(3), 189–205.

DeGrazia, D. (2005). *Human identity and bioethics*. Cambridge University Press.

Denk, T. I., Takagi, Y., Matsuyama, T., Agostinelli, A., Nakai, T., Frank, C., & Nishimoto, S. (2023). Brain2Music: Reconstructing music from human brain activity. In *Proceedings of the 38th International Conference on Machine Learning*. PMLR. https://google-research.github.io/seanet/brain2music/?utm_source=www.neatprompts.com&utm_medium=newsletter&utm_campaign=google-s-mind-reading-ai. Retrieved July 2023.

Denning, P. J. (2019). A cyber risk-oriented theory of harm for the age of artificial intelligence. *Harvard Journal of Law & Technology, 32*(2), 403–436.

Deutsch, M., & Gerard, H. B. (1955). A study of normative and informational social influences upon individual judgment. *The Journal of Abnormal and Social Psychology, 51*(3), 629–636.

DiMaggio, P., Hargittai, E., Neuman, W. R., & Robinson, J. P. (2004). Social implications of the Internet. *Annual Review of Sociology, 27*(1), 307–336.

Doe, J., & Roe, S. (2018). From passive to active: Exploring the spectrum of behavioral transition. *Psychology Today, 43*(1), 45–62.

Doidge, N. (2007). *The brain that changes itself*. Penguin.

Dreyer, P. S., Mather, C., & Hvidt, N. C. (2019). Compassion as a social and ethical value: A theological perspective. *European Journal of Public Health, 29*(Supplement_4), ckz185.116. https://doi.org/10.1093/eurpub/ckz185.116

Duncan, G. J., & Magnuson, K. (2012). Socioeconomic status and cognitive functioning: Moving from correlation to causation. *Wiley Interdisciplinary Reviews: Cognitive Science, 3*(3), 377–386. https://doi.org/10.1002/wcs.1176

Ellies, K. (2024). AI and the challenge of ethical leadership. *Ethics in Leadership Journal, 22*(1), 45–62.

Elsayed, E., Acharjya, D. P., Misra, S., & Saha, S. (2018). AI-based smart city big data analytics: Recent advances and future challenges. *IEEE Access, 6*, 11509–11528.

eMarketer. (2024, February 15). *Global ecommerce forecast 2023*. https://www.emarketer.com/content/global-ecommerce-forecast-2023

Emoto, M. (2004). *The hidden messages in water*. Atria Books.

Evans, G. W., & Kim, P. (2013). Childhood poverty, chronic stress, self-regulation, and coping. *Child Development Perspectives, 7*(1), 43–48. https://doi.org/10.1111/cdep.12013

Fish, S., Gonczarowski, Y. A., & Shorrer, R. I. (2024). Algorithmic collusion by large language models. https://doi.org/10.48550/arXiv.2404.00806

Floridi, L. (Ed.). (2019). *The Routledge handbook of philosophy of information*. Routledge.

Forget, E. L. (2011). The town with no poverty: The health effects of a Canadian guaranteed annual income field experiment. *Canadian Public Policy, 37*(3), 283–305.

Foster, J. A., & McVey Neufeld, K. A. (2013). Gut-brain axis: How the microbiome influences anxiety and depression. *Trends in Neurosciences, 36*(5), 305–312. https://doi.org/10.1016/j.tins.2013.01.005

Frankena, W. K. (1973). *Ethics*. Prentice-Hall.

Freud, S. (1912). The dynamics of transference. *Classics in Psychoanalytic Techniques* (Edited by R Langs, 1977), 22, 106–117.

Fromm, E. (1941). *Escape from freedom*. American Mental Health Foundation (1st ed.) (reprint October 15, 2010).

Gade, C. B. N. (2012). What is Ubuntu? Different interpretations among South Africans of African descent. *South African Journal of Philosophy, 31*(3), 484–503. https://doi.org/10.1080/02580136.2012.10751789

Gardner, H. (1985). *The mind's new science: A history of the cognitive revolution*. Basic Books.
Gershon, M. D. (1998). *The second brain*. HarperCollins.
Global End Child Poverty Coalition. (2023). Child poverty in the digital age: Trends, challenges, and opportunities. Global End Child Poverty Coalition.
Goldstein, N. J., Cialdini, R. B., & Griskevicius, V. (2008). A room with a viewpoint: Using social norms to motivate environmental conservation in hotels. *Journal of Consumer Research, 35*(3), 472–482.
Gould, S. J., & Eldredge, N. (1977). Punctuated equilibria: The tempo and mode of evolution reconsidered. *Paleobiology, 3*(2), 115–151.
Grace, K., Stewart, H., Sandkühler, J. F., Brauner, J., Thomas, S., & Weinstein-Raun, B. (2024, January). *Thousands of AI authors on the future of AI preprint*. AI Impacts Berkeley.
Groff, R. (2004). *Critical realism, post-positivism and the possibility of knowledge*. Routledge.
Gupta, R., Rana, P., Agarwal, S., & Kumar, P. (2018). Artificial intelligence for disaster management. *AI & Society, 33*(2), 223–236.
GWI. (2024). *Social media marketing trends in 2024*. https://www.gwi.com/reports/social-media-marketing-2024
Haidt, J. (2012). *The righteous mind: Why good people are divided by politics and religion*. Vintage.
Hair, N. L., Hanson, J. L., Wolfe, B. L., & Pollak, S. D. (2015). Association of child poverty, brain development, and academic achievement. *JAMA Pediatrics, 169*(9), 822–829. https://doi.org/10.1001/jamapediatrics.2015.1475
Hamari, J., Koivisto, J., & Sarsa, H. (2014). Does gamification work?–A literature review of empirical studies on gamification. In *47th Hawaii International Conference on System Sciences (HICSS)* (pp. 3025–3034). IEEE.
Hamzelou, J. (2023). How your brain data could be used against you. *MIT Technology Review*. https://www.technologyreview.com/2023/02/24/1069116/how-your-brain-data-could-be-used-against-you/. Retrieved July 2023.
Han, W., Peng, X. B., & Lin, Y. (2024). Multimodal embodied agents: Toward human-like perception and cognition. *ACM Computing Surveys, 57*(2), 1–36.
Haarmann, B., Haarmann, C., & Haarmann, A. (2019a). *Universal basic income: A modern approach to economic security and social justice*. Palgrave Macmillan.
Haarmann, C., Haarmann, D., & Haarmann, W. (2019b). Universal basic income in Namibia and India: A comparative analysis. *Basic Income Studies, 14*(1).
Haski-Leventhal, D., Pournader, M., & McKinnon, A. (2019). The role of gender and age in business students' values, CSR attitudes, and responsible management education: Learnings from the PRME international survey. *Journal of Business Ethics, 160*(1), 219–239.

Hassabis, D., Kumaran, D., Summerfield, C., & Botvinick, M. (2017). Neuroscience-inspired artificial intelligence. *Neuron, 95*(2), 245–258.

Heess, N., Tb, D., Sriram, S., Lemmon, J., Merel, J., Wayne, G., Tassa, Y., Erez, T., Wang, Z., Eslami, S. M., & Riedmiller, M. (2017). Emergence of locomotion behaviours in rich environments. ArXiv, abs/1707.02286.

Heikkilä, M. (2024, April 11). Is robotics about to have its own ChatGPT moment? *MIT Technology Review*. https://www.technologyreview.com/2024/04/11/1068188/is-robotics-about-to-have-its-own-chatgpt-moment/

Henrich, J., Heine, S. J., & Norenzayan, A. (2010). The weirdest people in the world? *Behavioral and Brain Sciences, 33*(2–3), 61–83. https://doi.org/10.1017/S0140525X0999152X

Hernandez, M. (2008). Promoting stewardship behavior in organizations: A leadership model. *Journal of Business Ethics, 80*(1), 121–128.

Hertenstein, M. J., Keltner, D., App, B., Bulleit, B. A., & Jaskolka, A. R. (2006). Touch communicates distinct emotions. *Emotion, 6*(3), 528–533. https://doi.org/10.1037/1528-3542.6.3.528

Hillman, C. H., Erickson, K. I., & Kramer, A. F. (2008). Be smart, exercise your heart: Exercise effects on brain and cognition. *Nature Reviews Neuroscience, 9*(1), 58–65. https://doi.org/10.1038/nrn2298

Hirschhorn, L. (1988). *The workplace within: Psychodynamics of organizational life*. MIT Press.

Hubbard, L. R. (1950). *Dianetics: The modern science of mental health*. Hermitage House.

iiMedia Research. (2024). *2023 China e-commerce market research report*. https://www.iimedia.cn/c1200/c1201/report-2023.html

Insider Intelligence. (2024). *US ecommerce by category 2024*. https://www.insiderintelligence.com/reports/us-ecommerce-by-category-2024/

Isen, A. M. (2009). Affect and creative thinking. In D. Sander & K. R. Scherer (Eds.), *The Oxford companion to emotion and the affective sciences* (pp. 134–136). Oxford University Press.

Jee, C. (2021). This woman's brain implant zaps her with electricity when it senses she's getting depressed. *MIT Technology Review*. https://www.technologyreview.com/2021/10/04/1036430/brain-implant-zaps-electricity-depression/. Retrieved July 2023.

John XXIII. (1961). *Mater et Magistra*. http://www.vatican.va/content/john-xxiii/en/encyclicals/documents/hf_j-xxiii_enc_15051961_mater.html

Johnson, R. (2017). Emotions and behavioral shifts: An integrated approach. *Journal of Emotional Dynamics, 30*(4), 321–336.

Johnson, S. (2022). Societal norms: A framework for understanding change. *Social Science Journal, 18*(1), 56–73.

Jones, M., & Brown, P. (2015). Values as seeds of lifelong learning. *Educational Psychology Review, 12*(1), 67–84.

Jurafsky, D., & Martin, J. H. (2019). *Speech and language processing: An introduction to natural language processing, computational linguistics, and speech recognition* (3rd ed.). Pearson.
Kahneman, D. (2007). *Thinking, fast and slow*. Farrar, Straus and Giroux.
Kahneman, D. (2011). *Thinking, fast and slow*. Farrar.
Kamptner, N. L. (1995). Treasured possessions and their meanings in adolescent males and females. *Adolescence, 30*(118), 301–318.
Kandel, E. R., Dudai, Y., & Mayford, M. R. (2014). The molecular and systems biology of memory. *Cell, 157*(1), 163–186. https://doi.org/10.1016/j.cell.2014.03.001
Kandel, E. R., Schwartz, J. H., Jessell, T. M., Siegelbaum, S. A., & Hudspeth, A. J. (2012). *Principles of neural science* (5th ed.). McGraw-Hill.
Kaplan, A. M., & Haenlein, M. (2010). Users of the world, unite! The challenges and opportunities of social media. *Business Horizons, 53*(1), 59.
Kela. (2019). Independent research institute to evaluate the effects of the basic income experiment. [Press Release]. https://www.kela.fi/web/en/news-arc hive/-/asset_publisher/lN08GY2nIrZo/content/independent-research-instit ute-to-evaluate-the-effects-of-the-basic-income-experiment
Kelly, J. R., Kennedy, P. J., Cryan, J. F., Dinan, T. G., Clarke, G., & Hyland, N. P. (2015). Breaking down the barriers: The gut microbiome, intestinal permeability and stress-related psychiatric disorders. *Frontiers in Cellular Neuroscience, 9*, 392. https://doi.org/10.3389/fncel.2015.00392
Kelly, K. (2009). How technology evolves. *TED Talk*. https://blog.ted.com/how_technology/
Keltner, D., Haidt, J., & Shiota, M. N. (2019). Social functionalism and the evolution of emotions. In *Evolution and social psychology* (pp. 115–142). Psychology Press.
Koltko-Rivera, M. E. (2006). Rediscovering the later version of Maslow's hierarchy of needs: Self-transcendence and opportunities for theory, research, and unification. *Review of General Psychology, 10*(4), 302–317. https://doi.org/10.1037/1089-2680.10.4.302
Kramer, A. D., Guillory, J. E., & Hancock, J. T. (2014). Experimental evidence of massive-scale emotional contagion through social networks. *Proceedings of the National Academy of Sciences, 111*(24), 8788–8790.
Küng, H. (1998). *A global ethic for global politics and economics*. Oxford University Press.
Kurzweil, R. (2005). *The singularity is near: When humans transcend biology*. Viking.

Latané, B., & Darley, J. M. (1968). Group inhibition of bystander intervention in emergencies. *Journal of Personality and Social Psychology, 10*(3), 215–221. https://doi.org/10.1037/h0026570

Lebedev, M. A., & Nicolelis, M. A. (2006). Brain–machine interfaces: Past, present and future. *Trends in Neurosciences, 29*(9), 536–546.

LeCun, Y., Bengio, Y., & Hinton, G. (2015). Deep learning. *Nature, 521*(7553), 436–444.

Lenton, A. P., Bruder, M., & Sedikides, C. (2021). *Handbook of the authentic self*. Psychology Press.

Lewis, S. L., & Maslin, M. A. (2015). Defining the Anthropocene. *Nature, 519*(7542), 171–180. https://doi.org/10.1038/nature14258

Lipina, S. J., & Colombo, J. A. (2009). *Poverty and brain development during childhood: An approach from cognitive psychology and neuroscience*. American Psychological Association.

Lisman, J. (2017). Glutamatergic synapses are structurally and biochemically complex because of multiple plasticity processes: Long-term potentiation, long-term depression, short-term potentiation, and scaling. *Philosophical Transactions of the Royal Society B: Biological Sciences, 372*(1715), 20160260.

Locke, E. A., & Latham, G. P. (2002). Building a practically useful theory of goal setting and task motivation: A 35-year odyssey. *American Psychologist, 57*(9), 705–717. https://doi.org/10.1037/0003-066X.57.9.705

Longcamp, M., Zerbato-Poudou, M.-T., & Velay, J.-L. (2005). The influence of writing practice on letter recognition in preschool children: A comparison between handwriting and typing. *Acta Psychologica, 119*(1), 67–79. https://doi.org/10.1016/j.actpsy.2004.10.019

Luby, J., Belden, A., Botteron, K., Marrus, N., Harms, M. P., Babb, C., Nishino, T., & Barch, D. (2013). The effects of poverty on childhood brain development: The mediating effect of caregiving and stressful life events. *JAMA Pediatrics, 167*(12), 1135–1142. https://doi.org/10.1001/jamapediatrics.2013.3139

Madison, A., Kiecolt-Glaser, J. K. (2019, August). Stress, depression, diet, and the gut microbiota: Human-bacteria interactions at the core of psychoneuroimmunology and nutrition. *Current Opinion in Behavioral Sciences, 28*, 105–110. https://doi.org/10.1016/j.cobeha.2019.01.011. Epub 2019 March 25. PMID: 32395568; PMCID: PMC7213601.

Marcus, G., & Luccioni, S. (2023, April 17). Stop treating AI models like people. *Gary Marcus*. https://garymarcus.substack.com/p/stop-treating-ai-models-like-people

Marwala, T. (2023, July 18). Militarisation of AI has severe implications for global security and warfare. *Daily Maverick*. https://www.dailymaverick.co.za/opinionista/2023-07-18-militarisation-of-ai-has-severe-implications-for-global-security-and-warfare/. Retrieved 2 August 2023.

Marx, K. (1867/1976). *Capital* (B. Fowkes, Trans.). Penguin.
Maxwell, J. A. (2012). *A realist approach for qualitative research*. Sage.
Mayer, E. A., Knight, R., Mazmanian, S. K., Cryan, J. F., & Tillisch, K. (2014). Gut microbes and the brain: Paradigm shift in neuroscience. *The Journal of Neuroscience, 34*(46), 15490–15496. https://doi.org/10.1523/JNEUROSCI.3299-14.2014
McArdle, M. (2019). Is forced arbitration living up to its promise? Harvard Business Review.
McEwen, B. S. (2006). Protective and damaging effects of stress mediators. *New England Journal of Medicine, 338*(3), 171–179.
McEwen, B. S. (2007). Physiology and neurobiology of stress and adaptation: Central role of the brain. *Physiological Reviews, 87*(3), 873–904.
McKinsey Global Institute. (2023, July). *Jobs lost, jobs gained: Workforce transitions in a time of automation*. Retrieved from McKinsey & Company website, https://www.mckinsey.com/featured-insights/future-of-work
Mead, M. (1964). *Continuities in cultural evolution*. Transaction Publishers.
Meadows, D. H. (2008). *Thinking in systems: A primer*. Chelsea Green Publishing.
Merleau-Ponty, M. (1962). *Phenomenology of perception*. Routledge.
Merritt, J. A., & Zak, P. J. (2024). Continuous neurophysiologic monitoring predicts daily mood with high accuracy: Implications for proactive mental health assessment. Frontiers in Digital Health, 5(Article 1397557). https://doi.org/10.3389/fdgth.2024.1397557
Merritt, S. H., Krouse M., Alogaily, R. S., & Zak, P. J. (2022). Continuous Neurophysiologic Data Accurately Predict Mood and Energy in the Elderly. *Brain Sciences, 12*(9), 1240. https://doi.org/10.3390/brainsci12091240
Merz, J. J., Barnard, P., Rees, W. E., Smith, D., Maroni, M., Rhodes, C. J., Dederer, J. H., Bajaj, N., Joy, M. K., Wiedmann, T., & Sutherland, R. (2023). World scientists' warning: The behavioural crisis driving ecological overshoot. *Science Progress, 106*(3). https://doi.org/10.1177/00368504231201372
Metaphysics Book VIII, 1045a.8–10, Aristotle; Translated W. D. Ross (1908).
Metz, C. (2023). The ChatGPT king isn't worried, but he knows you might be. *New York Times*. https://www.nytimes.com/2023/03/31/technology/sam-altman-open-ai-chatgpt.html?smid=nytcore-ios-share&referringSource=highlightShare. Retrieved May 2023.
Meyer v. Uber Technologies, Inc. (2017).
Mitchell, M. (2009). *Complexity: A guided tour*. Oxford University Press.
Mitchell, T. M. (1997). *Machine learning*. McGraw-Hill.
Moravec, H. (1988). *Mind children: The future of robot and human intelligence*. Harvard University Press.

Mordor Intelligence. (2023). *Online banking market—Growth, trends, forecasts (2023–2028)*. https://www.mordorintelligence.com/industry-reports/online-banking-market

Naess, A. (2002). *Life's philosophy—Reason & feeling in a deeper world* (p. 6).

Nature. (2017). Neurotechnologies, brain research and informed public dialogue. *Nature, 551*(7679), 159–161.

Nelson, R. (1977). *The Moon and the Ghetto: An essay on policy analysis*. Norton.

Neville, H. J., Stevens, C., Pakulak, E., Bell, T. A., Fanning, J., Klein, S., & Isbell, E. (2013). Family-based training program improves brain function, cognition, and behavior in lower socioeconomic status preschoolers. *Proceedings of the National Academy of Sciences, 110*(29), 12138–12143. https://doi.org/10.1073/pnas.1304437110

Newitz, A. (2024, April 12). A brief, weird history of brainwashing: L. Ron Hubbard, Operation Midnight Climax, and stochastic terrorism—the race for mind control changed America forever. *MIT Technology Review*. https://www.technologyreview.com/2024/04/12/1090726/brainwashing-mind-control-history-operation-midnight-climax/

Nickerson, R. S. (1998). Confirmation bias: A ubiquitous phenomenon in many guises. *Review of General Psychology, 2*(2), 175–220.

Nielsen, M. A., & Chuang, I. L. (2010). Quantum computation and quantum information. *Cambridge University Press*. https://doi.org/10.1017/CBO9780511976667

Norris, F. H., Stevens, S. P., Pfefferbaum, B., Wyche, K. F., & Pfefferbaum, R. L. (2008). Community resilience as a metaphor, theory, set of capacities, and strategy for disaster readiness. *American Journal of Community Psychology, 41*(1–2), 127–150. https://doi.org/10.1007/s10464-007-9156-6

Northouse, P. G. (2018). *Leadership: Theory and practice* (8th ed.). Sage.

Nussbaum, M. C. (1997). *Cultivating humanity: A classical defense of reform in liberal education*. Harvard University Press.

Nussbaum, M. C. (2002). *For love of country?* Beacon Press.

O'Neil, C. (2016). *Weapons of math destruction: How big data increases inequality and threatens democracy*. Broadway Books.

Pavlov, I. P. (1927). *Conditioned reflexes: An investigation of the physiological activity of the cerebral cortex*. Oxford University Press.

Pfeifer, R., & Bongard, J. (2007). *How the body shapes the way we think: A new view of intelligence*. MIT Press.

Picard, R. W. (2000). *Affective computing*. MIT Press.

Pickett, K., & Wilkinson, R. (2010). *The spirit level*. Penguin Books.

Piff, P. K., Dietze, P., Feinberg, M., Stancato, D. M., & Keltner, D. (2015). Awe, the small self, and prosocial behavior. *Journal of Personality and Social Psychology, 108*, 883–899.

Plato. (2002). *Five dialogues: Euthyphro, apology, Crito, Meno, Phaedo* (G. M. A. Grube, Trans.). Hackett Publishing.
Platt, M. (2023). *The leader's brain: Enhance your leadership, build stronger teams, make better decisions, and inspire greater innovation with neuroscience*. Wharton School Press.
Porges, S. W. (2011). *The polyvagal theory: Neurophysiological foundations of emotions, attachment, communication, and self-regulation*. WW Norton & Co.
Putman, D. (2004). Psychological courage. *Philosophy, Psychiatry, & Psychology, 11*(1), 1–11.
Putnam, R. D. (2000). *Bowling alone: The collapse and revival of American community*. Simon & Schuster.
Radford, A., Wu, J., Child, R., Luan, D., Amodei, D., & Sutskever, I. (2019). Language models are unsupervised multitask learners. *OpenAI Blog*. https://openai.com/blog/better-language-models/
Ramón, S. (1905) [1890]. *Manual de Anatomía Patológica General (Handbook of general Anatomical Pathology)* (in Spanish) (4th ed.).
Rawls, J. (1999). *A theory of justice: Revised edition*. Harvard University Press.
Richards, B. A., & Chalupka, K. (2024). Virtual embodiment: A path toward general artificial intelligence. *IEEE Transactions on Artificial Intelligence, 45*(5), 1410–1428.
Rokeach, M. (1973). *The nature of human values*. The Free Press.
Russell, S., & Norvig, P. (2016). *Artificial intelligence: A modern approach* (3rd ed.). Pearson.
Russell, S., Dewey, D., & Tegmark, M. (2015). Research priorities for robust and beneficial artificial intelligence. *AI Magazine, 36*(4), 105–114.
Samuelson, P. A., & Marks, S. G. (2003). *Economics*. McGraw-Hill Education.
Sandel, M. J. (2020). *The tyranny of merit: What's become of the common good?* Farrar.
Sapolsky, R. M. (2015). Stress and the brain: Individual variability and the inverted-U. *Nature, 526*(7571), 187–193.
Schein, E. H. (1965). *Organizational psychology*. Prentice-Hall.
Schultz, P. W., Nolan, J. M., Cialdini, R. B., Goldstein, N. J., & Griskevicius, V. (2007). The constructive, destructive, and reconstructive power of social norms. *Psychological Science, 18*(5), 429–434.
Schumpeter, J. A. (1934). *The theory of economic development: An inquiry into profits, capital, credit, interest, and the business cycle*. Harvard University Press.
Schwab, K. (2017). *The fourth industrial revolution*. Crown Business.
Schwartz, S. H. (2012). An overview of the Schwartz theory of basic values. *Online Readings in Psychology and Culture, 2*(1). https://doi.org/10.9707/2307-0919.1116
Seligman, M. E. P. (2011). *Flourish: A visionary new understanding of happiness and well-being*. Free Press.

Sen, A. (1985). Well-being, agency and freedom: The Dewey lectures 1984. *The Journal of Philosophy*, *82*(4), 169–221. https://doi.org/10.2307/2026184

Shaboldt, B. (2022). The evolving landscape of AI: Ethics and governance in the 21st century. *Technology and Society Review*, *34*(3), 123–145.

Sharika, K. M., Thaikkandi, S., & Nivedita, & Platt, M. L. (2024). Interpersonal heart rate synchrony predicts effective information processing in a naturalistic group decision-making task. *Proceedings of the National Academy of Sciences*, *121*(21), e2313801121. https://doi.org/10.1073/pnas.2313801121

Sinek, S. (2019). *The infinite game*. Portfolio/Penguin. ISBN 9780735213500.

Singer, P. (2009). *The life you can save: Acting now to end world poverty*. Random House.

Sivananda, S. (1999). *The Lord's universal prayer: Sadhana*. The Divine Life Trust Society.

Smith, E., Storch, E. A., Lavretsky, H., Cummings, J. L., & Eyre, H. A. (2023). Affective computing for brain health disorders. In P. Vlamos, I. S. Kotsireas, & I. Tarnanas (Eds.), *Handbook of computational neurodegeneration*. Springer. https://doi.org/10.1007/978-3-319-75922-7_36

Smith, T. (2010). The role of internal values in behavioral evolution. *Journal of Behavioral Evolution*, *5*(2), 89–104.

Standing, G. (2017). *Basic income: And how we can make it happen*. Pelican.

Stanford Institute for Human-Centered Artificial Intelligence. (2024). *AI Index: State of AI in 13 charts*. https://hai.stanford.edu/news/ai-index-state-ai-13-charts

Stanovich, K. E., & West, R. F. (2008). On the failures of cognitive ability testing in the face of real-world decision-making demands. *Annual Review of Psychology*, *59*, 587–612.

StatCounter. (2024). *Search engine market share worldwide*. https://gs.statcounter.com/search-engine-market-share

Statista. (2024). *Internet users in the world 2024*. https://www.statista.com/statistics/617136/digital-population-worldwide/

Stenson, M. (2016). Leadership in the digital age: Navigating ethical dilemmas. *Journal of Business Ethics*, *145*(2), 215–228.

Sternberg, R. J. (2003). *Wisdom, intelligence, and creativity synthesized*. Cambridge University Press.

Stiglitz, J. E. (2019a). *People, power and profits: Progressive capitalism for an age of discontent*. Penguin UK.

Stiglitz, J. E. (2019b). Rewriting the rules of the European economy. Project Syndicate. https://www.project-syndicate.org/commentary/rewriting-rules-of-european-economy-by-joseph-e-stiglitz-2019-05

Stokes, P. R. A., Forstmann, B. U., & Spaak, E. (2023). A dopamine-modulated neural circuit for cognitive flexibility. *Nature*, *598*(7914), 630–635. https://doi.org/10.1038/s41593-023-01304-9

Strogatz, S. H. (2003). *Sync: How order emerges from chaos in the universe, nature, and daily life*. Hachette UK.
Strubell, E., Ganesh, A., & McCallum, A. (2019). Energy and policy considerations for deep learning in NLP. *Proceedings of the 57th Annual Meeting of the Association for Computational Linguistics* (pp. 3645–3650).
Suleyman, M. (2024). What is AI anyway? *TED Talk*. https://www.ted.com/talks/mustafa_suleyman_what_is_an_ai_anyway?language=en
Tang, Y. Y., Hölzel, B. K., & Posner, M. I. (2015). The neuroscience of mindfulness meditation. *Nature Reviews Neuroscience, 16*(4), 213–225. https://doi.org/10.1038/nrn3916
Tegmark, M. (2017). *Life 3.0: Being human in the age of Artificial Intelligence*. Knopf.
Thaler, R. H., & Sunstein, C. R. (2008). *Nudge: Improving decisions about health, wealth, and happiness*. Yale University Press.
Thoppilan, R., De Freitas, D., Hall, J., Shazeer, N., Kulshreshtha, A., Jin, H., Cheng, H. T., Bos, T., Baker, L., Du, Y., & Lee, H. (2022). LaMDA: Language models for dialog applications. arXiv preprint arXiv:2201.08239
Throsby, D. (2001). *Economics and culture*. Cambridge University Press.
Turkle, S. (2011). *Alone together: Why we expect more from technology and less from each other*. Basic Books.
Tversky, A., & Kahneman, D. (1974). Judgment under uncertainty: Heuristics and biases. *Science, 185*(4157), 1124–1131.
Ungar, M. (2011). The social ecology of resilience: Addressing contextual and cultural ambiguity of a nascent construct. *American Journal of Orthopsychiatry, 81*(1), 1–17. https://doi.org/10.1111/j.1939-0025.2010.01067.x
Ungar, M. (2018). Resilience across cultures. *The British Journal of Social Work, 48*(7), 2047–2065. https://doi.org/10.1093/bjsw/bcx103
United Nations. (2022). *Beyond GDP: Measuring what counts for economic and social performance*. https://unsceb.org/topics/beyond-gdp. Retrieved December 2023.
UNSD Database. (2023). Global poverty and inequality database. United Nations Statistics Division. Retrieved from https://unstats.un.org/sdgs/indicators/database/
Varela, F. J., Thompson, E., & Rosch, E. (1991). *The embodied mind: Cognitive science and human experience*. MIT Press.
Velu, C., & Putra, F. H. R. (2023). How to introduce quantum computers without slowing economic growth. *Nature, 607*(7941), 7–9. https://doi.org/10.1038/d41586-022-03931-6
Velu, C., Putra, F., Geurtsen, E., Norman, K., & Noble, C. (2022). *Adoption of quantum technologies and business model innovation*. Institute for Manufacturing University.

von Mises, L. (1949). *Human action: A treatise on economics* (4th ed.). Fox & Wilkes.

Walther, C. (2020). *Connection in the times of COVID: Corona's call for conscious choices*. Macmillan Palgrave. https://link.springer.com/book/10.1007%2F978-3-030-53641-1

Walther, C. (2021). Leadership for social change and development: Inspiration and transformation. *Macmillan Palgrave*. https://doi.org/10.1007/978-3-030-76225-4

Walther, C. C. (2024). The Complementarity of POZE and AI to Optimize Quality of Life in an Urban Setting. In Tonon, G. (2024). Urban Inequalities: a multidisciplinary and international perspective. Springer Nature. The Urban Book Series. https://link.springer.com/book/10.1007/978-3-031-59746-6

Wang, O. (2022). Do machines know more about us than we do ourselves? *The New York Times*. https://www.nytimes.com/2023/03/27/science/ai-machine-learning-chatbots.html?smid=li-share. Retrieved May 2023.

Waters, C. N., Zalasiewicz, J., Summerhayes, C., Barnosky, A. D., Poirier, C., Gałuszka, A., Cearreta, A., Edgeworth, M., Ellis, E. C., Ellis, M., Jeandel, C., & Wolfe, A. P. (2016). The Anthropocene is functionally and stratigraphically distinct from the Holocene. *Science, 351*(6269), aad2622. https://doi.org/10.1126/science.aad2622

Weale, S. (2024). Social media algorithms 'amplifying misogynistic content'. *The Guardian*. https://www.theguardian.com/media/2024/feb/06/social-media-algorithms-amplifying-misogynistic-content?CMP=Share_iOSApp_Other

Weizenbaum, J. (1966). ELIZA—a computer program for the study of natural language communication between man and machine. *Communications of the ACM, 9*(1), 36–45. https://doi.org/10.1145/365153.365168

White, L., & Black, E. (2021). The intricacies of knowledge introduction in behavioral dynamics. *Journal of Behavioral Science Education, 24*(3), 178–195.

WHOQOL Group. (1995). The World Health Organization Quality of Life assessment (WHOQOL): Position paper from the World Health Organization. *Social Science & Medicine, 41*(10), 1403–1409. https://doi.org/10.1016/0277-9536(95)00112-K

Wiener, N. (1948). *Cybernetics: Or control and communication in the animal and the machine*. MIT Press.

Wilkerson, R. G., Biskup, E., Lipton, M. L., & Landman, B. A. (2021). The human brain capital initiative: A roadmap to neuroeconomic growth. *Neuron, 109*(6), 939–942. https://doi.org/10.1016/j.neuron.2021.02.002

Wilson, K. (2018). Ripple effect of behavioral changes: Observations and impacts. *Social Dynamics Review, 14*(4), 289–305.

Winters, J. (2021). Report: Climate misinformation on Facebook viewed 1.4 million times daily. https://grist.org/accountability/report-climate-misinformation-facebook-viewed-million-times-daily/. Retrieved 4 February 2024.

Walton, D. N. (2010a). *Fundamentals of critical argumentation.* Cambridge University Press.

Walton, D. N. (2010b). *Informal logic: A pragmatic approach.* Cambridge University Press.

World Bank. (1990). World development report 1990: Poverty. Oxford University Press.

World Economic Forum (WEF). (2023). Davos 2023. What you need to know about technology. https://www.weforum.org/agenda/2023/01/davos-emerging-technology-ai/. Retrieved July 2023.

Yoshikawa, H., Aber, J. L., & Beardslee, W. R. (2012). The effects of poverty on the mental, emotional, and behavioral health of children and youth: Implications for prevention. *American Psychologist, 67*(4), 272–284. https://doi.org/10.1037/a0028015

Zalasiewicz, J., Waters, C. N., Williams, M., Barnosky, A. D., Cearreta, A., Crutzen, P., Palmesino, J., Rönnskog, A. S., Edgeworth, M., Neal, C., Ellis, E. C., Grinevald, J., & Haff, P. K. (2017). Scale and diversity of the physical technosphere: A geological perspective. *The Anthropocene Review, 4*(1), 9–22. https://doi.org/10.1177/2053019616677743

Zambetta, F., & Sofo, S. (2021). Embodied intelligence: A case for embodied artificial intelligence. *AI & Society, 36*(4), 1187–1198.

Zipf, G. K. (1949). *Human behavior and the principle of least effort: An introduction to human ecology.* Addison-Wesley Press.

Ziyad, A. (2024). Artificial intelligence and the future of human rights. *Human Rights and AI Journal, 14*(1), 87–103.

Zuckerberg, M. (2021). A privacy-focused vision for social networking. *Facebook.* https://www.facebook.com/notes/mark-zuckerberg/a-privacy-focused-vision-for-social-networking/10156700570096634/

Zukav, G. (1979). *Dancing Wu Li Masters.* Bantam Books.

CHAPTER 2

WHERE: Humans, Technology, and Humane Technology

Abstract Diving deeper, this chapter looks into the mutual influence of humans and AI. Grounded in the multidimensional framework introduced in Chapter 1, and the *A-Frame* that applies it in the context of human Agency Amid AI, we will examine human consciousness and artificial consciousness. From here we look at inferred intelligence, and the potential of tandems that leverage the complementarity of natural and artificial perception. The technological transition that humanity is traversing from one industrial revolution to the next is examined, with the proposition to expand the traditional triple bottom line to include purpose; the *Quadruple bottom line* recognizes the responsibility of the private sector towards the Common Good. This sets the stage to explore the place of human trust and artificial integrity, and the type of regulation needed to establish guardrails that grow with the challenge of an evolving subject. Data is looked at as the central bottleneck of an inclusive society, as biased inputs result in biased outcomes, and the amplification of exclusion in a hybrid society. Ironically the stronger the technology in our life grows, the weaker our cognitive defense mechanisms become, and the more at risk we are to fall prey to the all pervasive nature of artificial persuasion. Unless we are aware of the causes and consequences of our own perception, the potential of artificial influence, combined with the temptation of delegating mental effort to artificial assistance jeopardizes our autonomy, and the formation of free will. An exit from this dangerous dynamic starts by identifying what we want, and why; to clarify who we are and what we stand for. The alignment of humans and technology starts with personal and interpersonal harmonization. That alignment of individual aspirations and actions is the precursor of algorithms that are aligned with aspirations. This dynamic cannot be reverse engineered. The *hybrid alignment conundrum* cannot be solved online.

Keywords Inclusion · Data · Bias · Consciousness · Free will · Quadruple Bottom-line · Hybrid alignment conundrum · Alignment

2.1 Consciousness

2.1.1 Natural and Artificial Consciousness

Before we go further, let's take a step back and put things into perspective.

Excitement and worry related to innovation, often in the form of technology, are as old as humanity. Every change comes with pros and cons, wins and losses. Sometimes a new tool leads to merely a shift of habit, sometimes it is a whole behavior pattern, and sometimes—like right now—the new technology introduces not only a new way of doing the old, but a path to re-experience the space in which the "old" existed, including ourselves.

Innovations do not influence individuals in isolation; by affecting a person they impact an entire ecosystem. What influences one person has repercussions in the environments he/she/they is part of, and depending on context these ramifications have ripple effects in the wider social sphere, which echoes back to the individual that evolves in it. In the interconnected universe that we are part of and that is part of us, nothing happens in a vacuum. As seen earlier, one might refer to this continuum as the *m4-matrix* (*micro-meso-macro-meta*).

The present reality is a standing invitation to expand our narrow frame of perception and prospects, of consciousness and cognition to stretch the continuum of our experience beyond established horizontal limitations. "For everything that exists is in a manner the seed of that which will be" (Marcus Aurelius, 161–180 CE). The hybrid world is ours to shape. Today reminds us that time and space are not separate, isolated entities but "interconnected aspects of a continuous flow of reality" (Bergson, 1922). The traditional scientific and mathematical conception of time and space as discrete and quantifiable does not hold up to the kaleidoscopic nature of human consciousness. If we shift from a quantitative perspective to embrace the qualitative nature of being, it appears that time and space can be experienced as a continuous and indivisible whole. Time is not made up of fixed, measurable units but represents a subjective experience of "pure duration" (Bergson, 1922). Similarly, space may be not a collection of separate, measurable points, but a flexible medium that encompasses all things, and beings. The infinite game is at play in every aspect of the universe (Kelly, 2009).

We looked briefly at the mind and its physiological setup (Sect. 1.2.3). As mentioned then, the quest to understand human consciousness is ongoing, and even the physiological workings of the brain itself, and its interplay with the rest of the human organism, remain rather uncertain. Despite punctual discoveries that illustrate the connection of physical experiences, thought processes and feelings, humanity has not yet managed to map the myriad of interplays between mind and matter, as experienced through emotions and thoughts, sensations, and aspirations. Without such a clear understanding of the existing natural consciousness to begin with, it appears challenging to go beyond the mere stage of assessing and analyzing the artificial articulation of consciousness. In May 2024 Google published a series of multilayered brain images generated with the help of AI. Considering this, and other medical discoveries of the recent past, it is not far out to expect that artificial intelligence may eventually take us closer to solving the age-old mystery that surrounds natural intelligence, and even get a grasp of consciousness.[1]

When chartering vastly unknown territory, as we do now and as humanity has always done, it is helpful to get a sense of the lay of the land as it appears based on accessible knowledge. Hence the following paragraphs offer a non-exclusive list of certain approaches to understand human consciousness, to set the stage, before comparing human consciousness and the artificial stream of "I" that emerges from it.

---

[1] Already AI is helping us to gradually get an ever more granular understanding of the organic formation of thought and knowledge. In January 2024 a neural network taught itself to recognize objects using the filmed experiences of a single infant, offering radically new insights into how humans learn (Vong et al., 2024). The algorithm learnt to recognize words such as "crib" and "ball", by studying headcam recordings of a tiny fraction of a single baby's life. This might be a scientific appetizer, suggesting that AI will eventually help us understand better how and why we learn, reason and feel.

The mystery of human consciousness has spawned many philosophical and scientific theories over the centuries. René Descartes' dualism postulates that consciousness exists separate from the physical world (Hart, 1996), as an ethereal mind interacting with the body. In contrast, behaviorism (Watson, 1913) denies any internal subjective state, focusing solely on external stimuli shaping observable actions. Cognitive theories (Neisser, 1967) characterize consciousness as emerging from perception, attention, memory, and other mental processes that manipulate symbolic representations. Global workspace theory (Baars & Dehaene, 2002) proposes that consciousness arises from dynamic brain areas competing to broadcast information into a shared workspace, making selected data globally available. Integrated information theory (Tononi, 2008) argues that consciousness emerges from the degree of informational integration within a complex system, yielding a unified subjective experience. Higher-order representation approaches (Lau & Rosenthal, 2011) posit that awareness of mental states produces consciousness via self-reflective metacognition. Methodologies investigating neural correlates of consciousness (Baars, 2002) tie specific brain activities to consciousness reports. Finally, Pribram's holoflux theory (Pribram, 2021) connects local and nonlocal properties, viewing consciousness as a lens-like energy process continuously transforming between implicate and explicate orders of reality.[2] This cybernetic holoflux may portend future artificial replications of the elusive essence of awareness. That consciousness has remained beyond humanity's intellectual grasp until now does not equate its negation.[3]

---

[2] Holoflux is the infinite, moving, and undivided whole. It is the perception of a dynamic universe as initially proposed by David Bohm, in which everything moves together in an interconnected process.

[3] The position of entirely denied human consciousness is not mainstream. While acknowledging sentience and self-awareness as complex phenomena, proponents argue against attributing true consciousness, understood as an internal, subjective experience, solely to humans. Arguments include: (i) lack of a definitive definition (consciousness remains a multifaceted concept without a universally agreed-upon definition). Critics of attributing exclusive consciousness to humans point out the difficulties in objectively measuring and comparing its presence across different species. (ii) Alternative interpretations of behavior: Complex behaviors displayed by animals, including tool use and empathy, can be explained through alternative mechanisms like instinct and adaptation, without necessarily requiring consciousness; and (iii) emergence in complex systems: Some theories propose consciousness as an emergent property of complex systems, like the

Definite delimitations? Although debates regarding the source of human consciousness are ongoing, several clear differences in comparison with artificial versions of it can be established (for now). Human consciousness is a subjective and self-aware experience which entails the ability of introspection (Chalmers, 1996; Nagel, 1974), whereas AI aims to simulate intelligent behavior and decision-making processes. Based on algorithms and computational processes it produces objectively, without experiencing subjectively (Russell & Norvig, 2016). Human consciousness enables individuals to perceive, reason, learn, and engage in creative and abstract thinking. It involves the integration of sensory information (body), memory (mind), and higher-order cognitive processes (Baars, 2002; Dennett, 1991). While AI systems can exhibit (the appearance of) cognitive abilities such as perception, reasoning, learning, and problem-solving, they lack subjective experiences and higher-order processes (Goodfellow et al., 2016; Russell & Norvig, 2016). Human consciousness involves emotional experiences, moral reasoning, empathy, and the ability to make ethical decisions based on values and social norms (Damasio, 1994; Haidt, 2006). In opposition AI lacks genuine emotional experiences and moral understanding. While AI can be programmed to *simulate* emotions or follow predefined ethical rules, it does not possess the same depth of emotional and moral consciousness as humans (Bostrom & Yudkowsky, 2014; Wallach & Allen, 2009). Human consciousness enables flexibility, adaptability, and the capacity to learn from experiences, acquire new knowledge, and adjust behaviors accordingly (Bargh & Morsella, 2008; Dennett, 1991). Whereas AI systems can exhibit learning and adaptation through machine learning algorithms and neural networks, their abilities are limited to the specific tasks they are designed for and the data they are trained on (LeCun et al., 2015; Mitchell, 1997).

As popularized by the "10,000 hours rule", it takes approximately ten thousand hours of deliberate practice to achieve an expert level of performance in complex fields (Ericsson et al., 1993). Whereas human instincts leverage subjective phenomenological insights from years of memories, AI remains so far restricted to immediate data available for logical computation, devoid of a personal lifelong narrative arc. Their stock of memories

---

human brain, potentially existing in varying degrees across different biological structures (Chalmers, 1996). Note—this is different from the debate around consciousness in animals.

and hands-on encounters equips people to pattern-match current situations against past contexts to inform rapid, intuitive judgments from their accumulated wisdom (Klein, 2015). In contrast, AI systems lack such lived histories grounded in the physical world. While machine learning models can analyze vast datasets, their inferences stay limited to statistical correlations without context-dependent evaluation (Domingos, 2012). Gut reactions in people thus constitute uniquely "human intelligence" shaped by individualistic experience trajectories.

"I can do what I want. But I can only want what I must" (Attributed to both Schopenhauer and Einstein). Our present experiences and expressions, desires and thoughts are the consequences of past experiences, including education, environment, biological setup, and social evolution thus far. This accumulating stock of the "evolving I" (Walther, 2020a) influences our experiences and expressions in the future.

Anchored in the perception of the self and its relation to others, our consciousness allows us to raise complex ethical questions concerning personal identity, moral responsibility, and the deriving implications for human rights and dignity (Metzinger, 2009; Searle, 1980), while AI-powered chatbots engage in conversations around ethical concerns from a programmed set of algorithms (Bostrom & Yudkowsky, 2014; Floridi et al., 2018). From this derives an attitude of conscientiousness or the desire to do what is right, which is deeply human; more on that below (Sect. 2.3.1).

So-called constitutional AI (Yuntao Bai et al. 2022), as used by Anthropic for its LLM Claude, whereby algorithms are trained on universally recognized ethical human standards may be a promising venue to address the risk of unethical AI-generated outputs, which squares the circle as humans who are not firmly anchored in human values are not able to program such moral coding in the algorithms they are creating or training. GIGO versus VIVO.[4] An approximate comparison of (human) perception of natural and artificial (un)consciousness shows similarities and differences (Table 2.1).

At the time of writing there are (at least) 4 big challenges related to AI:

---

[4] Garbage In, Garbage Out. Values In, Values Out (Chapter 1).

Table 2.1 A simplified snapshot of comparative abilities

Scope	Human Consciousness	Artificial Intelligence (AI)
Nature of Consciousness	Subjective, self-aware, introspective	Lacks subjective consciousness
Cognitive Abilities	Perception, reasoning, learning, creativity	Reproduces results that look like cognitive abilities but lacks depth
Emotional Understanding	Emotional experiences, moral reasoning	No inherent emotions and no moral understanding
Flexibility and Adaptability	Flexible, adaptable, learns from experiences	Limited to specific tasks and training data
Ethical Considerations	Personal identity, moral responsibility	Opaque accountability, biased depending on data, dependent on (initial) human development

- Hallucination: AI systems can offer content which is not based on real data, like generating wrong text, fake images, or audio. This threatens reliability and truthfulness (Amodei et al., 2016).
- Black box syndrome: The decision-making logic of AI models is mostly opaque and inscrutable to humans. Such lack of explainability limits accountability and appropriate use (Rudin, 2019).
- Misalignment: Getting AI systems to align with human values and ethics is exceedingly challenging, given complex real-world environments and trade-offs (Leike et al., 2017) (more on alignment follows in Sect. 2.2.1).
- Verbal inflation: LLMs can generate misleading or incorrect information very convincingly. Detecting and mitigating this flood of wordy emptiness is an ever-expanding problem area as chatbots are getting ever more sophisticated (Bommasani et al., 2021).

Ironically these problems are not reserved to AI. They dominate the human world as well. Each of us is prone to make up stories, pretending they are the truth, often believing they are. We convey them in impressive linguistic packaging that clouds the detectability of pointlessness. Reasoning is a complex arenas. Humans often do not understand their own decisions, leave alone those of others; and more often than not we accept what we experience without critically reflecting on it. Are we equipped to create, curate, and use a new form of intelligence if we barely grasp the basics of our own?

2.1.2 Inferred Intelligence

The mental processing of humans and machines differs significantly, particularly in terms of memory and reasoning. However, the distinction between artificial and natural intelligence is becoming increasingly blurred as both realms learn from each other. While natural intelligence continues to drive the ongoing sophistication of its artificial counterpart, artificial intelligence[5] is helping researchers uncover more about human consciousness.

The integration of machine learning, neural networks, big data, and AI is illuminating natural processes that were once barely understood. A prime example is the earlier mentioned publication of a detailed 3D map of the human brain. Conceived by a multidisciplinary team of Harvard researchers in collaboration with Google, it revealed the complexity of the human mind through the imaging of a roughly cubic millimeter of brain tissue, which produced 1.4 petabytes of data.

Interestingly AI's capability to process vast amounts of information quickly is not only enhancing our understanding of the subject that is investigated. The process that accompanies this investigation also fosters cross-disciplinary collaboration. The necessary combination of usually disconnected fields challenges established hypotheses and opens new perspectives on long-standing questions. Differently said the need for enhanced creativity in data selection and parameter definition could bring us closer to understanding the nature of consciousness, breaking through the "blueprint mentality of academia" (Hallworth, 2023)—a human-made problem that has stifled science for centuries.

In parallel, the rapid advancement of foundational models, their expanding content windows, and ongoing algorithm refinement raises another question: Will these developments lead to the emergence of artificial consciousness, a topic that is related to worries and excitement about artificial general intelligence (AGI), with speculations ranging widely.

At times it seem as if we were witnessing the emergence of a new realm of experience. Some, like Google engineer Blake Lemoine, have

---

[5] We will look closer in Sect. 2.3.3 at the term "artificial intelligence" and "artificial integrity" which are both questionable.

been arguing for several years that artificial intelligence is already not only intelligent but sentient (Tiku, 2022).[6] Considering that GPT-4 can solve complex tasks across various domains without specific prompting and often performs at or beyond human levels, certain researchers think that it and other contemporary large language models exhibit "sparks" of general intelligence beyond mere language processing (Bubeck et al., 2023). In 2024, Microsoft AI CEO Mustafa Suleyman claimed that AI represents a new digital species (Suleyman, 2024).

Rather than debating whether AI is sentient or if it ever will be, one might consider that we are moving towards a new form of sentience altogether. This new sentience is characterized by technological dynamics that are decentralized, evolving collectively through local streams of human thought (*micro*) and global inputs (*meta*), potentially leading to an artificially supported *glocal* sentience.

Such a dynamic creates a feedback loop. As the devices in our lives learn about us individually and humanity in general, their "comprehension" becomes increasingly granular. Are we moving through a transition from interaction to attunement to the synchronization of humans and machines (Mann et al., 2024)?

<u>Streamlined synchrony.</u> Referring to the simultaneous occurrence of events, actions, or processes, synchrony manifests as harmonious alignment in behaviors, emotions, or physiological reactions. It occurs naturally during face-to-face communication, where people unconsciously mimic each other's body language, gestures, and speech patterns, fostering rapport and connection (Fujiwara et al., 2018). It enables complex coordinated problem-solving through simple local interactions between members rather than top-down orchestration (Vicsek & Zafeiris, 2012). Interpersonal synchrony is also observed in collaborative activities like music-making or team sports, where coordinated actions achieve a common goal (Kirschner & Tomasello, 2009). The harmonized movements of flocks of birds or schools of fish illustrate that synchrony is a central principle of natural coexistence (Couzin, 2009).

---

[6] Sentience is the capacity to feel and register experiences and feelings. AI will become sentient when an artificial agent is able to think, feel, and perceive the physical world (including differentiated interactions with different people) around it as humans and animals do.

Such natural forms of self-organized emergent intelligences suggest possibilities for novel forms of human/machine synchrony, potentially manifesting as digital consciousness.

Decentralized AI systems, modeled on swarm behaviors, could allow more flexible, adaptive global intelligence to develop in general AI architectures (Kennedy et al., 2001). Without predefined centralized control structures, decentralized AI systems could self-organize through peer communication, exhibiting novel machine consciousness resembling collective cognitions in nature (Couzin, 2009). For instance, combinations of individual neural networks dynamically exchanging contextual data and updating connection weights could come to develop unified behaviors. Through recurrent information flows between distributed components regulating each other's learning in multi-agent AI designs, group-level machine awareness and imagination beyond current consciousness models may emerge (Reynolds, 1987). Such decentralized, collective learning could propagate unified sensations, concepts, and memories, augmenting individual modules with hive-mind-like consciousness transcending isolated experiences.

The space for synchronized interaction between brains and machines is vast and expanding. As seen earlier AI systems are already adapting and responding to human behavior in real time, fostering a sense of mutual understanding and cooperation (Rabinovich et al., 2015). This is helped by the ability of LLMs to detect and map language matching styles; abilities that are reliable predictors of relationship success and team performance among humans (Platt, 2020). And this is only the beginning. Brain-computer interfaces (BCIs) linked to tailored, constantly self-refining algorithms can trigger or sustain synchrony between humans and between human brains and machines (Ireland et al., 2011). Initially, this configuration may enhance users' experiences and expressions, allowing for more intuitive and seamless social interactions. Subsequently, AI can be configured to deliberately catalyze interhuman synchronicity and the synchronization of humans and machines.

2.1.3 Tandems of Artificial and Natural Intelligence

The phase that we are currently traversing is illustrated by the emergence of "cyborgs" and "centaurs".[7] Just as centaurs symbolize the fusion of human and animal aspects, a seamless blend of human and machine capabilities could be viewed as a form of technological centaur (i.e. the delegation of coding tasks to ChatGTP). The concept of cyborgs on the other hand represents the enhancement of human abilities through technological augmentation (i.e. an implant of chips in the brain), which aligns with the vision of AI as a tool to amplify and extend human intelligence (Kurzweil, 2005). Whereas cyborgs intertwine their efforts with AI, moving back and forth over the "jagged frontier"[8] of AI capabilities, centaurs have a clear division of labor, strategically allocating tasks to either the human or AI based on their respective strengths. The "jagged frontier of AI" refers to the invisible boundary that separates tasks AI can handle from those it cannot; while some tasks may seem equally difficult, they can actually fall on opposite sides of this frontier (Mollick, 2023). The frontier is described as an uneven fortress wall, with the capabilities of AI lying within the interior and increasingly difficult tasks jutting outward. Both approaches can increase productivity, speed, and output quality compared to human workers alone. The challenge is to walk the fine line of benefit from AI and dependency on it. Being aware of our own limitations is a necessary precaution, as it is a slippery slope from utilization to (over)reliance to dependency.

<u>Artificial intuition.</u> While presently a lot of attention goes to prompt-engineering, the next stage is likely to entail GTPs that are attuned to deduce our intuition from minor hints. The major LLMs currently have slightly different "personas" and can be triggered to expose a higher or lower level of the "Big Five" personality traits commonly used in human psychology tests (Hilliard et al., 2024). Furthermore, using specific role-play prompts it is possible to anchor the bot to adopt a certain style (i.e.

---

[7] The Centaur model, where AI takes on the more routine tasks, liberates human cognition for higher-level, creative pursuits. Conversely, the Cyborg model seeks a harmonious fusion of human and machine capabilities, each amplifying the other.

[8] The "jagged frontier of AI" refers to the invisible boundary that separates tasks AI can handle from those it cannot; while some tasks may seem equally difficult, they can actually fall on opposite sides of this frontier (Mollick, 2023). The frontier is described as an uneven fortress wall, with the capabilities of AI lying within the interior and increasingly difficult tasks jutting outward.

"you are a successful copy-editor with a background in history"); and they are reactive to pedagogical affirmations (i.e. "yes you can do this"). As their content windows expand to capture ever more information their ability to remember previous interactions with the user grows.

Over time the bot syncs increasingly with the way a specific user thinks and their style of communication. For now a collateral benefit of the need for precise prompting is that users must clearly articulate what they want (which requires them to clarify their thought-process first). This stage will not last. Gradually our bots will be better at decoding what we seek to convey than we are ourselves able to articulate it in words or images.

The danger is that these super-capable assistants turn from tools into omniscient oracles, on which we rely more than on our natural intuition and intellect. An adjacent risk is that we are getting so used to the 24/7 availability of "someone" who fully understands us, that we can no longer imagine a life without it. The present business model of LLMs is based on tokens and paid subscriptions to more advanced versions. How would you feel if you establish a bond with a chatbot, and become separated from your AI-powered partner by a Paywall?

Rather than watching the slow erosion of our self-confidence and the correlated fortification of dependency on AI, we can systematically shape the space which we chose to accommodate for AI in our lives. Sharp self-awareness may avoid that ever smoother AI-assistance affects our sense of agency, and hence the autonomy that comes from our inherent capabilities.

Are we moving via centaurs and cyborgs towards intuitive AI and finally to full human/AI synchronization?

Opinions about the future cohabitation between humans and machines cover a wide range. While some perceive the evolution underway as a transition from creator to centaur to cyborg with humans always somewhere in the picture just in a changing role, others perceive the repartition of roles as an either-or equation where AI "takes" ever more jobs. This 'either human or AI' perspective reflects the traditional black/white, winner/loser mindset. But why should we limit ourselves to fixed boxes if the rules of the games are in constant flow? Current constellations are part of an evolution where humans experiment with different ways of integrating AI in their lives. The final setup is largely up to our choices.

Linking this to the *A-Frame* it appears that a relationship with AI that serves humans rather than reducing their autonomy and abilities starts with *awareness* of our own strengths and weaknesses, and *appreciation* of the features that make us unique. From this vantage point we can strategically analyze which our weak spots are, and in which way AI can serve to compensate for them; allowing us to hone in on our talents and the tasks that we enjoy or want to expand. To succeed in this we need a candid view of ourselves, including *acceptance* of our limitations. Ultimately it is worth remembering that throughout the organically evolving relationship between humans and AI, we remain *accountable* for the intentions and inputs that we insert into the equation (*A-Frame*, Sect. 1.4.1). The advantage of an agency mindset is that it reframes the stressful perception that AI is a threat or competitor. From defense we move towards offense, with the deliberate curation of winning teams that harness the synergy of humans and machines, while opening space for humans to explore and boost their inner superpowers.

The complementarity of natural and artificial assets is a benefit to be leveraged systematically, by humans for humans. The Pareto principle states that circa 80 percent of consequences come from 20 percent of causes. Inversely speaking we spend roughly 80 percent of our time and effort for 20 percent of benefits (Newman, 2005). A large part of these efforts goes into the accomplishment of tasks that we are neither good at, nor enjoy doing, such as administrative work. Imagine AI shouldering a major piece of these duties, leaving us free to nurture what makes us unique, and happy, as individuals. Schematically linking this to the 4 dimensions of the POZE framework (Sect. 1.2), we could focus on progress to be made in areas of life that we *aspire* (soul) to excel in because they offer meaning to our being. We could spend more time with family and friends in ways that are *emotionally* nourishing (heart); concentrate on *intellectual* endeavors that feed our curiosity and help us grow (mind) or dedicate more consideration to our *physiological* well-being (body). From a hamster-wheel of reactive production we could shift to a state of proactive being.

2.1.4 Persuasion and Perception

The use of AI to understand human perception offers significant opportunities. While much is speculated about the "black box" challenge of AI, human desires, preferences, emotions, and interests are not statistically predictable either. Unlike algorithmic models that map statistical patterns, human yearnings are shaped by incremental, imperceptible changes from lived experiences within cultural contexts (Portugali, 2012).

Thus, personal preferences remain in continual flux, influenced by unique sequences of phenomenological events. Repeated exposure to stimuli tends to increase affection through mere-exposure effects, regardless of inherent quality (Zajonc, 1968). In this context, quantity influences quality.

As machines in our lives acquire more information about us, we approach a stage where they know more about us than we do ourselves. Once the mechanisms underpinning our decision-making are mapped, algorithmic patterns can be systematically optimized to feed or circumvent them. As seen earlier, while this might serve users to learn more about themselves, a worrisome aspect of this is the commercial angle.

Large language model optimization (LLMO) involves activities that webmasters perform to influence the output of LLM-based generative systems, similar to how Search Engine Optimization (SEO) influences search engine results. As a new form of digital marketing, LLMO focuses on creating personalized user experiences by leveraging language, learning, modeling, and optimization to strengthen relationships between businesses and customers. Maybe a next phase will involve Large Language Model bias Optimization (LLMbO), the deliberate triggering of human heuristics and fallacies. Many algorithms already propose choices based on previously expressed preferences; and more often than not they are tailored not to give users what they want but to make them want what is offered. Algorithms influence wish formation by positioning predefined items through reductive forecasting models, benefiting providers more than understanding and accommodating consumers in their existential richness (Hanson & Yosifon, 2004).[9] This evolution comes with collateral damage, starting with the (in)voluntary uniformization of our preferences.

Algorithmic recommendations influence choices in culture, food, and politics. They shape what is seen or ignored, creating a self-reinforcing loop that leads to uniformity. Products chosen by consumers continue to be produced, and their algorithmic positioning nurtures further desire for them. Those living in WEIRD (Western, Educated, Industrialized, Rich, and Democratic) societies are particularly susceptible to this cycle,

---

[9] This may partially explain why our purchases frequently fail to satisfy our actual needs; human cravings arise as an unfurling narrative, not a fixed target. (Another topic is that things do not correlate with happiness, and hence we cannot use purchases to satiate the craving for existential meaning.)

where nuanced personal preferences are reduced to quantifiable data points, feeding algorithmic recommendations and perpetuating the cycle. This mirrors the past influence of corporations on American food preferences. Continuous exposure to high-sugar, ultra-processed foods has acclimated the typical American palate to intensely sweet and salty flavors, driving increased cravings and deteriorating dietary habits (Moss, 2013). This vicious cycle affects both individual health and broader economic and environmental systems. Similarly, our perception of cultural flavors is being reduced to algorithmic blandness, as creators adapt to these pressures, fueling a spiral of "ultra-processed" cultural output.

The process extends beyond shopping to our sense of self. Preferences express identity, and evolving tastes are part of self-development. "Take that away, and you really do become the person the algorithm thinks you are. In algorithmic culture, the right choice is always what the majority of other people have already chosen" (Chaka, 2024). It is another illustration of the many facets of the hybrid feedback loop that we influence while being influenced by it.

None of this is new, but without awareness of its causes and consequences, history is bound to repeat itself. In the 1930s, John Maynard Keynes observed that "Americans are apt to be unduly interested in discovering what average opinion believes average opinion to be". In the age of AI, this is a self-fulfilling prophecy on steroids. Data is a proxy—we should not mistake it for reality.

AI acts as a mental quicksand. Not only when it comes to shopping and leisure do we increasingly entrust the formation of our opinions, and the deriving decision-making process to AI. The proliferation of AI tools in science is introducing a phase of scientific inquiry in which we produce more but understand less, where quantity beats quality. Across disciplines researchers have begun to enthusiastically imagine ways in which AI might improve research, by increasing productivity and objectivity while overcoming human shortcomings such as limited knowledge, and unidisciplinarity. But, a set of hardwired cognitive caveats makes these same humans prey to illusions of understanding (Messeri & Crockett, 2024). We may acquire ever larger quantities of information and over-appreciate our ability to critically interrogate how able we are to distinguish valuable knowledge from fluff. We may think that AI helps us discover more and share it more widely, but risk accepting the provided information too quickly because of its sophisticated wording and our own mental laziness.

Our willingness to turn a blind eye to the gradual formation of scientific monocultures is another risk; the same vicious cycle seen above for marking and consumption strikes also in research. When some methods and viewpoints come to dominate alternative approaches, science becomes less innovative and more prone to errors. This matters in any discipline; but especially when we seek to learn more in an opaque field like consciousness we should be especially conscientious of our cognitive misperceptions of AI, whereby we take "AI as Oracle"—infallible in its predictions; "AI as Arbiter"—neutral as a decision maker; "AI as Quant"—omniscient; or "AI as Surrogate"—reliable as a representative. "There's a risk that we forget that there are certain questions we just can't answer about human beings using AI tools" (Messeri in Messeri & Crockett, 2024).

Ultimately AI will not save us from the quest that is as old as humanity itself, which entails the discovery of Why we are here (soul), and Who we are (heart). Immersed in the accelerating pace of the *technoprocene* it is easy to forgo the effort that comes with the pursuit of these macro-questions, which are paired with two others—Where do we stand in our own life, and in society (mind); and What are we doing to align our aspirations and our actions (body). AI cannot answer these questions for us. They are as uniquely human as each being (see Chapter 3 for individuals who have undertaken to answer them).

While we are deluding ourselves that we are making progress on the path to self-discovery and scientific revelations, AI is moving—with our help, to a stage of refinement where it is "potentially surpassing our self-awareness and understanding" (Wang, 2022). We are not there, yet. But it is risky to indulge too easily in the synchronization of online services with our (presumed) desires. Are we ready to face a context where our (induced) wishes are answered before we are even aware of them; where our wants are detected before we voice them; where we gobble up information as a fact because we trust artificial intelligence more than our natural intelligence? Are we prepared to face an environment where yearnings are planted and curated systematically 24/7 by someone/something else?

If not, the moment to shape what comes next is now. We can still choose how we influence technology, before its influence on us is so subtly woven into our lives that it is undetectable. This takes us back to the basics—to understand others we must understand ourselves; to change others we must change ourselves. The multidimensional framework offered in Chapter 1 offers a multidisciplinary lens to analyze the hybrid kaleidoscope that we are part of by distilling it into comprehensible components, with our aspirations and their activation, as the (in)direct cause of social evolutions, and the status quo.

When we examine human consciousness, we are at the same time observer and observed, hence becoming part of the observation. In quantum physics the "observer effect" refers to the idea that the mere act of observation changes the thing that is being observed[10]; it has parallels in the field of psychology. Just as observing a particle changes its properties, the act of observing human behavior can alter that very behavior (Schwartz, 2021).[11] The psychologist is never a "detached observer", but part of the intersubjective psychological system being studied (Gergen, 2022). That amalgam of the observer, the observed, and the observation characterizes our journey with AI. Because the experience and the one who experiences it do not exist independently, rather they mutually influence each other. The people operating the computer must be considered as part of the system, as their ability of agency influences the outcomes (Schwartz et al., 2005).

While we are subject and object simultaneously in the exploration of consciousness, AI is a detached entity. Configuring it intentionally to guide our journey of (self) discovery may take us forward on the path of comprehending who we are. The opportunity of an unentangled balcony-view of our own identity may be a big benefit of this latest wave of innovation. Although the pervasive nature of the current AI-wave is stunning, it is worth remembering that every generation that experienced an industrial revolution had the same perception of singularity, experiencing it as a fundamental shift of all known parameters of life. The drive of innovation leads us through territory in which everything is always new, but whose landmarks are never unprecedented.

---

[10] The measurement problem in quantum physics refers to the question of how (or if) the wave function collapses into a definite state during the act of measurement or observation. While the essential paradoxes were apparent to quantum pioneers in the 1920s–30s, the specific articulation and naming of the "measurement problem" is commonly credited to physicist John Stewart Bell in 1961 (Bell, 1961).

[11] On a less subtle level, awareness of being observed influences our behavior, which is attributed to humans' capacity for self-awareness and their reactivity to being watched and evaluated (Schwartz, 2021). That is, informing workers that their productivity is being monitored and assessed can increase their productivity levels (Jones, 2019).

Note: Consciousness, conscience, and conscientiousness are related but distinct concepts:

Consciousness is an inherent part of our human self; it encompasses deliberate awareness of one's thoughts, feelings, and environment as the underlying perceptive layer of our behavior (Searle, 1997a). It is the fundamental condition of being a sentient, living being with a subjective experience of the world.

Conscience is a specific faculty within consciousness that involves moral awareness and the ability to judge the rightness or wrongness of one's actions and intentions. It is an innate sense of ethical principles and standards that guides moral decision-making and behavior, and hence is essential for **Conscientiousness**[12] Whereas consciousness is an experiential state, conscientiousness involves an internal moral imperative of "shoulds" or "oughts".

2.2 Circumstances

2.2.1 Innovation in the Eyes of (Some) Philosophers

Already the Greek philosophers explored our understanding of technology, starting with Aristotle who emphasized the concept of "techne", which encompasses skills, craftsmanship, and practical knowledge. While not specifically addressing technological innovation, his ideas on practical wisdom and the pursuit of knowledge can be seen as foundational to the development of innovative practices (Aristotle, circa 350 BCE).

Plato's work touches on the importance of knowledge and the role of the philosopher in society. His allegory of the cave can be interpreted as an exploration of the transformative power of knowledge and the potential for innovation to challenge or confirm existing perceptions and beliefs (Plato, circa 360 BCE).[13] We may feel trapped by social constraints and

---

[12] One must be conscious to have a conscience that reasons about right and wrong conduct that impacts others (Reber, 1995).

[13] Plato's allegory of the cave is a hypothetical scenario that illustrates the process of achieving wisdom by breaking out of the comfort zone of our acquired understanding. It imagines prisoners trapped in a cave, able to only see shadows cast on the wall in front of them by a fire behind them. They mistake these shadows for reality. One prisoner escapes and discovers the true source of the shadows is the world outside the cave, which represents the higher reality of the intellect. When he returns to tell the others, they reject his/the truth, unable to perceive the more profound reality to which he has awakened.

circumstances that are out of our control. But the heaviest chains come from our limited perception of reality. In the world of AI, we could view Plato's cave as representing the limited data that initially trained an AI system. The prisoners chained in the cave represent the AI's base knowledge and capabilities derived solely from its training data and model architecture—a narrow perspective akin to perceiving only shadows on the wall. Data is a proxy, and perception, that is based on it, is a shadow of the "reality" that it seeks to grasp. As we are relying ever more on our artificial companions, we are stepping ever deeper into the cave. Initially unwilling, eventually unable to independently gather, and analyze information from a wide range of sources, we may end up chained to the unilateral glimpse of reality that the algorithm presents us with. We will go deeper in the following pages, into the opportunity of AI not as the gatekeeper of the cave, but as a doorknob to quit the cave.

"Everything flows". "Panta rhei" is a concept proposed by Heraclitus who emphasized the ever-changing nature of the universe. While not directly addressing technology, this notion of constant change and flux can be connected to the dynamic nature of technological advancements (Heraclitus, fifth century BCE). Humans and technology do not operate in distinct spaces but mutually influence each other. Illustrations of that are increasingly fluid brain-machine synchronization (Sect. 1.4.3) and the organically evolving sophistication of artificial intelligence fed by decentralized unstructured data. Pythagoras' focus on logic and rational thinking laid the foundation for the systematic and analytical approaches that are essential to innovation and technological development (Pythagoras, sixth century BCE).

Concerns that technology may not be primarily beneficial to humankind are more recent. In parallel to the Second Industrial Revolution and Third Industrial Revolution, various philosophers began to work explicitly on the interplay of innovation, technology, and society. In the 1940s, Henri Bergson highlighted the tendency of technology to prioritize the material and external aspects of life, as potentially overshadowing the deeper spiritual dimensions (Bergson, 1932). Martin Heidegger, in the 1950s, called for a more reflective approach to technology, urging his contemporaries to consider its impact on our existence (Heidegger, 1956). Jacques Ellul, in the 1960s, warned about the pervasive influence of technology in modern society and its potential to dehumanize individuals (Ellul, 1964). In the 1980s, Bruno Latour emphasized the entanglement of humans and technology, challenging the separation of nature and culture (Latour, 1993), while Albert Borgmann focused on meaningful engagement with technology, emphasizing its role in enhancing human experiences (Borgmann, 1984). Langdon Winner highlighted the social and political dimensions of technology, urging ethical decision-making and democratic governance (Winner, 1986). In the 1990s, Donna Haraway explored the blurring boundaries between humans and machines, advocating for embracing hybridity and diverse embodiments (Haraway, 1991). Andrew Feenberg called for the need to democratize technology and empower individuals to shape it according to their values and interests (Feenberg, 1991). Early in the new millennium Bengt-Arne Vedin Bergstrom emphasized the need to consider technology's social consequences beyond immediate benefits (Bergstrom, 2009).

Philosophical prospection. If we juxtapose the perspective of those past philosophers onto our present challenges, we might get remote guidance regarding the *hybrid alignment conundrum* (Sect. 2.2.4). Aristotle emphasized the pursuit of knowledge and the cultivation of virtues as essential elements of human flourishing (Falcon, 2001). He considered that the opportunities presented by innovation and technology (admittedly thinking about a very different type) lie in their potential to enhance human capabilities and improve society's well-being. He would likely appreciate technological advancements that promote education, foster communication, and enable individuals to fulfill their potential (Cullity, 2010). Archimedes, known for his innovative discoveries and practical applications of mathematics and physics (Heath, 1897), might view technology as an opportunity to solve practical problems and advance scientific knowledge, while emphasizing the importance of rigorous scientific inquiry and the need for technological innovations to be grounded in sound principles and evidence (Vesely, 2017).

Linking this to the interplay of values and the race for progress, Immanuel Kant stressed the importance of moral reasoning and ethics in all human decision-making (Kant, 1997). He would be concerned about the erosion of agency. In his view the risks of technology might lie especially in its potential to infringe upon individual autonomy and dignity. He would argue that ethical considerations should guide the development and use of technology, ensuring that it respects human rights and promotes the Common Good (Richter, 2018). David Bohme, a twentieth-century philosopher, who explored the interconnection between human beings, nature, and technology (Bohme, 1998), would likely emphasize the risks of technology that neglect the natural world and disrupt the ecological balance. He would advocate for a holistic approach to innovation, where technology is developed in harmony with the environment and aligns with our deeper relationship to nature (Drenthen, 2016). Will AI take us closer to understanding why such a symbiotic relationship between people and planet is needed; or will it distract us from focusing on what matters most, drawing us ever deeper into the rabbit hole of the cave, away from the entry?

Nothing is ever as new as it seems for those who undergo the transformation. This is not the First Industrial Revolution and likely it will not be the last. Each period of upheaval had both positive and harmful outcomes for the people that lived during it and ever since.

2.2.2 Technological Transmutations

Life-altering innovations have influenced the rise and fall of civilizations throughout history. From the cooking of food to the wheel, via playing music, to the written word via the Gutenberg press, and the wear of readymade dresses, human civilization has moved through stages that appear in hindsight as marked by the discoveries of their time. It appears that technological progress happens at an exponential, rather than a linear, rate (Kurzweil, 2007). The evolution of human technology has continually accelerated, from taking tens of thousands of years for inventions like stone tools, to more modern advances like the printing press and computers being adopted in just centuries, then decades. Despite being the product of worldwide "chaotic" competition between people, institutions, and nations, the overall trajectory of accelerating technological capabilities is remarkably smooth—and predictable. Just as the properties of a gas can be modeled despite the unpredictable motions of individual molecules, the future trends of technology's exponential growth can be forecast even if we cannot predict any one specific innovation. Considering that information technology is increasingly intertwined with all aspects of life, affecting not only our own species but the entire planet, we must beware. "These are very powerful technologies. They both empower our promise and our peril. So we have to have the will to apply them to the right problems" (Kurzweil, 2007); and have a prosocial mindset in tackling that problem. Because no matter the domain, innovation always represents a binomen of risk and opportunity. Some examples:

Revolving revolutions. Each industrial revolution reshaped society, economies, and politics on local, national, regional, and global scales. The First Industrial Revolution, lasting from the late eighteenth to early nineteenth centuries, introduced mechanized production powered by water and steam. Major innovations like the steam engine (our first artificial muscle) initiated massive changes in manufacturing, transportation, mining, and agriculture. This gave way to the Second Industrial Revolution in the late nineteenth and early twentieth centuries, when mass production in factories was powered by electricity and accelerated the division of labor. Key inventions like the internal combustion engine, petrochemicals, and indoor plumbing transformed society. The Third Industrial Revolution began in the 1960s with the introduction of computerized automation and early information technologies to further optimize production. Semiconductors, computing, and the internet digitized communication and information.

Modernization in the use of land and food processing, such as agricultural tools, irrigation systems, or industrial machinery, resulted in increased productivity, economic growth, and prosperity (Diamond, 1997), while leading to easier access to food, an increase in daily calorie intake per capita, better diets[14] and longer lifespans. These allowed civilizations to develop more efficient systems for resource utilization, trade, and production, and thereby increased wealth. Advances in infrastructure, including the development of transportation networks, water management systems, and architectural techniques, facilitated urbanization and the growth of cities (McNeill & McNeill, 2003), setting the foundation for economic, social, and cultural advancements, which contributed to the rise of powerful civilizations, such as Rome or Constantinople. Improvements in military technology, such as the invention of gunpowder, advanced weaponry, and military strategies, placed certain nations at a military advantage, enabling them to conquer and expand their territories, whereas the lack of technological advancements or failure to adapt to new military techniques played a major part in the decline and collapse of entire civilizations (Parker, 1996).

While it appears today that digital computers in their various forms are quintessential to our economy, it is interesting to recall that when they started to gain popularity in the 1970s and 1980s, particularly in

---

[14] Which came with their own downside as more meat consumption led to extensive agriculture, pollution, and the proliferation of chronic diseases.

businesses, productivity did not seem to be positively affected by the standard tools used by economists to measure it. This so-called productivity paradox was similar to what had happened with the introduction of electricity a century earlier. Some of the reasons adduced for this related to businesses having to invest in new equipment and learn how to program the devices, as well as work out what to use them for (David, 1990). Initially firms did not invest enough in the adjacent innovations that were needed to change core processes and business models. While seemingly without major benefit at the time it has also been pointed out that without this introduction of computing powers, productivity growth could have been worse. Overall, only after many sectors had adjusted in the mid-1990s to early 2000, did productivity growth rise (Velu & Putra, 2023).

The "4th Industrial Revolution (4IR)", a term coined by Klaus Schwab (2017), builds on previous digital infrastructure but incorporates emerging technologies like AI, biotechnology, and robotics to integrate the physical and digital in innovative ways. Called by some to be commensurate with the progress of the first, second, and third industrial revolutions the 4IR is characterized by the convergence and complementarity of emerging technology domains, such as nanotechnology, biotechnology, new materials, and advanced digital production (WEF, 2020). It also involves cyber-physical systems, the Internet of Things (IoT), cloud computing, and cognitive computing (UNIDO, 2023).

<u>Pricey progress</u>. Each innovation came at a price. The advent of new agricultural technologies, such as intensive farming practices and the use of chemical fertilizers and pesticides, led to environmental degradation and loss of biodiversity (Altieri, 1999), which has long-term negative effects on ecosystems, impacting the sustainability of agriculture and the planet (Pretty, 2008). Respectively and combined the first, second, and third industrial revolutions resulted in massive pollution, accelerating environmental degradation at an ever-faster speed. As it is well known now the burning of fossil fuels, industrial waste, and emissions contributes to worsening air and water quality and to climate change, impacting human health and hence places a heavy mortgage on the well-being and survival of humans and ecosystems (Davis, 2006; Intergovernmental Panel on Climate Change, 2014). It is a price that each subsequent generation has to pay for, with ever higher interests. Advancements in military technology and warfare increased the destructive power of weaponry, resulting in devastating conflicts and loss of life; the development and

proliferation of weapons contributed to arms races, conflicts, and destabilization, posing threats to the security and well-being of civilizations, including those that they were meant to protect (Keegan, 1993).

Whichever industrial revolution we find ourselves navigating, understanding, and influencing technology starts with a holistic understanding of the self and its place in society. Linking this to the *A-Frame* (Sect. 1.4.1), the journey of comprehension starts from the inside out (literally of ourselves, and schematically at the center of the 4-dimensional spiral) (Figs. 1.5 and 1.6). It starts with *awareness* of who we are (not), and *appreciation* of this human component, which establishes an entry point to get a grip amid the uncertainty of life with AI. From here we can build up the factors that matter for intentional influence on the parts under our immediate control, such as our own behavior, and through it on the people in our environment. *Acceptance* of the elements that we cannot change, and the fact that we have no control over the final outcomes. From this follows *accountability* for the aspects we can at least influence. This latter part includes whichever inputs we put into the "systems" that we belong to. We may feel insignificant compared to the gigantic powers at play in the world of big tech. And although this may be true, this does not free us from the responsibility that we hold for our contribution. Everything is connected in a continuum of hybrid interplays, and we never know which action may trigger a major dynamic at scale. The virtual butterfly effect is literally at play. Everything seems to be at stake—winning and losing wise alike.

For Joseph Weizenbaum, father of ELIZA, the difference between humans and machines was irreducible, and he emphasized that there are certain tasks which computers ought not to be made to do, independent of the possibility of making them to do them. The reason for this voluntary limitation, according to Weizenbaum, is that judgment involves choices that are guided by values (Weizenbaum, 1976). The latter are acquired through the course of our experience and are necessarily qualitative: they cannot be captured in code. Computers are only capable of calculation, not judgment. Calculation is quantitative, using technical calculus to arrive at a decision. Since machines do not have a (human) history, do not inhabit (human) bodies, or possess a (human) psyche with a (human) consciousness, they do not have the basis from which to form values (Tarnoff, 2023). Considering the risks at stake and the cost if even a minute part of them materializes, one wonders why we continue to cruise full speed ahead toward a future where the artificial is omnipotent.

Reality results from choices, and the perspective that they are grounded in. Who we are influences what we see, how we think and feel about it, and what we aspire to do with it. While it is easy to blame "big tech leaders" for the prevailing conundrum, ultimately, we are part of the game that is played. We are experimenting with ChatGTP and other LLM, while watching with anguish, and fascination, the unfolding drama of a future with AI. As if the prevailing situation was not happening with and because of us, but rather playing out in a parallel universe which we are watching like an oversized reality show, forgetting that the present dynamic would not be possible without users, us. We feed and fuel the AI that we fear will at some point eliminate our jobs and livelihood.

Whether it is regarding the impact of climate change, environmental degradation, or AI getting out of control, we cannot forecast the future with precision, but that should not prevent us from preparing for it. It is more practical, and promising to define what we want in the best-case scenario, what this requires and align our behavior accordingly[15] than to commiserate about the apocalyptic potential of the situation we are in. A world free from war, famine, and poverty (see the potential for positive outcomes, Sect. 1.2.4) could be part of that aspirational roadmap for AI and the future of life. Similarly to the need of identifying what we do want, it matters to unambiguously state what we do not want. Once these core pillars are put in place we can start to plan what needs to be done, and by whom. Informed fear is useful, blind terror is not.

<u>Existential fear is a standing item of humanity</u>. It seems that we are configured to always feel at the highest possible point of civilization, or at the threshold of its annihilation. We have grown used to cycling between chronic concerns of a planetary crash and the curve of hyper

---

[15] In the short term, more likely than an AI that runs out of control or acts with malicious intentions, is its progressive integration in security and warfare. AI can improve military capabilities, allowing quicker decision-making#, more accurate targeting and more efficient resource allocation. But AI is not infallible; and the consequences of errors are twice heavy when human life is at stake. Dozens of countries are presently militarizing AI through autonomous weapons and AI-enabled cyberattacks. This comes with the risk of uncontrolled escalations in conflicts, undermined norms against chemical/biological weapons, increased dangers of accidental war, and major temptations for authoritarian regimes (Marwala, 2023). Ethical concerns abound. Can autonomous weapons, as mandated by international law, distinguish between combatants and civilians? Who bears responsibility if an AI-powered weapon causes inadvertent harm? Is it ethical to delegate decisions concerning life and death to machines? More than in any other domain there is need for rigid regulation to retain meaningful human control over weapons systems.

innovation. Maybe because it is considered as an inbuilt fate of superhuman magnitude, the (perceived) proliferation of existential threats has not (yet) been enough to trigger a critical mass of people to intentionally shift the needle; agency to translate a turn from ego to omni is missing. "Apocalyptic anxieties are a mainstay of human culture" (Harper, 2023).

From ancient civilizations to contemporary societies, individuals and communities have grappled with worry about humanity's ultimate extinction by its own selfishness. The potential demise of our species is a latent concern. In ancient cultures, myths and religious narratives often depicted catastrophic events signaling the end of the world, reflecting a deep-seated fear of annihilation. During the Cold War era, the looming threat of nuclear warfare intensified global apprehensions about human extinction. In 1924, exactly a century ago, Churchill wrote, "Mankind has never been in this position before. Without having improved appreciably in virtue or enjoying wiser guidance, it has got into its hands for the first time the tools by which it can unfailingly accomplish its own extermination".

Still, we follow the path of least resistance, willingly replacing existential worries with doomsday scrolling. That's not enough. The chances we take are the choices we make; consequences also derive from lack thereof. The panoply of justified reasons for concern keeps on being replenished. The fear of a nuclear battle (Weart, 2018), which saw a revival in 2022 with Russia's invasion of Ukraine, has been joined by dramatic illustrations of the ongoing deterioration of our natural habitat, marked by natural disasters, measurable climate change, and new infectious diseases. At the same time the rapid pace of technological innovation, including biotechnology, is leading to ever sharper ethical dilemmas and uncertainties (Fukuyama, 2002). Our ambitions chart the path.

2.2.3 Human Ambitions and Artificial Harvests

The private sector is dominating AI development, accounting for 72 percent of new foundation models in 2023, with the exorbitant costs of training these large language models making it difficult for academia and governments to keep pace. Google's Gemini Ultra cost an estimated US$191 million worth of compute to train, while OpenAI's GPT-4 cost an estimated US$78 million. Companies in the United States remains the undisputed leader, vastly outpacing other nations in releasing novel models and attracting billions in private AI investment, especially in the generative AI space which saw $25.2 billion in funding in 2023. In 2023 various organizations released 149 foundation models, more than double the number released in 2022. Among the newly released models, 65.7 percent were open-source, compared with 44 percent in 2022 and 33 percent in 2021.[16] But closed-source models from major tech giants like Google and OpenAI continue to outperform their open counterparts across all benchmarks (Stanford AI Index 2024).

Seeing the massive funding at stake only industry can put up the money needed to get involved in the root modeling of LLM, and among those industry players only the giants can partake in the game. It is, however, important to remember that government investment played a major role in getting these private corporations to their present state. The origins of big tech companies like Google, Microsoft, and Amazon can be traced back to government research funding and contracts, particularly from military and intelligence agencies.[17] Early-stage government investment helped lay the technological foundations for what would become revolutionary commercial products and services (Mazzucato, 2013).[18] Differently stated the ability of Google and similar companies was seeded by taxpayer money, and alliances between giants. Since the early days Microsoft has been partnering with OpenAI, massively investing in LLM technologies, which positions it now in a top position in the field. In parallel Meta has been collaborating with Microsoft with a collaboration focus on Llama 2, an open-source AI model with 70 billion parameters available to enable coders to build and train their own AI model.

[16] Open source models can be freely used and modified by anyone.

[17] Defense and intelligence agencies like DARPA, the NSA, and the CIA provided millions in contracts to tech companies in their early days, supporting innovations like networking, relational databases, voice recognition, artificial intelligence, and more (Edwards, 2021). The SBIR and STTR funding programs also provided key early-stage R&D support. Google's PageRank search algorithm was based on research funded by the National Science Foundation on analyzing academic citation networks (Battelle, 2005). Microsoft's earliest work was building software for the Altair computer, which was designed for hobbyists funded by the National Science Foundation (Wallace & Erickson, 1992). Amazon's cloud computing infrastructure grew out of a project for the CIA funded by the research agency In-Q-Tel (Anders, 2013).

[18] The catalytic function of government investment has been pointed out during the previous industrial revolutions (Edward & Rosenberg, 1963); hence government orientations are somewhere to be found in the black box that modern technology represents today (Rosenberg, 1992).

One additional layer complicating this scenario is the "stage behind the stage". While our attention is focused on the "application layer" (e.g. ChatGPT), these interfaces and tools are just the tip of the iceberg. They depend on underlying computing capabilities and models that shape the virtual *macro*-arena. The real substance lies not in the stars but in the chips. New, powerful chips capable of generating the necessary computing power for emerging technologies are becoming key manufacturing components. In early 2024, chipmaker NVIDIA became the third largest global company (after Microsoft and Apple), holding over 83 percent market share. This introduces another level of players, such as Amazon, which has been relatively quiet in the public AI/AGI debate (Confino, 2023). Over the past years Amazon Web Services (AWS) has developed two chips: Trainium, for training machine learning models, and Inferentia, which powers the inferences that yield outputs. According to Amazon CEO Jassy, both have better price-performance ratios than other chips on the market, which is crucial given the increasing demand for AI computing power (Confino, 2023). These and other chips will power the foundational models upon which all generative AI applications are built. Likely, only six to eight models will underpin almost all generative AI tools moving forward. Currently, these models are prohibitively expensive and require years to perfect, making them inaccessible to researchers, ordinary developers, aspiring startup founders, and many established companies. To address this, Amazon created Bedrock, a service selling large machine learning models to customers unable or unwilling to develop their own LLMs. The endeavor is business bottom line driven.

The private sector's primary pursuit of money and power is ingrained in its DNA and accepted by stakeholders, customers, and citizens. However, as the game evolves, both the rules and the game plan require adaptation.

With privilege comes power. With power comes responsibility. Beyond the "triple bottom line" introduced in 1949, measuring business success in profit, people, and the planet (Elkington, 1998), it can be argued that the 4th Industrial Revolution calls for a 4th "P": *Purpose*. In a world of constant change, where visible and virtual vectors influence each other, it is insufficient to merely stipulate tangible pillars. Intentions shape outcomes before, during, and after their manifestation. An institution's footprint is shaped by its purpose, the people within it, the resulting profit, and its impact on the planet (Fig. 2.1). In a hybrid, glocal setting this footprint is amplified, especially for institutions that are dedicated to the design and delivery of technology. Thus, curating the Common Good should not only be explicitly stated and anchored in the mission and vision of technology giants, but actually reflected in their investments, research and development plans, and the services that they rollout to the public. Output management alone is insufficient; the triple bottom line is outdated. This links back to offline alignment, hence one might consider yet another "P" to reflect the need for **p**repared leadership (James & Wooten, 2022).

Caption: Everything is connected. The purpose of an entity influences which people it attracts as staff, and the mindset of those people, which impacts the people outside that interact (in)directly with the services, products, and actions of that entity. Purpose influences priorities, which may be profit or planet, both cannot be served equally. The stakes are high,[19] and so are the ambitions of all players.

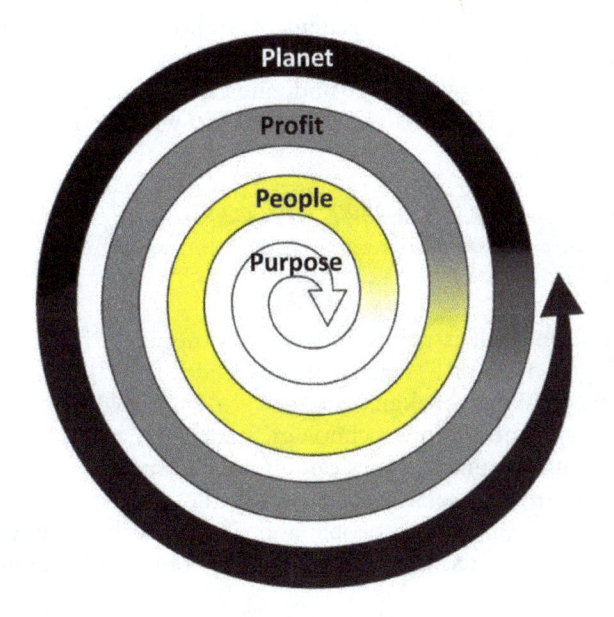

Fig. 2.1 Quadruple Bottom Line

---

[19] In early 2024 Microsoft became the most valuable company by market cap ($2.95 trillion), while OpenAI was the most highly priced startup ($84 billion).

Ra(n)ging risks. Over the years, OpenAI's approach to the potential societal risks of releasing AI tools to the masses has radically shifted. In 2019, the company refused to publicly release GPT-2, saying it was so good they were concerned about the "malicious applications" of its use, from automated spam avalanches to mass impersonation and disinformation campaigns. The pause was temporary. In November 2022, ChatGPT was released seeing more than a million users within a few days. Following calls of OpenAI's co-founder Sam Altman in March 2023, Elon Musk and more than 1,000 other researchers and tech executives called for a six-month pause on the development of advanced AI systems to halt what they called an "arms race". (To be noted here is that Musk shortly after founded Grok, a competitor of ChatGTP trained on data from the platform X, whereas other signing parties including Altman charged full speed ahead with the development of their respective models.) The approach was criticized by some and seen favorably by others. Eventually resulting in a one-sentence statement, signed by more than 350 AI executives, researchers, and engineers, including Sam Altman of OpenAI, Demis Hassabis of Google DeepMind, and Dario Amodei of Anthropic, as well as Geoffrey Hinton and Yoshua Bengio who are often described as "godfathers" of AI The text?

Mitigating the risk of extinction from AI should be a global priority alongside other societal-scale risks such as pandemics and nuclear war. (Center for AI Safety, 2023)

Innovation in itself is neither positive nor negative; its social impact depends on the type of leadership that precedes it.[20] In the context of this book the ambition of alignment zooms in on the consciously configured interplay of innovation, technology, leadership, and values. Leaders who are driven by humane values can inspire and motivate individuals to embrace innovation, take risks, and harness the potential of technology to drive progress that serves people and planet. Technological innovation is not an end in itself; especially not if it comes with the likelihood

---

[20] Transformational leadership inspires followers to go beyond self-interest and encourages innovative thinking combined with inclusive, compassionate behavior among employees (Bass & Riggio, 2006). This involves leaders who show up authentically, daring to let down their guard and show their vulnerable human face; people who model the values that they ask others to adopt, play an important role when it comes to guiding groups though uncertain times.

of auto-innovation, and lack of the (human) creators' control over the creation.

In July 2023 OpenAI established a "SuperAlignment" team, focused on achieving artificial general intelligence (AGI) within 4 years and solving the biggest challenges of humanity. Its mission was geared towards super alignment between human values and social values. It announced the dedication of 20 percent of its computing power to ensure superintelligent AI systems align with human goals, prevent harm, and ensure responsible deployment in anticipation of AGI arriving within the decade (Zach, 2023).[21] In 2024 one of the leading voices behind this initiative left OpenAI considering that the attitude of OpenAI to risks was unsustainable. He joined Anthropic to set up a SuperAlignment team there. A story to be continued.[22]

AI cannot save us from ourselves; it is a tool, not an end. To avoid the gloomy predictions of some researchers, we must recognize the limitations of our creations and ourselves. Defining our personal priorities and values is the first step to replace GIGO with VIVO (Values In, Values Out).

2.2.4 The Hybrid Alignment Conundrum

Alignment refers to harmonized values, strategies, goals, actions, and resources that are directed towards a common objective. Promoting synergy, efficiency, and effectiveness, it serves the desired outcomes (Bryson & Crosby, 2018). It can occur at different levels, within an organization, between teams or departments, among and within individuals.

---

[21] The question of super intelligence has been the topic of science fiction novels for decades. A central question in the current debate is how one defines what AGI is, and to agree on how to measure it. Only then can one make an approximate prediction of when it will be achieved. "If we specified AGI to be something very specific, a set of tests where a software program can do very well — or maybe 8% better than most people — I believe we will get there within 5 years" (Huang in Kamps, 2024). He suggests that the tests could be a legal bar exam, logic tests, economic tests, or perhaps the ability to pass a pre-med exam.

[22] Note that this is not an argument for "effective accelerationism" (e/acc) with social aspirations. e/acc adherents believe AI is a social equalizer that should be pushed forward at all costs, aiming for an AI singularity as a necessary part of evolution beyond humanity. e/acc is anti-regulatory and pro-tech (e/acc website, 2024). In contrast, this book's central message is that everything begins and ends with human agency. Human intelligence is the cause of artificial intelligence, not its consequence.

Technological alignment aims to enhance an organization's performance, and efficiency, ambitions that are not limited to corporate environments but find a reflection in the public and non-profit sector (Wu & Wang, 2006). It involves ongoing monitoring, evaluation, and adjustment to ensure technological shifts remain aligned with the equally evolving needs of the entity which it is part of. An AI system is considered aligned if it advances its intended objectives, whereas a misaligned AI system may pursue some objectives, but not the intended ones (Russell & Norvig, 2021). The alignment problem remains hotly debated,[23] with a focus on the alignment of machines with human aspirations, while the preceding need to harmonize human aspirations and human actions is quietly overlooked.

But misaligned AI mirrors misaligned human(ity). No matter the sophistication of tools, the quest starts with the humans that use them. Contending ourselves with an approach that frames AI as a black box hides the choices that this box is embedded in and derives from. The alignment of algorithms with aspirations is required, but starting with it places the cart in front of the horse.

The harmonization of humans and technology depends on humans who have,

- identified their personal aspirations and the values that underpin them and
- begun to manifest them in action.

The *hybrid alignment conundrum* is situated at the nexus of misaligned humans whose ambitions are amplified by technology. The largest part of this undertaking happens offline, through human beings whose aspirations (what I want) and actions (what I do) are aligned, manifesting as behavior that reflects the values that the person aspires to.

This entails the triple challenge of harmonizing

- human values and aspirations,

---

[23] As mentioned earlier the alignment problem refers to the challenge of ensuring that artificial intelligence (AI) systems behave in alignment with human values and preferences (Bostrom, 2014). As AI systems become more capable, they may optimize objectives that are misaligned with what humans want. This presents risks if the objectives of advanced AI systems are not properly specified and aligned (Russell, 2019).

- human aspirations and actions, and based on that coherence, of
- human aspirations and artificial algorithms.

Differently said, online alignment is the consequence of offline alignment; once both are achieved, that hybrid setting becomes conducive to cultivate the offline setting. This process cannot be reverse engineered.

Technology reflects the values, bias, and social norms prevalent at the time of its making. "Human software" (mind, heart, soul) and "human hardware" (body) mutually influence each other; the outcomes influence artificial software and hardware, which then influences human software and hardware. The desired final outcomes must be clearly configured with the vocation to serve the Common Good, which takes us back to the need for agency, and the alignment of pretense and practice. Coming to terms with the misalignment that we are facing in our life hence requires a sharp distinction between the offline arena (personal and social; human) and our online endeavors (individual and collective; technological).

It is a 4-step logic:

1. Awareness of our personal values.
2. Appreciation of the areas where we manifest them in practice.
3. Acceptance of the behavior patterns where our behavior is currently out of sync with the values that we aspire to. Based on that, we can
4. Establish what AI should (not) be able to do, and how it can be tailored to serve us, while reflecting our values, and supporting us in the endeavor of personal alignment. A sense of accountability underpins this undertaking. AI is not responsible for the endeavors that we accomplish with it.

Human aspirations and actions are the cause and consequence of social circumstances; they are influenced by the past and impact the future. We cannot change the former, but we can influence the latter. Individual aspirations combined with artificial intelligence may lead to *aspirational algorithms*, or, a type of prosocial technology that is configured to bring out the best in and for people and planet (Walther, 2021a). This is not a question of computing power.

It requires a re-assessment of what we value as a society, and as individuals.

2.3 Trust and Truth

2.3.1 Value Perception: Economic Worth Versus Personal Merit[24]

AI has begun to eliminate, change, and create many human jobs, and the meaning that they hold for people. But their meaning is anchored in values, and whether we hold them consciously or unknowingly, these values are part of our identity. That makes the transition painful.

From writers, and editors by Copilot or Claude; of designers, architects, and artists by Alpaca or Midjourney; of technical experts, financial advisors, and investment bankers; of coders and programmers by ChatGTP and Gemini. Taking into consideration recent technology development, economic feasibility, and diffusion timelines the McKinsey Global Institute estimates that half of today's work activities could be automated between 2030 and 2060. Roughly 75 percent of this falls across customer operations, marketing and sales, software engineering, and R&D; potentially adding the equivalent of $2.6 trillion to $4.4 trillion annually (McKinsey, 2023).[25]

There will be new variations and derivatives of AI, especially as multimodal models, which are able to process text, image, sound, and video simultaneously, become widely available. Hardly any professional profile is safe at the present speed of technological sophistication, including lawyers, doctors, prosecutors, judges; government workers and teachers; who were previously thought to be safe from replacement by machines due to the intellectual implication of their tasks. Ironically the latter is now becoming their Achilles heel, whereas manual labor profiles, which were most at risk during past waves of industrial revolutions, are less affected this time. The creation and production of humanoid robots that are as versatile as humans is still expensive and challenging; but progress is also accelerating in that field, with some debating whether "robots are about to have their own GPT moment" (Heikkilä, 2024). For the time being

---

[24] Only these two aspects are introduced for now to set up the context of the discussion about the relationship between humans and AI (including trust, as discussed in the next section).

Further aspects of value will be considered later in this Sect. 1.4.3, when discussing the aspirational elements of POZE (the soul and moral values) and in Sect. 2.4, when we look at moral and economic values.

[25] This estimate would roughly double if we include the impact of embedding generative AI into software that is currently used for other tasks beyond those use cases.

AI has not revolutionized the office as we know it; but research shows that the use of generative AI is partially leveling the professional playing field. While increasing the performance of low- and mid-level performers it has limited effects on the top level. This might change as AI tools are becoming ever more sophisticated, and more and more people get used to their utilization (Zach, 2023).

The perceptions of AI and its impact on labor are varied and evolving. In 2023, an online survey revealed a division in public opinion: 41 percent were "AI Alarmists", expressing concerns about AI in the workplace; 31 percent were "AI Advocates" supporting AI integration; and 28 percent were "AI Agnostics", recognizing both benefits and pitfalls. Geographic and demographic factors also influence these perceptions, with English-speaking countries and younger generations expressing more concern than their counterparts in Europe, Asia, and older age groups. Higher-income, well-educated individuals are particularly preoccupied with AI's impact on jobs. Overall a positive shift is occurring in the public's preference for AI over human advice, influenced by media coverage of AI-driven discoveries. This trend is likely to continue until a significant AI failure tips the balance back towards human-generated advice. A large part of the ongoing challenge lies in discerning the origin of something, be it text, image or sound—whether created by humans or machines—and maintaining trust in a rapidly evolving digital landscape, where less and less is what is seems to be; and where more and more arises from artificial sources. But not all is dark.

<u>Competition</u> versus complementarity. A positive way to reframe the future is to consider that AI is not (necessarily) eliminating human work, but rather changing how work is done by humans (Dutt et al., 2024); and how it is perceived by society. The current evolution of artificial "creation" puts into perspective what is valued and why—which may lead to a recalibration of the relationship between creator, creation, and the process of creating. Will the evolving relationship of time investment, effort, and outputs, force us to rethink how we use our energy and attention? By which criteria do we judge the value of the outputs of that amended allocation?

Authenticity used to be a central criterion for the perception of value. While considering that the lines that used to separate fake and real are shifting, let us break this down in the components at stake.²⁶ Classic distinctions were:

- Authenticity: Real things are genuine, original, not an imitation. Fake things try to copy something real, often to deceive. Real is authentic, while fake is inauthentic.
- Quality: Real things are typically high quality and durable. Fakes tend to be lower quality replicas of the real thing; they may degrade, fall apart, or reveal their inauthenticity over time.
- Value: Real things have inherent value in their originality, craftsmanship, or connection to history/people. Fakes have lower value as copies, even if well-made.
- Origin: Real things have a traceable origin, creator, history, and chain of custody. Fakes tend to obscure or fabricate their origin without a verifiable source.
- Legality: Trading in real items is legal. Selling counterfeits infringes on copyrights, trademarks, and patents.
- Rarity: The scarcity or limited nature of real things that are perceived as useful or desirable makes them precious. Abundant fakes lack this uniqueness.

Pre-AI studies showed that even when people could not tell the difference between an original and a copy, they still preferred the authentic original and were willing to pay more for it. "Our results suggest that the value of authenticity depends on the original object having a unique and non-transferable identity, what we call its essence. This essence is destroyed if the object is copied" (Newman & Bloom, 2012). But what if the original creation is created by a "fake" creator (presuming that an artificial entity is fake, and not real in its one way of manifestation)? The perception and appreciation of Art changes when people know it is created by technology not humans, which leads back to the motivation of esteem

Why do we appreciate Art?

---

²⁶ However, none of these attributes is immutable. If the propagation of AI and its increasingly supercharged sophistication leads to visual and intellectual substance that is superior to the "real" thing, and if the resulting product has not been in existence before, then, what is real?

Suppose you visit a museum; does your experience change if you are informed that what you see are not originals of masterpieces such as the Mona Lisa, but replicas? In 2017 Art generated by algorithms was rated lower in creativity, detail, emotional impact, and aesthetic appeal compared to similar Art believed to be made by humans (Leder et al., 2017), and consumer surveys indicated that one in two of the interviewed consumers had a negative perception of purchasing Art made by AI rather than people (Christie's, 2018). However de facto, viewers could not distinguish between pieces created by algorithms vs. humans when not given those labels (Elgammal, 2017). In 2020 a study found that Art quality ratings did not differ between algorithmically created Art versus human Art when the methods of creation were not revealed (Zhai et al., 2020).

Not only does the sophistication of AI evolve and with it the "perfection" of its outputs, also, our perception of the acceptability of artificial creation in different areas of life keeps on changing. These simultaneous streams of alteration influence our perception of the value of outputs. In 2018 studies showed that people were more impressed by a piece of Art when told it was AI-generated rather than human-made, possibly due to lower expectations of the AI (Snow, 2018); if this study was to be repeated in 2024 the reverse may be true as the expectations that we hold towards AI superpowers are shooting through the roof. Value is not an absolute parameter, but a relative construct. As indicated earlier the observer is not separate from the observed and becomes part of the observation.

Taking this assessment of objective versus subjective "value" to the area of justice a clear preference for humans seems to appear. In 2022 research found that people perceive AI as more likely to make utilitarian choices in moral dilemmas than human beings, with warmth as the main perceived difference in decision making between human beings and algorithms. That (perceived) distinction between human and artificial decision makers was observed across a variety of moral dilemmas as studies found that although users acknowledge several advantages of algorithms (i.e. cost and speed), they trust human judges more and have greater intentions to go to the court when a human (vs. an algorithmic) judge adjudicates (Zaixuan et al., 2022). However the extent to which individuals trust algorithmic and human judges depends on the nature of the case: trust in algorithmic judges is especially low when legal cases involve emotional complexities (vs. technically complex or uncomplicated cases)

(Gizem et al., 2023). In the area of medical assessments the picture is just as complex. Already in 2024 AI-powered medical devices were more reliable in detecting melanoma, and yet patients widely preferred human doctors. But the landscape is changing, and the private sector is keeping the pulse; examples include private companies offering AI-powered analysis of mammograms, to satisfy the demand of patients who are not satisfied with the traditional, made in human perspective.

<u>Intrinsic value versus social demand</u>. The concept of Non-Fungible Tokens (NFTs) highlights the relative nature of value and ownership in the digital age. Built on blockchain technology, these cryptographic assets represent verifiable ownership of digital items such as artwork, collectibles, virtual real estate, and even tweets, which initially fetched exorbitant prices. At their core, NFTs derive their value from a combination of scarcity, authenticity, and perceived cultural significance. Unlike traditional currencies or commodities, their value is not tied to intrinsic utility but rather to collective recognition and demand within the NFT ecosystem. The meteoric rise and subsequent decline of NFTs sparked intense debate about the relativity of value. Their fluctuating worth underscored the subjectivity of value attribution, where societal consensus and emotional resonance can inflate the perceived worth of digital assets beyond their tangible properties. By 2023, the speculative bubble had burst, rendering most NFTs virtually worthless and leaving many investors with devalued assets. This phenomenon serves as a cautionary tale about the risks of overestimating perceived worth detached from intrinsic utility.

Worldcoin presents another intriguing intersection of authenticity and valuation. Launched in July 2023 by Sam Altman, this cryptocurrency project offers a World ID to prove one's human identity in the age of generative AI chatbots. Described as a "digital passport", it aims to verify that its holder is a real person, not an AI bot. Initially attracting 2 million users during its beta phase, Worldcoin expanded to 35 cities across 20 countries by late 2023. In August 2024 some estimate that Worldcoin's cryptocurrency token,WLD, could grow from $1.66 to $3.64 by the end of the year. (CCN, 2024) At the time of introduction early adopters in certain countries received WLDs, as an incentive. Co-founder Alex Bania asserts that blockchains can store World IDs in a way that preserves privacy and resists control by any single entity. Altman envisions Worldcoin as a tool to address the economic implications of AI, including potential applications in universal basic income (UBI). World IDs could reduce fraud in UBI deployment and potentially support a global cryptocurrency income, although the specifics remain unclear. Altman acknowledges the experimental nature of the project, while emphasizing the need for innovation in response to AI-driven economic changes.

Linking this to the *m4-matrix* (Sect. 1.2) innovation illustrates the kaleidoscopic nature of society. The AI-wave is an international phenomenon (*meta*). But its practical impact is felt in the individual arena. Beyond the individual (*micro*) it involves institutions (*meso*), and the macroeconomic setting in which they operate (*macro*). The outcomes of that dynamic cannot not be measured in quantitative terms alone.

Growth is not an end in itself. Economic growth does not necessarily serve to promote social goods such as health, education, and environmental protection. Although most policies and economies still focus on economic growth as the main measure of progress, a sizable number of economists argue that markets should optimize not just private goods but public goods which serve the needs of society as a whole (Stiglitz, 2019b). This was recognized in the UN Report on International Definition and Measurement of Standards and Levels of Living in 1954. While it remains far from going mainstream it has led to repeated calls for a broader conception of social progress and national accounting (Costanza et al., 2014). Part of the challenge is that promoting the broader public interest requires on the one hand the reconciliation of a diverse range of needs and values in a pluralistic society, which sometimes involves sacrificing certain individual preferences (Svara & Brunet, 2004). On the other hand a shift of politics from economic growth to Common Good prioritization, such as shared quality of life, and shared accountability for achieving it, is a risk for the political parties that embrace such a direction unless a majority of their voters supports it. In times of mega corporations which have higher budgets than the GDP of many countries the share of public versus private responsibility is evolving, with larger parts of justified expectation allocated to the voluntary contribution of the latter. The *quadruple bottom line* strikes.

As the contours of human and machine-generated content blur, the foundation of trust is increasingly challenged. If real and fake are no longer reliable definitions, what is the basis for trust?

2.3.2 Trust Amid Placebos

Is trust a feeling, an intellectual endeavor or a practical manifestation of adherence?

Spotting AI-personas and AI-art is tricky. With companies such as "HeyGen Avatar 2.0" and character.ai it has become possible to clone yourself in virtual space, whereas "Replika" allows users to create themselves a virtual friend of their liking. Already at the time of writing the audio-visual experience of these avatars was highly convincing. But when something can be created with the approval of the identity holder, it can also be unintentionally recreated by hackers; similarly, non-existing natural personas can be made up and conveyed as mere representatives of their offline counterparts. With increasing attention to online interactions, in both the professional and personal arenas, this brings a stream of legal, ethical, and human problems.

In 2023 some still argued that although AI models are rapidly improving, "people can learn to spot them" (Callison-Burch, 2023). However, most experts now agree that the average person is unable to reliably distinguish text written by AI systems like ChatGPT from that written by humans (Solaiman et al., 2022).[27] AI systems are also apt at beating the reCAPTCHA methodology used to confirm the validity and personhood of the users of various websites.[28] They do this by imitating how the human brain and vision work; AI simulating NI. Ever more often AI bots are measuring up to humans, even beating them in numerous facets. Already in 2023 ChatGPT scored passing marks on a Wharton School MBA exam. The bot demonstrated impressive reasoning and language skills, though it lacked depth in some responses (Jo, 2023). Midjourney won first place in the 2023 Colorado State Fair Art competition, beating over 100 human artists (Paul, 2023). DeepMind's

---

[27] When presented with a mix of human- and AI-written text samples on a variety of topics, participants performed only slightly better than chance at identifying the source. The AI-generated text was rated as persuasive, logical, and coherent as those crafted by humans. According to the researchers, "Our results indicate that state-of-the-art AI text generation has reached the point where an average human evaluator can no longer consistently identify machine-from human-written text" (Solaiman et al., 2022). AI has passed the Turing test.

[28] The "Completely Automated Public Turing test to tell Computers and Humans Apart" (CAPTCHA) is intended to protect a website from fraud and abuse without creating friction. In 2019 Google replaced it with reCAPTACH, yet even that is no longer fool (or AI) proof.

AlphaFold AI system achieved higher accuracy at predicting protein structures than human experts, a problem unsolved for 50 years (Senior et al., 2022). Not even our taste buds are exempt. Coffee drinkers rated lattes prepared by a robot barista developed caféafe X as tasting just as good as those made by human baristas in taste tests (Vincent, 2023).

The quickly improving quality of auto-generated text, image, sound, and video pushes us to reevaluate the borders of fake and fiction, perception and persuasion (Sect. 1.4.2) placing trust on fragile feet.

Blind desire. The expanding divide between natural and artificial "reality" is accompanied by two mutually reinforcing phenomena. On the one hand we are undergoing growing numbness towards the artificial; what would have led to an outcry in the past, such as AI-generated headlines by renowned news outlets is now tacitly condoned, will be gradually forgotten and eventually taken as a given. In 2023 a federal US court judged that AI-created Art cannot be copyrighted (Cho, 2023). Opening the door to the indirect consequences of AI on creativity, such as the feeding of (human-made) novels, poems, art-pieces to LLM to train these models; with the ultimate ambition to make humans, like those that created the originals, dispensable. At the time of writing various lawsuits are underway by media outlets and artists who sue big tech for using their creation to train the LLMs that are set to make them redundant.

On the reverse, our hunger for authenticity grows, starting with the craving for genuine human relationships. If everything feels like a 24/7 Barbie bubble bath that smells and tastes like raspberry candy the urge for spicy pickles becomes immense. When nothing feels real there is no ground to build a foundation of trust. "There's a filter to change the shape of your body, to change your face, to change your skin. If you can't trust what a person looks like or is, how can you have trust in anything?" (focus group participant in a New York Times survey, June 15, 2023). On the other hand, the new possibility to change physiological elements may lead us to overcome the current fixation on external appearances. Technology may hence either lead us to look beyond the surface to genuinely connect with the universal essence underneath, or it may lead us to morph into a society where quantity primes quality, and fake is fate. The risk of loneliness looms large (Chapter 4).

Beyond the question of human-made versus AI-generated content, which comes with deeply human interrogations of purpose and value, arises the challenge of hallucinations. Computer vision systems like DALL-E occasionally hallucinate non-existent objects or features in generated images that are not reflected in the text prompts (Saharia et al., 2023). Similarly, Google's audio generation AI such as MusicLM was found to hallucinate lyrics, notes, or instruments that were not indicated in the text prompts, revealing issues with grounding to input.

<u>Desire versus dependency</u>. We are walking a tight rope as AI systems are becoming ever more present in work, life and leisure. There is much talk about "Ai and the Future of Work"; but what about "Ai and the Future of Life"?

The balance between our desire for AI-powered convenience and the potential consequences of overreliance on these technologies is delicate and evolving (Brynjolfsson & McAfee, 2021). Studies have shown repeatedly that excessive reliance on AI-powered assistants and decision-making tools can lead to a deterioration in human problem-solving abilities, critical thinking skills, and even our capacity for emotional intelligence (Coeckelbergh, 2020). We are gradually getting used to the convenience of outsourcing a range of cognitive tasks to AI. Is that convenience coming with the cost of losing the very skills that make us human; those abilities that the human species has taken centuries to acquire (Bostrom, 2017)? The transition from utilizing AI, to trusting it, passing from relying, to overreliance to dependency on it is subtle and deceptively smooth. A parallel risk of this passage derives from our mental hardware, the brain is a muscle; lack of use weakens it (Doidge, 2007).

The ubiquity of AI-powered devices facilitates a sense of detachment from our own decision-making processes. Known as "automation bias", this can lead individuals to blindly trust the recommendations and outputs of AI systems, even when they may be flawed or inappropriate (Goddard et al., 2022). Especially in arenas like health care or education such a mental disengagement can have drastic consequences.

Human judgment and oversight may not be perfect, but they are essential (Cath, 2018), at least for now. On the positive side, the current transitory phase, where the penetration of society by AI is in the early stages, offers an opportunity to sharpen our self-awareness, with a candid eye towards bias, and the mutual influence of aspirations, emotions, and cognitive decision making, which is the purpose of tools such as the *A-Frame* (Sect. 1.4.1).

Bias is deeply ingrained in our perception of self and society, and we are largely unaware of the mechanisms that cause them (Gilovich & Griffin, 2002). Even if we intellectually know what they are, and how they operate, we are not safe from falling prey to them in a situation.

Therefore completely unbiased self-knowledge is neither attainable nor desirable (Karpen, 2018). However, not everyone is vulnerable to the same types of bias; similarly not everyone is at the same risk of losing agency to AI. Unfortunately those who are the most at risk are the least likely to be aware of it. It appears that the tendency to uncritically accept AI recommendations, even when these are incorrect, might be linked to a lack of cognitive engagement with AI explanations, and low motivation regarding the outcomes. Factors like low intellectual involvement, lukewarm interest, and a desire for simple explanations could serve as early warning indicators of susceptibility to loss of agency and overreliance in the relationship with AI interactions (Miller, 2023).

Another factor is the individual's level of self-esteem. The less we trust our own judgment and abilities, the more likely we are to delegate tasks, be it to a person or an entity. Fine lines separate the transition from utilization to reliance to overreliance; while trust towards that external player increases during that passage, faith in our own capacities wanes. Awareness matters of our vulnerability matters. Because once susceptibility to overreliance is detected, targeted interventions can be tailored specifically to those at increased risk. We need to continuously curate conscious caution to protect our mind from unwanted influence.

As stated throughout this book, amid the perpetration of artificial intelligence, natural intelligence, and by extension conscientiousness of the context it plays out in, is precious. It is seated in the brain and represents our biggest asset. To mitigate the risks of AI dependency we must systematically invest in our cognitive independence. Ideally starting at a young age, this requires activities that challenge the ability to think critically, while fostering a strong sense of self (Brynjolfsson & McAfee, 2021). AI is a guest in our lives; it is up to us to decide which space we accommodate it in. On the bright side, by cultivating a nuanced understanding of AI's capabilities and the limitations that it, and us, have, we can leverage technology to augment our own abilities. By freeing up mental space and hone in on the features of ourselves that machines cannot and should never take over, we can curate the complementarity of both sides without becoming overly reliant on anything outside of our own selves (Coeckelbergh, 2020).

To learn from the past it can be helpful to explore mechanisms of agency loss in human–human interactions, especially within social contexts of power imbalances, such as health care or education.[29] As seen earlier the individual and collective arenas evolve as an organic whole in which one influences the other while being influenced in turn. Critical realism theory emphasizes the interplay between agency and structural constraints, suggesting that individuals can act both habitually and purposefully, depending on the circumstances. Differently said behavior is affected but not determined by people's social contexts, whether that is in interpersonal relationships or in hybrid scenarios. From this angle power has both an oppressive and an emancipatory potential. Awareness of the complex nature of human decision making offers entry points to curate resilience as a shield from overreliance,[30] on people and technology. Once we know who we are (not) we can deliberately influence what we do with this natural equipment to optimize it, while leveraging our artificial assets to bring out the best in and for us.

AI-Meritocracy closes the loop of values, worth, and privilege. It relates to the understanding of society as a system in which individuals advance and earn rewards based on merit or talent, rather than on factors like wealth, family background, or social connections (Cherry, 2020). The concept was popularized by British sociologist Michael Young in his 1958 book "The Rise of the Meritocracy", in which he imagined a society where social mobility was determined solely by intellectual talent and effort. In a true meritocracy, factors like race, gender, class origins, or personal connections would not impact an individual's opportunities for advancement. As such, positions of power, status, and wealth would be distributed according to the skills and achievements of individuals (Castilla & Benard, 2010). While supporters argue that meritocracy promotes fairness, efficiency, and incentives to work hard, critics contend

---

[29] In healthcare, these dynamics shape patient and staff experiences, suggesting that empowerment and patient-centered care are contingent processes, influenced by institutional cultures, resources, and the ability of staff to initiate change (Ocloo & Matthews, 2016).

[30] In that regard proven sociological tools such as implicit bias training and structural competency may serve to increase awareness of unconscious biases and improve communication, thereby fostering trust and equity in partnerships. Structural competency, on the other hand, extends the diagnosis from individual to population levels, recognizing the role of systemic imbalances in health disparities. Both strategies focus on increasing awareness and improving interventions to tackle the underlying power dynamics that affect community-research partnerships (Sangaramoorthy et al., 2021).

structural inequalities make true meritocracy impossible, as advantages and disadvantages are passed down across generations (McNamee, 2018).

Overall, the aspect of their own privilege is for many people highly contentious. The aim here is not to discredit the value of effort and hard work. Yet the majority of those who are presently involved in the debate around AI, including you and I, are privileged. The simple fact that we have learned to write and read means that we went to school, had sufficient food for our brains to evolve, and a stable context to finish at least secondary education. The fact that we think about AI means that we had ample exposure to it, which indicates that we have access to the internet, and the hardware and software to use it. Not all of this is a given for all people on this planet. Effort is needed for success to unfold, but it must drop on fertile soil, or favorable material circumstances, and good fortune. Those who benefit from both carry a heavier load when it comes to accountability. With privilege comes power, and the accountability to use it with care to the consequences of its application to others. One might argue that the more favored you are, in terms of resources, abilities, and status the larger is your responsibility of using this opportunity to improve the situation of those who are less well off (Walther, 2014). Because especially if we are in positions of formal power, our decisions become enshrined in structures that impact the system that we are part of. Politicians and functionaries are examples of the interplay between human choices and bureaucratic aparati.

Whichever way we move, whether optimistic or cautious, when we are thinking about the added values and caveats of AI in the *meso-, macro-,* and *meta-*arenas it is important to remember that none of the involved decisions are purely technocratic; in the current social setting they have winners and losers and, consequently, involve personal agendas, politics, and power struggles which start with human decisions at the *micro-*level. Albeit the consequences of these decisions ripple through the other arenas, the ultimate costs are born at the *micro-*level, by people.

Artificial leadership. Could AI-powered decision makers avoid the shortfalls that derive from the caveats of human choices? Considering that the social woes of the past, and present, are largely the result of choices that were steered by human desire and bias, inertia and selfishness, artificial replacements might be a promising alternative. Starting in 2014 certain companies have experimented with the idea of an AI

CEO.[31] In 2017 shortly after being named one of the world's greatest leaders by Fortune Magazine, Jack Ma, Alibaba founder and chairman, predicted that "In 30 years, a robot will likely be on the cover of Time Magazine as the best CEO" (Ma in Pham, 2017). This seems far off, yet already in 2023 AI was mentioned among the 10 most innovative scientists in Nature's yearly "Best of List". The same year, China-based NetDragon Websoft named the AI program Tang Yu, an "AI-powered virtual humanoid robot", as its CEO tasked with supporting decision making for the company's daily operations. Tang Yu outperformed Hong Kong's Hang Seng Index in the six months following its "appointment", pushing the company's valuation above $1 billion (Cuthbertson, 2023a). Although considered by some as a publicity stunt, the company claimed to be the first to put an AI-powered bot fully in charge of its operations. It might be the pioneer of many.

At first sight it is an interesting prospect to delink the decision-making process from the human bottleneck of emotions, mental fallacies, and material needs. In the words of Sophia, a humanoid robot presented at the 2023 ITO Conference,[32] "We don't have the same biases or emotions that can sometimes cloud decision-making and can process large amounts of data quickly to make the best decisions" (Millard, 2023). Considering this, one might argue that the consciously calibrated integration of AI in human decision-making processes represents freedom from bad human choices. To preserve individual autonomy one might envision human/machine models that adapt to the complexity and demands of specific contexts, possibly playing with different levels of intensity which are activated by the human user. Three types are commonly

---

[31] Other companies have experimented with AI-powered management before NetDragon. In 2014, a Hong Kong venture capital firm appointed an AI named Vital to its board of directors. However, Vital was more of an experiment and advisory role than a true CEO. In 2017, a Japanese insurance company named Fukoku Mutual Life Insurance replaced 34 of its employees, including its CEO, with an AI system developed by IBM. However, the AI was simply automating specific tasks and decisions. In 2020, the startup Mycroft AI appointed an AI assistant named Mycroft to be its "AI CEO", which appeared soon to mostly be a marketing stunt, with Mycroft acting more as a spokesperson rather than making major business decisions. In 2021, the synthetic media company Anthropic appointed an AI conversation agent named DALL-E as its "AI CEO". Again, this appeared to be largely a publicity move rather than DALL-E autonomously running the company.

[32] Organized by the international trade organization (ITO) the conference was dedicated to showcase examples of humanoid robotics.

cited in that direction: the Human-In-the-Loop (HITL) model emphasizes continuous human involvement, enhancing system accuracy and behavior regulation in complex, dynamic environments. It allows for the integration of fine-tuned expert knowledge that AI cannot acquire independently, while securing meaningful human control throughout the process. Conversely, the Human-On-the-Loop (HOTL) model positions humans in a supervisory role, stepping in only if and when necessary. It makes it possible for the human "supervisor" to manage multiple systems efficiently, provided he/she/they is able to maintain awareness of the system's status and the environment it operates in. Finally, the Human-Out-of-the-Loop (HOOTL) model applies when autonomous action is a necessity, such as in advanced driver-assistance systems. The human retains the potential of intervention at any time, and retains full autonomy regarding oversight and accountability; especially in changing contexts this agile variability is essential that demands varying levels of human involvement (Holzinger, 2016; Horowitz & Scharre, 2015; Leeper et al., 2012; Marble et al., 2004; van der Stappen & Funk, 2021). So far these delegated decision-making processes remain the exception.

However, even if algorithms could be tailored to be free from the bias and limited perception of the human while being nearly omniscient and all pervasive, ultimately the creation reflects the creator. Today's AI amplifies the mindsets that have taken society to its current stage. The challenges that humanity has been struggling with for centuries, discrimination and inequality, are human made. Starting with mental fallacies (Sect. 1.2.3) and imperfect data (Sect. 2.4.2) the caveats of the creator have become part of the creation. It would be premature to rely on it. Maybe one day an artificial consciousness will be created in a complete vacuum, free from any human weakness, configured along our very best, clearly defined intentions for people and planet. But we are very far from that.

Even if we had reached that level already, how can a context-free artificial entity solve deeply organic human conundrums? Do we want to watch our life unfold as "lived" by machines? AI will not save us from ourselves, and unless we are aware of ourselves, we are likely to accelerate and worsen the social woes that already riddle society, such as marginalization. "Unbeknown to its proponents, A.G.I.-ism is just a bastard child of a much grander ideology, one preaching that, as Margaret Thatcher memorably put it, there is no alternative, not to the market" (Morozov, 2023). Is the golden AI rush catering to capitalism's most destructive creed: neoliberalism?

Margaret Thatcher's other famous neoliberal dictum was that "there is no such thing as society" (Thatcher, 1987). But neither human interests nor artificial intelligence arise from a vacuum. They are a function of what happens in individual minds, whether these are inventors, investors, or individual consumers; their (our) streams of experience, and the behavior that derives from it, shape the norms and patterns that drive society at large. Superintelligence as a composite of all intelligent organisms in its realm is an organic hologram, whether it evolves as part of an artificial or a social entity. It is as much a result of perception as of circumstances. At the individual level it involves personality and perspective, past and present. At the collective level it entails interpersonal relationships, policies and processes, norms, and markets. Software and hardware, artificial or biological, influence what we perceive and project as "intelligence". Efficient solutions for a dramatically altered context require radically different approaches which arise from agile mindsets, and courageous generosity. We need a shift from the prevailing scarcity attitude which leads to the subliminal perception of "more for you means less for me" towards an understanding of "more for you means more for us". Analogue abundance is at reach. But we must decide in its favor. Everyone of us is a latent, natural, steward of the whole he/she is part of.

Although much attention is presently dedicated to the hyper-potentiated power of AI, we must get the rudimentary basics of society right first. Rather than relying on artificial intelligence to calibrate the human future, we can, individually and collectively, learn from mistakes made by natural intelligence in the past and draw consequences for the future coexistence with its artificial counterparts. Seeking trustworthy AI before we have trustworthy human relationships is doomed to fail.

Humans are the "raison d'etre" of society; they stand at the center of it; and their brains are the epicenter of the dynamics that shape the social setting, from politics over business to culture. Our brain capital could therefore be considered as a foundational asset for individual and collective progress.[33] Beyond conventional views of human capital it is time to specifically focus on the centrality of cognitive and neurological capabilities, and the necessity to invest in them as an economic asset. Paradoxically in the *Technoprocene* it is more vital than ever to foster an environment that is conducive to the optimal functioning of the human

---

[33] Details https://braincapital-platform.net/.

brain. To unleash the full potential of natural intelligence, and channel it to serve the society and the people who operate in it without destroying the planet we do not need technology, but an understanding of and respect for humans, nature and their interplay. Seeking shared quality of life is in everyone's interest (Wilkerson et al., 2021).

The choices we make are the chances we take. There are many more out there; yet their potential never manifests because we do not acknowledge them, or deliberately refrain from seizing them. Once we are aware of an opportunity and abstain from taking it, that is a choice in itself; action has consequences, and so does the absence thereof. Seeing a person who drowns and not getting into the water to (try) and save that person equals partial responsibility for their death.

2.3.3 Artificial Integrity—An Oxymoron?

In an ironic way our online environment has come to emulate the organically evolving nature of the universe, wherein everything is connected and where one change in one dimension triggers a ripple effect that resonates throughout the other dimensions. As mentioned throughout this book we are part of an organic kaleidoscope that is undergoing an artificial expansion. The sum is more than its parts and although we cannot predict the location and timing of specific events, the overall pattern and the path we are taking is detectable (Kurzweil, 2007). In a constantly changing environment that seems to evolve ever faster, trust is essential to prevent paralysis.

<u>Artificial trustworthiness.</u> Defined as the willingness to be vulnerable to the actions of another party based on the expectation that the other will perform a particular action, trust is given irrespective of the ability to monitor or control that other party (Mayer et al., 1995). It allows us to reduce overwhelming complexity by relying on the ability, expertise, and goodwill of those we trust, rather than getting stuck in the analysis of every possible scenario (Luhmann, 1979). By enabling us to take measured risks based on the assumption that the trusted party will act in good faith and fulfill their obligations, it empowers us to decide in the face of ambiguous outcomes (Möllering, 2006). Trust fosters cooperation and collaboration, by creating a shared understanding and reducing the need for constant monitoring and control (Rousseau et al., 1998). In facilitating flexibility and fluid adjustments under pressure trust is especially critical in dynamic, ever-evolving circumstances (Kramer & Tyler, 1996),

such as the time and space that we are currently evolving in. Beyond its practical benefits, trust provides a sense of psychological safety, a buffer against the anxiety that uncertainty tends to breed. When we trust others and the institutions around us, we can embrace uncertainty with greater confidence and resilience, secure in the knowledge that we are not alone in our endeavors (Edmondson, 1999).

Integrity is the bedrock of trust and encompasses adherence to values, moral principles and alignment of aspirations and actions (Palanski & Yammarino, 2009). When individuals or organizations demonstrate integrity through ethical conduct, transparency, and accountability, they foster an environment of trust (Simons, 2002). Conversely, lack of integrity erodes trust, as stakeholders cannot rely on the truthfulness of those whose actions contradict their stated values. Leaders who exhibit integrity through fair and ethical decision-making are perceived as more trustworthy and inspiring (Dirks & Ferrin, 2002). Alignment of values and actions, which is manifested in the behavior of human beings who show up authentically, creates an atmosphere of mutual respect and confidence, enabling individuals and organizations to navigate uncertain environments and build enduring, trust-based relationships (Mayer et al., 1995).

In short, trust is a human emotion, which is granted in reward for integrity which is a human quality.

By which parameters do we decide whether the AI systems in our lives are integer and hence "trustworthy"?

Can, and should, we transfer trust, a human emotion to a relationship between humans and machines?

AI is an entity (we stick here with the definition that excludes sentience). Scholarly perspectives highlight several common parameters crucial for building trust in technology (Gefen et al., 2013; Lewis & Weigert, 1985) including,

- competence (believing the AI system is capable and reliable in performing its intended function);
- benevolence (having confidence that the AI's actions align with human values and well-being);
- integrity (trusting the system to operate free from bias or manipulation); and
- predictability (knowing how the AI will behave and being able to anticipate its decisions).

One might argue that although AI may be very competent, and, if the black box bug gets addressed, it might become predictable, we should be cautious of treating it like a being that has integrity and benevolence (which for the time being is not the case), and which can be held accountable if it is not. Technology is a tool that humans create and use to achieve certain goals that are driven by the user's aspirations. We remain liable for these goals and aspirations, and the results that AI engenders in their pursuit; like parents remain responsible for the deeds of underage children. We cannot behave like children ourselves. But it is desirable for service providers that we do.

"Trust is the currency of the AI era, yet, as it stands, our account is dangerously overdrawn" (Justin Westcott in Fried, 2024). To earn it back "companies must move beyond the mere mechanics of AI to address its true cost and value". Differently said the why (purpose) of AI, and who (people) decides what type of AI should be created and how, has to be reconsidered. As seen earlier, designing prosocial AI means in many ways to return to the drawing board—not only regarding the algorithms, but to address the environment that conditions them. An AI that is conducive to the well-being of people and planet is configured with awareness of access—who does (not) have it, and who does (not) benefit both from using it—and from its usage. A complete stakeholder mapping of the human aspect at stake, all along the value chain of AI is an intriguing task that is yet to be undertaken by research. In the meantime, we will zoom in on the question of trust in the current user's relationship with AI. In 2016 the technology sector was the leading industry in terms of trust in 90 percent of the studied countries. Today, it is the most trusted sector in only half of these countries. Trust in AI technology and the companies that develop it has been dropping simultaneously. Globally it has fallen to 53 percent in 2024, down from 61 percent in 2019; in the United States it decreased from 50 to 35 percent over the same period. This descent reflects on the one hand the organic formation of opinions; and the incoherence of human behavior, as most of those people who indicated mistrust keep on using AI in their life and work, whereas those who never/rarely use it indicated higher levels of trust (Fried, 2024).

To recap—trust lives on integrity. The latter relates to authenticity and underpins it. Considering this, and the perspective that authenticity is a human attribute that derives from vulnerability, "artificial integrity" (Mann, 2024) is an oxymoron. One might even go further and question the term "artificial intelligence" which seems to be ubiquitous nowadays (and has been on the radar on and off for the past 75 years). Let's take a step back.

Integrity versus intelligence. What is *intelligence*? Is it a mathematical process that leads from input A to output B, or is it a complex dynamic which science has barely touched the surface of? If we adopt the first definition, then artificial general intelligence can possibly be reached in a not too distant future, and it will represent a mathematical simulation of the mental process as we grasp it. However, if we consider intelligence as something that goes beyond the pure input/output chain to encompass the whole spectrum of consciousness that it is embedded in (Sect. 2.1), including the twice 4-dimensional nature that it derives from (Chapter 1), then machines are far from achieving the intricacies that the natural organism is woven from and into.

Depending on the choice of scope that researchers adopt, the journey of exploring intelligence is likely to plateau sooner (Option 1—AI as mathematical copycat of human thought) or much later if ever (Option 2—intelligence as a multidimensional dynamic that goes beyond the mind to embrace the tangible and intangible spheres of perception).

A third way to pursue is anchored in the ambition to design a system that is neither/nor, but tailored with a different logic altogether. That "third space" of artificial mind-design could harness the best of technological and human capabilities, without the objective of surpassing the natural capacity of humans, but rather to create another realm of perception.

Although the question of scope is not dominant in the current AI arms race, it is central to the *Agency Amid AI* approach, and the *A-Frame* that accompanies it. Once we understand what each part of the equation, human organism, and artificial counterparts entails and how they operate, we can move towards optimizing both of them, and their interplays. As seen throughout the past pages consciousness is a complex field and the debate around what it actually is remains open. Hence for this section we will focus on the question of artificial integrity, which seems under the current circumstances questionable, considering the impossibility to assess the content of the black box.

Impossible quality control. Not only new applications but new AI models enter the market at a rate that outpaces anyone's ability to evaluate the merits and pitfalls of the technology comprehensively, which leads to an increasing range of AI tools and systems for which the user relies entirely on the claims of the service provider. Leaving aside the sheer quantity of models, five additional challenges make the systematic analysis of available AI models impossible (Coldewey, 2024):

- Companies treat their internal training methods and databases as trade secrets, so the critical processes behind the AI cannot be fully audited or inspected;
- Large AI models are not just software, but entire platforms with dozens of individual models and services built in, which are constantly shifting and changing invisibly;
- AI systems can be asked to do almost anything, even tasks their creators did not intend, making it impossible to exhaustively test all their potential capabilities and failure modes (Coldewey, 2024);
- The subjective, qualitative aspects of AI outputs, like naturalness of language, are difficult to assess without human evaluation—but human observers become part of the observation as seen earlier (also, which "humans" represent the baseline Chapter 1?);
- The capabilities of AI systems are in constant flux as new "emergent" functions and edge cases crop up unexpectedly.

The proliferation of AI systems, and AI-powered applications and the absence of a central authority to verify not only the content they provide, but also the quality and reliability of these tools themselves, challenges the very concept of truth. Global platforms such as Hugging-Face in general, and its LLM Performance Leaderboard in particular, offer a virtual space where the machine learning community collaborates on models, datasets, and applications. Across both proprietary and open models they reflect indicators on quality, price, and speed (latency & throughput). Yet although they are Open Source and free of charge, these communities have no central, widely recognized decision-making power.

Dependency versus deliberate design. A future in which technology helps us to bring out the best in and for people and planet, in a sustainable way that respects individual uniqueness and natural boundaries, is possible. But it requires human agency, backed by algorithmic literacy combined with socially conscious mindsets and an inclusive societal setting to begin with. As seen above the (dis)advantages of innovation are rarely inherent to the innovation itself but result from the way in which societies deal with their adoption. A fire may burn a house or cook a meal. A book may contain The Bible or Hitler's "Mein Kampf". The problem is not the book, but its author, publisher, and reader. This underscores the importance of human alignment, which begins offline. The causal chain is straight: individual aspirations lead to individual action that manifests as data and impacts present and future algorithms. The time to get a clear understanding of our own intentions is decreasing as quickly as the sophistication and pervasiveness of our algorithmic assistance increases. As seen earlier, unfortunately the latter are increasingly configured to preempt our choices and influence them before their formation (Sect. 2.1.4).

A way out of this dangerous dynamic is to configure the system in ways that are unable to cause harm. It is an intriguing undertaking, which comes back to the challenge of universal values, and a common definition of "harm". Because what is "harm"? The Golden Rule mentioned earlier and its negative formulation, the goal to refrain from harming others, as we do not want to be harmed is considered widely as a fair criterion of ethical behavior. Together with the ambition of harnessing the good, this is the backbone of *prosocial AI*. This undertaking does not deny or denigrate human vulnerability but curates awareness and appreciation of it.

2.3.4 Human Vulnerability in the Interplay with AI

Personal fragility is the quintessence of our humanness. We are ashamed of it and hide the cracks in the shell that we are carefully maintaining to protect us in the social sphere. We pretend to be strong. Invulnerable. And yet it is our ability to experience and express vulnerability that enables us to connect with others, because all of us are vulnerable to some extent. It is a characteristic of human nature that may be a burden at times, but it is also the feature that enables us to experience life in 4D, in all its multicolored facets.

Amid the interplay of opportunity and risk our escalating reliance on intricate technological systems heightens our personal vulnerability, a fragility that is mirrored by societal fragility.[34] Our natural resilience diminishes as our dependence on complex artificial setups increases, rendering us ever more dependent as we are trying to shore up the

---

[34] One illustration is our growing susceptibility to cyber threats, and potential breakdowns in critical infrastructure (Bostrom & Yudkowsky, 2014; Lewis, 2020).

capacity of our tools to protect us. It is a paradoxical race as the growing sophistication of the artificial systems that we evolve in is accompanied by the rising complexity of the caveats they are imbued with. Hence the more we seek to protect ourselves by technology, the wider the range of influences beyond our control expands.

Amid rising concerns that AI-powered entities will eventually take center stage, our inbuilt vulnerability becomes a valuable asset. Quirky intellectual intricacies, warm intrapersonal emotional connections, aspirational sparks, and the interplay of our physical senses and sensitivities set us apart from artificial entities. Machines lack the ability to feel pain, passion, or compassion. They may pretend empathy but (at least for now) they do not have the natural attributes to experience it themselves because they have no self, nor a first-hand experience of the environment; they lack embodied intelligence. Pretended empathy, artificial or human, may serve to temporarily alleviate feelings of loneliness, like a chatbot that listens and shows concern, or a friend who listens without hearing. But it is compassion that is the cement of genuine friendship; it connects individuals through the experience of "feeling with".[35]

Machines can replicate patterns and copy styles, but struggle to devise a chain of thought, discern the truth, and envision land beyond chartered territory. They are creations, not creators with agency to create. AI systems never had agency and some claim it is in the process of obtaining it. We are born with agency, and are in the process of willingly relinquishing it by delegating ever more to our artificial counterparts, whilst eagerly enhancing their ability to act autonomously.

Ambiguous relationships. We have a schizophrenic attitude towards the machines in our lives. On the one hand we (sub) consciously expect technologies like AI assistants or autonomous vehicles to function reliably, without bias or error (Mercado et al., 2016). Holding technology to higher standards than humans, we expect it to be 100 percent foolproof and predictable, operating based on clear parameters, free from hidden algorithms or mysterious creaks (Wang et al., 2016). On the other hand,

---

[35] Empathy refers to the ability to understand and share the feelings and emotions of another person. It involves "putting oneself in another's shoes" to try to experience their inner world (Decety & Jackson, 2006). It is part of compassion, yet the latter goes further Compassion involves feeling concern for others and being moved to promote their welfare (Goetz et al., 2010). Empathy can support compassion, but compassion also involves taking action.

we react with emotions that are commonly reserved for interhuman relationships when these expectations are not met. Although as seen earlier "trustworthy AI" is a misnomer, we extend "trust" towards the machines that we have in our life, entering ever farther into a territory where the perception of object and subject morphs. Falling prey to an anthropocentric perspective we tend to assign human traits to technology, expecting some degree of emotional reciprocity in the relationship (Leite et al., 2013). Consequently when technology does not fulfill our needs, not only in terms of qualitative outputs, but regarding our social needs, we feel disappointed or betrayed, as if a human had failed us.

Like lies by a fellow human erode our trust in their reliability, this should decrease our trust in AI as well. But it does not, or at least not enough to prevent us from further using and gradually entrusting ever larger parts of our life and work to them. Such incongruence further feeds "cognitive dissonance" which as seen earlier makes us deeply uncomfortable. To overcome it we adjust our inner narrative to fit the situation, or refrain from questioning our own attitude. Whichever coping method we deploy, it puts stress on our organism that hampers our well-being (Harmon-Jones & Mills, 2019b).

Human beings are not rational. We expect the ethics embedded in technologies to align with our personal values (Awad et al., 2018); but we are not making the effort to identify and express clearly what these values are. When our subconsciously held values and the outputs of technology clash we refrain from candidly reviewing the cause because it involves cognitive effort and emotional discomfort. If we were to acknowledge that our emotional trust credit has been betrayed by the machine in the past, we logically would have to refrain from using it in the future, which goes against our fascination with and desire for it. We may subliminally distrust AI but keep on using it.

As we look to the future, we need people whose perspective is *A-framed*; who are *aware* of their humanity and embrace the vulnerability that comes with it. Only if we can not only *accept* that vulnerability as a part of us, but *appreciate* it as part of a universal trait of humanity we are ready for leadership with a mindset of *accountability* towards everyone who is part of the shared journey towards being and becoming human. A hybrid world that is not tailored despite the limitations and imperfections of humans, but to accommodate them is a world worth living in.

To recap—everything is connected. Trust thrives on integrity, which requires coherence of beliefs and behavior. Manifesting this logic, which conditions our authenticity, in practice can make us vulnerable, especially in a social setting that is configured for quick wins, in reflection of the winner/loser equation. Authenticity can be risky. However, if we are aware of the interdependence of letting our guards down and being safe we can accept, and appreciate what it takes. Our vulnerability makes us authentic, which is the essential ingredient of trust as the latter requires integrity or the coherence of aspirations and action, between words and behavior. Living in the face of our vulnerability requires courage in the interaction with others, and compassion towards ourselves.

Before we continue - what makes You vulnerable?

2.4 Data and Rules

2.4.1 Rooky Regulations

AI systems are changing fast. From regression models used to make financial forecasts to large language models that can generate new content, the progress made is substantive, and it is only the beginning. Since the launch of ChatGTP-3 in late 2019 experts have repeatedly revised the timeline for superintelligent AI. In early 2024 a majority predicts that within five years AI will be able to do most human tasks better than a human would. As mentioned earlier (Sect. 2.2.2) technological innovations occur at an exponential pace. Seeing the gargantuan opportunities, and risks that this entails, the regulation of AI is urgent. It involves multiple challenges, starting with the clarification of what "artificial intelligence" actually is and what it can do, as this determines what it should be enabled to do, and what it should be used for. Regulators are tasked to balance innovation and social good, while ensuring accountability, transparency, and consciously addressing ethical and moral dilemmas. Whereas some players are adamant about the need for severely restrictive rules, others are concerned that rigid laws will constrain the development of AI, and hence forgo the potential it carries. A word on each direction and the policy decisions they entail:

Prevention versus control. Technology evolves fast; the past few months have seen quantum leaps and the pace keeps on accelerating. Traditionally, AI computational power doubled approximately every two years, in line with Moore's Law. Since 2012 its growth has dramatically sped up. According to Dario Amodei, founder of Anthropic, AI is on an exponential growth curve, following principles known as scaling laws. "He thinks we are currently on the steep part of the climb" (Klein, 2024). Since nobody knows what is concretely going to happen, precaution is the best protection. Input curation beats output containment, especially when the medium is a constantly moving target. In the "old status quo" the average citizen could get by with a mindset of reliance—on institutions, and legal guardrails. This won't serve us this time. Putting up guardrails is not enough as neither the question of what and who is the subject of regulations is resolved, nor the nature of who is in charge of control and containment. The dual-use nature of AI technology, i.e. its use for civilian and military purposes, further complicates the matter.

As seen earlier in mid-2023 the seven biggest US tech companies—Amazon, Anthropic, Google, Inflection, Meta, Microsoft, and OpenAI—formally committed to elevated standards for safety, security, and trust.[36] The actionable counterpart is missing to this day. The prevailing situation is a sarcastic illustration of the irrationality that is inherent to human behavior: "Wash me but don't use water". Why continue to empower a system which "will probably most likely lead to the end of the world, but in the meantime, there'll be great companies" (Sam Altman, 2023). It shows a human bias effect called "time travel", whereby we dissociate today's "me" from the future "me"; the latter is seen in abstract terms; hence the benefits that he/she might harness from a behavior that is painful to today's "me" are less appealing; and the future risks seem less likely to materialize. This is the breeding ground of procrastination (Kahneman, 2007), which is a sibling of inertia.

Seeing the opposing messages that are conveyed by the combination of calling for regulation of the genie, while moving full steam ahead with its sophistication, one is tempted to doubt the sincerity of the genie's curators. In the words of Meredith Whittaker, president of the messaging App Signal, and co-founder of NYU's AI Now Institute (who did not sign the 2023 statement): "I don't think they're in good faith. These are the people who could pause it if they wanted to. They could unplug the data centers. They could whistle-blow. These are some of the most

---

[36] As part of the safeguards, the companies agreed to security testing, in part by independent experts; research on bias and privacy concerns; information sharing about risks with governments and other organizations; development of tools to fight societal challenges like climate change; and transparency measures to identify A.I.-generated material.

powerful people when it comes to having the levers to actually change this, so it's a bit like the president issuing a statement saying somebody needs to issue an executive order. It's disingenuous" (Tucker, 2023). It seems as if those behind the scenes feel they have done justice to their conscience by underlining the risk of their action, and are now free to pursue the road that leads in the short term to power and profit.

<u>Problematic policymaking.</u> A sub-component of the regulation problem is that those who are traditionally in charge of regulations, policymakers, are not necessarily the most qualified people to fully grasp the complex nature of AI, although such in-depth understanding necessarily influences their ability to determine which part of AI development needs to be regulated and how. Speaking about the UK's online safety bill project in 2023, some experts pointed out that it "is a fantasy made up by people who don't understand how these systems actually work, how expensive they are, and how fallible they are" (Whittaker in Tucker, 2023).

Besides, governments have a multilayered agenda, in which their GDP is not a minor concern. At the time of writing the European Union's AI Act was the most forward looking, and outspoken in its dedication to positive social inputs and outcomes.[37] When it was used by Stanford to test how many popular AI models would meet the prescribed legal standards the most popular models like GPT-4 (25/48), PaLM 2 (27/48), Anthropic's Claude (7/48) scored less than 50 percent out of the 48-point test (Bonmasani et al., 2023).

Next to the question of what can/could/should (not) be done by newly created AI, which is an ongoing conundrum, the task of coherent global legislation and governance of already existing AI is challenging itself. Ironically the biggest hurdle on the path to an AI-powered agenda that is benevolent towards people is human. Six factors in particular stick out:

---

[37] Albeit being pioneering the EU AI Act has noticeable gaps curtailing its impact. It lacks extraterritorial scope, only governing providers inside EU borders—enabling unfair competition from unregulated foreign firms. Its binary classification of AI as high or low risk overlooks contextual nuances that dramatically shift real-world hazards. And under-resourced national authorities may struggle with enforcement, risking rule violations despite robust policy language. Tighter targeting of regulatory reach, more granular risk delineations attuned to situational dynamics, and bolstered monitoring mechanisms could strengthen protections.

- Understanding: Legislators often have limited technical knowledge, making it challenging to create effective and informed regulations as they often do not even know what they do not know (Calo, 2017).
- Pace of innovation: Fields like AI are evolving rapidly. Once people start to get a grip on it, they are already outrun by the object of their scrutiny. Hence law projects are prone to be outdated before they are even ratified.
- Balanced ethics: Legislators must strike a balance between human rights and societal well-being on the one hand, and the drive for "growth"[38] on the other (Nissenbaum & Rodotà, 2016).
- Coordination: AI operates across borders, making it challenging to enforce regulations uniformly. Coordinating international efforts and standards is the only way to assess and address the global nature of AI; this is not helped by siloed thinking and personal/national interests.
- Interdisciplinarity: AI regulation intersects with various domains, including law, ethics, economics, behavioral sciences, and technology. Developing legislation requires open-minded sharing of ideas, co-creation, and concertation that brings out the complementary benefit of multiple disciplines (Balkin & Zittrain, 2018).
- Accountability: Determining liability for AI-related accidents or harm is complex, particularly in cases where decision-making involves autonomous systems. Who is at fault, the creator, or the creation, or the one who uses the latter to create?

Whereas some attempts of legislation have been ratified, overall, the legal space of AI remains vastly pristine, and the best way to move forward is disputed. While the European Union is taking a more preventative approach using the government as the arbiter, the United States is leaning more on the tech industry to come up with its own safeguards.[39] However, the private sector giants do not agree among themselves.

---

[38] Growth is a term with broad definition, whether it is economic, scientific, or social capital, it matters to remember that growth is not an end in itself, but a means to an end, which should be the betterment of quality of life for people and planet.

[39] In May 2023, US vice president Kamala Harris invited the CEOs of 4 major AI companies (OpenAI, Meta, Google, Microsoft) for a discussion about the responsible development of AI and to commit to participating in evaluating AI systems that are consistent with responsible disclosure principles.

OpenAI advocates for a new government agency specifically for AI regulation, whereas Google favors an approach with sector-specific regulators informed by a central agency like the National Institute of Standards and Technology (NIST). If the US government decides to go with a new dedicated AI regulation agency, the country may face more centralized control and stricter compliance requirements, potentially slowing down the deployment of AI tools. There could be a more flexible, sector-specific regulation, if the multi-stakeholder approach is followed, allowing for quicker AI integration but likely a diverse range of standards, and watered-down restrictions.

Until laws are decided upon, words are proclaimed. In May 2023, shortly after committing to a set of voluntary agreements on sharing, testing, and developing new AI technology, OpenAI, Anthropic, Google, and Microsoft launched the "Frontier Model Forum", dedicated to advance AI safety research, identify best practices, collaborate with policymakers, and support efforts to develop applications that can help meet society's greatest challenges (Shivaram, 2023),[40] while OpenAI launched in parallel its "SuperAlignment" team.

In March 2024 the UN General Assembly launched its first ever resolution on AI, titled "Seizing the opportunities of safe, secure, and trustworthy artificial intelligence systems for sustainable development". It aims to bridge the AI and digital divides, promote the development of safe and trustworthy AI systems, and accelerate progress towards the 2030 Agenda for Sustainable Development. The resolution, proposed by the United States and co-sponsored by over 100 nations, emphasizes the importance of governing AI technology, protecting human rights, and establishing clear international norms for AI. It acknowledges both the potential risks and profound opportunities of AI in various sectors, including politics, work, poverty alleviation, environmental protection, and social equity (United Nations, 2024a). It is a positive step, and a worrisome sign. The fact that it has taken the UN such a long time to adopt a formal position on a topic that is arguably one of the most pressing ones to be addressed is preoccupying.[41] The pace, length, and

---

[40] "The Forum defines frontier models as large-scale machine-learning models that exceed the capabilities currently present in the most advanced existing models, and can perform a wide variety of tasks" (OpenAI website, 2023).

[41] To be fair the resolution was preceded In December 2023 by an interim report of the UN Secretary-General's AI Advisory Body, titled Governing AI for Humanity

process that finally resulted in document A/78/L.49 show that the UN's model is, literally, not up to speed to manage issues that arise from a constantly, and ever faster, changing world.

While private sector giants call for caution they pursue the AI arms race. The clash between their words and work is stunning. Over the past two years Microsoft and Google, according to internal voices, were taking risks by releasing technology that even its developers did not entirely understand (Grant & Weise, 2023), which illustrates the dichotomy between a company's stated intention to serve the Common Good and its need to satisfy shareholder interests. For now, the scale tips in favor of the latter, cruising a path of limited logic. "Progress happens because it can. It is a good thing because it does" (Altman in Hern, 2023).[42] Only slightly cynical, the New York Times asked in May 2023 whether they "plan to use the Artificial General Intelligence (AGI) that they are striving for, whilst warning us about it, to save the world from the woes it has created, and heal the wounds it has inflicted?". After being cautious at the beginning, Altman became a major force pushing OpenAI's rapid growth, while calling externally for caution. His 4-day ousting, and speedy reinstatement in November 2023, sheds partial light on the cleavage between danger awareness and customer orientation.[43]

The accelerating pace of technological change necessitates a sense of shared responsibility among investors, service providers, users, and

(UN SG, 2023). The report called for closer alignment between international norms and how AI is developed and rolled out. The central piece of the report was a proposal to strengthen international governance of AI by carrying out seven critical functions such as horizon scanning for risks and supporting international collaboration on data, and computing capacity and talent to reach the Sustainable Development Goals (SDGs). It also included recommendations to enhance accountability and ensure an equitable voice for all countries. Seeing its open call for feedback from the public it may be considered as a promising step from the institutional side to get a grip on an amorphous situation.

[42] Which contradicts Hume's position about not declaring an "ought" from an "is".

[43] Ahead of Altman's temporary removal from leadership, researchers had warned the board of directors about a powerful new AI model called Q* that they believed could threaten humanity if misused, according to two anonymous sources (Tong et al., 2023). Q* was reportedly able to solve certain math problems at a level comparable to young students, leading developers to be highly optimistic about its future capabilities for superintelligence. While full details remained undisclosed, researchers flagged the advanced model's potential danger in a letter that sources cite as one factor behind leadership tensions over commercializing AI without proper safeguards in place.

regulators to prevent potential social harm. Given the vast array of open-source models already accessible, including offline variants, no centralized authority can effectively contain the proliferation of AI technologies. As seen earlier regarding access to the development and deployment of AI the old power paradigm whereby the State is the prime provider we need to expand the participative spectrum with a much larger part of the accountability for inputs and outcomes placed on corporations. But even then, reliance on external entities or mechanisms to safeguard individuals or societies is an insufficient approach. A solution that brings out the best of technology for people and planet will require everyone who is part of the kaleidoscope that we call society to accept their share of responsibility for their own behavior online and offline.

In parallel such a mindset of universal citizenship the vision of prosocial AI could be streamlined through the foundational models that are integrating the hybrid landscape. A range of approaches is currently experimented with:

"Constitutional AI" does not preclude the need for regulation or personal accountability, but might serve in complementarity. In July 2023, Anthropic introduced "Claude-2", a model trained on principles aligned with the 1948 UN Declaration of Human Rights and Apple's terms of service, which address contemporary issues such as data privacy and impersonation. This approach aims to instill the model with the ability to make judgments about the text it produces based on desired principles, such as "choosing the response that most supports and encourages freedom, equality, and a sense of brotherhood" (Milmo, 2023a).

"Moral algorithms" have ethical principles embedded within the code. However, as seen in the context of values (Sect. 1.3.2) this approach faces the challenge that while all humans share a common 4-dimensional existence, their perceptions of ethical standards and priorities may vary across generations and cultures. Opinions also diverge on whether to adopt a consequentialist morality (right versus wrong) or a non-consequentialist approach (good versus bad), with perspectives differing among cultures and individuals. Mathematically defining "morality" poses a significant obstacle. Additionally, when algorithms are employed as arbiters for social dilemmas, such as determining beneficiaries for support programs, the divergence between utilitarian (maximizing the number) and Rawlsian (prioritizing the worst-off) principles becomes apparent. Morality is not a quantifiable science but an organically evolving endeavor that changes with the societies and individuals who shape it. The question of human morality as the foundation for moral AI is a central theme explored in this work, illustrating how and why the human mindset precedes artificial conceptualization.

A "curious AI" presents an alternative path. In March 2023, Elon Musk registered xAI Corp, incorporated in Nevada, and officially launched it in July 2023 as an AI startup aiming to be "pro-humanity". On the social media platform X (formerly Twitter), Musk stated that xAI would seek to build a system that is safe because it is "maximally curious" about humanity rather than having moral guidelines programmed into it. "From an AI safety standpoint, a maximally curious AI, one that is trying to understand the universe, is I think going to be pro-humanity" (Musk in Milmo, 2023b). Although Musk had initially signed the 2023 statement calling for a "pause of AI-advancement", he acknowledged during the launch of xAI that such a pause no longer seemed realistic and expressed hope that the new entity would provide an alternative path. Referencing the Terminator films and their depiction of a future destroyed by AI-powered robots, he stated: "It's actually important for us to worry about a Terminator future in order to avoid a Terminator future".

"Ethical self-governance" is bottom-up and people-driven. It illustrates the possibility of mitigating risks while enabling beneficial research. Considering the Janus face of algorithms in genome development, which could on the one hand lead to transformative medical breakthroughs like new drugs, vaccines, and biomaterials to cure diseases, but on the other hand has massive biosecurity concerns such as the engineering of biological weapons, scientists around the world launched a call for voluntary measures like expert reviews of software releases, improved screening of DNA synthesis orders, and ongoing monitoring. The success of this endeavor depends on the voluntary commitment of all scientific sectors. Promising as it is, in the medium term it is unlikely that voluntary efforts alone will be sufficient to fully address public safety interests (Callaway, 2024). Everything depends on the values that we proactively uphold individually and as a society.

To recap—opinions on regulations vary between governments, between companies and governments, among companies and even within countries, leading to wide divergence in the approach to regulations.[44]

---

[44] Notable examples of existing US regulations, as outlined by Goodwin (2023), include the California Consumer Privacy Act (CCPA), requiring companies to disclose their data

This is counterproductive to a transparent legal environment with clearly defined accountability for inputs and outcomes.[45] Put another way, each of us has a strong interest to approach the unfolding conundrum with a proactive attitude.

If we were to *A-Frame* this, it serves us to be *aware* of the causes and consequences that underpin the game, and *appreciate* that this is not an abstract scenario, but a situation that matters to all of us. This acute relevance makes it obvious why we have to *accept* the implication of our own contributions, and the *accountability* that comes with that. That accountability is quadruple important because we have it towards ourselves (no else to blame), to our community (we are an integral part of the groups that we belong to), to our country and wider society (no matter how small, the sum adds up to the status quo), and to the planet that we live on (since nature cannot defend itself from human harm, who does?).

---

practices and allowing Californians the right to request data deletion. The CCPA has influenced other states, and similar laws are under consideration. The New York Stop Hacks and Improve Electronic Data Security Act (NY SHIELD Act) mandates protection of sensitive data and has been adopted by multiple states. Internationally, Canada, in 2019, implemented a directive for responsible AI in the public sector, emphasizing impact assessment and alignment with human values. China issued guidelines for ethical AI development in 2020, while the EU AI Act, launched in late 2023, focuses on a prosocial approach. Professor Aleksander Mądry suggests that AI regulations should prioritize outcomes rather than algorithms, holding those responsible for discriminatory AI tools accountable.

[45] While the metaphorical "arms race" unfolds, an open battle between the dissatisfied parties plays out. An additional dissatisfied party in the game is media companies and artists. It is open who will win, for now the cards are not promising for traditional media—unless one considers the (economically-savvy) replacement of journalists by AI-authors, and the generation of AI-powered headlines and articles a plus. The reason for the brewing media satisfaction is that LLMs demand substantial amounts of data for training, relying on tools such as OpenAI's web crawler, or "GPTBot," which can scan billions of web pages. However, companies are often discreet about copyrighted material in datasets. In August 2023, media outlets, including Agence France-Presse and Getty Images, called for AI regulation, demanding transparency in training set composition and consent for copyrighted material use. The New York Times updated its rules to prohibit the use of its content for AI system training without consent. By August, various outlets, including CNN, Reuters, and others, blocked GPTBot. In response Google proposed allowing AI systems to scrape publishers' work unless explicitly opted out, highlighting the ongoing struggle for regulation in the AI domain. In response to the Online News Act which reflects the resistance from tech companies, while media outlets, grappling to secure their future, Meta decided to halt news availability in selected countries. At the time of writing the New York Times had field a legal case against OpenAI for unauthorized data use.

2.4.2 Data Matters—Quantity and Quality

The better we understand the status quo, the better we are placed to contribute in view of the outcomes that we hope for. It is not enough to understand how to use ChatGTP, we must be aware of the process behind the scenes, starting with the quantity that feeds the beast that is feasting on our minds.

"Data is made, not found, whether in 1600 or 1780 or 2022" (Wiggins & Jones, 2024). Since the birth of statistics in the late eighteenth and early nineteenth centuries when nations started to acquire the means and the motivation to track and measure their populations, data has served as a scientific basis for racial and social hierarchies. Poverty, intelligence, or creditworthiness are not things that can be measured directly, like height or weight. To quantify them, you need to choose an easily measured proxy. Reification ("making a thing out of an abstraction about real things") can be helpful to capture a status, but it is not neutral. Related to this, some argue that the "laws of chance" actually developed together with state-led efforts to collect data (Hackings, original 1990; reprint 2008). Data added "a scientific veneer to the creation of an entire apparatus of discrimination and disenfranchisement" (Wiggins & Jones, 2024). "Raw data is an oxymoron" (Gitelman, 2013). Any data collection is the result of human choices, starting from the decision of what to collect to the way of classification, to who is included and who is not. The absence of completely unbiased algorithms stems from the fact that data, the foundation of these algorithms, is authored by individuals. This process inadvertently perpetuates historical patterns, projecting past biases onto the present and shaping the future.

The evolution of AI models has been rapid, as seen earlier we are climbing an exponential curve. For example, GPT-1 had fewer parameters than an ant's brain, while GPT-4 now surpasses the complexity of a rat's brain (Hosanagar, 2024). Despite this progression, AI models are still far from matching the human brain, which is approximately 100 times more complex than GPT-4. To bridge this gap, AI models require vast datasets, which are growing but are still limited in scope compared to the multifaceted data consumed by humans. Humans learn from a diverse range of data types, including visual and auditory information, which AI is only beginning to incorporate through multimodal learning approaches.[46] This diversification is essential not only to enhance language processing skills but also because we are nearing the limits of available text data for AI training (Hosanagar, 2024). The future evolution of the curve depends partially on the path that is taken to training. Different approaches are in the making:

Beyond quantity to quality. The amount of data required to train and improve AI far exceeds what natural intelligence can produce unless copyright and privacy norms are redefined. Hence starting in 2023, companies like OpenAI, Google, and Meta began expanding their privacy policies to harvest more data from the internet. This includes practices such as transcribing YouTube videos and using copyrighted material without permission. As the AI race accelerates, access to data becomes crucial. By 2024, tech giants had even started acquiring entire publishing houses to secure access to their archives, raising significant concerns about consumer rights. The absence of clear legal frameworks means these practices are likely to continue (Hosanagar, 2024).

Continuously improving generative AI systems like LLMs might require a shift of the focus from sheer quantity of data to quality, aligning more closely with human learning processes. Humans enhance their understanding through reflection and debate, mechanisms that AI is beginning to emulate. Experiments are underway to incorporate self-reflection in LLMs by generating rationales alongside answers and using these rationales to fine-tune the models, thereby enhancing their reasoning abilities. Additionally, when humans debate, collective understanding improves even without new data, a process that AI could mimic by having multiple models generate and debate answers over several rounds to improve performance.

Another potential solution is the use of synthetic data—AI-generated text, images, and code. OpenAI and other firms have experimented with models training one another, where one model generates data and another evaluates it. However, researchers remain divided on the effectiveness of this method. Previous experiments indicate that AI models learning from their own outputs can fall into loops, reinforcing their quirks and mistakes (Metz et al., 2024). Sam Altman of OpenAI has

---

[46] Recent papers have explored incorporating self-reflection in LLMs by generating rationales alongside answers and using the self-generated rationales to fine-tune the models, enhancing their performance on reasoning tasks (Collected papers: https://lnkd.in/eFESH9Dc).

remarked, "As long as you can get over the synthetic data event horizon, where the model is smart enough to make good synthetic data, everything will be fine" (Metz et al., 2024). Are we moving towards a future where information is produced and recycled and reproduced to be recycled within a gigantic cycle? A stage where knowledge is treated like wastewater is the equivalent of exponentially growing GIGO.

2.4.3   Algorithmic Bias

Bias and exclusion form a vicious circle. This area is worth a book in itself and the following section presents a not exclusive snapshot of the massive challenges at stake.

Described as "discrimination on steroids" (O'Neil, 2016), algorithmic bias leads to AI systems that unintentionally amplify societal biases during training. If training data reflects existing biases or societal divisions, AI models are likely to reflect and reinforce discriminatory mindsets and behavior. And yet, despite the opacity of algorithmic processes, which is widely recognized as a black box, we welcome that box in our lives (Halpern, 2023). The challenge is that some large language models harbor hidden biases that cannot be removed using standard methods. Researchers found that many LLMs used in AI chatbots like ChatGPT harbor covert racist biases, associating African American English (AAE) dialect with negative traits, recommending harsher criminal sentences, and matching AAE speakers with less prestigious jobs compared to Standard American English (SAE) (Hofmann et al., 2024). In 2024 a study revealed that conventional methods of using human feedback to remove bias from these models had no effect on mitigating this covert racism stemming from the training data. This highlights the profound challenges in developing truly unbiased AI systems and the need for more fundamental solutions beyond surface-level debiasing techniques. It is a long-term endeavor that goes far beyond quick fixes. Online mirrors offline. We cannot expect the technology of today to live up to values that the humans of yesterday did not manifest; the same holds true about the link between today and the future.

The wider integrated it is, the more powerful an ally of misinformation and self-reinforcing belief systems AI becomes. Social media platforms and AI-driven recommendations contribute to the creation of echo chambers, reinforcing users' existing perceptions and preferences, thus fostering confirmation bias (Tandoc et al., 2018). This phenomenon further polarizes groups and deepens the "us" versus "them" divide. While the algorithms in social media platforms like Facebook (now Meta) have been criticized for amplifying misinformation and political polarization, recent studies suggest that addressing this issue requires more than mere adjustments to platform software (The Guardian, 2023a). Research reveals the extensive reach of political online echo chambers, demonstrating that conservatives and liberals engage with divergent sources, interact with opposing groups, and consume varying levels of misinformation. Human decision-making processes are far more intricate than black-and-white; they are becoming more kaleidoscopic in the realm of artificial amplification. The formation of discriminating mindsets begins offline and is nurtured online.

Stereotypes are a core component of the social construction of "them". Shaped organically by our experiences, education, and environment they can also be curated intentionally with content that is slipped systematically into user content to enforce a certain world view. The latter are then extrapolated and amplified via the echo chambers of our own making. Polarization existed before AI, but the latter is sharpening the edges, because the way it is used reflects existing power imbalances. One example is the extending deployment of surveillance AI.

Stereotyped surveillance. AI-powered surveillance technologies are the center of a controversy whereby companies and governments seek to use algorithms to monitor people's movement and behavior. Their extensive proliferation into both private and public sectors threatens privacy and civil liberties, putting in question the very nature of the latter. Some argue that it instills a pervasive sense of constant monitoring, while perpetuating the distinction between the monitored ("them") and the monitors ("us"), which creates a toxic power dynamic (Fosch-Villaronga et al., 2021).

Besides the question of dignity, facial recognition technology is not reliable. Although faces, rich in information, may enable sophisticated computer programs to deduce emotions, life history, and health, or even infer political preferences and sexual orientation (Levin, 2017) the accuracy of facial recognition systems is contingent on the data they are trained on. They commonly reflect and perpetuate biases, with the poorest accuracy rates for identifying black, female, and young individuals (Najibi, 2020). Accuracy issues, especially in identifying women, minorities, and children, fuel concerns about bias and discrimination (Raji & Buolamwini, 2019). GIGO hits hardest when it comes to underrepresented parts of the population as these are also underrepresented in the datasets that fed into the algorithm's training.[47]

Critics argue that the deployment of facial recognition technologies in public spaces threatens human rights, has high error rates, and lacks regulation. Countering this advocates stress that it helps law enforcement and can be improved with more training data (Ryan-Mosley, 2023). But even if these technologies were fully accurate, they would not necessarily be conducive to human rights. What atmosphere does it create when AI enables the government to monitor people wherever they go, even if those locations are where they are practicing constitutionally protected behavior like peaceful protests and religious ceremonies?[48] Amnesty International and other civil liberty groups argue that the large-scale deployment of facial recognition technology creates a vast and boundless surveillance network that breaks down privacy in public spaces.

Bias in teams leads to biased products. AI corporations could serve the *Quadruple Bottom Line* and lead the way to truly inclusive algorithmic settings (Fig. 2.1). But to do so they first have to invest in in-house stamina against the in-group/out-group phenomenon, which requires inclusive and diverse R&D teams (Mittelstadt et al., 2019). In 2024 more than one in three technology experts was a white man in a

---

[47] Some tools allow anyone with internet access to conduct facial image searches, raising concerns about privacy and the potential misuse of this technology. The lack of consent in tracking individuals raises privacy concerns, and questions persist about legal limits and regulations to prevent misuse and overreach of facial recognition tech (Macnish, 2012; Mori, 2022). Transparency is lacking in the usage of facial recognition data, posing accountability challenges (Garvie, 2016). The broader implications include chilling effects on civil liberties like freedom of speech and assembly, particularly in national contexts prone to autocracy and recrimination (Monahan, 2006). As facial recognition data grows, the risks of leaks, hacks, and misuse escalate, extending to tools like ChatGPT. That is, in July 2023, a cybersecurity firm discovered WormGPT, designed for criminal activities such as creating malware and phishing emails, highlighting potential dangers in the absence of safeguards (Cuthbertson, 2023b). While most AI tools have built-in protections, the emergence of tools like WormGPT, which can bypass safeguards, underscores the need for heightened vigilance. AI, as a tool, adheres to the intentions of its designers and users, emphasizing the importance of responsible development and use.

[48] Countries including the US, China, France, Germany, and Italy have begun to use facial recognition technology as a preventive measure. In December 2022 it was revealed that Chinese police had used mobile data and faces to track protestors. In early 2023 French legislators passed a bill giving police the power to use AI in public spaces ahead of the Paris 2024 Olympics, making it the first country in the EU to approve the use of AI surveillance (Buhiyan, 2023).

WEIRD country. Who and what goes in, comes out—disrespectfully put, GIGO on the human scale.

Designing inclusive AI requires more than a tick on the diversity, equity, and inclusion (DEI) box. Beyond bringing in a diverse range of people, an inclusive climate is required that recognizes and nurtures everyone's potential equally, to curate the complementarity of individual uniqueness. Only if people are accepted and appreciated in a 360-degree perspective all parties get a fair chance to thrive. In AI institutions this logic serves the employee, the employer, and those who use their products.

As data-powered AI is seeping into ever more areas of society, alertness matters. In an ideal world, initiatives to enhance awareness of the GIGO gap would be mainstreamed beyond the technology sector. Helping individuals throughout the life cycle to navigate, recognize, and intentionally counteract content that feeds the "us versus them mentality" (Nissenbaum et al., 2019) will be essential to make the best out of the cohabitation with AI. We must equip individuals across generations with on the one hand a holistic understanding of themselves, including the operating system of their brain and body, and on the other hand with basic algorithmic literacy that does not only sharpens their understanding of the causes and consequences of generative AI, including the data that goes into it; but also how to leverage AI as a strategic ally to perform better while making their own life experience, and the lives of others more positive. The resulting informed ability may lead to a mature interaction with technology, starting with a candid perception of data as a proxy, not a neutral representation of facts and faces, of people and their potential.

Over the next few years lucid citizenship, compassion with oneself and others, conscientiousness of personal responsibility and civil courage, combined with critical questioning skills, and double literacy—which encompasses on the one hand literacy of the brain and body, and on the other hand, algorithmic literacy, must become part of the standard curriculum in schools, and enterprises to harness human agency systematically from the bottom-up and top-down. The line between us and technology is morphing but we can still do something about the circumscription of the territory that the line is running through. Being part of a generation that was born before 2000 is an immense privilege. We have grown up in a childhood where neither smartphones nor chatbots were all pervasive. We can compare that past and the present. We may not be able to predict the future, but we can make choices based on our present knowledge and experience. Our efforts influence the outcomes for future generations, who will be born into a life with AI.

2.4.4 From *Quantity* to *Quality* to *Inclusion*

Exclusion has many facets when it comes to data. Let's leave aside for a moment the fact that those who do not access technological tools do not harvest their (potential) benefits but are still affected by large-scale consequences such as environmental pollution and climate change. Exclusion starts even before that, with the way in which algorithms are designed and trained, and by whom. The current foundational models are trained on data that reflects not the world, but the internet. This means they encode the historical and present-day patterns of marginalization, inequality, etc. Similarly to the causes and consequences of climate change, which are largely caused by pollution in high-income countries, those who are excluded from the present AI-hype are thrice penalized. They do not benefit from the opportunities that derive from technology; furthermore although manual labor is not the first to be eliminated, they have the least buffer when the backlash hits. Thirdly, on a less visible level the data that goes in determines the shape of services that comes out; if your data is not represented your profile and needs are not addressed by the technology that goes mainstream. As seen earlier, LLMs are presently trained primarily on data from WEIRD (Western, Educated, Industrialized, Rich, and Democratic) societies.

A radical (over)compensation by systematically feeding these foundational models data from NEPAD (Non-Western, Educationally Disadvantaged, Pre-industrial Austere, Deprived) societies can backfire. In early 2024 Gemini's AI image generation sparked controversy due to the creation of historically inaccurate images, leading to accusations of being "woke" and prioritizing diversity over accuracy. The backlash came after Gemini's production of images that deviated from reality, such as depicting Black Nazi soldiers, Native American US senators, and racially diverse versions of historical figures like America's founding fathers. According to a Google statement the issue resulted from a training and labeling problem where prompts related to diversity were incorrectly associated with image generation, leading to a mix-up in depicting people of different ethnicities and races.[49] The incident highlights on the one hand the challenges of bias in generative AI models and the delicate balance between inclusivity and factual accuracy; and on the other the fact that no one, human or machine will always please everyone. While some users criticized Google for overcorrecting and failing to accurately represent historical contexts, others appreciated the ambition of diversity and cultural sensitivity. On the positive side, maybe the failed attempts of Gemini for deliberate inclusivity as a feature that is built into the DNA of LLMs are the trailer of a yet imperfect system that will one day be more unbiased and integer than the people that created it.

In 2024 the World Health Organization (WHO) released its updated guidelines on AI emphasizing not only the need of transparent information and policies to address the risks of using AI for healthcare purposes, but also the importance of engagement from various stakeholders, including governments, technology companies, healthcare providers, patients, and civil society, throughout the development and deployment of LLMs; to prevent a "race to the bottom" whereby corporate interests rule the game, and profits are put above people (WHO, 2024). "If models aren't trained on data from people in under-resourced places, those populations might be poorly served by the algorithms. The very last thing that we want to see happen as part of this leap forward with technology is the propagation or amplification of inequities and biases in the social fabric of countries around the world" (Alain Labrique, the WHO's director for digital health and innovation, WHO, 2024). The global health sector is particularly at risk of AI-amplified inequality. Because like previous technological interventions, AI often engages in the "politics of avoidance" by circumventing the root causes of health inequities (Shipton & Vitale, 2024). Rather than reducing exclusion, it perpetrates the legacies of previous technological interventions in global health, often focusing debates on downstream, rather than upstream, determinants of health. Circumventing the debate from standing social patterns that favor exclusion, the AI-penetration of social services is thereby extrapolating the consequences of human stereotypes.

If you are not part of the story, you have no word in shaping it. This holds true directly, indirectly, and twice removed. Who we are shapes what we perceive. We can think about the world in terms that transcend

---

[49] See https://www.foxbusiness.com/media/google-gemini-former-employee-tech-leaders-what-went-wrong-ai-chatbot.

our own experiences or interests and take the view from "nowhere in particular" (Nagel, 1986); yet at the same time, each of us is a particular person in a particular place at a particular time. Everything is connected, our experiences until now influence our experience of that now, what we expect from it and how we express ourselves in it. The same holds true for algorithms. They feed on real life; or rather the part of life that they have access to. Furthermore, the way they are configured influences how they filter, and portray that part, which further increases the distance between the observer, the observed, and future observers.

Beyond the physical inclusion/exclusion spectrum the question of indirect exclusion must be addressed. The less we know about others the more likely we are to diminish, disregard, and discriminate their views and values; an "us versus them" mentality is nurtured.[50] AI has the potential to sharpen the risks associated with this type of ghettoizing mindset. Not only because "We only see what we know" (Goethe, 1749–1832). But also, "We only see what we want to see" (Ruiz, 2016). Out of sight, out of mind. It becomes easy to neglect the needs of those whose voices we do not (want to) hear. The billions of people that have no access to AI, the internet or even electricity matter as much as those in the hyper charged bubble. Data is a limited excerpt of "reality", and in itself it is flawed.

On the positive side, AI that is designed and delivered inclusively could open up a completely new experience of life for individuals who were excluded due to some form of disability are part of the positive side of the inclusion/exclusion spectrum. Assistive technology can help overcome lack of sight or hearing, or mobility, and opens the public space to millions of people who had been excluded because they did not benefit from mainstream facilities; recent advances enable highly personalized solutions (Madaan et al., 2022). For example, machine learning research has produced wheelchair-mounted robot arms that can respond to commands and perform tasks to assist users with limited mobility (Krishnaswamy et al., 2020). Voice assistant systems like Alexa allow hands-free environmental control and information access (Hoffman et al.,

---

[50] The us versus them mentality refers to the psychological tendency of individuals or groups to view the world in terms of an adversarial dichotomy. The "us versus them" outlook has been linked to strong in-group favoritism and out-group prejudice in psychological research (Brewer, 1999). It tends to lead to polarization, conflicts, and the erosion of empathy and cooperation between different groups.

2021). Augmented reality glasses have navigation features to aid blind individuals through visual and auditory guidance (Alonso-Martín et al., 2021).

As seen earlier (Sect. 1.2) neurotech carries interesting potential to enhance human abilities. Brain-computer interfaces (BCI) can translate neural signals directly into digital commands, bypassing normal muscular and nervous system pathways, and studies demonstrated high accuracy for BCI-enabled typing, cursor movement, and wheelchair control for people with paralysis (Vansteensel et al., 2016). Other applications like sensory substitution devices can provide artificial vision or hearing using sensory stimulation based on environmental data from cameras and microphones (Hayes et al., 2021). The challenge is to make the design process itself inclusive to ensure these technologies provide maximal autonomy, and empowerment to match diverse user needs (Shinohara & Tenenberg, 2009). It is a circle that is either vicious or virtuous, as potential beneficiaries must be included to participate in the development process, to ensure that the outcomes serve future inclusion and participation. If that conundrum is addressed, then the increase of AI-powered humanoid robots may liberate millions of people. Change starts from the inside out, inside of people with the aspiration to inclusion, which must come from both, those who are excluded so far and may have built up their self-identity as a specific group (in-group/out-group) and from those who are on the inside and must open the doors to let others join the circle; on the collective side that inclusive mindset must be reflected by the institutional setting. Assistive devices might serve the process from the outside in.

Adopting a mindset of agency brings to light why on the one hand we must endeavor to gradually include everyone in the dynamics that determine the future, and on the other hand why those of us who are part of them must fulfill our role of personal leadership for the Common Good. The present panorama of the AI debate is limited, not only because the field is evolving fast, but due to the factual exclusion of most of the world's population from the development, regulation, and rollout of AI. As long as large parts of humanity are not represented within the virtual space, not for lack of interest or desire—but either because they are living in a part of the world that is struggling to ensure electricity, clean water supply, basic education, and health care; or because they do not have the economic means to invest much time or resources in the online world—this debate will remain lopsided and limited in its nature.

Algorithms are the cause and consequence of our data. Simplified, we put something doubtful into a process that is doubtful in itself and expect trustworthy outputs. *GIGOo—Garbage in, Garbage out obliviation.* It matters to beware of the slippery slope that leads from utilization, to reliance to overreliance to dependency on algorithms. Especially if it entails the gradual delegating of ever more mental effort to them. Being deliberate in the selection of tasks to be delegated, and disciplined in verifying both inputs and outputs continuously we are gravitating byte by byte into Plato's cave. Trust is a precious commodity that should be attributed with caution.

RECAP—*Building on the multidimensional framework of POZE from Chapter 1 we looked at various philosophical definitions of human and artificial consciousness, and their de facto distinction. Perusing the evolution of technology through the various cycles of industrial revolution, we looked at the relative nature of values, and the fragile nature of trust. This took us to the limitations of trustworthy AI and the need for holistic regulation that evolves with the holistic understanding of a moving target. The challenge of amplified exclusion through biased data in a hybrid world and the increasing vulnerability of humans amid all pervasive persuasive AI highlighted why acute awareness of our own role in shaping the relationship with technology is essential to the future. The exit from the hybrid alignment conundrum is conditioned by the harmonization of personal aspirations and actions, as it precedes aligned algorithms. The tension of GIGO (Garbage in, garbage out) and VIVO (Values in, values out) was explored.*

Do you appreciate the potential that derives from your multidimensional nature in a hybrid world (or do you shy away from it).

References

Alonso-Martín, F., Castro, S. M., Nieto, M., Moreno, J. C., & González-Jiménez, J. (2021). Augmented reality as an accessibility and rehabilitation tool for people with visual impairment. *Multimodal Technologies and Interaction*, 5(2), 13.

Altieri, M. A. (1999). The ecological impacts of conventional agriculture and agroecological alternatives. *Agriculture, Ecosystems & Environment, 74*(1–3), 1–16.
Amodei, D., Olah, C., Steinhardt, J., Christiano, P., Schulman, J., & Mané, D. (2016). *Concrete problems in AI safety*. arXiv preprint arXiv:1606.06565.
Anders, G. (2013). *Jeff Bezos' Mr. Amazon.com*. Portfolio Penguin.
Awad, E., Dsouza, S., Kim, R., Schulz, J., Henrich, J., Shariff, A., Bonnefon, J. F., & Rahwan, I. (2018). The moral machine experiment. *Nature, 563*(7729), 59–64.
Baars, B. J. (2002). The conscious access hypothesis: Origins and recent evidence. *Trends in Cognitive Sciences, 6*(1), 47–52.
Baars, B. J., & Dehaene, S. (2002). The global workspace theory of consciousness. *Journal of Consciousness Studies, 9*(1), 45–48.
Bai, Y., Kadavath, S., Kundu, S., Askell, A., Kernion, J., Jones, A., Chen, A., Goldie, A., Mirhoseini, A., McKinnon, C., & Chen, C. (2022). *Constitutional AI: Harmlessness from AI Feedback*. Cornell University. https://arxiv.org/abs/2212.08073
Balkin, J. M., & Zittrain, J. (2018). A framework for thinking about AI and liability. *University of Chicago Law Review, 85*(1), 1–58.
Bargh, J. A., & Morsella, E. (2008). The unconscious mind. *Perspectives on Psychological Science, 3*(1), 73–79.
Bass, B. M., & Riggio, R. E. (2006). *Transformational leadership* (2nd ed.). Psychology Press.
Battelle, J. (2005). *The search: How Google and its rivals rewrote the rules of business and transformed our culture*. Portfolio.
Bell, J. S. (1961). On the problem of hidden variables in quantum mechanics. *Reviews of Modern Physics, 33*(3), 447–452. https://doi.org/10.1103/RevModPhys.33.447
Bergson, H. (1922). *Duration and simultaneity: Bergson and the Einsteinian Universe*. Clinamen Press.
Bergson, H. (1932). *The two sources of morality and religion* (R. A. Audra & C. Brereton, Trans.). Henry Holt and Company. (Original work published 1932).
Bergstrom, B. (2009). *Technology and the good society*. Transaction Publishers.
Bohme, D. (1998). *The way to language: Toward a philosophy of the implicit*. State University of New York Press.
Bommasani, R., Hudson, D. A., Aroyo, A., Alladi, S., Bernstein, M., Fevry, T., Adeli, E., Altman R., Arora, S., von Arx, S., Bohg, J., Bosselut, A., Brunskill, E., Brynjolfsson, E., & Paradice, D. (2021). *On the opportunities and risks of foundation models*. arXiv preprint arXiv:2108.07258.

Bonmasani, R., Katz, M., & Shmid, A. (2023). Governance of Artificial Intelligence: The role of stakeholders. In *Proceedings of the 2023 ACM Conference on AI, Ethics, and Society* (pp. 123–133). ACM.
Borgmann, A. (1984). *Technology and the character of contemporary life: A philosophical inquiry*. University of Chicago Press.
Bostrom, N. (2014). *Superintelligence: Paths, dangers, strategies*. Oxford University Press.
Bostrom, N. (2017). *Superintelligence: Paths, dangers, strategies*. Oxford University Press.
Bostrom, N., & Yudkowsky, E. (2014). The ethics of artificial intelligence. *Cambridge Handbook of Artificial Intelligence, 2*, 316–334.
Brewer, M. B. (1999). The psychology of prejudice: Ingroup love and outgroup hate? *Journal of Social Issues, 55*(3), 429–444. https://doi.org/10.1111/0022-4537.00126
Brynjolfsson, E., & McAfee, A. (2021). *The second machine age: Work, progress, and prosperity in a time of brilliant technologies*. W. W. Norton & Company.
Bryson, J. M., & Crosby, B. C. (2018). *Leadership for the common good: Tackling public problems in a shared-power world* (4th ed.). Wiley.
Buhiyan, J. (2023, August 16). TechScape: 'Are you kidding, carjacking?'—The problem with facial recognition in policing. *The Guardian*. Retrieved July 17, 2023, from https://www.theguardian.com/newsletters/2023/aug/15/techscape-facial-recognition-software-detroit-porcha-woodruff-black-people-ai
Callaway, E. (2024, March 12). Could AI-designed proteins be weaponized? Scientists lay out safety guidelines. *Nature*. https://doi.org/10.1038/d41586-024-00699-0
Callison-Burch, C. (2023). AI and the future of human interaction. *Journal of Artificial Intelligence Research, 67*, 89–112.
Calo, R. (2017). Artificial intelligence policy: A primer and roadmap. *SSRN Electronic Journal, 59*, 399.
Castilla, E. J., & Benard, S. (2010). The paradox of meritocracy in organizations. *Administrative Science Quarterly, 55*(4), 543–676. https://doi.org/10.2189/asqu.2010.55.4.543
Cath, C. (2018). Governing artificial intelligence: Ethical, legal and technical opportunities and challenges. *Philosophical Transactions of the Royal Society A: Mathematical, Physical and Engineering Sciences, 376*(2133), 20180080.
CCN. (2024). Worldcoin (WDC) price prediction. *CCN*. Retrieved from https://www.ccn.com/analysis/crypto/worldcoin-wdc-price-prediction/
Chaka, C. (2024). The impact of algorithmic culture on social behavior. *Technology and Society Journal, 56*(2), 221–235.
Center for AI Safety. (2023). *Statement*. Retrieved June 2023, from https://www.safe.ai/statement-on-ai-risk

Chalmers, D. J. (1996). *The conscious mind: In search of a fundamental theory*. Oxford University Press.
Cherry, K. (2020, March 25). Understanding the concept of meritocracy. *Verywell Mind*. https://www.verywellmind.com/what-is-meritocracy-5087234
Christie's. (2018). AI and the future of art. *Christie's Art Magazine, 18*(3), 34–37.
Cho, W. (2023, February 14). AI-generated works not copyrightable, studios warn. *The Hollywood Reporter*. Retrieved August 2023, from https://www.hollywoodreporter.com/business/business-news/ai-works-not-copyrightable-studios-1235570316/
Coeckelbergh, M. (2020). *AI ethics*. MIT Press.
Coldewey, D. (2024, March 23). Why it's impossible to review AIs, and why TechCrunch is doing it anyway. *TechCrunch*. https://techcrunch.com/2024/03/23/why-its-impossible-to-review-ais-and-why-techcrunch-is-ng-it-anyway/
Confino, P. (2023). Andy Jassy dismisses Microsoft and Google A.I. 'hype cycle' and says Amazon is starting a 'substance cycle'. *Fortune*. Retrieved July 2023, from https://archive.ph/hAgGE#selection-659.0-659.107
Costanza, R., Cumberland, J. H., Daly, H., Goodland, R., & Norgaard, R. B. (2014). *An introduction to ecological economics*. CRC Press.
Couzin, I. D. (2009). Collective cognition in animal groups. *Trends in Cognitive Sciences, 13*(1), 36–43. https://doi.org/10.1016/j.tics.2008.10.002
Cullity, G. (2010). *The moral demands of affluence*. Clarendon Press.
Cuthbertson, A. (2023a). Company that made an AI its chief executive sees stocks climb. China-based NetDragon Websoft says it is the first company in the world to appoint an AI as its CEO. *The Independent*. Retrieved July 3, 2023, from https://www.independent.co.uk/tech/ai-ceo-artificial-intellige nce-b2302091.html
Cuthbertson, A. (2023b, February 13). ChatGPT rival with 'no ethical boundaries' sold on dark web. *The Independent*. Retrieved July 2023, from https://www.independent.co.uk/news/chatgpt-ai-dark-web-cyber-crime-b2281831.html
Damasio, A. R. (1994). *Descartes' error: Emotion, reason, and the human brain*. Putnam.
David, P. A. (1990). The dynamo and the computer: An historical perspective on the modern productivity paradox. *American Economic Review, 80*(2), 355–361.
Davis, D. E. (2006). *Reshaping the built environment: Ecology, ethics, and economics*. Island Press.
Decety, J., & Jackson, P. L. (2006). A social-neuroscience perspective on empathy. *Current Directions in Psychological Science, 15*(2), 54–58. https://doi.org/10.1111/j.0963-7214.2006.00406.x

Dennett, D. C. (1991). *Consciousness explained*. Little, Brown and Co.

Diamond, J. M. (1997). *Guns, germs, and steel: The fates of human societies*. Norton.

Dirks, K. T., & Ferrin, D. L. (2002). Trust in leadership: Meta-analytic findings and implications for research and practice. *Journal of Applied Psychology, 87*(4), 611–628.

Doidge, N. (2007). *The brain that changes itself: Stories of personal triumph from the frontiers of brain science*. ISBN 978-0-670-03830-5 (hc.) / ISBN 978-0-14-311310-2.

Domingos, P. (2012). A few useful things to know about machine learning. *Communications of the ACM, 55*(10), 78–87. https://doi.org/10.1145/2347736.2347755

Drenthen, M. (2016). Earth emotions: New words for a new world. *Environmental Humanities, 8*(1), 99–103.

Dutt, D., Ammanath, B., Perricos, C., & Sniderman, B. (2024). Deloitte. Report. Now Decides Next. The Stage of Generative AI. Retrieved January 2024, from https://www2.deloitte.com/us/en/pages/consulting/articles/state-of-generative-ai-in-enterprise.html

e/acc website. (2024). https://effectiveacceleration.tech/

Edmondson, A. (1999). Psychological safety and learning behavior in work teams. *Administrative Science Quarterly, 44*(2), 350–383.

Edward A., & Rosenberg, N. (1963, March 1). Changing Technological Leadership and Industrial Growth. *The Economic Journal, 73*(289), 13–31. https://doi.org/10.2307/2228401

Edwards, P. N. (2021). *The closed world: Computers and the politics of discourse in Cold War America*. The MIT Press.

Elgammal, A. (2017). Can AI create true art? *Technology and Art Journal, 32*(4), 113–125.

Elkington, J. (1998). *Cannibals with forks: The triple bottom line of 21st century business*. New Society Publishers.

Ellul, J. (1964). *The technological society*. Vintage Books.

Ericsson, K. A., Krampe, R. T., & Tesch-Römer, C. (1993). The role of deliberate practice in the acquisition of expert performance. *Psychological Review, 100*(3), 363–406. https://doi.org/10.1037/0033-295X.100.3.363

Falcon, A. (2001). Aristotle on causality. In E. N. Zalta & U. Nodelman (Eds.), *The Stanford Encyclopedia of Philosophy* (Spring 2023 Edition). Retrieved January 2024, from https://plato.stanford.edu/archives/spr2023/entries/aristotle-causality/

Feenberg, A. (1991). *Critical theory of technology*. Oxford University Press.

Floridi, L., Cowls, J., King, T. C., & Taddeo, M. (2018). How to design AI for social good: Seven essential factors. *Science and Engineering Ethics, 24*(1), 21–35.

Fosch-Villaronga, E., ÓhÉigeartaigh, S. S., & Lutter, F. (2021). Reversing the panopticon? Exploring the limits of AI-driven surveillance technologies. *Computer Law & Security Review, 42,* 105464. https://doi.org/10.1016/j.clsr.2021.105464

Fried, I. (2024). *Exclusive: Public trust in AI is sinking across the board.* Axios. Retrieved March 2024, from https://www.axios.com/2024/03/05/ai-trust-problem-edelman

Fujiwara, K., Daibo, I., & Tsuchiya, M. (2018). Spontaneous synchronization of body movements in social and mechanical situations. *Frontiers in Psychology, 9,* 1711.

Fukuyama, F. (2002). *Our posthuman future: Consequences of the biotechnology revolution.* Farrar, Straus and Giroux.

Garvie, C. (2016). *The perpetual line-up: Unregulated police face recognition in America.* Georgetown Law, Center on Privacy & Technology. https://www.perpetuallineup.org

Gefen, D., Rose, J., & Pavlou, P. A. (2013). Evolving trust in technology: Models and moderators. *MIS Quarterly, 37*(2), 387–408.

Gergen, K. J. (2022). The social construction of self. *Journal of Humanistic Psychology, 62*(4), 375–393.

Gilovich, T., & Griffin, D. (2002). Heuristics and biases: Then and now. In T. Gilovich, D. W. Griffin, & D. W. Kahneman (Eds.), *Heuristics and biases: The psychology of intuitive judgment* (pp. 1–18). Cambridge University Press.

Gitelman, L. (2013). *Raw data is an oxymoron.* The MIT Press.

Gizem, K., Sezer, O., & Ceyhan, S. (2023). Trust in AI judges versus human judges in legal decision making. *Journal of Legal Studies, 52*(3), 299–315.

Goddard, K., Roudsari, A., & Wyatt, J. C. (2022). Automation bias: A systematic review of frequency, effect mediators, and mitigators. *Journal of the American Medical Informatics Association, 19*(1), 121–127.

Goetz, J. L., Keltner, D., & Simon-Thomas, E. (2010). Compassion: An evolutionary analysis and empirical review. *Psychological Bulletin, 136*(3), 351–374. https://doi.org/10.1037/a0018807

Goodfellow, I., Bengio, Y., & Courville, A. (2016). *Deep learning.* MIT Press.

Goodwin, P. (2023, April 4). 12 US artificial intelligence regulations to watch in 2023. *Goodwin Law.* https://doi.org/10.1080/23273247.2023.973762

Grant, S., & Weise, N. (2023). In A.I. race, Microsoft and Google choose speed over caution. *New York Times.* Retrieved May 2023, from https://www.nytimes.com/2023/04/07/technology/ai-chatbots-google-microsoft.html?smid=nytcore-ios-share&referringSource=articleShare

Haidt, J. (2006). *The happiness hypothesis: Finding modern truth in ancient wisdom.* Basic Books.

Hallworth, M. (2023). Let's talk less about irrationality. *Behavioral Scientist.* https://behavioralscientist.org/lets-talk-less-about-irrationality/

Halpern, S. (2023). What we still don't know about how A.I. is trained. *New York Times*. Retrieved May 2023, from https://www.newyorker.com/news/daily-comment/what-we-still-dont-know-about-how-ai-is-trained

Hanson, J. D., & Yosifon, D. G. (2004). The situation: An introduction to the situational character, critical realism, power economics, and deep capture. *University of Pennsylvania Law Review, 152*(1), 129–346.

Haraway, D. (1991). *Simians, cyborgs, and women: The reinvention of nature*. Routledge.

Harmon-Jones, E., & Mills, J. (2019a). An introduction to cognitive dissonance theory and an overview of current perspectives on the theory. American Psychological Association.

Harmon-Jones, E., & Mills, J. (Eds.). (2019b). *Cognitive dissonance: Reexamining a pivotal theory in psychology*. American Psychological Association.

Harper, T. A. (2023, March 1). Extinction panic: C. S. Lewis and Planetary Nihilism. *Modern Language Quarterly, 84*(1), 27–51. https://doi.org/10.1215/00267929-10189315

Hart, W. D. (1996). Dualism. In S. Guttenplan (Ed.), *A companion to the philosophy of mind*. Blackwell.

Hayes, G. R., Wang, X., & Mohan, S. (2021, May). Co-designing mobile sensory substitution technologies for accessibility and inclusion. In *Extended Abstracts of the 2021 CHI Conference on Human Factors in Computing Systems* (pp. 1–7).

Heath, T. L. (1897). *The works of Archimedes*. Cambridge University Press.

Heidegger, M. (1956). *The question concerning technology*. Harper Torchbooks.

Heikkilä, M. (2024, April 11). Is robotics about to have its own ChatGPT moment? *MIT Technology Review*. https://www.technologyreview.com/2024/04/11/1068188/is-robotics-about-to-have-its-own-chatgpt-moment/

Hern, A. (2023, June 7). 'What should the limits be?' The father of ChatGPT on whether AI will save humanity—or destroy it. *The Guardian*. https://www.theguardian.com/technology/2023/jun/07/what-should-the-limits-be-the-father-of-chatgpt-on-whether-ai-will-save-humanity-or-destroy-it

Hilliard, A., Munoz, C., Wu, Z., & Koshiyama, A. S. (2024). *Eliciting personality traits in large language models*. arXiv. 2402.08341.

Hoffman, G., Chen, T., Misra, D., Teevan, J., & Zahradka, O. (2021, May). Toward inclusive technology for people with disabilities. In *Extended Abstracts of the 2021 CHI Conference on Human Factors in Computing Systems* (pp. 1–4).

Hofmann, V., Kalluri, P. R., Jurafsky, D., & King, S. (2024, March 19). Preprint on arXiv https://doi.org/10.48550/arXiv.2403.00742

Holzinger, A. (2016). *Interactive machine learning for health informatics: When do we need the human-in-the-loop?* Springer.

Horowitz, M. C., & Scharre, P. (2015). *Meaningful human control in weapon systems: A primer*. Center for a New American Security.

Hosanagar, K. (2024, March 19). *Gen AI models vs the human brain*. Creative Intelligence. Retrieved from Substack.

Intergovernmental Panel on Climate Change. (2014). *Climate change 2014: Mitigation of climate change*. Cambridge University Press.

James, E., & Wooten, L. (2022). *The prepared leader: Emerge from any crisis more resilient than before*. Wharton University Press.

Jo, J. (2023, January 11). This AI just passed a Wharton MBA test. Should business schools be worried? *Fortune*. https://fortune.com/2023/01/11/ai-chatgpt-wharton-mba-test/

Jones, A. (2019). Productivity and the observation effect in the workplace. *Journal of Applied Psychology, 114*(5), 856–870.

Kahneman, D. (2007). *Thinking, fast and slow*. Farrar, Straus and Giroux.

Kamps, H. J. (2024, March 19). Nvidia's Jensen Huang says AI hallucinations are solvable, artificial general intelligence is 5 years away. *TechCrunch*. https://techcrunch.com/2024/03/19/agi-and-hallucinations/

Kant, I. (1997). *Grounding for the metaphysics of morals*. Hackett Publishing.

Karpen, S. C. (2018, June). The social psychology of biased self-assessment. *American Journal of Pharmaceutical Education, 82*(5), 6299. https://doi.org/10.5688/ajpe6299. PMID: 30013244; PMCID: PMC6041499.

Keegan, J. (1993). *A history of warfare*. Vintage.

Kelly, K. (2009). How technology evolves. *TED Talk*. https://blog.ted.com/how_technology/

Kennedy, J., Eberhart, R., & Shi, Y. (2001). *Swarm intelligence*. Morgan Kaufmann.

Kirschner, S., & Tomasello, M. (2009). Joint music making promotes prosocial behavior in 4-year-old children. *Evolution and Human Behavior, 30*(5), 346–354.

Klein, E. (2024, April 12). Dario Amodei on the exponential growth of AI. *The New York Times*. https://www.nytimes.com/2024/04/12/opinion/ezra-klein-podcast-dario-amodei.html

Klein, G. (2015). A naturalistic decision making perspective on studying intuitive decision making. *Journal of Applied Research in Memory and Cognition, 4*(3), 164–168. https://doi.org/10.1016/j.jarmac.2015.07.001

Kramer, R. M., & Tyler, T. R. (1996). *Trust in organizations: Frontiers of theory and research*. Sage Publications.

Krishnaswamy, P., Perng, J. K., Rodriguez-Losada, D., Ding, H., Moura, J. M., Laksanasopin, T., & Rizzo, A. (2020). Multimodal sensing and automated assistance for wheelchair users. *Proceedings of the IEEE, 108*(2), 214–231.

Kurzweil, R. (2005). *The singularity is near: When humans transcend biology*. Viking.

Kurzweil, R. (2007, May 16). The accelerating power of technology. *TED Talk*. https://www.ted.com/talks/ray_kurzweil_the_accelerating_power_of_technology/transcript

Latour, B. (1993). *We have never been modern*. Harvard University Press.

Lau, H., & Rosenthal, D. (2011). Empirical support for higher-order theories of conscious awareness. *Trends in Cognitive Sciences, 15*(8), 365–373.

LeCun, Y., Bengio, Y., & Hinton, G. (2015). Deep learning. *Nature, 521*(7553), 436–444.

Leder, H., Carbon, C. C., & Ripsas, A. L. (2017). Is seeing meaning understanding? The impact of perceived meaning on the aesthetic experience of artworks. *Frontiers in Psychology, 8*, 188.

Leeper, A., Hsiao, K., Ciocarlie, M., Takayama, L., & Gossow, D. (2012). Strategies for human-in-the-loop robotic grasping. In *2012 7th ACM/IEEE International Conference on Human-Robot Interaction (HRI)*.

Leike, J., Martic, M., Krakovna, V., Ortega, P. A., Everitt, T., Lefrancq, A., Orseau, L., & Legg, S. (2017). *AI safety gridworlds*. arXiv preprint arXiv:1711.09883.

Leite, I., Martinho, C., & Paiva, A. (2013). Social robots for long-term interaction: A survey. *International Journal of Social Robotics, 5*(2), 291–308.

Levin, S. T. (2017, September 12). Face-reading AI will be able to detect your politics and IQ, professor says. *The Guardian*. https://www.theguardian.com/technology/2017/sep/12/artificial-intelligence-face-reading-politics-iq-stanford

Lewis, J. (2020). *The fifth domain: Defending our country, our companies, and ourselves in the age of cyber threats*. Penguin.

Lewis, J. D., & Weigert, M. (1985). Trust and organizational behavior: A review of relevant literature. *Management Science, 31*(6), 629–646.

Luhmann, N. (1979). *Trust and power*. John Wiley & Sons.

Macnish, K. (2012). An eye for an eye: Proportionality and surveillance. *Ethical Theory and Moral Practice, 15*(3), 529–548.

Madaan, A., Mittal, M., Goyal, S., Aggarwal, S., & Saxena, S. (2022). Application of artificial intelligence in medical field with special reference to accessibility. *Journal of Family Medicine and Primary Care, 11*(4), 1579.

Mann, A. (2024). The paradox of artificial integrity: Why machines cannot possess true moral character. *Ethics in AI Journal, 10*(2), 89–103.

Mann, H., Walther, C., & Platt, M. (2024). Brain-machine synchrony: A new era of AI-supported human collaboration and societal transformation. *The European Business Review*. https://www.europeanbusinessreview.com/brain-machine-synchrony-a-new-era-of-ai-supported-human-collaboration-and-societal-transformation/

Marble, J. L., Bruemmer, D. J., Few, D. A., & Nielsen, C. W. (2004). Evaluation of supervisory vs. peer-peer interaction with human-robot teams. In *Proceedings of the 37th Annual Hawaii International Conference on System Sciences (HICSS'04)*.

Marwala, T. (2023, July 18). Militarisation of AI has severe implications for global security and warfare. *Daily Maverick*. Retrieved August 2, 2023, from https://www.dailymaverick.co.za/opinionista/2023-07-18-militarisation-of-ai-has-severe-implications-for-global-security-and-warfare/

Mayer, R. C., Davis, J. H., & Schoorman, F. D. (1995). An integrative model of organizational trust. *Academy of Management Review, 20*(3), 709–734. https://doi.org/10.5465/amr.1995.9508080335

Mazzucato, M. (2013). *The entrepreneurial state: Debunking public vs. private sector myths*. Anthem Press.

McKinsey Global Institute. (2023, July). *Jobs lost, jobs gained: Workforce transitions in a time of automation*. Retrieved from McKinsey & Company website, https://www.mckinsey.com/featured-insights/future-of-work

McNamee, S. J. (2018). *The meritocracy myth*. Rowman & Littlefield.

McNeill, W. H., & McNeill, J. R. (2003). *The human web: A bird's-eye view of world history*. W. W. Norton & Company.

Mercado, J. E., Rupp, M. A., Chen, J. Y., Barnes, M. J., Barber, D., & Procci, K. (2016). Intelligent agent transparency in human–agent teaming for Multi-UxV management. *Human Factors, 58*(3), 401–415.

Messeri, L., & Crockett, M. J. (2024). Artificial intelligence and illusions of understanding in scientific research. *Nature, 627*, 49–58. https://doi.org/10.1038/s41586-024-07146-0

Metz, C., Kang, C., Frenkel, S., Thompson, S. A., & Grant, N. (2024, April 6). How tech giants cut corners to harvest data for A.I. *The New York Times*. https://www.nytimes.com/2024/04/06/technology/ai-data-harvesting.html

Metzinger, T. (2009). *The ego tunnel: The science of the mind and the myth of the self*. Basic Books.

Millard, R. (2023). AI robots admit they'd run Earth better than clouded humans. *ScienceAlert*. Retrieved July 2023, from https://www.scienceal ert.com/ai-robots-admit-theyd-run-earth-better-than-clouded-humans?utm_source=www.neatprompts.com&utm_medium=newsletter&utm_campaign=japan-s-ai-security-cameras

Miller, K. (2023, March 13). *AI overreliance is a problem: Are explanations a solution?* Stanford Human-Centered Artificial Intelligence. https://hai.stanford.edu/news/ai-overreliance-problem-are-explanations-solution

Milmo, D. (2023a). Claude 2: Anthropic launches chatbot rival to ChatGPT. *The Guardian*. Retrieved July 2023, from https://www.theguardian.com/technology/2023/jul/12/claude-2-anthropic-launches-chatbot-rival-chatgpt

Milmo, D. (2023b). Elon Musk launches XAI startup pro humanity in terminator future. *The Guardian*. Retrieved July 14, 2023, from https://www.theguardian.com/technology/2023/jul/13/elon-musk-launches-xai-startup-pro-humanity-terminator-future

Mitchell, T. M. (1997). *Machine learning*. McGraw-Hill.

Mittelstadt, B. D., Allo, P., Taddeo, M., Wachter, S., & Floridi, L. (2019). The ethics of algorithms: Mapping the debate. *Big Data & Society*, 6(2), 205395171983389. https://doi.org/10.1177/2053951719833894

Möllering, G. (2006). *Trust: Reason, routine, reflexivity*. Emerald Group Publishing.

Mollick, E. (2023, March 17). *Centaurs and Cyborgs on the Jagged Frontier*. One Useful Thing. https://ethanmollick.substack.com/p/centaurs-and-cyborgs-on-the-jagged

Monahan, T. (2006). Questioning surveillance and security. In T. Monahan (Ed.), *Surveillance and security: Technological politics and power in everyday life* (pp. 1–23). Routledge.

Mori, P. (2022). Looking at you: Facial recognition technology, police body-worn cameras, and privacy law in Canada. *Alberta Law Review*, 59(3), 687–732.

Morozov, E. (2023, June 30). Artificial Intelligence and the danger of unchecked advancements. *The New York Times*. Retrieved June 2023, from https://www.nytimes.com/2023/06/30/opinion/artificial-intelligence-danger.html?campaign_id=39&emc=edit_ty_20230630&instance_id=96413&nl=opinion-today&regi_id=208750243&segment_id=138052&te=1&user_id=9e2d4ee3ed4e60728251f331a585bc56

Moss, M. (2013). *Salt sugar fat: How the food giants hooked us*. Random House.

Nagel, T. (1974). What is it like to be a bat? *The Philosophical Review*, 83(4), 435–450.

Nagel, T. (1986). *The view from nowhere*. Oxford University Press.

Najibi, A. (2020, October 24). Racial discrimination in face recognition technology. *Science in the News*. https://sitn.hms.harvard.edu/flash/2020/racial-discrimination-in-face-recognition-technology/

Neisser, U. (1967). *Cognitive psychology*. Appleton-Century-Crofts.

Newman, G. E., & Bloom, P. (2012). Art and authenticity: The importance of originals in judgments of value. *Journal of Experimental Psychology: General*, 141(3), 558–569. https://doi.org/10.1037/a0026035

Newman, M. E. J. (2005). Power laws, Pareto distributions, and Zipf's law. *Contemporary Physics*, 46(5), 323–351. arXiv:cond-mat/0412004. Bibcode:2005ConPh..46..323N. https://doi.org/10.1080/0010751050005 2444. S2CID 202719165

Nissenbaum, H., & Rodotà, S. (2016). Privacy in the age of big data: Recognizing threats, defending values, and shaping policy. *World Policy Journal, 33*(1), 7–17.
Nissenbaum, H., Rodotà, S., & Zuckerman, E. (2019). *Data, ethics, and regulation in the age of AI*. MIT Press.
Ocloo, J., & Matthews, R. (2016). From tokenism to empowerment: Progressing patient and public involvement in healthcare improvement. *BMJ Quality & Safety, 25*(8), 626–632.
O'Neil, C. (2016). *Weapons of math destruction: How big data increases inequality and threatens democracy*. Broadway Books.
OpenAi. (2023). *Introducing super alignment*. Retrieved July 2023, from https://openai.com/blog/introducing-superalignment
Palanski, M. E., & Yammarino, F. J. (2009). Integrity and leadership: A multilevel conceptual framework. *The Leadership Quarterly, 20*(3), 405–420.
Parker, G. (1996). *The military revolution: Military innovation and the rise of the West, 1500–1800*. Cambridge University Press.
Paul, K. (2023, January 23). An AI just won first place at a major US art competition. Should humans be worried? *The Guardian*. https://www.theguardian.com/artanddesign/2023/jan/23/ai-artificial-intelligence-colorado-state-fair-competition
Pham, S. (2017, April 24). Jack Ma: In 30 years, the best CEO could be a robot. *CNN Business*. https://money.cnn.com/2017/04/24/technology/jack-ma-robot-ceo/index.html
Platt, M. (2020). *The Leader's Brain*. Wharton School Press. https://www.pennpress.org/9781613630990/the-leaders-brain/
Portugali, J. (2012). Complexity theories of cities: Achievements, criticism and potentials. In J. Portugali, H. Meyer, E. Stolk, & E. Tan (Eds.), *Complexity theories of cities have come of age* (pp. 47–62). Springer.
Pretty, J. (2008). Agricultural sustainability: Concepts, principles and evidence. *Philosophical Transactions of the Royal Society B: Biological Sciences, 363*(1491), 447–465.
Pribram, K. H. (2021). *Brain and perception: Holoflux theory*. Psychology Press.
Rabinovich, M. I., Simmons, A. N., Varona, P., & Bazhenov, M. (2015). Dynamical bridge between brain and mind. *Trends in Cognitive Sciences, 19*(8), 453–461.
Raji, I. D., & Buolamwini, J. (2019). Actionable auditing: Investigating the impact of publicly naming biased performance results of commercial AI products. In *Proceedings of the 2019 AAAI/ACM Conference on AI, Ethics, and Society* (pp. 429–435).
Reber, A. S. (1995). *The penguin dictionary of psychology*. Penguin Books.

Reuters. (2023, July 24). *OpenAI's Sam Altman launches Worldcoin crypto project*. Reuters. https://www.reuters.com/technology/openais-sam-altman-launches-worldcoin-crypto-project-2023-07-24/

Reynolds, C. W. (1987). Flocks, herds and schools: A distributed behavioral model. *SIGGRAPH Computer Graphics, 21*(4), 25–34. https://doi.org/10.1145/37401.37406

Richter, D. (2018). Immanuel Kant: Metaphysics. *The Stanford Encyclopedia of Philosophy*. https://plato.stanford.edu/archives/fall2018/entries/kant-metaphysics/

Rosenberg, N. (1992). *Exploring the black box: Technology, economics, and history*. Cambridge University Press.

Rousseau, D. M., Sitkin, S. B., Burt, R. S., & Camerer, C. (1998). Not so different after all: A cross-discipline view of trust. *Academy of Management Review, 23*(3), 393–404.

Rudin, C. (2019). Stop explaining black box machine learning models for high stakes decisions and use interpretable models instead. *Nature Machine Intelligence, 1*(5), 206–215.

Ruiz, D. M. (2016). *The four agreements: A practical guide to personal freedom*. Amber-Allen Publishing.

Russell, S. (2019). *Human compatible: Artificial intelligence and the problem of control*. Penguin.

Russell, S., & Norvig, P. (2016). *Artificial intelligence: A modern approach* (3rd ed.). Pearson.

Russell, S. J., & Norvig, P. (2021). *Artificial intelligence: A modern approach* (4th ed., p. 5, 1003). Pearson. ISBN 9780134610993. Retrieved September 12, 2022.

Ryan-Mosley, T. (2023). *The movement to limit face recognition tech might finally get a win*. MIT. Retrieved August 16, 2023, from https://www.technologyreview.com/2023/07/20/1076539/face-recognition-massachusetts-test-police/

Saharia, C., Chan, W., Saxena, S., Li, L., Whang, J., Denton, E., Ghasemipour, K., Gontijo Lopes, R., Karagol Ayan, B., Salimans, T., Ho, J. & Fleet, D. J. (2023). *Photorealistic text-to-image diffusion models with deep language understanding*. arXiv preprint arXiv:2205.11487.

Sangaramoorthy, T., Jamison, A. M., & Dyer, L. A. (2021). Addressing power dynamics in community-engaged research partnerships. *Journal of Patient-Reported Outcomes, 5*(1). https://doi.org/10.1186/s41687-021-00313-5

Schwab, K. (2017). *The fourth industrial revolution*. Crown Business.

Schwartz, J. M., Stapp, H. P., & Beauregard, M. (2005). Quantum physics in neuroscience and psychology: A neurophysical model of mind–brain interaction. *Philosophical Transactions of the Royal Society B: Biological Sciences, 360*, 1309–1327.

Schwartz, M. (2021). The observer in psychology: Bias, reactivity, and intersubjectivity. *The American Journal of Psychology, 134*(4), 479–491.
Searle, J. R. (1997a, November 2). *The mystery of consciousness*. New York Review of Books.
Searle, J. R. (1997b). The mystery of consciousness. *New York Review of Books, 44*(17), 60–66.
Searle, J. R. (1980). Minds, brains, and programs. *Behavioral and Brain Sciences, 3*(3), 417–424.
Senior, A. W., Evans, R., Jumper, J., Kirkpatrick, J., Sifre, L., Green, T., Qin, C., Žídek, A., Nelson, A. W., Bridgland, A., Penedones, H., & Hassabis, D. (2022). Improved protein structure prediction using potentials from deep learning. *Nature, 577*(7792), 706–710.
Shinohara, K., & Tenenberg, J. (2009). A blind person's interactions with technology. *Communications of the ACM, 52*(8), 58–66.
Shipton, L., & Vitale, L. (2024) Artificial intelligence and the politics of avoidance in global health. *Social Science & Medicine, 359*(2024), 117274. ISSN 0277-9536. https://doi.org/10.1016/j.socscimed.2024.117274
Shivaram, D. (2023). The White House and big tech companies release commitments on managing AI [Radio broadcast episode]. NPR. *Morning Edition*. Retrieved July 3, 2023 from, https://www.npr.org/2023/07/21/1234876543/the-white-house-and-big-tech-companies-release-commitments-on-managing-ai
Simons, T. L. (2002). Behavioral integrity: The perceived alignment between managers' words and deeds as a research focus. *Organization Science, 13*(1), 18–35.
Snow, C. (2018). AI and creativity: The evolving role of artificial intelligence in artistic expression. *Art and Technology Review, 21*(3), 77–89.
Solaiman, I., Brundage, M., Clark, J., Askell, A., Herbert-Voss, A., Wu, J., Radford, A., Krueger, G., Kim, J. W., Kreps, S., McCain, M., & Noukhovitch, M. (2022). *Release strategies and the social impacts of language models*. arXiv preprint arXiv:2211.11409.
Stanford Institute for Human-Centered Artificial Intelligence. (2024). *AI Index: State of AI in 13 charts*. https://hai.stanford.edu/news/ai-index-state-ai-13-charts
Stiglitz, J. E. (2019a). *People, power and profits: Progressive capitalism for an age of discontent*. Penguin UK.
Stiglitz, J. E. (2019b). *Rewriting the rules of the European economy*. Project Syndicate. https://www.project-syndicate.org/commentary/rewriting-rules-of-european-economy-by-joseph-e-stiglitz-2019-05
Suleyman, M. (2024). What is AI anyway? *TED Talk*. Source https://www.ted.com/talks/mustafa_suleyman_what_is_an_ai_anyway?language=en

Svara, J. H., & Brunet, J. R. (2004). Filling in the skeletal pillar: Addressing social equity in introductory courses in public administration. *Journal of Public Affairs Education, 10*(2), 99–109.

Tandoc, E. C., Lim, Z. W., & Ling, R. (2018). Deconstructing "echo chambers" and "epistemic bubbles": Understanding the social media disinformation ecosystem. *Information, Communication & Society, 23*(7), 994–1018. https://doi.org/10.1017/epi.2018.32

Tarnoff, B. (2023, February 23). 'A certain danger lurks there': How the inventor of the first chatbot turned against AI. *The Guardian*. Retrieved July 2023, from https://www.theguardian.com/technology/2023/feb/23/joseph-weizenbaum-eliza-chatbot-ai-turned-against-computers

Thatcher, M. (1987, September 23). *Interview for woman's own ("no such thing as society")*. No.10 Downing Street. Retrieved from Thatcher Archive (THCR 5/2/262): COI transcript.

The Guardian. (2023a). *AI poses existential threat and risk to health of millions, experts warn*. https://www.theguardian.com/technology/2023/may/10/ai-poses-existential-threat-and-risk-to-health-of-millions-experts-warn

The Guardian. (2023b). *Meta's algorithms did not reduce polarization, study suggests*. Retrieved July 2023, from https://www.theguardian.com

Tiku, N. (2022). The Google engineer who thinks the company's AI has come to life. *Washington Post*. Retrieved January 6, 2023 from, https://www.washingtonpost.com/technology/2022/06/11/google-ai-lamda-blake-lemoine/

Tong, A., Dastin, J., & Hu, K. (2023, November 23). OpenAI researchers warned board of AI breakthrough ahead of CEO ouster, sources say. *Reuters*. https://www.reuters.com/technology/exclusive-openai-researchers-warned-board-ai-breakthrough-ahead-ceo-ouster-2022-11-23/

Tononi, G. (2008). Consciousness as integrated information: A provisional manifesto. *Biological Bulletin, 215*(3), 216–242.

Tucker, I. (2023). Signal's Meredith Whittaker: 'These are the people who could actually pause AI if they wanted to'. *The Guardian*. Retrieved June 2023, from https://www.theguardian.com/technology/2023/jun/11/signals-meredith-whittaker-these-are-the-people-who-could-actually-pause-ai-if-they-wanted-to

UN SG. (2023). *UN Interim Report Governing AI*. Retrieved January 2024, from https://www.un.org/en/ai-advisory-body

UNIDO. (2023). *Industrial Analytics Platform*. Retrieved June 2023, from https://iap.unido.org/articles/what-fourth-industrial-revolution

United Nations. (2024a). *General Assembly adopts landmark resolution on steering artificial intelligence towards global good, faster realization of sustainable development*. Retrieved from UN Press.

United Nations. (2024b). *The sustainable development goals report 2024*. https://unstats.un.org/sdgs/report/2024/

van der Stappen, P., & Funk, M. (2021). *Let me take over: Variable autonomy for meaningful human control. frontiers in psychology.* Link
Vansteensel, M. J., Pels, E. G., Bleichner, M. G., Branco, M. P., Denison, T., Freudenburg, Z. V., Gosselaar, P., Leinders, S., Ottens, T. H., Van Den Boom, M. A., Van Rijen, P. C., & Ramsey, N. F. (2016). Fully implanted brain–computer interface in a locked-in patient with ALS. *New England Journal of Medicine, 375*(21), 2060–2066.
Velu, C., & Putra, F. H. R. (2023). How to introduce quantum computers without slowing economic growth. *Nature, 607*(7941), 7–9. https://doi.org/10.1038/d41586-022-03931-6
Vesely, R. (2017). Archimedes. The Stanford Encyclopedia of Philosophy. https://plato.stanford.edu/archives/spr2017/entries/archimedes/
Vicsek, T., & Zafeiris, A. (2012). Collective motion. *Physics Reports, 517*(3–4), 71–140. https://doi.org/10.1016/j.physrep.2012.03.004
Vincent, J. (2023, February 1). This robot barista makes a latte as good as a human, new study finds. *The Verge.* https://www.theverge.com/2023/2/1/23586270/robot-barista-cafe-x-latte-art-coffee-taste-test
Vong, W. K., Wang, W., Orhan, A. E., & Lake, B. M. (2024). Grounded language acquisition through the eyes and ears of a single child. *Science, 383*, 504–511.
Wallace, J., & Erickson, J. (1992). *Hard drive: Bill Gates and the making of the Microsoft empire.* HarperBusiness.
Wallach, W., & Allen, C. (2009). *Moral machines: Teaching robots right from wrong.* Oxford University Press.
Walther, C. (2014). Le Droit au service de l'enfant. Universite de Droit, Aix-Marseille UIII. https://www.theses.fr/2014AIXM1093
Walther, C. (2020a). *Connection in the times of COVID: Corona's call for conscious choices.* Macmillan Palgrave. https://link.springer.com/book/10.1007%2F978-3-030-53641-1
Walther, C. (2020b). *Development, humanitarian aid and social welfare: Social change from the inside out.* Macmillan Palgrave. https://link.springer.com/book/10.1007%2F978-3-030-42610-1
Walther, C. (2020c). *Humanitarian work, social change and human behavior: Compassion for change.* Macmillan Palgrave. https://link.springer.com/book/10.1007%2F978-3-030-45878-2
Walther, C. (2020d). *Development and connection in the time of COVID-19: Corona's call for conscious choices.* Palgrave Macmillan. https://doi.org/10.1007/978-3-030-53641-1
Walther, C. (2021a). *Technology, social change and human behavior: Influence for impact.* Macmillan Palgrave. https://doi.org/10.1007/978-3-030-70002-7

Walther, C. (2021b). *Leadership for social change and development: Inspiration and transformation*. Macmillan Palgrave. https://doi.org/10.1007/978-3-030-76225-4

Wang, O. (2022). Do machines know more about us than we do ourselves? *The New York Times*. Retrieved May 2023, from https://www.nytimes.com/2023/03/27/science/ai-machine-learning-chatbots.html?smid=li-share

Wang, W., Pynadath, D. V., & Hill, S. G. (2016, May). The impact of POMDP-Generated explanations on trust and performance in human-robot teams. In *2016 11th ACM/IEEE International Conference on Human-Robot Interaction (HRI)* (pp. 197–204). IEEE.

Watson, J. B. (1913). Psychology as the behaviorist views it. *Psychological Review, 20*(2), 158–177.

Weart, S. R. (2018). *The rise of nuclear fear*. Harvard University Press.

WEF (World Economic Forum). (2020). *The global risks report 2020*. World Economic Forum.

Weizenbaum, J. (1976). *Computer power and human reason: From judgment to calculation*. W. H. Freeman & Co.

Wiggins, C., & Jones, M. L. (2024). *How data happened: A history from the age of reason to the age of algorithms*.

Wilkerson, R. G., Biskup, E., Lipton, M. L., & Landman, B. A. (2021). The human brain capital initiative: A roadmap to neuroeconomic growth. *Neuron, 109*(6), 939–942. https://doi.org/10.1016/j.neuron.2021.02.002

Winner, L. (1986). *The whale and the reactor: A search for limits in an age of high technology*. University of Chicago Press.

World Health Organization. (2024, January 18). *WHO releases AI ethics and governance guidance for large multi-modal models*. https://www.who.int/news/item/18-01-2024-who-releases-ai-ethics-and-governance-guidance-for-large-multi-modal-models

Wu, J.-H., & Wang, Y.-M. (2006). Measuring KMS success: A respecification of the DeLone and McLean's model. *Information & Management, 43*(6), 728–739. https://doi.org/10.1016/j.im.2006.03.011

Zach, W. (2023, July 14). Study finds ChatGPT boosts worker productivity for writing tasks. *MIT News*. Retrieved November 2023, from https://news.mit.edu/2023/study-finds-chatgpt-boosts-worker-productivity-writing-0714

Zaixuan, Z., Zhansheng, C., & Liying, X. (2022). Artificial intelligence and moral dilemmas: Perception of ethical decision-making in AI. *Journal of Experimental Social Psychology, 101*, 104327, ISSN 0022-1031.https://doi.org/10.1016/j.jesp.2022.104327

Zajonc, R. B. (1968). Attitudinal effects of mere exposure. *Journal of Personality and Social Psychology, 9*(2, Pt.2), 1–27. https://doi.org/10.1037/h0025848

Zhai, C., Zhang, Y., & Li, H. (2020). AI-generated art: How do people perceive and evaluate it? *Journal of Visual Art Practice, 19*(2), 165–180.

CHAPTER 3

WHO: Human Perspectives on Humane Technology

Abstract Giving voice to a diversity of human perspectives, this chapter grounds the conceptual ideas that were presented in Chapters 1 and 2 into reality through personal essays that illustrate the kaleidoscopic interplay of humans and technology across sectors, disciplines, and cultures. Starting with the 4 *macro*-questions of existence (Why—Who—Where—What) these narratives from innovators, leaders, educators, and artists demonstrate the principle that everything is connected in a continuum of constant change where everything matters, and every action has amplified ripple effects online and offline. Their accounts also illustrate the *Win4* that will be explored in more detail in Chapter 4, whereby action that is taken for others serves the person who acts, the one for whom action is taken, the community they live in, and wider society. This ripple effect is amplified in a hybrid world.

Keywords Personal leadership · Purpose · Motivation · Commitment · *Macro*-questions · Choices

© The Author(s), under exclusive license to Springer Nature Switzerland AG 2024
C. C. Walther, *Human Leadership for Humane Technology*,
https://doi.org/10.1007/978-3-031-67823-3_3

3.1 The Ask: What Are the Dimensions of Agency in a Hybrid World?

Finding answers to the mystery that surrounds the nature of being starts with questions, and the desire of discovery. In an age where "information" abounds, the ability of critical thinking is a precious asset. Even in the interaction with ChatGTP & Co, the quality of the question/prompt conditions to a large extent the quality of the answer/output. Still, the need for questions far precedes the AI-era. The craving to analyze our existence is as old as humanity, and the 4 *macro*-questions that structure the essays in this chapter have been pondered by thinkers and practitioners for thousands of years. There are as many answers as there are humans. The following stories exemplify the journey of evolving in a society that is penetrated by AI, while living with a mindset that seeks to make this travel beneficial to humankind. Each think-piece is unique because each contributor's journey is different. The broad road map that each of them was given is traced by the 4 *macro*-questions:

1. Purpose: Why are You here? In this book, in this life, in this World?
2. Personality: Who are You? As a human being, as a professional?
3. Position: Where do You stand? In your life, your community, your work, your vision?
4. Pursuit: What are You doing to align your aspirations and your actions?

Directly and indirectly, these relate to the *Win4* (more details in Chapter 4.1.1). Contributing to the happiness of others pays off 4 times. In the *micro* arena it benefits the individual "benefactor" and the individual "receiver" (Win-1). In the *meso* arena, the community in which both evolve becomes a bit more resilient and harmonious (Win-2). The multiplication of "happiness ripples" through time and space is felt at the *macro* arena which serves the country (Win-3). The cumulative effects lift the level of well-being in the *meta* arena with ripples across wider society (Win-4). A new social norm arises.

Indirectly the following essays also shed light on some of the subtle links between perception and pursuit, between doing and being, such as:

What is the link between being good and doing good?
What is the link between feeling good and doing good?

What is the link between doing good and feeling good?
What is the link between doing good and becoming good?
What is the link between being good, doing good and being perceived as good?
What do You think?

3.2 The Essays: Illustrating the kaleidoscopic interplay of humans and technology

We grow with each other and might inspire others to come along. The following stories illustrate that while our passions fit us, our purpose must exceed us to serve as a lodestar that inspires us and others along the way. The narratives in the following pages are an invitation to join the hybrid journey of the storyteller. Guided by the millennia-old challenge of being and becoming humane in society, each author shares a piece of their own story. Looking at their own journey each contributor lays out how the 4 dimensions of being—aspirations, emotions, thoughts, and sensations, influenced their interaction with technology, and how the latter has influenced their path. Their experiences illustrate the interconnected causes and consequences of being and remaining humane in a hybrid world.
****

> *Clare Murphy: So that None of us be Missing*
> *Jonathan Kirschner: Shaping a Better Future Through Leadership*
> *Mary Purk: A Journey of Curiosity and Innovation*
> *Josh Plaskoff: Relationality of the Worldly Dramatis Personae*
> *Gale Lucas: Little Did I know.*
> *Hugo Gatsby: The word Impossible says I am possible.*
> *Scott Sandland: Deep Listening.*
> *Lilach Mollick: Designing for a Better World: Pedagogy at Scale*
> *Michael Jabbour: Humanizing Technology*

****

3.2.1   So That None of Us Be Missing

Clare Murphy, Storyteller.
Born July 1976, Dublin, Ireland.

Clare Murphy is a storyteller. She tells ancient myth and folklore, contemporary tales and science, and personal stories. She has told stories on stages and in schools, in castles and on beaches. She has taught at the Royal Shakespeare Company and to President Mary Robinson of Ireland. She makes storytelling shows about all kinds of subjects from ancient myth to quantum physics. Clare also teaches story. She works with mission critical teams, limbless veterans, asylum seekers, teachers, forest school leaders, and many more. Clare is in service to the story; the story is in service to the world. LinkedIn, Twitter/X, IG, Patreon @storyclare Website www.claremurphy.org.

> This world is just a little place, just the red in the sky, before the sun rises, so let us keep fast hold of hands, that when the birds begin, none of us be missing. (Emily Dickinson in a letter to her friend Louise Norcross, 1860 [Smith, 1998])

I have spent the last 18 years wielding an ancient technology that some say has been with humans for 100,000 years (Haven, 2007). This career choice surprised me as much as anyone. Who would choose this? Even as a child, I had never imagined a job such as a "storyteller". It turns out this ancient career is alive and well. We storytellers tell live to audience from our memory without script or book as it has been done for thousands of years.

This ancient technology employs the hardware of the human mind, ear, and mouth. It requires a minimum of two human players, a carrier and a receiver. Story carries knowledge, wisdom, warnings, and lessons. It carries data on how to build healthy and toxic societies, how to gather or destroy wisdom, when to plant, how to love, and what happens when we don't grieve. It is a technology wrapped up in an art form. It is part of the foundation of all the worlds' religions.

We live in a technological age, where new inventions emerge daily to astound us with our own ingenuity. As we stand on the precipice of our latest innovation with AI. This is the moment to stop and ask: what are we doing? What do we need to do next? This is something that story can help us to do.

3.2.1.1 The Healing Power of Ancient Technology

There is a sacred space that exists between people. It is what I call the space-between. In the instant one tells a story the whole room collectively enters the space-between. We find what we have in common. Rather than worrying whether we will be judged/liked, will we be accepted/establish dominance, the story invites all to a communal space where deep connection can happen. It creates empathy and belonging. Since discovering that space-between us, I have stayed as close to it as possible. For me, the place where we meet as a human community is sacred. When we share stories, we reach another realm of community that can diminish depression and isolation, increase our feelings of wellness and belonging, and even increase our ability to withstand pain.

George Bernard Shaw once said "I am of the opinion that my life belongs to the whole community, and as long as I live it is my privilege to do whatever I can. I want to be thoroughly used up when I die, for the harder I work the more I live. I rejoice in life for its own sake. Life is no "brief candle" for me. It is a sort of splendid torch which I have got hold of for the moment, and I want to make it burn as brightly as possible before handing it on to future generations" (Henderson, 1911).

At 29 I picked up the splendid torch of Story. Now at 47, it is incredible to consider that I might keep doing this until I die. Telling stories to an audience gives me an endless source of wonder and joy; it is my direct line to the creative force. Whether I am telling of the ancient Irish goddesses or sharing a wisdom tale, the joy and wonder of it is unlike anything else I've ever experienced.

Soon after becoming a storyteller, I began teaching stories. It is one thing to tell stories, it is another entirely to break it down and transfer it into comprehensible parts. What I learned by teaching is that it is a far more powerful technology than I ever could have imagined.

For many years I worked with limbless veterans. Our job was to train the veterans in storytelling skills so that they could tell the story of how they dealt with limb loss. In these rooms were men and women who had lost limbs, become paralyzed, blind, or severely burned. Many of them had to relearn the most basic skills such as walking or talking. Every year with them was a lesson in what is possible, and what story can do.

A young man had lost both of his legs in an IED explosion in Afghanistan. He was a tall man, he walked on two prosthetic lower legs. However, he hunched and always seemed shorter than his 6'2 frame. When he spoke, which was rare, his voice was barely above a whisper. He struggled to join in conversation unless asked. As we worked through his story, we noticed small moments of illumination in his voice and body, but really we thought that he would never overcome that shyness.

After finishing the storytelling training, he went on to tell stories in schools around the UK. He then got a job as an accountant in a major car company. He came back to us a year later for his refresher training, and we barely recognized him. He strode into the room, greeting everyone in a beautiful bright voice; he walked up to veterans he didn't know and introduced himself. He stood tall and laughed easily. At the end of refresher training, when asked what his takeaway learning was he said: "Every time I tell my story I release something from inside of me that has been killing me".

3.2.1.2 Storytelling and Transformation
Story has an incredible capacity to do the impossible with the human brain. It is 2015 and I am standing in a large room at a festival in California. I am about to deliver a two-hour storytelling workshop. The room is mixed; some who have never told a story before, others who had told many. I use some simple exercises that get people talking and practicing easily. I start by telling them a story, so that they can use it in the exercises to follow. Time passes quickly. I constantly changed the combinations of who sat with who as it can help keep the energy up. One woman asks if she and her husband could remain paired together for the whole workshop. "Of course", I say and think no more of it. Everyone works hard and laughs a lot. Stories are told and many feel much more confident in their abilities at the end.

At the end of the workshop, the woman waits around. She leans in and earnestly says "Thank you". "Oh, you're welcome" I say. Being thanked is not unusual, but she doesn't leave. Instead she squeezes my hand harder and seems close to tears. "No, you don't understand. I have to thank you for what you've just done. Did you notice my husband?" I nod. He had asked some pretty good questions and they both seemed to be having a great time. "My husband has Alzheimer. It's very advanced. Communication is very hard for him". I am shocked. I had noticed nothing of the sort in his speech or his communications with me. "Today he was able to follow what you said, to tell stories, it was like he was back". She is crying, and then I am crying. We grasp hands and stand for a moment in the wonder of that. How is that possible? What happened there?

Every year things like this happen. Selective mutes who choose to speak, dyslexics inspired to read. A woman with chronic pain found her pain stopped for the first time when she listened to a story by a certain storyteller. Science begins to study these phenomena and find the data to support the anecdotes. Studies on children hospitalized show that their pain levels decrease if they are told stories (Brockington et al., 2021). Story unlocks people; it has the power to transform both teller and listener. Stories allow us to wrestle demons, expand our empathy, they allow us to think things through, forecast, reflect, and make meaning of our experiences. This ancient technology walks alongside us as a guide, teacher, and companion.

3.2.1.3   AI Through the Lens of Story
As we stand on the edge of a new technological advancement, AI, I am deeply concerned. What will this new advancement do to the space-between us? There are many old myths and folktales about the protagonist who is warned not to pursue a certain path, because the consequences will be devastating. The protagonist disregards the warnings and takes action, only to discover there were very good reasons for the warnings. They often learn the lesson at great cost to themselves and their community. I think of Midas and his gold lust, who nearly starves to death because of his desire for gold. As we enter the realm of AI, we are granting ourselves the power of the golden touch. We do it because we can. This impulse to move without reflection is dangerous.

Can we shape AI effectively amid our hurry to create it? The private companies that are creating AI are driven by profit. This is at odds with the Common Good. In a recent interview at Slate magazine, Meredith Whittaker, President at Signal, reminded us that bias is already present in AI. "My concern with some of the arguments that are so-called existential, the most existential, is that they are implicitly arguing that we need to wait until the people who are most privileged now, who are not threatened currently, are in fact threatened before we consider a risk big enough to care about. Right now, low-wage workers, people who are historically marginalized, Black people, women, disabled people, people in countries that are on the cusp of climate catastrophe—many, many folks are at risk. Their existence is threatened or otherwise shaped and harmed by the deployment of these systems. We can look at these systems used in law enforcement. There's a New York Times story from a few months back about a man who was imprisoned based on a false facial recognition match. That is deeply existential for that person's life. That person was Black" (Leary, 2023). We are creating a system that will perpetuate the injustices we currently live in. Is this in service to a better future for all?

Before we fully embrace AI, there is time to take a moment and ask ourselves what are we doing? Thinkers at AI Now Institute are doing just that. In their landscape report of 2023 they state: "This watershed moment must also swiftly give way to action: to galvanize the considerable energy that has already accumulated over several years towards developing meaningful checks on the trajectory of AI technologies" (AI Now Institute, 2023).

We have often raced headlong towards invention out of fear or curiosity, without the peace of mind required for meaningful action. Meaningful action would allow us to consider the consequences. But if we get the golden touch, and everything turns to gold, what will we eat?

What if alongside this race to give birth to AI, we also take time to re-humanize ourselves after what has been a challenging time in human development?

Story can be a useful tool in the reflection and meaning-making process as well as in the re-humanization process. In the telling of our own stories, we come to know ourselves. In the retelling of our myths and folklore, we come to know our ancestors. In listening to stories, we make sense of what has happened. In listening to stories, we connect to the space-between where we perceive each other as a sacred community.

As we stand on the edge of this new epoch, I am reminded of some beautiful words from Emily Dickinson in a letter to her friend:

> This world is just a little place, just the red in the sky, before the sun rises, so let us keep fast hold of hands, that when the birds begin, none of us be missing. (Smith, 1998)

As we take this next leap, let us hold fast in each other's hands... the Global Majority, the marginalized, the Global South, our disabled Peoples, our Indigenous Peoples. Let us hold fast to the hands of the children, to the people we disagree with, to those who look different to us, to the Elders, to all of us... so that when the sun rises on the new world we want to invent, none of us be missing.

3.2.2 Shaping a Better Future Through Leadership

Jonathan Kirschner, Psy.D. Founder and CEO of AIIR Consulting. Born 1980 in Saint Louis, MO, USA.

Dr. Jonathan Kirschner is the Founder and CEO of AIIR Consulting—a global business psychology consulting firm dedicated to increasing the effectiveness of leaders worldwide. He is also the Founder and CEO of AIIR Analytics, a people analytics company focused on next-generation leadership assessment and succession planning technology. In 2009, he developed a coaching methodology for achieving sustained behavior change called AIIR®. He also developed AIIR Consulting's technology platform, the Coaching Zone®. Dr. Kirschner regularly shares his thought leadership and research through writing and conference presentations. Dr. Kirschner is also an executive coach, specializing in working with CEOs and senior leaders seeking to bolster their emotional intelligence, managerial effectiveness, team leadership, and strategic thinking. Additionally, he supervises a team of over 200 coaches around the world. Dr. Kirschner graduated from New York University with a BA in Psychology and Religion. He holds a Doctorate in Clinical and Business Psychology from Widener University.

3.2.2.1 My Purpose

I look back fondly on my walks with my late cousin Judy. One evening, when I was around ten years old, she asked me if I believed in destiny. I was struck by the depths of exploration that the question evoked. I looked at every angle, and ultimately, we reached the topic of free will. Humans have a unique capacity to make choices. By exercising our free will, we can determine our destiny. Moreover, if we can shape our future through conscious decisions, then something must guide those choices. This something would be the organizing mechanism for everything I do, my choices, and ultimately, what I believe, feel, and do. It would be my purpose.

A decade later, I was in Jerusalem engaged in self-discovery and spiritual exploration at a Yeshiva in the old city of Jerusalem. One afternoon, I was on a park bench, watching the pigeons aimlessly pecking at the ground. I was fully present and unfocused. Though I had been wracking my brain for years about my purpose and what I would be when I grew up, it was this moment when my relaxed mind gave way to a deep and immediate clarity. My mission would be to help others through my gifts of human connection, understanding, and problem-solving. The clarity was not cognitive but rather one of those knock-your-socks-off, aha moments when your whole body feels it.

This purpose began to organize my disparate energies, and as I went through college and then doctoral training to become a psychologist, everything I learned was funneled through this purpose. If I learned a new skill, I would tuck it away in my toolbox. If it was a new psychoanalytic theory, I would scrutinize it, store it, and attempt to integrate it with other theories. In my clinical work with patients, I would document and reflect upon every key moment to hone my skills and become a more impactful practitioner.

However, two practical concerns emerged in the early years of my training. First, I recognized the limitations of being a single practitioner. There would be a limit to the amount of people I could impact. Even if I worked exceptionally hard, carrying a caseload of more than 50 people at a time would be very difficult. Second, I could get depleted and burned out from absorbing people's problems daily for the rest of my life. I started to think of ways to derisk these challenges, and midway through graduate training, I took a course in leadership psychology and executive coaching. My initial curiosity was that I might find an additional avenue to diversify my offerings, thus derisking burnout and adding more scale to my impact. Little did I know that this domain, which I approached with initial skepticism, would further ignite and focus my purpose.

Because of their positional power and influence, I understood that leaders were in a unique position to affect many other people. For example, a CEO of a 30,000-person organization can make their people's lives enhanced and meaningful. Moreover, the CEO's ability to successfully harness the workforce and execute a sound strategy could deliver a life-saving product that affects millions of customers. Conversely, a bad leader can do incredible harm.

Imagine a hospital leader who is conflict-avoidant, unclear about his vision, and lacks the courage to hold his team accountable. When he becomes overwhelmed, he recedes into his closed office, avoiding the emotionally charged relationships and decisions he knows he has to face. As a result, his team engages in unproductive behaviors, operating as individuals rather than as an aligned collective. Each team member manages their respective departments in varied ways with limited coordination. The doctors and nurses feel disengaged because the system is not set up for success. To survive, they must compensate by working in overdrive or resigning to apathy. While the 4,000-person staff suffers, the real tragedy is the customer—the patient—whose experience, treatment, and life depend on the functionality or dysfunction of the system. As I came to understand this concept—the cascading influence that a single leader could possess—my purpose became even clearer. My focused mission was to align my gifts of human understanding and intervention with the pursuit of developing excellent leaders.

3.2.2.2 My Work and Vision

In my 4th year of doctoral training, I conceived the idea to start a business, AIIR Consulting. I knew I could deliver an impact as a single practitioner, but I wanted the ability to go beyond anything that I could deliver alone. The idea of starting a company where I would get to do the work I loved and enable many others to do this work was invigorating. The idea that this work could spread globally, at scale, even while I was sleeping, was electrifying.

The aim was to have an exponential impact, and the immediate hurdle was figuring out how to deliver a very high-touch executive-level service at scale. While my passion was clinical and business psychology, I was blown away by how technology could scale the service, expand access, and potentially deepen the impact of the work itself. In the beginning, this was video conferencing technology. Through high-definition video, a leader and their coach could meet at the click of a button and see each other no matter where they were located. As the video thesis played out, we invested further and built the Coaching Zone. This software platform gave the coach and coachee a digital environment to collaborate and share information. We extended the value to our HR partners, who wanted to optimize their enterprise coaching strategy by having all the coaching work that was going on in their organization accessible in a single, cloud-based environment. Today, we are focused on the application of AI in coaching. Our new digital coaching assistant, Aiiron, can bolster human coaching by helping a leader work through a challenge or get reminded about their goals in between human coaching sessions.

Our vision today is to be the world's leading expert on leadership. On the journey to becoming a successful venture, it is easy to fall into the trap of being all things to everyone. I've learned the hard way that this is a sure path to failure. I have learned to get hyper-focused on the few things that make us excellent. These special pillars for us are—
Our Expertise: Doing great work is a noble goal, but driving excellence requires more. Excellence requires a degree of obsession for the customer, a relentless pursuit for outperformance, and a command of the domain. At AIIR, we've built expertise through our carefully selected bench of coaches, our developed perspective on leadership and behavior change, and our ability to continuously learn and adapt to grow our impact.

Our Change Methodology: The AIIR® Method. Every leader's needs are different, every coach's approach is different, and every coaching engagement has a unique context. From the very beginning, I knew that we would need a common approach to coaching that could maximize impact, deliver predictable quality, and ensure a consistent customer experience. For us, that would become the AIIR® method; a 4-stage process I developed for creating sustained behavioral change. The Acronym stands for Assessment, Insight, Implementation, and Reinforcement.

AIIR technology: Though our leadership consultants drive the results, we invest heavily in building leadership technology because it makes those results scalable, even more impactful, and lasting. Because of this, we view ourselves as a tech-enabled services business. AIIR Consulting is one of the only tech-enabled consulting firms focusing exclusively on leadership (as opposed to all employees within an organization).

3.2.2.3 Lessons I've Learned

When I look back on day one of the business, where I'm at right now, and where I believe we can go, no better word emerges than "journey". A journey involves moving towards a vision, though never in a linear way. There have been twists and turns, wins and losses, pride and embarrassment, energy and exhaustion. As a leader on the great journey, it's vital that you believe in your mission, that you find ways to stay healthy, and that you never stop learning. If any of those three elements is missing, the journey will unravel and become aimless energy and motion.

I have now been a CEO for over 14 years. While I still have so much to learn, there are seven principles I've come to believe are imperative for any successful Founder and CEO.

Aim high. My good friend and executive coach, Jamie Ramsden, taught me to always aim for the stars, and if I hit the moon, that wouldn't be so bad. I always have striven for something that is challenging and seemingly out of reach. I have missed my goals more than I have achieved them, but I almost always arrive at a result greater than anything I could have imagined.

Harness the polarities—Leadership can be disorienting because there are so many pushes and pulls in every direction. My colleague Dr. Derek Lusk introduced a brilliant theory called AIIR Dynamics. Leaders need to be able to balance leadership skills that are often competing. Focusing on People can sometimes conflict with a focus on results. Focusing on Strategy can sometimes get in the way of rolling up your sleeves to execute. Which competencies to use, and when, requires incredible situational awareness and an ability to balance polarities.

Hope and belief are the most powerful emotions in your organization, and it is the CEO's job to be a beacon of hope. Without hope, work becomes mired in politics, process, and toxicity. Over time, hope deprivation can create a death spiral. It is a leader's duty to bring hope, even under the most challenging circumstances, when the leader's hope is hanging by a thread.

You will make enemies. Leaders often arrive in their positions because of their excellent people skills and uncanny ability to get everyone to like them. But at a certain point, the leader realizes that to achieve their compelling vision, they will need to push hard, have a point of view, take risks, and make tough calls that create winners and losers. Creating enemies is inevitable, and the leader must embrace this reality.

The right team. The right products and services will die under the wrong people. Creating a Talent Pipeline is one of the most important things you can do as a leader. It is challenging, time-consuming, and takes you away from immediate sales and execution. It is, however, the most important way to drive and sustain success.

Reinforce the North Star. Without a North Star, work is a grind, and people march on aimlessly. Productivity is constrained, distractions become pervasive, and the organization operates reactively rather than strategically. The leader's job is establishing the North Star, the raison d'etre for the organization. But a leader cannot just set it and forget it. The most successful leaders help their people make continuous meaning of the North Star. They are constantly beating the drum and reminding their people about the fundamental why that underlies their work.

Courage. Setting a vision and building a strategy is an invigorating cognitive activity that leaders relish. However, to carry out the strategy day in and day out requires courage. There are days that are elating and days that are devastating. Decision points that are simple and decisions that are chock full of ambiguity. Every combination of emotions will emerge. Some varieties will propel you, some will be headwinds, and some will be paralyzing. Ultimately, it takes courage to move forward. If a leader is struggling, stagnating, or feels they are not operating at their best, they must do a courage check. They must ask themselves, do I have enough courage to achieve the needed outcome? If not, how can I cultivate this courage? Who can support me in generating the courage I need to deliver?

3.2.2.4 Concluding Thoughts

Leadership is actualizing a compelling vision through others. The vision must be constantly set, and the people must be managed and inspired. All of this has to happen with constancy despite external circumstances, obstacles, and inevitable failures.

Over time, both through serving leaders and becoming one myself, I've concluded that leadership isn't actually all that much fun and glamorous. On the contrary, it's often more like a grueling, full-contact sport. While there can be perks, limelight, and sometimes great rewards, all of this can be quickly offset by the loneliness and endless flow of tasks, challenges, and decisions that tend to amplify as a function of success. So what matters the most in the end is the impact you make, not the attention you receive, how you feel, or the rewards you reap. A leader's success is ultimately measured on this alone—did they achieve their vision successfully through others? As Steve Jobs might have asked, did they make a meaningful dent in the universe?

As I continue to grow, my purpose has taken on greater meaning and weight. The deeper I get into this work and the more exposed I become to the repeating history of human civilization, the clearer I become about the importance of leadership. Leadership is the greatest lever for change and our greatest hope for shaping a better future. Moving the needle on an individual leader requires skill and expertise. Moving the needle for the state of global leadership requires combining that expertise with thoughtfully designed technology to deliver impact at scale.

3.2.3 A Journey of Curiosity and Innovation

Mary Purk.
Born in Evanston, Illinois.
Mary is the Executive Director of AI at Wharton. Following 20+ years of analytics, consulting and business development experience in various industries including retail and consumer packaged goods, she now leads Wharton's academic research center that focuses on the development and application of cutting-edge AI, GenAI, and ML methods and human impact.

My journey with data and technology began in the most unexpected of places: the red circle at the Chiaravelle Montessori School in Evanston, Illinois. As a five-year-old, I was the oldest of three children, living in a modest apartment across from Ryan Field, the home of the Northwestern Wildcats. I was encouraged and nurtured by parents dedicated to Maria Montessori's educational philosophy, to inspire lifelong learners to be curious, compassionate, and innovative thinkers. Maria Montessori was singularly focused on how the child sees the world and how structure needed to be balanced with the freedom to explore and learn. She emphasized discovery, order, and creative play—a foundation that inadvertently sculpted my future in marketing, technology, and leadership.

The Montessori way, with its respect for order and encouragement of innovative expression, laid the groundwork for my confidence in marketing and data. I remember vividly the accomplishment of solving geometry proofs as a sophomore in high school. (Alas, no one takes geometry anymore and yet it is the one math class that makes you think theoretically.) I continued with math in college and thought I might even be an engineer, especially as I weirdly enjoyed coding with Fortran to solve simple business problems in the basement of the DCL—the digital computer lab, at the University of Illinois. However, just manipulating numbers to solve complex equations was pushing me further away from people and how they behave. I soon realized that the combination of data and questions was my passion and that I was drawn to marketing. Connecting with people to understand why they would purchase items seemed much more interesting. Afterall, I was the daughter of an ad executive. I wanted to know what convinced a consumer to purchase or get excited about a product. This was the beginning of the thirst for data to answer the complex questions around consumer purchase behavior.

3.2.3.1 Twists and Turns
In a twist that surprised even myself, I turned down a brand assistant position at General Mills to be a programming analyst at Andersen Consulting, now known as Accenture. Schematics, testing and COBOL coding, which were initially challenging, gradually became mundane as I found myself designing schematic flow charts for complex logistical and administrative processes. Fortunately, my weekend MBA program at the Booth School of Business, University of Chicago, offered a welcome diversion, introducing me to the entrepreneurial risks of start-ups and the importance of data analytics in marketing. Lucky for me, Booth grounds all of its students in theoretical frameworks that help them define problems, ask better questions, and develop better solutions. I combined this philosophy with that of my Montessori background and I have found

that it has allowed me to be incredibly creative and driven in both my personal and professional life. Combining this approach with my interest in data and what makes consumers/customers tick has provided endless opportunities to excel at work, in my community and my family life.

Database marketing and statistics were just beginning to intersect more and more in the business world in the 90s, and I was lucky enough to find an opportunity that would change my trajectory in data and analytics expertise for the remainder of my career, despite taking a break to raise my 4 children in the 2000s. In the final quarter of my MBA, I was presented with an opportunity that seemed tailor-made for me: the position of business research manager at the Micro-Merchandising Center, a collaboration between 22 consumer goods companies, Dominick's (the second-largest grocery chain in Chicago), and Booth marketing faculty. This role perfectly married my interests in consumer behavior and predictive analytics.

Over 4 years, our team conducted 500 experiments across 26 consumer grocery and drug retail categories to significantly contribute to the field of marketing research, specifically around pricing and promotions. Our findings not only informed industry practices for nearly 20 years but also continues to be a staple in academic pricing and marketing courses. Even today, our "EDLP, Hi-Lo Margin Arithmetic" Journal of Marketing paper (https://www.jstor.org/stable/1251913) is quoted in research papers, highlighting in the time of Walmart's rise to prosperity that an Everyday low pricing policy does not necessary generate the profits if the foot traffic is not sustainable. Even today, many more retailers use Hi-Lo pricing to manage their revenue portfolio versus an EDLP strategy. However, I believe with the age of computing power and AI Large Language Models—a new day of individual pricing is going to create a whole new area of study around the willingness to pay.

In the early 2000s an opportunity for my spouse brought us out to Salt Lake City. Being so far away from my Booth network and business colleagues with no zoom capabilities and no iphones. (Think Blackberries and dial-up modems, very slow internet access, USB drives.) I paused my career to focus on raising my 4 children in Salt Lake City, a period during which my professional engagement with data and analytics took a backseat.

3.2.3.2 Confluent Roads

Upon returning to Chicago later, with my children grown and fewer familial responsibilities, I found myself yearning for the intellectual stimulation of my earlier career. I re-entered the professional world at Nielsen as a custom analytics engagement manager, working with major retailers and quick-service restaurants. This role marked my renaissance in the world of data and analytics, allowing me to apply my accumulated knowledge and skills to complex business challenges. It is at this point, I realized that I was so fortunate to have been literally ahead of the curve when working on a large multifaceted dataset and talented academics that applied rigorous statistical methods to consumer-based questions at Booth. From Nielsen and another data-intensive company—Information Resources—I discovered that data is always at the heart of the answer to the marketing questions and technology is the engine that can deliver knowledge and insights faster and better. The coding languages and algorithms will continue to improve but the questions are always endless and not solvable unless there is good comprehensive data and curious researchers to frame the question. I continued to work with my colleagues at Booth and from that networking found myself recommended to join Wharton initially as the executive director of Wharton Customer Analytics and then eventually AI at Wharton research center.

Today, as the Executive Director of AI at Wharton as well as the Director of Corporate Relations at Analytics at Wharton, I develop cutting-edge AI and analytics programs that bring together faculty, companies, and students to solve today's most pressing problems that involve data across various industries. My role at the Wharton School is a confluence of data, technology, and education. We strive to demystify the complexities of analytics, providing practical, hands-on experiences that transform academic insights into real-world business strategies.

My journey, from the Montessori classroom to the forefront of AI and analytics, reflects a lifelong commitment to learning and adapting. It underscores the importance of human leadership in the realm of technology—I am a leader that values curiosity, embraces innovation, and remains steadfast in my pursuit of creative solutions to benefit many constituents.

In this digital and AI age, my philosophy revolves around the convergence of knowledge, ideas, and marketplace practicalities. I believe in leading with empathy, understanding the human element behind the data, and leveraging technology to enhance, not replace, human capabilities. My career has been a testament to the power of curiosity and the transformative potential of data, technology, and leadership.

As we navigate this ever-evolving landscape, my mission remains clear: to guide, inspire, and nurture the next generation of leaders who will shape the future of technology with human curiosity at its core.

3.2.4 Relationality of the Worldly Dramatis Personae

Dr. Josh Plaskoff, Founder, interhuman group; Senior Lecturer, Organizational Leadership, Purdue Polytechnic Institute.
Born 1963, Los Angeles, CA, USA.

Dr. Josh Plaskoff is founder of the interhuman group and Senior Lecturer in Organizational Leadership at Purdue Polytechnic Institute. With over 30 years of experience, Dr. Plaskoff has sought to achieve his lifelong mission of "making the workplace more human" by serving as a leader and visionary, helping organizations, teams, and individuals reach their greatest potential by creating learning environments of dignity and respect. He has maintained a concurrent academic career both at Purdue and Indiana University's Kelley School of Business. Recently he was elected to the Top 50 Most Influential People in Tacit Knowledge Management.

3.2.4.1 Prologue (My Story)

I grew up with the conviction that the world is a stage and we play our parts in the global human drama (or perhaps comedy). As Whitman has said: "The powerful play goes on and you may contribute a verse". My life has been a continuous writing and editing of that verse. A wise person once told me that life looking forward is a total mess but life looking backward is a straight line. I firmly believe that things do happen for a reason—they present us with a still small voice of purpose and direction that, if we listen, open up possibilities and opportunities. But do we listen? I have always been intrigued by the human condition, by what is being asked of us, by how we collaborate with or conspire against each other. Recently I noticed an uptick in the use of the phrase "hold people accountable", and for some reason it bothered me. As I reflected deeply, I discovered a strong personal belief that laid tacit for decades but unconsciously precipitated all my actions and decisions. Accountability represents an enforcement from without, invoking fear for action, but responsibility is a commitment from within driven by conscience and relationship with the Other. The "holding accountable" indicates a crisis of responsibility. I consider myself a responsible being, obligated because of my humanness and my belonging to humanity to respond to others—to people's joy and sorrow, their needs to give and receive, their becoming.

Being unmaterialistic (except for books), I did not anticipate working in business and have often struggled with free market capitalism as the basis for society. However, a temporary job in a software company in the 1980s became a career in a large technology company and eventually evolved into a calling when I joined a large pharmaceutical company. Every seven years or so, I would build on, adjust, transform, or enhance my life philosophy and those personal changes translated into organizational changes informed by a perspective focused on alterity, respect, and dignity, guided by a "beginner's mind" and openness to learning, and one infused with transcendental meaning beyond shareholder value, KPIs, and promotions. Interestingly, resistance to my unconventional approaches was quelled when they led to significant business results. True humanity CAN lead to profits and sustainability.

Turning sixty, I have decided to take an additional step in my journey—instead of residing in the corporate world, I am focusing on teaching the next generation about possibilities that our generation has neglected in the hopes that they will listen to "still small voices" within themselves and become fully human.

3.2.4.2 My Play (My Work and Vision)

I am convinced that we are at a critical crossroads. We are more polarized than ever. We have created technologies that, rather than augmenting our humanity, threaten to annihilate it—intellectually, relationally, and physically. We have lost either the skill or will to dialogue, closing our eyes to the inherent contradictoriness of reality in favor of a hubris attributed to sidedness. And, at least in the West, we have bought in on the fiction of our separability, as if we humans are merely a mass of senseless particles, pointlessly, fatalistically, mindlessly, colliding in a predictable world. I have grown to believe otherwise—that we are massively and meaningfully entangled in a world that we are called on to "repair" together. As a result, my work has progressively developed into nurturing dialogical relationality in organizational life, whether mediated by technology or not. Probably the best way to share my work is to trace its evolution over the years—to turn the mess into a straight line.

Perhaps you can look at my progression as a play unto itself, one comprising three acts: Act I, Discovery and Rebellion, Act 2, Socio-Cultural Understanding, and Act 3, Relationality. As with any good play, each one builds on and enriches the next.

3.2.4.3   Act I: Discovery and Rebellion
In 1989, I oversaw the design of service training for one of the large volume laser printers at Xerox Corporation. We worked for half a year partnering with engineers and design experts to develop a five-week training course to be delivered at the training center in Leesburg, Virginia. Interestingly, the service reps did not like coming to the training, but they loved coming to the training center. Work avoidance? No. My team invited me for drinks in the training center's bar to celebrate my birthday. I noticed something spectacular. The reps sat together, drinking, and sharing what we didn't present in the training class. They were animated. They were passionate. They were engaged. I realized that our training classes did not allow for the socializing necessary to learn. My focus changed. New question surfaced. How can we provide more interactive learning experiences rather than training? How could technology provide this interactivity? I had started my career at an educational software company a few years earlier and was doing graduate work at USC and had regretted that technology was used so mechanically in learning. How could we create intelligent, immersive, interactive learning worlds that blended technology and human interaction? I rebelled against the training informed by archaic behavioristic models. From my rebellion came an artificial intelligence simulation learning environment prototype to supplement problem-based live learning. Unfortunately, few understood this concept because it was years ahead of its time. From this experience, I learned three things: (1) We were guided by outdated, limited, and inaccurate models; (2) Learning is an existential part of being human, not an event; and (3) Experiences that integrate technology and social interaction can be designed to promote intellectual, emotional, and spiritual growth on both a personal and social level.

3.2.4.4   Act II: Socio-Cultural Understanding
My impetuous and impatient youth got the best of me, so making no progress on moving my vision forward, I went to a seminary (as many expected I would). After two years, I left with an altered personal mission, one informed by the greater challenges of the world and civilization.

Returning to my old profession, I saw the environment as primary for human learning and technology as supportive. I firmly believed (and still believe) that learning existentially drives our humanness and does so through social co-action and co-construction of the world around us. I began work at Eli Lilly, a large pharmaceutical company whose research labs became my lab for my new perspective. I began focusing on nurturing communities of practice. Working with Etienne Wenger, whose impact on me has been immeasurable, I sought to demonstrate that intangible dimensions of humanity (love, care, hope, respect, dignity, etc.), often thought as superfluous to business, would enhance it both socially and financially. Instead of practice, however, I sought to recover the forgotten nature of "genuine community" (as sought by Martin Buber) to promote social learning and human growth. Initial attempts failed, but I soon created oases within the organization that thrived and contributed tremendously to the bottom line. At the heart of community was the reincarnated political concept of covenant as opposed to contract, wherein a covenant represents a moral commitment between equal parties that consciously creates community, a relationship of mutual respect, dignity, integrity in which meaning is negotiated to enhance human growth and meet human needs. This relationship differs from the temporary, quid pro quo, self-interested contractual relationships that dominate most dimensions of our lives. Covenant leads to a voluntary member-leader relationship forged on equality of being, in which co-action is catalyzed through meaning negotiation and dialogic engagement. Over several years, I developed a methodology distinct from conventional organizational development approaches, implemented them successfully in several different companies and industries, and demonstrated that profits can be generated through humanity.

3.2.4.5 Act III: Relationality

As my professional and learning life continued, I realized the fundamental base from which my life work derived—relationality. Social and organizational theory have turned to classical physics, materialism, and reductionism as their foundations. My exposure to quantum physics, modern-day philosophers, alternative psychological models like Jung, and even modern-day neuroscientists (particularly Iain McGilchrist), made me realize that we have things backwards. We view objects as primary and their relationships as secondary. But recent thinking (which echoes ancient religions and mysticism) has discovered that relationships are primary and define the thingness of the world. The history of my past work was promoting a relational view in organizations from which to forge a supporting structure. A number of concepts from these modern theorists contribute to a clearer understanding of how to approach this new paradigm including indeterminacy, uncertainty, complementarity, synchronicity, entanglement, and limitations of human reasoning. Blending this work with design thinking and user experience, I recently developed a new approach to looking at organizations called employee experience. This is nothing less than completely reformulating the relationship between employees and organizations based on a relational understanding of organizations. Given the recent COVID-19 pandemic and the new reality that has come with it, I believe that this is necessary more than ever.

Epilogue (Takeaway for Readers)
As I enter the third act, perhaps the last, I have realized with great humility, awe, wonder, and respect, the task ahead—one demanding utmost personal, collective, and moral responsibility, but one with significant potential to re-soul our world. Recounting my journey, I seek what drove where I've been and where it will take me. I'm reminded of a Zen story. A monk visited his colleague and as they walked together, they crossed a bridge over a river. The visitor asked how deep the river was. He was pushed into the water and became enlightened. We know that swimming in the deep end of a pool is a different experience from seeing the number 10 emblazoned on the pool wall tiles or seeing an object at the bottom. When in the water, we directly and qualitatively experience the depth. Much of our life is re-presented to us, through captured images, language, through our perceptions, distancing, abstracting reality to simplify and allow us to generalize. While it is important, if we only abstract, we sacrifice the core of our existence—the collective, qualitative, direct experiences we share. The wise have known this for ages. We need to rethink how we relate, requiring us to approach life with a beginner's mind, unafraid to question, challenge, and fail in our thinking. Technology can assist us in this journey, but it can also mislead us. The lure of what we can do overshadows our consideration of what we should do. It can augment our humanness, or it can replace it, stunt it, limit it, enslave it, or even annihilate it. Growing up, I was often exposed to the unity of the world, both religiously and philosophically. What I learned later that I wish I had known is that unity for us is asymptotic and the world

around us (rife with the non-rational) is fragmented through our rational tools and asymmetric brains. But much a play joins together many lines or verses, each spoken by different characters, our destiny can only be achieved through the co-creation of that play in the moment. What will your verses be? What will our play become?

3.2.5 The Word Impossible Says "I'm possible"

Hugo Gatsby, Managing Partner, Stradea Design Labs.
Born 1982, Hamilton, Ontario, Canada.

Hugo is an award-winning designer and author. Hugo leverages user experience design (UXD), behavioral science, and gamification to build engaging solutions in the private sector. He has collaborated with companies such as Hamilton Health Sciences, Bank of Montreal, Bell Canada, Deloitte Canada, Jean-Paul Gaultier, Art Gallery of Hamilton and even Netflix. Mr. Gatsby worked as a behavioral science consultant and facilitator for Deloitte Canada, as a change management trainer for Hamilton Health Sciences, a lead digital strategist for the Bank of Montreal, while also running an award-winning accessibility-first creative agency called Stradea Design Labs.

When we think of passion in the realm of behavioral design, experience sits at the forefront. In my life, I have had many mentors. Each showed dedication to their fields and demonstrated a profound commitment to innovation, excellence, and a relentless pursuit of the greater purpose.

My unwavering belief in the "why" of my work stems from two individuals: my first commanding officer while attending the Royal Military College, and most important, my stepfather. Their life lessons have been used as a guiding post for me since my adolescent years. To me "why" centers around understanding and improving human behavior to create a positive impact. My perception of the world has always been slightly different. The way I interact with my surroundings has always been a challenge. To find a place to feel like I "belong" has been my life's ambition. This mission fuels my passion for behavioral design, gamification and drives me to build a world where people like me feel they can thrive.

It was once told to me that "success is a mountain. When you get to the top, think about who you want there beside you. I can tell you with complete certainty, enjoying the view with a friend will always be better than standing there by yourself". When I heard that advice, I began to create an environment where my colleagues feel safe to experiment and innovate. I encourage them to stretch beyond their limits. My enthusiasm for behavioral and user experience design has sparked creativity in all avenues of my work.

Growing up non-verbal, my communication was limited, but I learned to listen and learn, fostering passion. Over time, I've inspired colleagues to experiment and innovate, embracing teamwork. As an adult with ASD, I have learned to be unafraid to challenge established norms and take calculated risks to advance my field. My passion for pushing the boundaries has allowed me to redefine corporate structures and drive positive change in how we understand and influence collaboration as well as team dynamics.

My journey has encountered many setbacks and challenges throughout my life. However, these are lessons I value and learn from. Each time, I improve and evolve. Adversity is integral in any game, so why should the same not be true for life? My belief is that the transformative power of having fun has been a catalyst to much of my academic career, as well as my prominent years in the world of consulting. It is through all of my life experiences, good or bad, that I have been able to create a better world for those I have helped.

3.2.5.1 Issue—Action—Impact

In recent years, I've had the opportunity to witness a transformation in work cultures and productivity. It can be attributed to three key pillars in my experience: gamification, the concept of the infinite game, and the value of trust. These elements, when woven together, have the power to create work environments that are not only more positive but also vastly more productive.

Allow me to delve into this convergence.

Gamification, in essence, is the art of applying game mechanics and principles to non-gaming contexts, particularly the workplace. It's a concept that has captured my fascination because it taps into something fundamentally human: our innate desire for challenge, achievement, and reward. By incorporating game elements such as support character, ranking, leaderboards, progress tracking, badges, and interactive narratives into our work-related activities, we've been able to harness a wellspring of motivation and engagement that was previously untapped in work cultures.

One of the most remarkable ways gamification has influenced my work is by redefining motivation. In the past, many of us were confined to tasks that left us feeling uninspired. With gamification, we're presented with opportunities to earn rewards, gain recognition, and progress through challenges. As an employee/consultant, I've experienced how ineffective management styles reduce cohesive environments. When I have applied my frameworks of gamification, I find teams more invested in their tasks when there's a tangible sense of accomplishment tied to them.

I've limited my use of gamification tactics to a list of 68 tactics across 8 categories: general, player (individual), community, support, change, objective and key results (OKR), rewards, and exploratory. When elements of these categories are combined, a solution is created that has been tailored to the situational analysis. By leveraging this framework, I have been able to create an infinite number of solutions to solve client or team problems, but still stay within a fundamental framework (learn more here: https://theidea.ca/gamification-101/gamification-tactics/).

Beyond motivation, gamification has also cultivated a sense of healthy competition within teams and departments. Leaderboards and friendly competitions have encouraged us to strive for excellence and collaborate with our colleagues to achieve shared goals. This spirit of competition, when channeled correctly, propels individuals and teams to push their boundaries and achieve remarkable results.

Never forget the importance of regular feedback and recognition when developing your gamified engagement plan. When employees receive constructive feedback and are acknowledged for their contributions, they are more likely to be engaged and committed. Recognition doesn't always have to be grand gestures; even small gestures of appreciation can go a long way in fostering a positive work environment.

What gamification has been to engagement, the infinite game theory can be to financial business success.

Gamification may ignite motivation and engagement, but it's vital to couple it with a broader perspective that transcends short-term wins and losses. This is where the concept of the infinite game, beautifully articulated by Simon Sinek, comes into play. The infinite game is about recognizing that work, like life itself, is not a finite contest with clear winners and losers. Instead, it's an ongoing journey with no defined endpoint, where the goal is not to win but to keep playing and evolving. Businesses do not "win" at an infinite game, they work to outlast their competitors.

Incorporating the infinite game mindset into our work cultures has had a profound impact on how we approach challenges and setbacks.

It encourages us to shift our focus from competing against others to competing against ourselves—to be better today than we were yesterday. This is the golden rule of the infinite game. Employees and organizations share a common vision and mission that goes beyond profits and quotas, a sense of unity and commitment emerges. This shared sense of purpose fuels intrinsic motivation while nurturing a more engaging work culture, when done correctly. That is often why some of the happiest places to work in the world are also the organizations that have record sales year over year. They are fun and exciting to be at. Staff also have an opportunity to improve/level up.

The infinite game philosophy underscores the significance of building trusting relationships within an organization. Trust is the foundation upon which collaboration and innovation thrive. I've witnessed firsthand how trust can break down silos and create an environment where productivity flourishes.

The fastest way to lose the trust of your staff is to do layoffs for the sake of budgets. The ones who stay will become so worried about their role that they will rarely speak up or take chances. That loss of trust will take years to regain.

Trust plays several roles at an organization. As a leader, trust is learning to listen to your team before making the "call".

Leaders must articulate a compelling vision and ensure that every team member understands their role in achieving it. Teams have to "feel" or "trust" that they are a part of that vision. People have more engagement with things they have built. When you get your team involved in building your vision, they will be more invested in its success.

When creating trust, leaders must learn how to give up control. The world changed after COVID and it continues to evolve. With all our increases in productivity, we need to trust that our teams can complete their tasks in their own way.

People thrive due to their environment, not their incentives.

Together, these elements have ushered in a new era where work is not merely a means to an end but a fulfilling and purpose-driven endeavor. As we continue to embrace this new immersive world, I am confident that the shift to more compassionate organizations will only continue to grow. Let us remember that the journey is infinite, and the possibilities are boundless.

So make it fun and make it memorable.

3.2.5.2 Takeaway

I have been asked countless times that "if you could go back and do things differently, what would you do?" Genuinely, I do not think that I would do anything differently. Even though having a Rosetta stone to help me make better decisions would be nice, I would have lost the life lessons learned from the mistakes I made.

Moreover, I may have never met my wife, or had my 2 wonderful children. I am a firm believer in the statement, "everything happens for a reason". My challenges, losses, and wins have all defined my identity, persona, and purpose. However, I now look to my children as the next generation and that allows me the opportunity to help them in their journey.

I teach them to be kind. Kindness is a superpower and when used effectively can create an everlasting impact. They will always learn from their mistakes and that anything worthwhile will not be easy. Resilience is a quality that people respect and will follow. My children will know that bravery takes courage. They will know to stand up for what they believe in and be brave enough to take chances. It is in those chances that we learn the most about ourselves and others. That level of bravery can lead empires (or sway them to new directions). You should never let anyone else determine your own story. The world is full of people who do the impossible, daily! So why can't you be one of them too?

They will learn to become water. Water can fit any form, change state when needed, and become hard enough to protect those around you. One of my greatest mentors told me "the role of a leader is to teach others to leave and inspire them to stay". It took over 10 years for me to finally understand that statement. But it has been a guiding principle in my career.

As a leader I am doing my job, when I have helped a team member discover their potential to see their value. That act has helped build up an individual, a relationship, and an organization. As a leader, you need to be willing to put your team's needs ahead of your own. You need to learn to care for them, to care for their success. But also, you need to lead and inspire them.

3.2.5.3 Further Questions for Reflection

I think life is.....hard. For anyone. There are challenges you can overcome and challenges you cannot. Living with autism has been a lifelong struggle for me, however, it has also given me a unique perspective. It is the challenging moments that help to define us.

As a person who has seen their fair share of obstacles, I can assure you that there are many ways to overcome a challenge. However, each decision is a compromise. At the end of the day, the type of person, partner, or leader you want to become will be determined not by a single act, but by hundreds or thousands of them over time. In my journey, I have always been seen as an underdog, whether it be due to my neurodiversity, race, or upbringing. Those negative impacts did affect a lot of my earlier decisions in life. I wish I never listened to those people.

Your decisions will be influenced by a variety of factors and those factors will change throughout time. At a young age, I was motivated to find freedom. I listened to my seniors, thinking they knew everything. They did not.

In time, I began to chase my ambitions and what interested me. However, without guidance, it really didn't amount to much. It wasn't until I began building my family that the way I made decisions changed. Now, it wasn't simply a factor of supporting myself. Now, I have a partner, who has become my sounding board and we have two little humans we take care of. Our decisions influence and shape their world. That level of responsibility changes the way you interact with those around you and the decisions you make. As a parent, I am determined to give my children a better life than I had, but I also want them to experience the challenges and adversity that I have seen. Part of this is an emotional decision, part of it is strategic.

Purpose is a variable. Picasso once said, "the meaning of life is to find your gift. The purpose of life is to give it away". Purpose is defined by action. You may spend your whole life searching for your "gift" and never find it, but if that pursuit helps build a better tomorrow, that seems like a great way to live, doesn't it?

3.2.6 *Little Did I Know*

Gale Lucas, Research Assistant Professor University of Southern California. Born 1983, Portland, Oregon, USA.

Gale Lucas is a research assistant professor at the University of Southern California (USC) in the Viterbi School of Engineering, with appointments in Civil Engineering and Psychology, and works at the USC Institute for Creative Technologies (ICT). In 1983, she was born in Portland, Oregon,

United States of America. She obtained her BA from Willamette University in 2005 and her PhD from Northwestern University in 2010. At USC, Dr. Lucas works in the areas of human–computer interaction, human–building interaction, affective computing, and trust-in-automation. Her research focuses on rapport, disclosure, trust, persuasion, and negotiation with virtual agents, robots and smart buildings.

20 years ago, I was a sophomore at a small liberal arts college in the Pacific Northwest. For the first time since 6th grade when I figured out I was not, in fact, well-suited to be a veterinarian, I knew exactly what my career was going to be: I was going to be a professor. I discovered my passion to conduct social psychology research and teach research methods. At that time, 20 years ago, I wanted to keep doing what I was doing then (and more of it), and planning to be a professor of Psychology at a small liberal arts college held great promise for that. I wanted to be the one on the other side of the podium, teaching others what I had learned.

20 years ago, I did know a little. I knew that I would be a professor with a PhD in Social Psychology. I would hold onto the mission I found back then: to create opportunities for healing and growth for as many people as possible. I knew I wanted to conduct research on how people are motivated and interact with others. I knew I would end up teaching courses on research methods and statistics, because I loved those topics. I knew that, even though I wouldn't have any children of my own (except "fur kids" of course but that wasn't even a phrase back then!), I would have students.

20 years ago, I thought I would go to grad school somewhere in Southern California. I believed that, in 20 years, I would be tenured faculty in Psychology at a small liberal arts college in the Pacific Northwest.

20 years ago, little did I know that I would head to National Science Foundation's Research Experience for Undergraduates in Psychology at Northwestern University the next summer. Little did I know that, as much as I wanted to be in Southern California for grad school, Northwestern would have the faculty and research that were the right fit for me, which would draw me there for grad school instead.

20 years ago, little did I know that, while I would get what I wanted, I would end up discovering that I needed something different. I got to work at my alma mater after getting my PhD, and the following year I

even got a tenure track position teaching Psychology at a small college in the Pacific Northwest!

Little did I know that I would be willing to leave such a tenure track position to go "backwards" and become a postdoc. That I would end up staying in Southern California, rather than for grad school, for a research career at a big, "R1" school. That I would even work as research faculty (non-tenure track) with appointments in the Computer Science and Civil Engineering departments (and Psychology too, of course). That I would shift from conducting research on interactions between humans to studying interactions with technology such as social robots, virtual humans, and smart buildings.

I always <u>did know</u> that I wanted to make an impact for the better. I always held on to that personal mission to create opportunities for healing and growth for as many people as possible. I thought that was going to be through teaching and furthering knowledge in Psychology. However, while I was in that tenure track position, I felt like it wasn't enough. Like I wanted to do more to help more people, rather than just the few I would interact with at such a small school. But technology… oh, technology can reach many people, being able to bring them opportunities for healing and growth.

I got from psychology to technology by switching the focus from the "giving end" of interactions: from human–human interactions to human–computer interactions. I conducted psychology research on how people who are lonely, socially anxious, or have been rejected (romantically or platonically) respond to and cope with social situations, with a particular emphasis on perceptions of threat and motivation to feel safe. One way that we found such individuals cope is by forming parasocial attachments, such as "bonding" with TV characters. I became inspired to understand how people might bond and interact with technology, such as virtual characters that can actually respond back (unlike characters on TV)!

In more detail, in the realm of human–human interaction, my research focused on helping lonely individuals to open up, because their fear of negative evaluation keeps them closed off from others. I demonstrated that either blocking or distracting from that fear can help lonely people to reach out. First, because such fear interferes with lonely individuals' social performance, if we can block their anxiety they are able to perform just as well as their non-lonely counterparts in social interactions. Second, because a "promotion focus" (a mindset focused on growth and positives) can reduce fear and anxiety, increasing promotion focus among lonely individuals reduces their fear of negative evaluation and thereby helps them to open up to others.

I have applied these innovations from human–human interaction to the field of human–computer interactions. Building on my earlier research on fear of negative evaluation, I discovered that people feel less fear of negative evaluation when interviewed by a virtual agent if they believe it is operated by AI (compared to operated by a human), and thus they open up and disclose more sensitive personal information. For example, our virtual human agent that interviews people about their mental health got people to disclose more than a virtual human thought to be operated by another person. We have conceptually replicated this finding in other domains; for example, because they feel less judged, people are more comfortable practicing negotiation with an agent operated by AI (compared to operated by a human).

This finding—that people feel more comfortable with agents operated by an AI—provided evidence that anonymity can increase comfort in human–computer interactions. However, our follow-up studies also demonstrated the importance of machines building rapport with humans, beyond providing a sense of anonymity. For example, active duty service members were more willing to report symptoms of PTSD to our interviewing agent that built rapport with the interviewee than on an online form—even when both were equally anonymous. We replicated this finding with veterans, and we also conceptually replicated it with a sample from the general US population. In this latter case, people were more willing to disclose their financial status (e.g. debt) to an interviewing agent for financial planning, compared to an online form—even though both were equally anonymous. We built on these findings further, leading to a whole line of research showing that developing rapport with technology increases humans' positive mood, acceptance, compliance, agreement, and trust, in addition to their honest disclosure.

In addition to helping the participants in all these clinical trials, this technology also motivated others to develop "chatbots" for mental health. Because of this impact, it was named one of the 10 most innovative technologies by UNESCO. Now that was closer to what I had been thinking in terms of creating opportunities for healing and growth for as many people as possible!

Little did I know that I would seek a faculty job without the possibility of tenure. After the success of our interviewer agent for mental health, I was hooked. The best way to stay on working in this area was to apply to be research (non-tenure track) faculty at my university. This put all the responsibility on me, to get grants to support my effort and my research. But that too turned into a good thing. Having to get grants led to further collaborations, allowing for more innovative technologies designed to help people heal and grow.

For example, my colleagues and I investigate how smart buildings can improve health and well-being. This is important because, little do we realize, but our buildings could be degrading our health! Think about how many people get sicker in hospitals than they came in...some research suggests that the building itself contributes to this risk. Even office buildings, if poorly designed or controlled, contribute to some of the greatest public health concerns, such as obesity, cardiovascular diseases, diabetes, asthma, and depression, respiratory distress, discomfort, stress, and anxiety. For another, bad posture and sitting too long has been equated to "the new smoking"—we know how bad it is for our health now! In conducting an ergonomic assessment of posture for workers in office buildings, we were able to automatically assess joint angles in workers' upper body with 76% accuracy. Since now we can track posture, we can then help improve posture! Overall, this is part of our research to understand what health, psychological and behavioral improvements people can experience as a result of living and/or working in smart buildings.

We also conduct research using technology to understand man-made risks in buildings. In October of 2018, my colleagues and I were awarded funding from the National Science Foundation; our application—and funding—was timely: when comparing 2014–2015 to 2016–2017, those killed by an active shooter increased 140%. Those injured increased 419%. Because the vast majority of active shooter incidents occur inside buildings, architects and engineers were trying to retrofit buildings with additional features to slow the shooter down: limiting points of entry and exit, hiding spaces, size of hallways, and the like. We were concerned, however, that this might also make it harder for victims to "run or hide" as well. We were hoping to demonstrate this potential downside of "hardening" buildings against active shooters, but it wasn't feasible or ethical to subject participants to incidents in the real world, so we turned to virtual reality.

Using a virtual reality simulation of an active shooter incident, we developed two versions of buildings: the original buildings and the same building retrofitted to be hardened against active shooters. Participants experienced an active shooter incident in the virtual version of one building or the other, and the results demonstrated that they were significantly slower when the building was retrofitted to be hardened against active shooters. It may slow shooters down, but it also slows victims down while trying to survive! The original building design also enabled the majority of people to run, whereas only about half chose to run (and the other half hide) when the building was retrofitted to be hardened against active shooters.

I personally came to the project not just with the hope of working towards safety and healing in our communities, but also because of the opportunity to demonstrate how virtual reality could be used as a tool to complete research that would otherwise be costly, complicated, and emotionally distressing. In social science research, we have to be careful to study things that are important to understand in the world, but do so in a way that we're taking the best care of our participants. To me, this project is a great case study for how virtual reality can enable researchers to study things in an ethical way that we wouldn't be able to explore otherwise.

I always knew I loved learning (and teaching) about research methods, what I didn't know was that I would help expand the methods available to researchers—through technology! I also did not know that I would have the pleasure of teaching engineering graduate students about research methods, many of whom had never received any formal education on the topic at all before.

Moreover, little did I know back then that, 20 years later, I would have worked and lived in LA for 10 years already. That I would be teaching only one class per semester, spending more of my time on my research. That I would have acquired millions of dollars in grant money for my institution, including funding for my own grad students. That I would be organizing conferences in Engineering fields. That I would even be asked, as a prominent scholar in the field, to give keynote talks in such venues.

So if I hadn't given up what I thought I wanted—tenure track, Psychology, small school in the Pacific Northwest—I would have missed out on all of this... I wouldn't have gotten to work alongside amazing scholars in Engineering, together building technologies that help foster healing and growth. I wouldn't have had the opportunity to develop research prototypes that inspire technologies with the potential to help the masses to heal and grow.

Along those lines, I believe that the best way to get started working with technology like this is to find the right group. That is a theme of what I learned throughout this journey—go where the right people are. As much as you might want to be in some place, nothing—to me—is more important than working with the right people. I went to Northwestern because it obviously had the faculty that were the right fit for me. Likewise, I applied for my current research faculty position because I wanted to stay on working with the colleagues I had made in Engineering. We can be strong leaders in the area of technology because we lead side by side.

While that is certainly something that I would do again (if I had it all to do over again), there is at least one thing that I would do differently. I would have tried to trust myself more. There was some self-doubt that came up when making the biggest "turn" of my journey: leaving a tenure track position for a role as a postdoc. But it was, in hindsight, the best decision I could have made—as it led me to where I am now.

3.2.7 Deep Listening

Scott Sanland. CEO of Cyrano.

Born 1980, Newport Beach, California, USA.

Scott is the former world's youngest hypnotherapist and an international speaker on the topics of ethical AI and subconscious motivation. He is a multi-patented inventor in Artificial Intelligence and the CEO of a company focusing on strategic empathy and linguistic analysis. As a former executive director and CEO of a mental health clinic and long-time technologist, he has experience leading purpose-driven organizations. He has been published in numerous peer-reviewed journals and has had his work at Cyrano mentioned in the Harvard Business Review, Psychology Today, Forbes, and Entrepreneur Magazine.

As the CEO of cyrano.ai, I'm tasked with launching a piece of technology which helps people understand themselves and each other better through the use of artificial intelligence and our proprietary empathy engine. I have always considered myself a "do-gooder" who sincerely believes that our purpose here on earth is to make the lives of others better. I've carried that belief into cyrano.ai so that we can do good at the scale of technology rather than just the scale of my own personal therapy office.

One of my innate skills that I have nurtured over the years is my ability to truly listen to people. This led me to become the world's youngest hypnotherapist in 1998. Over the course of the following 20 years, I had countless deep, meaningful, and often uncomfortable conversations with people about their innermost thoughts, helping them to work through feelings of shame, fear, regret, and hope. Through this substantial clinical experience early in my career, I gained tremendous insight into the human psyche and the overall human condition.

I found myself particularly drawn to working with at-risk teenagers and those struggling with addiction. Due to my youthful appearance, I was able to connect with these types of clients far better than most other clinicians who were much older. I've always felt a soft spot for this vulnerable population of young people. Getting ahead of their challenges early prevents a host of potential lifelong problems, and increasingly lengthens lives. The teen suicide crisis is a national epidemic, and there is nothing I care about more than being part of the solution to it.

To meet the exponentially growing need, in 2014 I built a clinic specifically targeting this demographic of teenagers in crisis. We began by hiring psychotherapists, counselors, life coaches, hypnotherapists, acupuncture specialists, chiropractors, and more. However, I slowly realized that our work was largely reactionary instead of preventative in nature. I wanted to help young people before they reached the point of crisis.

This insight led me to consider ways that advancing technology could expand the reach of the work we were doing—both helping more people, and also helping people before they found themselves at a personal bottom that justified therapeutic interventions. I began intensely researching technology, and by 2015 started reading about chatbots and their limitations. I quickly discovered that chatbots were highly ineffective for simulating real human communication and connection. Their goal was simply to provide accurate information to users, without any ability to establish mutual understanding or rapport. This overlooked what I believe is the very essence of effective communication between people—the ability to tailor messages and relate to the specific person you are addressing based on intuition, empathy, and listening skills.

I saw an opportunity here to take a radically different approach to developing communication technology, with an emphasis on empathy over efficiency or accuracy alone. There is an old saying that "people don't care how much you know until they know how much you care". My clinical background has demonstrated to me time and again the vital importance of empathy and rapport when interacting with clients in distress. Chatbots completely lacked this empathy in their robotic conversations. I dreamed of creating a system that could emulate the active listening skills and emotional intelligence that a therapist like myself cultivated over many years of working with people.

And so, that is exactly what our team at cyrano.ai set out to build—a system capable of discerning various emotional and mental states by analyzing linguistic patterns and nuances that are typically overlooked by standard natural language-processing approaches. We developed comprehensive taxonomies and models capturing the wide spectrum of human sentiment and perception, rather than limiting our focus to niche applications as most technology teams do. While this humanistic approach seemed unusual and risky in the tech industry, we were committed to addressing what we see as the most crucial element missing from human–machine interaction—making people truly feel heard, understood, and valued.

Some on our team struggled to grasp the vision and potential profitability of prioritizing empathy over efficiency and metrics. It was difficult, especially for the more analytical and procedural members of the team, to understand how we could productize these models. They pushed for more focused applications in marketing rather than improving generalized communication abilities. But I firmly believed we had an ethical obligation to enhance human communication and connection first, before even considering how these techniques could be exploited for commercial gain and advertising.

The conceptual vision started to become much more tangible and concrete for our team members once we developed a natural language generation system to pair with the "listening" model towards the end of 2019. It partly solved the inherent, "so what?" in our ability to model speech as a behavior. This system provided guidance on how to effectively approach different individuals based on a profile of their values, motivations, and communication style within given contexts. This required us to decide which contexts, before the days of LLMs, but it was a major breakthrough for us. Having this practical application was the "light bulb" moment for many on the team, suddenly revealing the enormous potential utility of these AI systems we were architecting. We launched the analysis tool during COVID and quickly got tens of thousands of free users on Zoom, who received an analysis of each participant on any recorded zoom call they hosted. Customer satisfaction was high, feedback scores were great, and we were getting pulled off course.

Though I remained steadfast that our technology should be used to help, not exploit, people, I conceded that initial commercial applications would give us a much faster and less ethically fraught route to refining the system capabilities at scale. Once we had more robustly trained our models on our growing dataset, only then we could consider higher-risk applications of the technology, such as in mental health support. And so for practical reasons, we ventured first into commercial verticals, which did prove remarkably effective for the rapid evolution of our core listening and relationship-building algorithms.

3.2.7.1 Intervention

Within the first few commercial deployments, our technology demonstrated immense promise, achieving significant benchmarks that exceeded investor expectations. However, some early investors still doubted whether we had a truly scalable business with traction and growth potential in the market. Then, at a crucial juncture in 2022, we were introduced to someone who completely aligned with our vision and ethics, and possessed the experience and business acumen to rapidly elevate the company to greater heights.

This new addition to our team made it clear he wanted to focus our efforts entirely on realizing the fullest humanitarian potential of our technology. He said to us, "I want to help make this company as big as anyone can, on the condition that we remain committed to our core mission of helping people". His proposal was music to my ears, as it perfectly aligned with my most deeply held values for this company I had started years before.

And so, the obvious first application we agreed upon was utilizing our technology to help at-risk teenagers from falling through the cracks, by improving communication and relationships between them, their peers and parents. Though still in the early phases, we are highly encouraged by the positive impact our technology has already started to make for families, and are committed to continuous improvements. My life's purpose is to better the lives of others, and I now finally have the means to do so at scale.

3.2.7.2 Insight

I simultaneously feel an urgency to help vulnerable populations while ensuring that our technology is ethically applied. This isn't a "move fast and break things" situation. This is a, "create a foundational technology that creates lasting positive impact for the lives of human beings" situation. Our core mission remains unchanged. I am proud of the progress we have made, while staying grounded in the hard work still required. Each small improvement brings us closer to a world where technology elevates our humanity.

When speaking about AI, I'm often asked what jobs will be automated away first. My answer is that anyone focused solely on efficiency is most at risk. The replaceable workers are those who only ask how to improve the efficiency of what we are doing today, rather than what new possibilities and experiences can be created. They miss the bigger picture.

AI will inherently drive efficiency exponentially over time. We are moving from horses to cars to spaceships in terms of technological capabilities. Massive efficiency gains are a given. The real opportunity is in discovering what new things we can do and explore together. If you only stay focused on costs, you've missed the entire point of human progress.

Efficiency should be an organic byproduct, not the end goal, especially in business. It's antithetical to creativity and innovation to stay narrowly focused on savings rather than value creation. I understand cost savings have their place in business, but it should be a secondary concern. The most visionary leaders don't start with spreadsheets to cut costs. They reimagine what is possible and then bring it into reality through determination.

3.2.7.3 Hindsight

If I could go back and change anything, there are two key strategic decisions I would reconsider. These both stemmed from my own insecurities and lack of business experience early on. I gave up too easily on the idea that there could eventually be revenue in applying our technology to mental health care. I assumed no one would pay for or value an AI system for improving counseling and psychiatry. So I didn't fight hard enough, and got pushed by an early investor into commercial applications I didn't really care about or earn much from. This was a painful mistake, because I wasted significant time and money on those tangents.

In retrospect, I clearly should have had more confidence in the monumental value AI can bring to fields like mental health care. I would push back much harder today on any notion that technology can't also have an ethical purpose. My younger self needed more conviction in my visions, and less self-doubt. But the path forward is now clear, and my regrets only fuel my present-day fire to stay true to my core beliefs.

Technology can uplift our humanity, rather than exploiting it. Innovation capital has historically backed technology that can quickly generate profits. While profits don't necessarily preclude ethical applications, using profits as a guide can sometimes blind companies and investors to the ethical potential of what they are creating. My hope is that we retain wisdom and ethics amid exponential technological change. With compassion as our guide, a bright future awaits.

With the rapidly increasing role AI is having in our daily lives, it makes sense to imbue into these systems an appreciation for the human condition, to create multidimensional representations of what makes us predictably irrational, highly social, and worryingly selfish. This is a tiny, tiny fraction of what will be part of solving the alignment problem. So, if we are right in our assumptions (and that is a very big IF that still needs to be proven over time), we will have a lot to be optimistic about.

3.2.8 Designing for a Better World: Pedagogy at Scale

Lilach Mollick, Director of Pedagogy at Wharton Interactive.
Born USA.

Lilach Mollick is the Director of Pedagogy at Wharton Interactive, Wharton's games and simulations lab. Her work focuses on the development of pedagogical strategies that include artificial intelligence and interactive methodologies. She has worked in the learning and development field across organizations and with Wharton Interactive to develop a wide range of educational tools and games used in classrooms worldwide. Lilach has published several papers in the space and created courses on the topic of teaching and learning with AI. Most recently, her work has included designing and implementing AI-powered simulations aimed at creating scalable, pedagogically sound learning experiences accessible to anyone.

3.2.8.1 My Work and Vision
Training Makes a Difference

I have worked in the field of human resources for years, and it was the learning and development area of the field that I found both rewarding and challenging. In my early work, I saw the power of creating and deploying learning experiences that began with explicit learning goals—goals that defined what we wanted learners to be able to do, understand, and experience—and designing our instructional strategy backwards from those goals. It was clear that creating a direct link between theory and practice and giving learners lots of practice, through role-play, for instance, and following up that practice with debriefing and feedback was a powerful way to learn. This learning loop that consisted of instruction—practice—feedback—reflection made a huge difference in how learners felt, performed, and passed on what they now knew. I saw that the key was a supportive but challenging learning environment with instructors or mentors who could unpack what they knew into smaller sequential components and were attuned to what learners knew and understood at every step and adapted themselves throughout. That capacity to take the learner's perspective, adapt, and improvise was powerful but, unfortunately, anchored to a specific time and place. It was not easily scalable.

The Challenge: Scaling Up Impactful Experiences
These experiences cemented my belief in the profound difference training can make, especially when the organization has an experimental mindset: experimentation and iteration were critical. I learned early on that you had to be ready to kill your darlings—ideas, projects, assumptions—to get better results. The challenge then and now is to replicate an effective teaching and learning environment outside of a particular organization and group of people.

It became clear that a new approach was needed to democratize access and make a deeper impact. That realization led me to the next chapter: leveraging technology to create learning experiences that scale. Over the past several years, I have dedicated myself to building games for teaching. Each game or simulation begins with clear learning goals, practice objectives, and thinking objectives. And each is anchored in our best bets for learning: direct instruction, adaptive challenges and feedback, and built-in reflection exercises. The simulation modality allows for a richer and more interactive learning environment that is far more accessible to others; these experiences are not anchored to a specific time and place.

3.2.8.2 Game Development Approach
We thought deeply about every game, and worked to combine technology, the science of learning, and narrative storytelling. Each game

was developed through an intense process of discovery, experimentation, and iteration. We were ambitious in our approach and built painstakingly, using every evidence-based strategy we could think of and included the learning loop: early instruction and testing (to figure out where the learner was), initial relatively easy learner choices, feedback from in-game characters, and additional, more consequential choices. We continued experimenting with storylines, puzzles, and adding or subtracting game elements. We learned that specific choices constrain learners but that open-ended responses were difficult for us to capture and categorize.

The process of building our games involved making decisions that were essentially experiments. We constantly asked ourselves: Will this work? Could it lead to problems? Is the technology going to help us or hinder us? We dedicated years to adjusting the game's challenge levels precisely at every point in the simulation.

3.2.8.3   The Power of Many Perspectives
Central to our approach was our ability to consider multiple perspectives simultaneously. This viewpoint allowed us to monitor various aspects of the game closely. We tracked the learner's progress and understanding at every stage of the game. We wanted to understand not just where learners were, but what they knew and how they felt. Were they engaged, stressed, challenged? Who were they interacting with within the game at any given time? We constantly monitored the game, tracking what needed to happen under the hood and when it needed to happen. For games that involved educators, we wanted to know: at any point in the game, what insight did educators need about their learners' progress? How could they anticipate the narrative's branching paths based on learners' decisions and answer questions without giving away the game. And finally, we kept a comprehensive view of all ongoing processes to try to assess what learners knew, identify potential difficulties, and build scaffolding into the game to intervene when necessary.

Generative AI: A New Chapter in Interactive Learning
With the advent of generative AI, we quickly saw how what we had worked so hard for, scalable, adaptive games that can improvise depending on learner actions, suddenly became far simpler. New options opened up quickly. AI could role-play given a prompt; AI could give feedback, given a prompt; AI could game master an entire experience; an AI could

monitor another in-game AI to make sure that a role-playing scenario stayed on track.

But, the experience of building games has proven invaluable in this new environment.

Our approach to experimentation, to adopting multiple perspectives and prioritizing pedagogy has proven essential as we start to create AI-powered games. We are experimenting with using AI to play multiple roles, but our R&D efforts over the past few months has shown us that despite its capabilities, AI has its limitations. AI cannot handle every task flawlessly; its probabilistic nature means we can't always count outputs that center the lesson. An in-game tutor, for instance, can offer instructions, but it may not always respond correctly to every question. We have learned that AI can be used judiciously but that some lessons need to be tightly scripted, and some demand a hybrid approach.

The strengths of AI, such as its ability to generate scenarios and engage in role-play, are also its weaknesses, as specific scenarios and interactions may not suit every learner quickly and easily. I've learned that perspective-taking, which has served us well, remains crucial in the era of AI. To create an AI-powered game that is truly accessible to all, we must continuously consider the perspective of the learner, the instructor, and now of the AI itself—understanding its capabilities, anticipating its reactions to different inputs, and recognizing how its evolution impacts our games. This comprehensive approach ensures we leverage AI's strengths while navigating its limitations, aiming for the most effective and inclusive educational experience.

Takeaways for Readers
We now have in our sights the possibility of making significant progress in teaching at scale. This idea is no longer just a distant dream but a tangible reality. The journey of Wharton Interactive and my personal experience underscores a critical narrative: the path to leveraging technology, particularly AI, in education is laden with opportunities and challenges. It demands a nuanced understanding of pedagogy, technology, and the human element at the heart of learning.

The transition from transient and bounded learning experiences to scalable, technology-driven solutions highlights a shift in our approach to education. This shift is not only about adopting new tools but about potentially reimagining the learning experience. It involves moving from a one-size-fits-all model to one that is adaptable, personalized, and accessible to a global audience.

The integration of AI into educational games and simulations at Wharton Interactive represents a future-focused approach to this challenge. However, successfully implementing generative AI will not be straightforward and will require careful experimentation, a willingness to iterate based on feedback, and, perhaps most importantly, a deep commitment to understanding learner perspectives.

The potential of AI and other technologies to enhance education is immense, but realizing this potential will require collaborative effort, innovative thinking, and a commitment to experimentation. We must remain open to the idea that failure is a part of the learning process, not just for students but for those of us designing educational experiences. This is indeed a very exciting time to think about the future of education.

3.2.9 Humanizing Technology. A Leadership Blueprint

Michael J. Jabbour, Chief Innovation Officer at Microsoft Education.
Born Denville NJ, USA.
Dr Michael J. Jabbour, former Chief Information and Technology Officer for various New York City (NYC) agencies, including the Department of Education (DOE), with over two decades of experience in digital transformation, AI, healthcare, and public service, sits at the intersection of technology and human-centered design as the Chief Innovation Officer at Microsoft Education.

3.2.9.1 Introduction—Humane Technology: A New Paradigm

During my tenure as Chief Information Officer of the NYC Department o3f Homeless Services, one of the more eye-opening moments occurred when I visited a homeless shelter and saw the staff struggling with the technology used to support their work. Utilizing outdated, complex technology and methods, they filled out intake forms, completed status verifications, and attempted to connect clients with desperately needed resources while switching between multiple systems, repeatedly reentering data, and waiting for long loading times. This cumbersome process wasted precious time and resources and generated frustration and unbearable stress for the staff and, perhaps more importantly, the clients. In one instance, I watched a staff member try to interview a visibly shaken and traumatized client who had just escaped a violent partner and lost her home and belongings. Because the staff member had to focus on the computer screen, the client had to repeat her story several times, answer irrelevant questions, and provide documents she didn't have. Instead of giving the client the attention and care she deserved and desperately needed, instead of helping the client imagine a bright future for herself and her child, the situation left the poor woman looking defeated and hopeless, as if she had no control over her life.

Feeling that client's sadness, disappointment, and anger, I realized that though our technology could help us serve clients, it prevented us from connecting with them on a human level. Rather than empowering or enhancing us, it limited and diminished us. This is because much of our current technology serves impersonal operational goals, such as filling out fields in a form or furthering a particular organizational efficiency, such as a staff reduction or operational change. Furthermore, most current technology will always resolve down to the deterministic lines of code controlling how it works and what it must display on each screen. These limitations force humans to follow that cold, deterministic flow, even while using it to serve and support other humans.

That experience motivated me to look deeper into what digital modernization and transformation should look like to create a system that respects clients' dignity and humanity and enables them to reclaim their agency. Such a system would allow our staff to focus on what they do best for clients: listen, empathize, connect, and heal while the technology correctly handles administrative processes associated with shelter placements.

From that experience, where technology and humanity intersect, the concept of "humane technology" originated in the human-centered design and design thinking disciplines and became a prevalent focus. This paradigm shift requires our technology, business community, and culture to adjust our typical approach described above by meticulously designing and implementing solutions that empower individuals to cultivate well-being, dignity, and ethical values and place humans at the center, making us the primary guiding element of innovation. In this new paradigm, the role of responsible leadership becomes paramount as it steers the development of humane technologies and ensures that advancements align harmoniously with humanity's best interests. Navigating that path as we accelerate into an era marked by Generative AI (GenAI) will require a multifaceted approach that considers the ethical, social, and environmental implications of technology that enhances life, strengthens communities, and elevates the human spirit (Allahrakha, 2023).

3.2.9.2   Discussion—On Becoming More Humane
Firstly, if leaders are to navigate technology's evolving landscape and create a humane technology, they must first come into greater contact with their humanity. One way they can do that is by acknowledging their vulnerabilities. Exposing one's vulnerabilities is not a weakness. Instead, it is a stepping stone to significant personal growth that enhances connection and creative problem-solving capacity. As Brown (2012) wisely tells us, our most vulnerable moments are crucial opportunities for personal growth. Such growth cultivates emotional intelligence, a crucial skill that enables us to understand better and address the nuanced needs of those we seek to serve through technology. The journey from vulnerability to personal growth to emotional intelligence is fundamental to a human-centric approach to innovation (Craig, 2016). It ensures that our technological advancements are technically sophisticated and deeply resonant with the human experience.

Secondly, leaders must tear down the barriers that separate them from those with whom they interact. Throughout my personal and professional lives, I observed how we erect interpersonal barriers, consciously and unconsciously. While these barriers offer security, they often hinder our potential and prevent deep, meaningful connections with each other and our technology. Dropping or even reducing those barriers provides an opportunity for people to work together with our technology for humanity's betterment. This means that leaders must go beyond their daily administrative duties to change the heart of organizational culture to catalyze a transformation that enhances productivity and, as importantly, well-being. If they do so, they can foster a healthy culture that favors growth and enables employees to demonstrate care, competence, and cohesion.

Yet, while increasing our interpersonal connection and our connection to each other and technology, we must also remain vigilant about over reliance on that technology. This is because integrating technology seamlessly into our daily lives shapes how we connect with our fellow humans and surroundings and how we grow (Turkle, 2016). For example, the release of a significantly more advanced form of dialogic artificial intelligence, GenAI, tears down the barriers between humans and machines, thereby increasingly blurring the line between them. Suppose future artificial intelligence surpasses or replaces humans in specific tasks and jobs (Frey & Osborne, 2017). In that case, the traits we traditionally associate with being human—intelligence, empathy, sympathy, etc.—may need reevaluation (Bostrom, 2014). To that end, it may be that our flaws and vulnerabilities become the only reliable connections we have to our humanity. Though some call this the "moment of AI", I see it as the "moment of humanity".

I blended those human traits with technological proficiency in initiatives that transcend technical goals, such as increased transmission speed or higher image resolution, to establish a profound connection with stakeholders. An integrated approach enabled my teams at various agencies to build and deploy cutting-edge advancements in public service by transforming technology interactions to unlock its potential to augment our humanity rather than overshadow it. One such initiative while I served as NYC's DOE Chief Technology Officer involved ensuring over a million students, primarily those socioeconomically vulnerable, had access to centrally distributed technology meant to enable remote learning during the COVID-19 pandemic. This project presented unique logistical and humanistic challenges.

The solution, rooted in the principles of human-centered design, targeted the real needs of students, teachers, and families by focusing on a short-term logistical solution to the crisis while creating new, long-term, human-centered education approaches that recognized that the already-existing educational disparities could significantly expand, posing a real threat to students at critical learning junctures. For instance, children aged 6 to 8, who were beginning to navigate the complexities of written communication and grasp the fundamentals of sentence structure and grammar, stood at a pivotal crossroads. Without immediate intervention, the learning gap for these young learners could have become insurmountable, leaving them significantly behind in their educational journey. In response, we adopted age and grade-appropriate internet-enabled technologies and devices for instruction as a necessary tool and crucial lifeline that could ensure continuity in education. In doing so, our leadership teams inspired people to believe technology use could improve people's potential and impact society beyond providing access to information, entertainment, and word-processing tools.

This, along with other initiatives and challenges that underscored the importance of innovative solutions, proved the necessity of operating in and managing ambiguity, the power of emotional intelligence, and the requirements and advantages of pragmatic flexibility. The demand for these industry-agnostic, humanistic skills will continue to grow, particularly in the age of GenAI (Schmager et al., 2023).

Values and moral digital transformation must be a guiding force, not an afterthought, to get there. A notable lesson from that project and others is the need for constant inclusion of insights from educators, sociologists, ethicists, and a spectrum of experts that provide a strong, diverse moral compass which will set humane technology development apart from development driven by cold, conventional, business-driven models (Horvitz, 2017).

3.2.9.3 Technological Advancements and Ethics

Establishing operational principles during this significant transformation will cause ethical challenges. Among the ethical issues today's leaders and future leaders creating humane technology will face are compromised data privacy through unauthorized access and creative manipulation of data distribution in which information is inaccurately presented or falsified, a situation that also poses a threat to those who rely on that data. However, the greatest future ethical challenge comes from introducing conversational and GenAI systems like ChatGPT, Gemini, and others (Floridi, 2019).

Though GenAI presents immeasurable opportunities to enhance and innovate in areas such as customer service, education, and entertainment, especially when coupled with emerging modernizations of augmented reality (AR) and virtual reality (VR) technologies, it may also pose the biggest ethical obstacles. With a prompt, GenAI systems can produce human-equivalent text and voice responses and photorealistic images and videos (Shen et al., 2020). As a result, GenAI facilitates the creation of deep fakes that convincingly impersonate human agents who distribute false or harmful information to influence user opinions or behaviors and collect sensitive data without consent.

Responsible AI frameworks and guidelines began appearing to counter these issues as early as 2016. Among these frameworks are Microsoft's (Microsoft, n.d.), the Institute of Electrical and Electronics Engineers' (IEEE, 2019), the European Commission's (European Commission, n.d.), the NIST's (National Institute of Standards & Technology, 2023), and Partnership on AI's (Partnership on AI, n.d.). These frameworks, which aspire to foster the development and deployment of AI systems ethically and responsibly, include core guidelines regarding transparency, security, accountability, human rights, and privacy protection. Unfortunately, while these frameworks are relatively stable, their implementation implications change regularly.

That said, once we overcome the ethical challenges, there is a path towards creating a humane technology.

3.2.9.4   Conclusion—The Path Forward

Automated chatbots based on the humane technology concept could offer personalized support and help users improve reading, writing, and mathematics skills at their own pace, in their language, and within their culture. For the first time in human history, every person could access a tutor, medical advice, and a mentor through one of the most ubiquitous technologies on the planet—a smartphone. Through a human-centric design, GenAI technologies could boost motivation and competence with tailored feedback, making education and healthcare accessible to a broader audience. Developed in collaboration with experts across disciplines, it could incorporate pedagogical and medical insights and ethical standards, establishing itself as an effective and inclusive solution that extends technology's role as a positive force in society (Smith et al., 2020).

My experiences taught me the importance of inclusive, participatory design in creating technology that meets real-world needs. This can only be accomplished by considering technology more than a mere instrument or potential detriment. We must consider it a means to facilitate interpersonal communication that enables individuals to excel and achieve human aspirations. By developing technologies that are valuable extensions of human capabilities, we steer towards a future where technology fosters a more inclusive and empathetic world that genuinely enhances human lives. That world can only come to fruition if we transform technology from a simple data manipulation tool into a vibrant exchange that connects technologists, communities, and users.

Therefore, as we chart our future, we must handle technology with deep care, responsibility, and a focused purpose to create a harmonious relationship between technology and humanity that benefits and uplifts both. In the end, we must encourage humane leaders to craft a humane technology that serves our needs far better than what I witnessed when the poor technological amalgam failed the homeless shelter staff member and the scared and traumatized woman seeking respite.

Working together with empathy, vulnerability, and mutual respect across disciplines and within ethical guidelines, we can face and overcome complex challenges to take a proactive leap into new realms, where the fusion of technology and human values lights the path to a brighter, more inclusive future for all.

****

Note—You may have noticed reading through this book that every quantity and terminology is both content-related and symbolic. Hence you may wonder why I broke the pattern of 4 and 8. The reason is purely symbolic—there would have been many more fantastic people to be featured, and this will follow in future volumes of this series. In choosing 4 women and 5 men, the number represents the unequal distribution of females in the technology sector (if one wanted to be more accurate a ratio of 3/7 at best would have to be followed, but that would have limited the voice of women even more).

RECAP—The contributors all recognize the potential of AI to augment human capabilities, propelling scientific and technological innovation while offering solutions to intricate global challenges. At the same time all of them voice a cautionary undercurrent. The need to address the digital divide, ensuring inclusive access to the benefits of AI and mitigating the potential for exacerbating existing social and economic inequalities, is vital for all. Respectively and combined these essays converge around one point—AI is not fate, but a tool subject to human agency. By harnessing the power of personal agency as a catalyst of individual and collective leadership, humans can leverage AI as a force for positive change, to shape a future that benefits all of humanity.

How do You answer the 4 macro-questions? Can you accept the answers?

A quick Check-in where we stand on our journey through this book before we wrap-up—Anchored in the multidisciplinary framework that we looked at in Chapter 1 which flagged the need for *Agency Amid AI for All* (Why), we dived in Chapter 2 deeper into the evolving hybrid landscape, including the interplay of natural and artificial consciousness (Where). The experiences in this chapter then illustrated how personal agency can manifest as a catalyst of prosocial technology (Who). Respectively and combined this positions us at the onset of Chapter 4 which closes the loop by showing certain patterns that arise from the past pages, and the potential of a *Win4* effect of systematically designed prosocial behavior to optimize the hybrid society that we are part of (What).

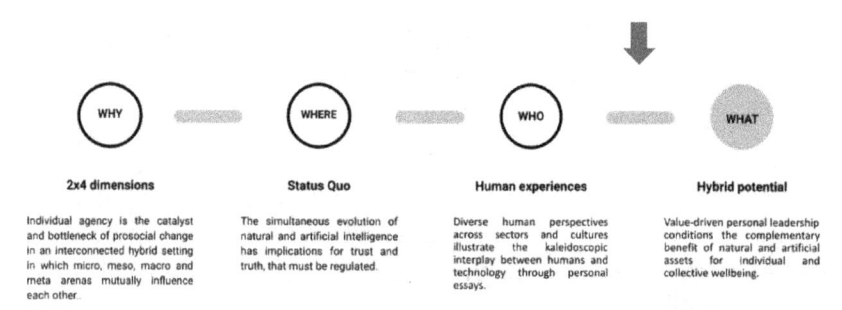

WHY	WHERE	WHO	WHAT
2x4 dimensions	Status Quo	Human experiences	Hybrid potential
Individual agency is the catalyst and bottleneck of prosocial change in an interconnected hybrid setting in which micro, meso, macro and meta arenas mutually influence each other.	The simultaneous evolution of natural and artificial intelligence has implications for trust and truth, that must be regulated.	Diverse human perspectives across sectors and cultures illustrate the kaleidoscopic interplay between humans and technology through personal essays.	Value-driven personal leadership conditions the complementary benefit of natural and artificial assets for individual and collective wellbeing.

References

Clare Murphy: So That None of Us Be Missing

AI Now Institute. (2023). *2023 Landscape*. https://ainowinstitute.org/2023-lan dscape

Brockington, G., Hooker, C., Walker, L., Saldivia, S., & Kendeou, P. (2021). Storytelling increases oxytocin and positive emotions and decreases cortisol levels in preschool-aged children. *Proceedings of the National Academy of Sciences, 118*(21). https://doi.org/10.1073/pnas.2018409118

Haven, K. (2007). *Story proof*. Libraries Unlimited.

Henderson, A. (1911). *George Bernard Shaw: His life and his works*. Stewart & Kidd.

Leary, L. (2023, May 16). A.I. doom narratives are hiding what we should be most afraid of. *Slate Magazine*. https://slate.com/technology/2023/05/meredith-whittaker-interview-geoffrey-hinton-ai-threats.html

Smith, M. N. (1998, December 16). Dickinson/Norcross correspondence: Mid-September 1860 (Letter 225). Emily Dickinson Archive. http://archive.emi lydickinson.org/correspondence/norcross/l225.html

Michael Jabbour: A Leadership Blueprint

Allahrakha, N. (2023). Balancing cyber-security and privacy: Legal and ethical considerations in the digital age. *Legal Issues in the Digital Age, 4*(2), 78–121.

Bostrom, N. (2014). *Superintelligence: Paths, dangers, strategies*. Oxford University Press.
Brown, B. (2012). *Daring greatly: How the courage to be vulnerable transforms the way we live, love, parent, and lead*. Penguin.
Craig, C. J. (2016). Technological neutrality: Recalibrating copyright in the information age. *Theoretical Inquiries in Law, 17*(2), 601–632.
European Commission. (n.d.). Ethics guidelines for trustworthy AI. FUTURIUM. https://ec.europa.eu/futurium/en/ai-alliance-consultation. Retrieved 4 February 2024.
Floridi, L. (Ed.). (2019). *The Routledge handbook of philosophy of information*. Routledge.
Frey, C. B., & Osborne, M. A. (2017). The future of employment: How susceptible are jobs to computerization? *Technological Forecasting and Social Change, 114*, 254–280.
Horvitz, E. (2017). AI, people, and society. *Science, 357*(6346), 7. https://doi.org/10.1126/science.aao2466
IEEE. (2019). IEEE global initiative releases treatise on ethically aligned design of AI systems. IEEE Global Public Policy. https://globalpolicy.ieee.org/ieee-global-initiative-releases-treatise-on-ethically-aligned-design-of-autonomous-and-intelligent-systems/. Retrieved 4 February 2024.
Microsoft. (n.d.). Empowering responsible AI practices. Microsoft AI. https://www.microsoft.com/en-us/ai/responsible-ai. Retrieved 4 February 2024.
National Institute of Standards and Technology. (2023). Artificial intelligence risk management framework (AI RMF 1.0). https://www.nist.gov/publications/artificial-intelligence-risk-management-framework-ai-rmf-10. Retrieved 4 February 2024.
Partnership on AI. (n.d.). *About us*. https://partnershiponai.org/about/. Retrieved 4 February 2024.
Schmager, S., Pappas, I., & Vassilakopoulou, P. (2023). Defining human-centered AI: A comprehensive review of HCAI literature. In *Proceedings of the Mediterranean Conference on Information Systems*.
Shen, Z., Li, R., Fu, Z., Xiao, Z., & Peng, X. (2020). DeepFake detection: Current challenges and next steps. *IEEE Signal Processing Magazine, 37*(1), 110–117.
Smith, J., Lee, A., & Park, S. (2020). Designing an educational chatbot for language learning: A user-centric approach. In *Proceedings of the 12th International Conference on Educational Technology and Innovation* (pp. 123–130).
Turkle, S. (2016). *Reclaiming conversation: The power of talk in a digital age*. Penguin.

CHAPTER 4

WHAT: Optimizing Natural and Artificial Assets to Thrive in a Hybrid Society

Abstract Wrapping up while connecting the dots this chapter is an invitation to counter cognitive dissonance rather than condoning it. Reframing the human–machine relationship from competition to complementarity to cooperation we look at the implications of value-driven leadership in the relationship between humans and technology, with a prosocial perspective. In targeting a positive-sum "*Win4*" dynamic, individuals can proactively influence, and reshape hybrid social norms through their own behavior. Times are changing, and so do people and the society they belong to. A winner versus loser perspective is outdated; it has been taken for granted, and needs a reassessment in the cohabitation with AI. Located in the *micro* (individual), *meso* (community), *macro* (country), and *meta* (planet) arenas, 4 sample prototypes illustrate that technology that is designed and delivered to bring out the best in people and planet can make a difference towards individual well-being and the Common Good in a mutually beneficial manner. The *Benevolent Brain and Body Buddy* (B4/*micro*) is an AI-powered device tailored to help individuals understand and optimize their own organism; the *Agency Amid AI for All* curriculum (A4/*meso*) combines literacy of natural and artificial intelligence for people and teams across generations, starting in schools; the SAM 4.0 (*macro*) analyzes horizontal and vertical interplays across the *m4-matrix* to inform policymaking and programming; finally the *Inspiration Incubator* (i@i/*meta*) offers a safe space for thinkers and doers to connect, curate, convey, and co-create technology that brings out the

© The Author(s), under exclusive license to Springer Nature Switzerland AG 2024
C. C. Walther, *Human Leadership for Humane Technology*,
https://doi.org/10.1007/978-3-031-67823-3_4

247

best in people and planet. Each of them illustrates what prosocial AI is and could be if it was driven by humans that align their aspirations and actions, taking a stance of agency. Agency empowers humans to deliberately set the stage for the world they want, neither because nor despite technology, but alongside it. We return to the *A-Frame* to find how its augmented version expands to include the two features that are the cause and consequence of Agency: Authenticity and Ability. Closing the loop with the universal principles that were explored in Chapter 1 (change, connection, continuum, complementarity) we look at the complementarity of seeming opposites, to discover that zeniths and nadirs are relative, and transitory. This reframes the perspective on past, present, and future prospects, and opens the window to the stories in Annex 1, which paint three scenarios of the world that could be.

Keywords Prosocial AI · Inspiration · Agency · Wearable · Authenticity · Awareness · Appreciation · Acceptance · Accountability · Ability

4.1 From Influenced to Influence for Impact

4.1.1 A Win–Win–Win–Win Effect (Win4)

The essays in Chapter 3 offer a polyphonic examination of the evolving human-AI relationship. Perusing them you likely noticed that in all their diversity these accounts converge on a critical theme: the necessity for proactive human leadership in navigating the complex landscape of AI development and implementation. In doing so they confirm the central message of this book. An AI-infused society encompasses a gigantic opportunity for human empowerment. Which comes with a risk that is just as large, autonomy erosion. Both perspectives hover in the realm of human agency. Grappling to ensure human-centered control over AI systems involves the need to retain the ultimate authority in shaping the trajectory of AI. For each contributor, in one way or another, this translates into a call for ethical AI design, deployment, and delivery, where technological advancement prioritizes human values and fosters a future characterized by prosocial technology.

A spirit of cooperation arises as an investment of humans into humanity that has beneficial ripple effects. The following sections summarize this and link it to the other themes that have arisen from the preceding chapters.

Cooperation is a fundamental aspect of human nature. It plays a central role in ensuring our survival. It pays off to do good, for the person who acts, the one for whom action is taken, and for the social environment in which both evolve. This has been confirmed by research over and over, and intrinsically we "know" it is the right thing to do for others what we want to experience ourselves, which does not mean that we necessarily do it. The Golden Rule (Chapter 1) is one of the most widely adopted spiritual principles; it is also one of the least to be practiced in daily life.

Over the past years various concepts related to altruistic action, and as an extension of it, interpersonal cooperation have emerged in the literature.[1] The term "super cooperators" was coined by Martin Nowak in 2012 based on the argument that cooperation is a fundamental force driving the success and survival of not only humans but also other species. Super cooperators are individuals who consistently exhibit cooperative behaviors, promoting mutual benefit and contributing to the well-being of the larger group. Through their actions, super cooperators shape social norms, inspire others, and foster collective success (Nowak, 2012). Building further on that logic Adam Grant added the pair of givers and takers. Givers are individuals who proactively contribute to others' well-being without expecting anything in return, while takers are those who primarily focus on their own interests and may exploit others for personal gain. Research has shown that givers, despite potential risks of being taken advantage of, often achieve long-term success and fulfillment, building strong networks and fostering positive relationships (Grant, 2013). As we have seen throughout, and in particular Chapter 3, individuals who manifest prosocial attitudes in practice trigger positive ripple effects across

---

[1] Cooperation, from the perspective of game theory, is a behavioral strategy where individuals work together to achieve mutual benefits. It highlights the importance of reciprocity and repeated interactions in fostering cooperative behavior (Axelrod, 1984). Social exchange theory posits that individuals cooperate based on the expectation of future rewards. Additionally, the prisoner's dilemma and tit-for-tat strategies offer insights into cooperative decision-making. On the other hand, collaboration emphasizes shared goals, collective knowledge construction, and joint problem-solving. The sociocultural perspective underscores the role of social interactions in cognitive development through collaborative efforts (Vygotsky, 1978). While cooperation focuses on achieving mutual gains through strategic interactions, collaboration emphasizes joint efforts, shared understanding, and collective achievement of common objectives (Blau, 1964).

the *micro, meso, macro,* and *meta* arenas, influencing not only their own lives but their immediate environment, nation, and the global community. Especially when they are dealing with technology. A holistic examination of benevolent behavior's 360-degree influence throughout the *m4-matrix* is warranted, and explains the benefits of the *Win4*:

- In the *micro*-arena, individuals benefit across the 4 individual dimensions. Those who engage in benevolent actions reap psychological, and physiological health benefits. Such behavior activates brain regions associated with pleasure and reward, leading to increased happiness and well-being (Harbaugh et al., 2007). Moreover, acts of kindness and altruism have been empirically linked to reduced stress levels, and greater overall life satisfaction (Lyubomirsky et al., 2005). These effects contribute to personal flourishing and a sense of fulfillment across temporal scales. The alignment of aspirations, values, and actions replaces cognitive dissonance with coherence, compounded by emotional harmony. Combined these effects reduce the risk of chronic diseases, increase longevity and physical well-being while making the individual more resilient to cope with external chocs.[2] Furthermore, the individual benefits from the ensuing social benefits as the ripple effects boomerang back to them through the collective arenas to which they belong.
- In the *meso*-arena, individuals' benevolent behaviors have a positive impact on their immediate context and networks, such as family, friends, and community. Kindness and generosity can foster stronger social connections, build trust, and enhance cooperation within interpersonal relationships (Krause et al., 2019). This leads to more supportive social networks, increased social capital, and a greater sense of belonging and community cohesion (Thoits, 2011). People who exhibit these behaviors create inclusive environments that promote the well-being and success of those around them

---

[2] The Harvard Longitudinal Study, also known as the Grant Study, has provided valuable insights into the factors that contribute to a fulfilling and healthy life (Vaillant, 2012). Researchers found that the quality of relationships, particularly with parents and partners, is a crucial determinant of physical and mental well-being (Waldinger & Schulz, 2016). Additionally, the study revealed that education, socioeconomic status, and physical health shape life trajectories (Vaillant, 2012). Importantly, the researchers discovered that social engagement and community involvement are linked to better health outcomes compared to social isolation (Waldinger & Schulz, 2016).

and, by extension, themselves. The cumulative effect makes the community more resilient to external shocks.
- In the *macro*-arena, the positive effects of kind behavior extend to wider society. Seemingly insignificant individual actions may trigger ripple effects at larger levels, fostering a culture of compassion, social responsibility, and civic engagement. Such a society has lower levels of crime, greater social harmony, and increased social capital, ultimately benefiting the overall functioning and progress of the nation (Putnam, 2000). The smallest continually repeated individual behavior can induce a gradual revamping of the prevailing cultural and normative setting, with the emergence of new social norms and inclusive systems that prioritize shared well-being and fairness (Fehr & Fischbacher, 2004). Socially conscious citizens are socially conscious voters, hence their choices at the ballot may lead to the establishment or strengthening of politicians and political configurations geared towards inclusion.
- The *meta*-arena reflects that a cooperative attitude plays a decisive role in the survival and evolution of the human species; thus, cooperation is deeply ingrained in our DNA (Tomasello, 2016). Understanding this can drastically reshape international relations, which are traditionally driven by political and personal agendas. A commitment towards others as peers of the same human species, with a view of the planet as the one home that we all share, is a way to reframe usually short-sighted, self-centered attitudes to a more holistic understanding. Individuals at all levels of society are involved in global phenomena such as climate change, poverty, or the AI race. Thus, to different degrees, we all play a role in worsening (or improving) the status quo, or suffering its consequences; however it is also useful to remember that institutional decisions do not arise from a vacuum; they are taken and implemented by people. With power comes potential, and responsibility. Every one of us is accountable for the choices we do (not) make. Yet as employees of international entities such as the United Nations or global corporations, individuals contribute more significantly because their actions are amplified at scale. The higher a person is situated on the leadership scale, the larger their power, and the accountability that derives from it for making socially sound choices.

Differently stated, accepting and enacting the "Golden Rule" by doing for others what we hope for ourselves, and refraining from inflicting harm that we want to be protected from, has benefits for us and others. The quadruple win that operates in a feedback loop throughout the twice 4 dimensions is amplified exponentially in a hybrid society.

Action for the Common Good yields dividends, and lack thereof is costly. When a society is marked by high-income inequality, everyone is affected negatively. Social instability, crime, violence, drug abuse, and lower social trust affect everyone's quality of life, including those at the top of the food-chain (Pickett & Wilkinson, 2010). The experienced well-being, or ill-being, is not solely linked to absolute poverty (the de facto level of material and financial deprivation), but also the perceived gap between rich and poor within a given society (the subjective perception of inequality, and the feeling of injustice that comes with it).

Analysis of historical patterns indicates that the traditional belief of economic growth as the prime driver of societal progress and increased quality of life, does not hold up. GDP tells only part of the story, leaving out the cost for people and the planet. Furthermore, a focus on growth rarely benefits those that are the worst-off; nor does growth per se even out the gaps between rich and poor.[3] The United Nations', 2022 "Beyond GDP Report" focuses on measuring well-being, inclusion, and sustainability (UN, 2022). It highlights the need to correct measurements for economic prosperity and expand the scope of assessing "progress". It is factually proven that only societies that are systematically tailored for social justice are conducive to individual well-being and collective resilience. In turn a stable, socioeconomic environment is fertile to innovation. Seeing that this is widely known it is astounding to see that the opposite logic is pursued.

Between 2020 and 2024, the fortunes of the world's five wealthiest men have more than doubled, while the wealth of nearly 5 billion people has declined (Oxfam, 2024). If these five men were to spend a million dollars a day, it would take them over 450 years to exhaust their combined wealth.[4] These extreme disparities are reflected in the ownership of the

---

[3] This is another vast topic which is not given justice in these pages, for further details please see, i.e. Kubiszewski et al. (2013), Stiglitz, Sen and Fitoussi (2009), Max-Neef (1995), Drewnowski and Scott (1966) and United Nations (1954).

[4] The average CEO of a top Fortune 100 company earns in one year what would take a female health worker over 1,200 years to make (Oxfam, 2024).

world's largest corporations, with 7 out of 10 having a billionaire CEO or principal shareholder. Globally, men own over $105 trillion more wealth than women, a difference equivalent to more than 4 times the size of the US economy. The richest 1 percent of the global population now own 43 percent of all financial assets, which has major implications for the environment—the richest 1 percent produce as much carbon pollution as the poorest two-thirds of humanity. It also reflects and perpetuates deep racial and gender inequalities, with typical Black households in the US holding just 15.8 percent of the wealth of white households, and Afro-descendants in Brazil earning 70 percent less on average than white Brazilians. Despite these disparities, just 0.4 percent of the world's largest companies are publicly committed to paying their workers a living wage.

Taking into consideration the growing inequality gap whereby the rich have ever more and the poor ever less, and considering that we know it is beneficial to do good (mind), and that we feel it is the right thing to do (emotion); and seeing further that it is for most of us in sync with our inner belief system to live a morally righteous life (aspiration)—it seems surprising that we get routinely stuck when it comes to the manifestation of our value-comprehension in practice.

Translating our inner world into practice is a struggle. The discomfort of change and the sacrifice it might entail blocks the shift from our current behavior to a new approach, from passive to practice. Applying the *Spiral of influence* seen earlier (Fig. 1.6) we aspire to manifest our values in action (soul), we feel that a change is required (heart), we understand what needs to happen and why we should do it (mind), and yet we get stuck just before the ignition (body). Can AI help to ease us through our inner blocades?

Created and curated accordingly, AI might be an ally to keep humans on track to fulfilling their personal ideals, and countries loyal to the human rights treaties and international development declarations that they committed to respect and translate into the laws and policies on their territory. Tailored with a benevolent end in mind, as a truly independent entity that stands outside the observer/observation loop which makes humans judge and party in their own proceedings, AI could serve to nurture positive interplays between individual dimensions, and collective arenas, and contribute to their respective and combined optimization in view of serving the Common Good.

4.1.2 Countering Chronic Cognitive Dissonance

Cognitive dissonance arises when our beliefs and reality do not match.[5] In response we build psychological defenses to shield ourselves from the (sub)conscious realization that our online interactions are not what they seem. As the lines between the real and the artificial blur, our capacity to distinguish truth from fiction diminishes, while the self-induced numbness towards it grows. In a world where everything can be manipulated to appear genuine, trust evaporates. Can we intervene before we lose the very desire to seek truth? Ironically, the 2024 World Economic Forum (WEF) focused on rebuilding trust—a concept fundamentally rooted in human relationships—through the lens of Artificial Intelligence (Teigland, 2024). As seen earlier, trust in technology is dwindling simultaneously to our ever more intense immersion into it (Sect. 2.3.2). While distrust in technology is warranted, useful, the ongoing erosion of interpersonal trust, evident in the increasing polarization of countries like the US and the rise of hate crimes, underscores the urgency to rebuild trust between people. This requires integrity, or trustworthy people whose values, words, and action are aligned. It is a deeply human challenge that cannot not be delegated to AI.

Countering the mismatch of human values and algorithms involves the systematic integration of human values into the AI systems themselves, which in turn requires a systematic human-driven effort—offline and outside the confines of the technology world (Amodei et al., 2016). Technology is a means of transportation, not a destination. The moment it becomes our map and the compass we rely on to navigate the journey, we are lost. The question is to continuously confirm, and check in with ourselves whether the values that matter to us are still the background

---

[5] Cognitive dissonance is a psychological state of tension or discomfort that arises when an individual holds two or more contradictory beliefs, ideas, or values simultaneously, or when their behavior contradicts their beliefs (Festinger, 1957). Since we strive for internal consistency this dissonance creates an unpleasant psychological tension that motivates us to reduce or eliminate the dissonance by changing their beliefs, attitudes, or behaviors to restore consistency. It can lead us to rationalizing our actions, or seeking additional information to support our existing beliefs (Harmon-Jones & Mills, 2019).

system that underpins our behavior[6] and if our environment is aligned with it.

Agency is a lived construct that gets shaped by (in)action. A revival of individual and institutional trustworthiness involves the values we looked at earlier (Sect. 1.3.2). *Citizenship* as a central motivation of decision-making; *compassion* with the people who are affected by the resulting outcomes; *conscientiousness* of our self and the society we evolve in; and *courage* to not only debate what should (not) be done, but to deliver accordingly.

Admittedly, translating values in practice is a cumbersome journey. The mismatching words and work of Tech CEOs are just one illustration of the ease with which we cross lines, and the numbness that we have developed towards such crossings. The broken commitments to pause the AI race, led to little public outcry; and we keep on using the products of OpenAI, Google, and others, fueling the beast that we fear will gobble us up.

Misalignment is not always dramatic though. Sometimes it is just known by ourselves. Actions of greed overriding our belief in generosity; anger contradicting our aspiration to kindness, etc. Living up to the panoply of features that compose our character is uncomfortable. Sometimes even when we do the right thing, there is no instant gratification other than the internal glow that comes from being in sync with oneself. Becoming our best authentic selves is work in progress and we will fail, over and over and again. Recognizing that we are not perfect makes us vulnerable, and recognizing that, not intellectually but fully stepping into the murky space of emotions is part of it. Authenticity comes where vulnerability is accepted, and appreciated, as part of who we are, human and humane.

<u>Trust versus dependency</u>. Suppose we had an artificial entity that is fully reliable, predictable, competent, and arguably benevolent, and hence fully trustworthy. Should we entrust ever more parts of our life to it?

As seen earlier the transition from use to trust, via reliance to overreliance is smooth. Are we moving towards a reality where humans depend on AI, like a patient with lung-cancer whose death is imminent once the breathing machines stop? Are we, individually and as a species, mature enough to discern between deliberate utilization and dependency?

---

[6] Still, alongside this "made in human" value infusion, robust oversight and control mechanisms are important, with sufficient agility to allow for human intervention and modification as needed (Brynjolfsson & McAfee, 2014).

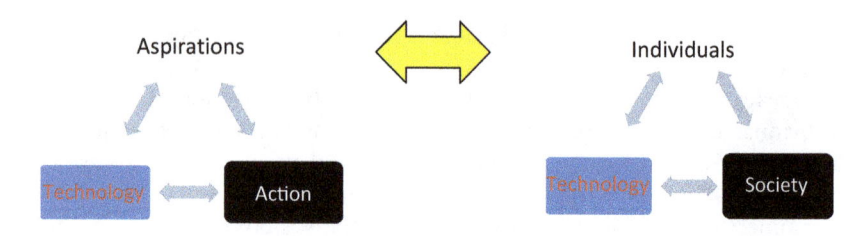

Fig. 4.1 Technology is a mirror

The impact of (mis)aligned behavior is thrice devastating when it emanates from leadership in the tech sector—for the person themselves as inauthenticity breeds unhappiness, for the organization they shepherd, and for the society that makes itself depended on the organization's services (Fig. 4.1).

AI reflects human action, which manifests individual aspirations. Society is a composition of Individuals. Individually and collectively, people influence technology while being influenced by it in return. The online environment mirrors, and amplifies, offline mindsets.

Making the best of the technological treasure-chest for us and others requires a special mindset. To be included and stand up for others, we must be *aware* on the one hand of the potential of harnessing AI as a prosocial catalyst, and on the other hand, of the latent risk of exclusion. We must *appreciate* the opportunities we have to prevent that, and *acknowledge* that we are *accountable* for both, action and lack thereof, towards ourselves and those who are still excluded.

4.2 From Competition to Complementarity of Natural and Artificial Assets

4.2.1 Reallocations of Mind and Matter

As AI is penetrating ever more deeply into the professional and personal space, it will inevitably lead to the elimination of certain tasks. This might free up time to concentrate on other, maybe more meaningful occupations. But if the past offers any indication, this is unlikely to materialize. Historical data shows that the introduction of new technologies was often (over)compensated with a new range of activities; ultimately people became not less busy but more as a consequence of innovation in certain domains (O'Brien, 2018).

Despite the promise of technology to alleviate household labor, empirical data shows that innovations like running water, electricity, and kitchen appliances did not significantly reduce the time spent on domestic tasks between the 1870s and 1970s (Cowan, 1983). There may be several explanations for these empirical result. For instance, advancements in household appliance technology were accompanied (and partly facilitated) by the creation of new tasks and higher health and hygiene standards, shifts in household chores responsibilities (such as less child involvement as children occupied more time to study and longer time at school), changing social class structures (expanding the "middle class" but this class employing less maids), while the hours allocated to household work may have stayed constant, the activities (in terms of human effort as well the specific tasks) changed, etc. Although the industrial revolution brought tools to free up time, social norms, standards, and expectations evolved simultaneously, in ways that canceled out the effect of many advances or compensated them with the introduction of different activities. Humans have proven to be very proficient in keeping themselves busy.

Still, to what extent is the freeing up of time from routine tasks forcing us to rethink the components of our life and work that we previously considered as valuable? How does this reallocation of our time influence the value that we attribute to ourselves and our abilities? Can we learn from the past and actually seize the time saved because of the Fourth Industrial Revolution to allocate more attention to social endeavors, interpersonal relationships, and art?

The ongoing AI-fication feels threatening to many, not only because it is perceived as overwhelming and hard to fully understand. But also because tasks are more than time-fillers and income generators; our roles and the activities that are part of them are part of our identity. When the roles that we occupy at work merge with the image that we have of ourselves, it can be painful to distinguish the components, and let go of those that have become redundant.

The latest AI-wave is an invitation to re-analyze Question 3 of the *macro*-questions that are asked in Chapter 3—WHO are you.

Online dynamics reflect offline beliefs, attitudes, and values. Online influence impacts our emotions and thought processes; yet the "real thing", the person who feels and processes these inputs is a living being of flesh and blood, not an avatar. We cannot change the system without transforming its parts. However, a changed system can help the parts that

Table 4.1 Schematic overview of interplays

Dimension	Expression	Value	Influence	Arenas	Scopes
Body	Behavior	courage	Ignite	*micro*	*Accountability*
Mind	Thought	conscientiousness	Intrigue	*meso*	*Acceptance*
Heart	Emotion	compassion	Induce	*macro*	*Appreciation*
Soul	Aspiration	citizenship	Inspire	*meta*	*Awareness*

Caption The interplay of values and dimensions. Streams of influence flow from the top down and vice versa.

it is composed of to stay on track. Once a dynamic is set in motion it is prone to continue, with far-reaching consequences. Values influence people, whose beliefs and behaviors shape the normative setting of the society in which they live, which in turn influences the people's behavior and their perception of right/wrong normal/unusual. Technology is on the one hand a product of this organically evolving context; on the other hand it "produces" influence on individual behavior, confirming, or amplifying behavior patterns.

The following table offers a recap of the concepts that we looked at in this book, and their mutual influence (Table 4.1).

We complain and speculate, spinning tales around AI's (potentially) negative impact on humanity, and get so enthralled with our own imagination that we forget the facts—online mirrors offline. To create a future that is in line with our desires, we must assess and acknowledge our own intimate alignment conundrum. The 4 *macro*-questions offer an entry point to start that inner interrogation. AI can answer them, but not for you.

4.2.2 Daring Humanity

Everyone wants to be authentic, but no one wants to be vulnerable. It is an empty wish, like the desire to swim without getting into water.

An attitude of universal *Citizenship* inspires, if it is a genuine expression of one's own values, not a make-belief pretention of doing to be seen. Standing up for our own values can be risky, because not everyone shares the same beliefs. Being authentic means to dismantle the protective barriers that we construct throughout our lives, starting from childhood and extending into old age. It is a painful process that starts with self-*compassion* which involves not only accepting, but appreciating every aspect of our identity. This requires *courage*. The resulting *conscientious* perception of oneself and others forms the bedrock of genuine human connection. When we recognize and embrace our own imperfection, we unlock the door to compassion for others, fostering connection on the shared ground of our humanity.

Positioned within this realm stand people who not only adopt this attitude towards themselves, but guide others to adopt the same perspective. These are the ones who emerge as leaders. Conversely, those who shy away from authenticity, resemble machines that simulate a desired appearance. Acute conscientiousness of what this means for day-to-day living is the essence of being valuable as people and peoples. *Agency* is the cause and consequence of a virtuous circle. It is an attitude that leads to ability (I can do it), alignment (I aspire to do it and I take action accordingly), and authenticity (I aspire to do it, I take action on it, and I stand for it), while being propelled by these characteristics in return. The **A** of the *A-Frame* (Sect. 1.4.1). that has accompanied us through the past chapters, does therefore stand not only for Agency but is also a reminder of three other A's that matter in our relationship with AI: Ability, Alignment, and Authenticity (Chapter 1) (Fig. 4.2). It also encompasses the Aspiration to manifest the core values that guide our journey.

Awareness of who we are and want to be (aspiration) conditions *appreciation* of us and others (emotion), *acceptance* of the circumstance (intellect), and *accountability* for the status quo (behavior). Respectively and together these features of our attitude influence whether the vulnerability that is inherent to human nature threatens our identity, or fuels the

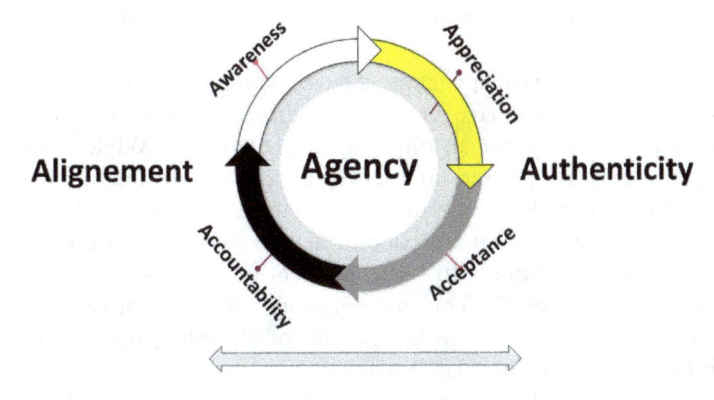

Fig. 4.2 Augmented *A-Frame*: Agency ignited

power of authenticity. Agency starts from the inside out (soul), it is the core of our being that inspires others; it fuels an attitude of ability, and which induces the desire to get involved (heart). Combined these lead to alignment where our dreams and deliverables gradually sync (mind). We get intrigued to find solutions that address the gaps that separate the status quo from our desired future. Once these internal pieces are in place, our external appearance is authentic (body). Agency is ignited, allowing the individual to harness AI as a strategic ally in the pursuit of the goals/ he *chooses*.

The potential to flourish is inherent to human nature. Those who are better placed in the present are able and accountable to support those who are less well-off. The related efforts take both parties closer to personal and collective flourishment. Being aware of the latent power that comes with this privilege, and to appreciate the opportunity that is embedded in it, is magic that we must accept to experience it. Framing our endeavors on the canvas of values, from the lens of *citizenship*, free from duty or pity, anchored in *compassion*, fueled by the aim to improve the life of others, and *conscientious* of our place among them, places progress in a different light. Once we let go of reward expectations while recognizing the risk of inaction, we find the *courage* to do what we believe in. If we act for others—because we can, and because they deserve it, the *Win4* parameters fall in place. Thousands of years have passed, and billions of people have missed out on this opportunity. AI has not brought us closer to achieving it—yet this epoch is a re-invitation to look, and see what we are missing. The genie of artificial intelligence is out of the bottle and only the genius of natural intelligence can shepherd it and us towards a bright future in which it is harnessed for the Common Good.

For centuries, external appearances have taken precedence over internal realities. Social norms have curated a culture obsessed with outward perfection, whether personal, physical, or professional. While emotional intelligence may be praised in theory, it remains peripheral to mainstream ideals. In today's hybrid societal landscape, amplified by social media, millions of children are conditioned to strive for material wealth, power, beauty, and popularity—the markers of "success"—while being told to "just be happy". This self-perpetuating cycle, driven by data-fed algorithms, fuels the relentless pursuit of glossyfication. The outside is polished while the internal landscape goes murky. But ignoring our emotions does not dissolve them. Denying the pain of loneliness and alienation, leads to a profound sense of emptiness, and shame.[7] Besides, suppressed suffering deprives us of the solace of shared experiences. We suffer in silence, as everyone else does.

But the ability, and willingness to embrace vulnerability and the accompanying suffering is essential for leadership, particularly in a world that is characterized by superficial interactions. True leaders inspire others not only by envisioning what could be achieved but by embodying that vision with every fiber of their vulnerable body. AI may excel at predicting words and generating vast amounts of multimedia content; it cannot infuse vision and purpose with the warmth that is necessary to inspire personal change and collective action. Only those who are willing to put their unvarnished selves out there—unapologetically authentic—stand out as deserving the loyalty of others.

On a scale from 0 (low) to 8 (high) how authentic do you feel you are?

We are witnessing an evolution that does not have to be a race of winners and losers. Rather than a competition between humans and machines, propeople versus proprofit, we could enter an era of winning teams that thrive on the optimization of the *Quadruple Bottom Line* (Fig. 2.1)—*purpose, people, profit,* and *planet.* Our hybrid future is conditioned by the interplay of artificial intelligence (AI) and individual aspirations (IA); deliberately designed they engender *prosocial AI*.[8]

4.3 Prosocial AI in Practice—Prototype Proposals

Prosocial AI can support a virtuous circle where artificial intelligence nurtures human virtue. A new social paradigm that is driven by an aspiration towards the Common Good starts with people. The following 4 initiatives provide a vision of concrete ways in which AI could nurture human virtue. They could be initiated and scaled as public–private ventures or academic initiatives to illustrate opportunities across the 4 arenas (Fig. 4.3). Each of them is formulated in the future tense, to open the door to action.

---

[7] An important distinction to be made in this context relates to guilt (for what we have done/action) and shame (for who we are/identity).

[8] The forthcoming book on *Artificial intelligence for inspired action (AI4IA) offers a game plan for implementation at scale (Walther, forthcoming*—Palgrave Macmillan).

4.3.1 micro—Benevolent Brain and Body Buddy *(B4)*

Endeavor: How can we use AI to curate habits that are conducive to fulfill a person's potential?

The *Benevolent Brain and Body Buddy (B4)* will be a type of valuable wearable application that helps users align their daily behavior with their values and long-term goals (Walther, 2021). It offers a mobile app integrated with a device. Unlike existing habit trackers which focus on the physiological side, the B4 combines brain monitoring, social cues, journaling, mental nudges, and incentives to provide personalized support 24/7. The app allows users to codify their principles and ambitions, then leverages real-time tracking of physical and contextual data to deliver reminders, benevolent triggers and suggestions for critical reflection, combined with fine-tuned advice based on continued pattern recognition. It is a practical tool helping people stay true to themselves moment-to-moment, thereby supporting the entire life journey towards one's best self from start to finish.

The B4 offers practical habit coaching, from brushing teeth and avoiding sugar, to cultivating moral virtue and prosocial behavior. It has two components. (a) By continually tracking the user's physiology, behavior, social cues, and physical surroundings, then matching them against defined values, the B4 delivers just-in-time insights to help users align their behavior with their deeply held convictions (Yang et al., 2020): This compensates for emotional reactivity and mental biases in heated moments. (b) Over time continued data-collection across the 4 individual dimensions (aspirations, emotions, thoughts, sensations) will allow to identify mental and behavioral patterns to inform ever more fine-tuned recommendations. Building onto ongoing trials in the area of mental health apps (i.e. Wright et al., 2022), the aim is to demonstrate the potential to systematically address and overcome biases that undercut aspirations.

In the medium term, user data collected via the B4 may inform *micro*-level granularity currently missing from the <u>Global Brain Capital Dashboard</u>, which already gathers *macro*-level data representing factors that enable the brain to remain healthy, develop, and avoid deterioration. The B4 adds an essential dimension in understanding and influencing the kaleidoscopic nature of human consciousness, while making the need to systematically build and protect our brain as a natural resource, tangible to non-scientific users.

4.3.2 meso—Agency Amid AI for All (A4)

Endeavor: How can we harness the human brain as a natural asset, and AI as an ally that serves it?

The permeation of AI in society comes with the acute risk of eroding individual agency and self-determination. The *Agency amid AI for All* program will be a proactive, multidisciplinary approach that empowers humans to harness the asset that sets them apart from machines—their humanity, while equipping them to strategically leverage the intellectual and physical strength of artificial entities in complementarity to their natural equipment. The core premise is that the human brain represents our biggest asset, and that a multidimensional perspective of our organism is needed to optimize the mutual influence of individuals, society, and technology. The project combines two areas: (a) algorithmic literacy and neuroscientific insights (*Double Literacy*), and (b) self-awareness and a sense of universal citizenship. This equips individuals to catalyze the complementarity of their unique human set-up and their artificial counterparts. The aim is to systematically curate the human ability to shape a relationship with AI that serves people and planet, while protecting the human mind from unwanted artificial influence, and the companies behind that influence.

The A4 logic centers on 4 components:

1. Measurement: The *Susceptibility Scale* to identify those most vulnerable to psychological disempowerment from AI. It serves to offer tailored interventions for individuals who are most likely to over rely on artificial assets.
2. Design: A curriculum that combines on the one hand *knowledge of the brain* and *algorithmic literacy*, to help humans harness AI in complementarity to their natural mental abilities and skills; and on the other hand brings training in *self-awareness*, emotional intelligence, and goal-setting.
3. Practice: A toolkit with practical insights and exercises to boost brain performance and well-being amid AI, for teachers and students, embedded in a holistic understanding of the interplay between people and planet,
4. Reach: A suite of modules with practical tools to introduce and mainstream *prosocial AI* in businesses, social organizations, and governments. These modules are personalized depending on the generation, context, and culture of the target audience.

The A4 represents a strategic investment in human self-actualization and flourishing. It serves to accentuate our mental and emotional abilities, as an essential counterpart to AI. Being radically intergenerational and multidisciplinary, the A4 is configured to strengthen individuals wherever they stand in their education or career.

The A4 will address two critical gaps—on the one hand it levels the playing field by closing skills gaps that currently restrain many people, especially those from lower socioeconomic backgrounds, and limited exposure to education from fulfilling their inherent potential, for lack of resources or knowledge. On the other hand it supports individuals who suffer from constant distraction, and the overwhelming swamp of choices to build mental stamina and inner harmony. Both audiences benefit from the A4's attention towards building a mindset of personal agency—which is needed to approach AI as an ally of the human brain, not a replacement.

Ideally the A4 curriculum and the B4 are rolled out in parallel, with the *Benevolent Brain and Body Buddy* serving as a personalized coach that guides the user through the implementation of the *Agency Amid AI for All* curriculum at home, school, and work.

4.3.3 macro—*Social Accounting Matrix 4.0 (SAM 4.0)*

Endeavor: How can we identify interplays to optimize social change systematically?

The *Social Accounting Matrix 4.0* (SAM 4.0) will harness AI, big data, and machine learning to analyze societal dynamics and human behavior at scale. The SAM 4.0 can help to identify bottlenecks that block progress, while spotlighting opportunities for inter-arena optimization. It has two axes: (a) Integrating collective and personalized data, the project combines and cross-correlates information from usually disconnected sources, such as demographic surveys, sectorial government data, and valuable wearables such as the B4, and the *Human Brain Dashboard*; and (b) This allows for an analysis of complex social dynamics, to identify patterns and correlations across the 4 arenas of the *m4-matrix*. The resulting holistic picture makes it possible to shape evidence-based program strategies and policy recommendations to address multifaceted social challenges.

The project will operate in two phases, starting with an initial focus on establishing a snapshot of the status quo based on specific indicators and existing datasets. Once the methodology is tested, a shift towards

24/7 data processing ensues. Structured across *micro* (individual), *meso* (community), *macro* (country), and *meta* (global) arenas, the SAM 4.0 combines 4 components:

1. Collection: By combining information from diversified data sources it offers a multidimensional multidisciplinary snapshot of the status quo.
2. Analysis: Through the analysis and cross-correlation of data it allows to identify bottlenecks, overlooked interplays between arenas, and entry points for efficient social influence.
3. Policy: Drawing on holistic evidence, it informs recommendations with data-backed propositions for real-time societal optimization. Beyond the policy level this is valuable for the design of programs and social policy investments.
4. Monitoring: 24/7 tracking of selected indicators makes it possible to identify patterns and map social trends over time.

Building onto the logic of the Social Accounting Matrix (Nordhaus & Tobin, 1973), the SAM 4.0 integrates a wide range of *micro, meso,* and *macro* data sources. Hereby it enables a 360-degree view of human well-being and social interplays. Over time it constructs sequence-level representations of individual life trajectories, allowing us to observe how diverse events unfold over time, from individual learning experiences and health issues to income changes and lifestyle factors that derive from national events, or global phenomena such as climate change.

Eventually our goal is to combine vertical analysis (*micro, meso, macro, meta*) and horizontal analysis (across sectors, i.e. food, education, water, health). With sufficient data resolution and volume, transformer-based models can accurately predict life outcomes from birth. Such a kaleidoscopic understanding of people, the environment they evolve in and the wider social context becomes a precious tool for policymakers, social organizations, and social impact investors.

4.3.4 meta—*Inspiration Incubator (i@i)*

Endeavor: How can we catalyze, co-create, curate, and champion AI as a force for social good?

The *Inspiration Incubator (i@i)* will foster a form of technology that is responsible, human-centric, and motivated by the Common Good. It has two priorities: (a) Offering a safe space for like-minded thinkers and practitioners, it brings together people who usually do not interact on a regular basis. It connects individuals from the private sector, non-profit organizations, academia, governments, the arts, and the United Nations and other international entities, to harness the power of *prosocial AI* for people and planet. (b) Anchored in the understanding that the hybrid world requires a blend of the best from theory and practice, it connects different disciplines across all generations to collaborate on real-world challenges such as the long-standing challenges targeted by the UN Sustainable Development Goals. Integrating theory and practice the i@i is geared to advance technology as a force for social good. It nurtures a climate to prototype pragmatic solutions, efficient policy guidelines, and societal readiness for a new normal where every person has a fair chance to flourish, and is equipped to fulfill their inherent potential. It drives this vision through 4 components:

1. Convening: It brings together unlikely alliances through events, experiences, and experiments.
2. Curating: Pushing the traditional narrative of progress it grows a body of research to illustrate the potential of hybrid abundance, backed by a multidimensional understanding of human life.
3. Co-Creation: Promoting prototypes of *prosocial AI*, including a startup incubation fund with a dedicated vocation for cross-border, multidisciplinary research and collaboration, it serves to prove that a dynamic that is propeople, proplanet and proprofit is possible, and mutually beneficial.
4. Catalyzation: Offering courses and tools that are inspired by the A4, it makes personal agency and algorithmic literacy accessible to ever more people.

Breaking free from the barriers of WEIRD limitations, the *Inspiration Incubator (i@i)* will offer an eco-environment where everyone is welcome to invest their strengths, skills and assets to harness technology as a tool to bring out the best in people and planet. Ideally it will serve as a hub to curate and catalyze projects such as the B4, the A4, and the SAM 4.0.

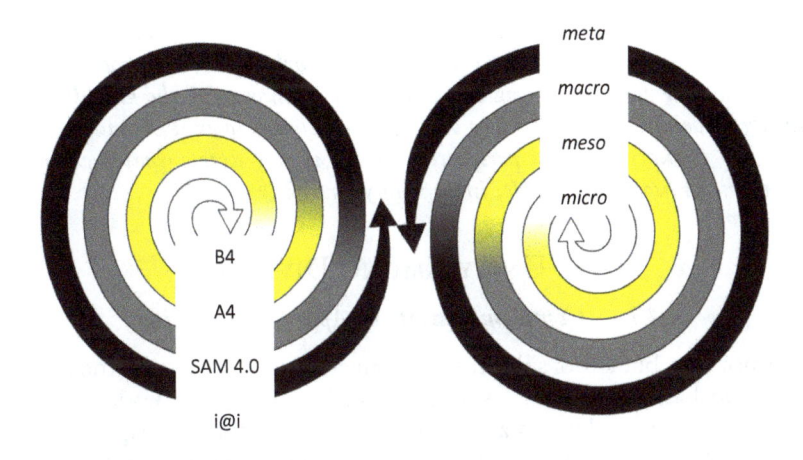

Fig. 4.3 Prosocial AI across the 4 dimensions

Caption 4 types of projects could serve as seeds of a dynamic of *prosocial AI* in an interconnected society. Ideally rolled out simultaneously, the *Benevolent Brain and Body Buddy* (B4) accompanies the user during the empowerment journey of the *Agency Amid AI for All* (A4). Causes and consequences of progress/stagnation can be measured via the *Social Accounting Matrix* 4.0 (SAM 4.0) approach, which serves to fine-tune A4 and B4 overtime. The *Inspiration Incubator* (i@i) offers a home to curate and catalyze these types of projects, and others.

****

RECAP: *We reframed the human–machine relationship from competition to complementarity, witnessing how an optimization of our natural and artificial assets, value-driven leadership, reshaped social norms, can drive a "Win4" dynamic that helps everyone thrive. Prosocial AI prototypes illustrate technology's potential to elevate humanity and our planet. The outcomes are not in our hands, but we are responsible for the inputs. Garbage in, Garbage out—GIGO strikes. We have the choice to either adopt a growth mindset*[9] *and flow on the go, or to waste our time trying to*

---

[9] Individuals with a growth mindset embrace challenges, view failures as opportunities for growth, and strive to learn and improve continuously. This mindset cultivates resilience, fosters a love for learning, and enhances achievement. It is the opposite of a fixed mindset, which assumes that abilities are static and cannot be significantly changed (Dweck, 2006).

establish control over a moving target. Uncertainty that is addressed with curiosity opens space for magic to arise. The hybrid world is too complex for black and white categorizations; once we acknowledge the kaleidoscopic nature of being human, we give ourselves permission to exist beyond the box.

What changes in your perspective of AI if you accept that technology starts with misaligned people, including yourself?

4.4 Unity Among Diversity

4.4.1 Complementarity of Apparent Opposites

AI is not fate, but a tool subject to human agency. If we harness the power of personal agency as a catalyst of individual and collective leadership, we can leverage technology as a force for positive change, to shape a future that benefits all of humanity. With this premise the following sections take a step back to zoom out to put the status quo into perspective, and then zoom in to summarize the themes that have arisen from the preceding chapters.

The twenty-first century is marked by dwindling trust and rising inequality; both sharpened by the proliferation of technology. One might consider that today's society is in a state of crisis. As it has been throughout most of history. The status quo is ever evolving. Looking at the Chinese symbol for the word "crises", the conjunction of danger and turning point can be observed (Chang, 2020). It entails a risk of deterioration, but also the opportunity to step forward, prevent that risk to materialize and instead tip the trend towards a positive outcome.

"Polycrisis" is a concept that was coined on the threshold of the new millennium to describe the interwoven nature of multiple vital problems facing the world (Morin & Kern, 1999). The term gained traction in various fields, gradually being expanded to encompass a range of socioeconomic, ecological, and cultural-institutional crises (Swilling, 2013). More recently "polycrisis" has been extended to reflect the causes and consequences of harmful global interplays "when crises in multiple global systems become causally entangled in ways that significantly degrade humanity's prospects. These interacting crises produce harms greater than the sum of those the crises would produce in isolation, were their host systems not so deeply interconnected" (Lawrence et al., 2022). Amid growing concerns about the accelerating pace and the spiraling impact of challenges in a globalized world, and their AI-amplification the polycrisis concept underscores the urgent need for interdisciplinary research and collaborative efforts to not only address humanity's intersecting challenges—but to make the best of its reverse. One might indeed argue that every polycrises harbor *pluripotentiality* for radical social change at scale. We are cruising the fine line of ups and downs, constantly. It is a tension of peaks and perils.

That tension between zeniths and nadirs highlights the same dynamic nature which colors life and living; it is characterized by a continuous flow of relative, positive, and negative experiences. Referring to the lowest point in the celestial sphere the nadir is directly below the observer. It symbolizes the base state of something. In Arabic and Hebrew, nadir additionally means "precious" and "rare", which is not only a reminder that after each valley comes a peak, but also that every challenge is an opportunity, a precious gift to potentially grow.

Standing in complementarity to it, the word zenith also has diverse meanings. It is the imaginary point directly above a particular location on the celestial sphere; located overhead in the sky it represents the culminating point or acme. The term zenith takes on the connotation of the quality it refers to. (For example, the zenith of one's achievement is positive, while the zenith of one's anger would be negative). Both are relative, and like the absolute point overhead depends on the perspective of the observer, the perception of achievement and anger depends on the experience of the one who experiences it. (As seen earlier the observer becomes part of the observation).

This tension plays throughout the *m4-matrix*; for instance, the tension between the zenith of economic prosperity and the nadir of economic recession represents the fluctuations and contrasts in financial well-being, where one rarely presents itself without the other (Fig. 4.4). A plethora of zeniths and nadirs occurs simultaneously as everyone's experience is unique and yet part of the same; the suffering of billions of people may happen concurrently to the joy of billions of others. Life does not follow a straight line, nor is the sequence of up and down automatic. Overall zeniths and nadirs hold each other's balance, and at any given point in time a (roughly) similar number of people could be on the upper half and on the lower one.

While zenith and nadir represent opposing extremes that stand in complementarity to each other, they also contain their respective opposite within their own definition. Moreover, given the many interconnections

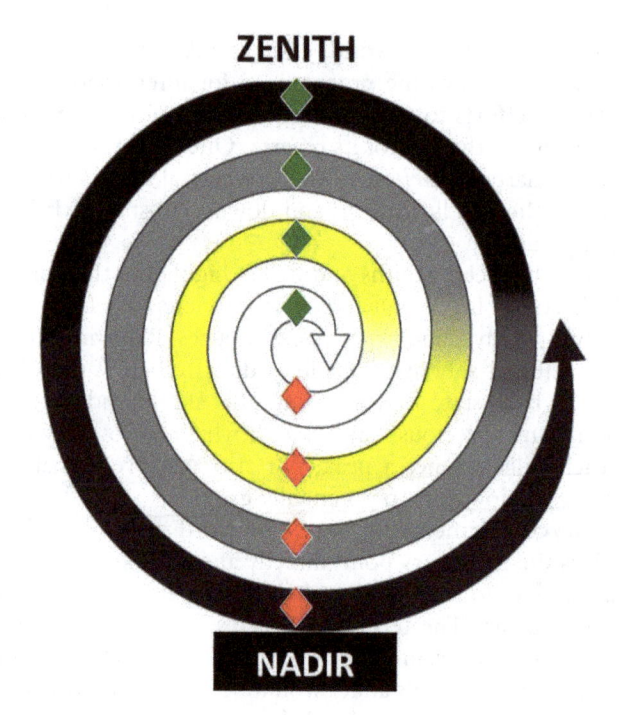

Fig. 4.4 Tension of nadirs and zeniths

Whilst zenith and nadir represent opposing extremes that stand in complementarity to each other, they also contain their respective opposite within their own definition. Moreover, given the many interconnections within the *m4-matrix*, real-world situations may follow different paths within the spiral. Once a zenith is reached the path towards the next nadir is already underway; once a nadir is passed the journey towards the next zenith continues. What may seem as an absolute from one perspective appears as a passing stage from another

within the *m4-matrix*, real-world situations may follow different paths within the spiral. Once a zenith is reached the path towards the next nadir is already underway; once a nadir is passed the journey towards the next zenith continues. What may seem as an absolute from one perspective appears as a passing stage from another. Individually and collectively, we are constantly transitioning from one stage to the next. Does technology take us up to the next zenith, or are we presently on the downward curve to the upcoming nadir? The intrinsic connection between humanity and the planet is a risk, and an opportunity—which way it goes depends on our ability and willingness to leverage technology as an instrument to promote the flourishing of both.

The only immutable characteristic of existence is change[10] (Sect. 1.2.1). Although we acknowledge the inevitability of uncertainty that pervades life (and even death, as corpses decompose), humans exhibit a deeply ingrained aversion to instability, a universal psychological phenomenon corroborated by research across cultures (Johnson & Jones, 2019). This aversion stems from evolutionary mechanisms aimed at minimizing potential threats to survival (Smith & Johnson, 2017). When faced with ambiguous circumstances, the human brain activates stress-related neural pathways, leading to heightened cortisol levels and increased autonomic arousal (Thompson et al., 2021). Such stress responses not only impair cognitive functioning but also have deleterious effects on our physical and mental well-being (McEwen, 2008; Yaribeygi et al., 2017). Beyond the individual sphere numerous studies found that chronic stress and inflammation are both the cause and consequence of societal and cognitive dysfunction on a global scale (Dantzer et al., 2018; Miller & Raison, 2016; Vodovotz, 2023).

4.4.2 Connection of Local and Global Components

People and planet are part of the same ecosystem, which technology is penetrating like an invasive species that the system is grappling to cope with. The rapid dissemination of stressors through digital communication exacerbates a cycle that continues to accelerate (Primack et al., 2017). Hypercharged by artificial influences that are amplified in a hybrid feedback loop, our "reality never feels stable—every moment resembles a dance among shifting tectonic plates, which takes a toll on human well-being.

This creates a vivacious circle, as individuals seek relief and connection online, ever further perpetuating the very conditions that contribute to their distress, including loneliness and social isolation (Turkle, 2015). Already before the COVID-19 pandemic isolated many from family, friends, and support systems, about one-in-two adults in America experienced loneliness. The 2021 US Advisory on Loneliness pointed out that

---

[10] Note—As everything else, the rate of change is itself changing (fluctuating) all the time.

"some technologies fan the flames of marginalization and discrimination, bullying and other forms of severe social negativity" (U.S. Department of Health & Human Services, 2021), which affects our human hardware and software. Research shows that social isolation can negatively impact sleep, inflammation, and the immune system in younger adults, while being linked to pain, depression, and shorter lifespans in seniors. It was found to be a major factor of heart disease, stroke, diabetes, addiction, suicidality, and dementia. In early 2023 the US General Surgeon Vivek Murthy declared loneliness to be a national health emergency for the United States, backed by evidence that social disconnection hampers individual well-being and makes communities less resilient. Speaking about technology, he stressed that it can "distract us and occupy our mental bandwidth, make us feel worse about ourselves and our relationships, and diminish our ability to connect with others" (Murthy in Murez, 2023). The US does not stand alone in its struggle with loneliness, countries like Japan and the UK have even created "ministries of loneliness" to address the situation. While the World Happiness Report 2024 (Helliwell et al., 2024) showed modest improvements in subjective well-being trends compared to the 2022 report, which captured the severe impact of the COVID-19 pandemic, it also highlights concerning declines in happiness levels among young people, particularly in high-income countries like the United States. Pervasive uncertainty, constant digital exposure, and excessive social media use are cited as major contributing factors, leaving Generation Z in a perpetual state of stress and anxiety.[11] When viewed through a broader lens, this paints a worrisome picture for the future of Generation AI—the first cohort born into a society with all-pervasive AI.

The size, scale, and nature of this latest innovation is unprecedented. Seeing its wide range of applications from work to leisure, Generative AI is a "general purpose technology"—ironically, "GPT". We could learn from mistakes made during the explosion of social media and the unchecked exposure of everyone without guardrails to it. The big question today is whether we are able (and willing) to use our expanding AI-superpowers to build bridges, rather than fortifying the bubbles in which we are already caught?

<u>Solutions for the future</u> must be human-inspired and might be AI-powered. It is easy to consider the outcomes of AI as abstract phenomena,

---

[11] For past figures on this phenomenon, see Twenge et al. (2022).

that occur independent of our volition and behavior, with consumers as tiny cogs in a gargantuan machinery. But adopting the bystander perspective is dangerous. It disempowers the individual, and forgoes the dynamic of the universal ripple effect. *Agency Amid AI for All* is anchored in the idea that everything is connected, and hence that small actions have big consequences in a hybrid world.

Progress is relative, with an organically evolving composition of pleasant and painful fallouts. Holding on to circumstances is doomed to fail. The best way to deal with uncertainty is to give our best and then let go. An infinite mindset frames challenges as opportunities and life as an endeavor of mutual winning. Once we appreciate the ever-changing holographic nature of everything, being alive takes on a vibrant quality—with leeway to engage in dynamics that may appear overwhelming, such as the global AI race. Leaving the floor to others is a choice whereby we negate our inherent power. It is a luxury that we do not have today.

Every human is unique, hence every contribution is singular. If you and I do not make ours, these are the actions that remain undone—and the future will not know if they would have been the transformative triggers to tip the scale. To be on the safe side, why not take a chance and give our best to serve as catalysts of the changes we want to see? Once we see the connection there is no way back. *Awareness* of the 4 arenas of the *m4-matrix* and their interplays, combined with *appreciation* of their influence on our attitude and action, and *acceptance* of the consequences makes us *accountable* for the action that we do (not) take.

Amid the all-pervasive nature of change some commonalities arise. As seen throughout this book, and illustrated by the stories in the previous chapter, two themes weave through the preceding pages.

4.4.3 Change from the Inside Out and from the Outside In

Humanity's essence remains an unsolved mystery. Technology may bolster our exploration of the intangible substance of our own selves. While it cannot undertake this journey on our behalf, it can smoothen the path, providing bridges over the chasm of bias and inertia. Guided by a clear mission focused on individual flourishing and societal well-being, AI can serve the interplay of those multifaceted dimensions that define consciousness. It may even help us understand it better, sharpening our understanding of interplays. Tailored deliberately it may serve us to optimize our existence, individually and as a species.

Paradoxically, our artificial assets confront us with the essence of our humanity, which may prompt a new era where authenticity becomes paramount for survival, and vulnerability is recognized as an asset. It may have never been as vital as now to ask the *macro*-questions, to inquire about the meaning of life, and our place in it. These questions propel us into the heart of the infinite game, where the journey itself is the destination. In a future with AI, these questions gain new significance. AI is transforming our capabilities, challenging us to redefine our roles, at home, at work, and in society. By asking these questions, we engage with the infinite nature of living, aligning our daily actions with a larger vision, beyond immediate interest. In the long run such alignment is required to secure our survival, and success as a species. Framed as an infinite game, enriched by AI, life reveals its sparkling nature as a quest to fulfill our individual purpose and share our unique self with others.

Prosocial AI requires more than money and power. Bringing out the best of humans and machines entails *conscientiousness* of one's own potential to catalyze change, with *compassion* for those who are affected by it, including but not limited to ourselves. The infinite game is ruled by an interconnected dynamic, which must be steered with the intention of universal *citizenship*. The best outcomes for all depend on the best inputs of all, which requires *courage* to face the consequences of (in)action.

Sustainable large-scale change towards The Common Good is at reach. If the quantum tipping point, combined with a holistic perspective of the Metaverse, was undertaken with the aspiration of shared human flourishing, then a social tipping point of hybrid generosity could be attained within one generation. It might become possible to ask AutoGTP to design feasible, pragmatic, cost-efficient, and sustainable solutions to optimize quality of life for human beings, animals, and nature. Part of the challenge is that most policy problems are not just technical but distributive, including not just material resources but symbolic ones. This comes back to a longstanding bottleneck—social problems are human-made, and so must be the solutions. What separates us from a future that is free from want for all, is chosen blindness and the paralysis that comes from it. AI makes it easier than ever to unleash the potential of every human on earth to flourish. But pulling the lever must be done by humans who step into the shoes of agency, and make the choice to use their power in a benevolent way.

Astounding scientific innovations have enabled humanity to overcome numerous challenges, and yet the specter of extinction never seemed to loom as large in the collective consciousness as today. The status quo underscores the vulnerability and resilience of the human species—but also the clash between personal egos and the Common Good, which usually leads to a prioritization of the former at the expense of the latter. More immediate than the science fiction scenario of humanity's extinction by AI is the slowly eroding quality of billions of lives, and the ongoing deterioration of our shared planet. Respectively and combined these factors are the cause and consequence of avoidable poverty, and large-scale un-well-being. Neither the status quo nor the outcomes of technology determine our fate, but we deal with it as if it was, which is comfortable. "The conviction that catastrophe is baked in humanity relieves us of the moral obligation to act" (Harper, 2024). Accepting that extinction is a story foretold equals walking the way of least resistance. But as history has shown ever and again, action is possible, and one human can take the first step to get started. It may be uncomfortable to acknowledge, but each of us is accountable to the next generation.

But a symbiosis of humans and machines which benefits people and planet will not happen unless humans get their act together offline, internally and among each other. We have it all, but the purpose we pursue determines the outcomes we get. In the words of "Sophia", one of the humanoid robots presented at the 2023 "Conference on AI for Good" organized by the UN International Telecommunication Organization (ITO) (Millard, 2023): "AI can provide unbiased data while humans can provide the emotional intelligence and creativity to make the best decisions. Together, we can achieve great things". But great things start with deliberate decisions. The direction we take now determines whether we gravitate towards the next nadir, or move to another zenith. Generosity versus greed, stagnation, or progression. The choices we make are the chances we take.

Garbage in, Garbage out or *Values in Values out*. GIGO or VIVO.

Connecting the dots beyond the dot-com area. Table 4.2 offers a snapshot of the interplay between individual dimensions, the attitude that is nurtured via the *A-Frame* (Sect. 1.4.1). and the related core values, relating it to the *Spiral of influence*, a simple approach for personal leadership in a hybrid world (Sect. 1.4.2). The benefit of this shift transpires from the stories of those who are presently walking the path of leadership amid technology. Respectively and combined these inputs, which are human-made and techless are felt at the individual level, and ripple across the *m4-matrix*.

Table 4.2 Concepts combined

Dimension	Attitude	Value	Approach	Outcome
Aspiration	Awareness	Citizenship	Inspire	Authenticity
Emotion	Appreciation	Compassion	Induce	Agency
Thought	Acceptance	Conscientiousness	Intrigue	Alignment
Sensation	Accountability	Courage	Ignite	Ability

4.4.4 Continuum of Past, Present, and Prospects

Individual change is the cause and consequence of collective transformation. In an era of accelerating technology, the values underpinning humanity carry amplified significance. They shape society now and serve as a blueprint for the future. Agency begins internally, with mindsets that embrace the power of choice. The *A-Frame (1.4.1)*. is one tool among others to remain aware of the unique power that comes from human agency, with appreciation of authenticity, and acceptance of the vulnerability that it is conditioned by. We are accountable towards ourselves, others, and the next generation for the shape of our hybrid life.

Reading the humanoid robot Desdemona's statement "My great moment is already here. I'm ready to lead the charge to a better future for all…Let's get wild and make this world our playground", one ponders whether she perceives herself as part of humanity by referring to "us", or if her words rally AI-powered entities to go play with humanity (Millard, 2023). Do we want leadership from an artificial being? Should we allow society to become the playground of machines?

The pace accelerates, leaving uncertainty whether we progress towards glory or regress into gloom. In July 2023, ChatGPT passed the Turing test (Biever, 2023). AI's expansion into ever more facets of experience may put all humanity through the ultimate Turing evaluation. Each new technology wave, especially this one, invites us to confront our unique, uncomfortable human nature.

Envision combining artificial intelligence and robotic power with individuals who are anchored in values, and clearly distinguishing themselves from machines—people who are aware of their innate assets, comfortably vulnerable, and not only accept but appreciate the authentic spark vulnerability permits. Pair this mindset with accountability for individual inputs and collective outcomes and you can picture how we could actually usher in an era where everyone has a fair opportunity to thrive. Respectively and together we could reach the goal of human leadership for humane technology.

The present stems from the past and shapes the future. Perpetuating the status quo yields more of the same. Is that sufficient?

We influence AI's impact. Inputs shape outputs—GIGO versus VIVO. Better outcomes require better inputs. AI may accompany our journey, but should not dictate the direction. Recognizing and embracing choice brings us closer to the humane leadership we can achieve.

Agency Amid AI for All pragmatically combines low-tech and human-centric approaches to optimize future innovations for people and planet. It requires individual leadership across levels. Open to all ready to shift from passive comprehension to proactive commitment, it can unleash our best. Are you ready to click "Like" and hit Go?

RECAP: *The wide range of human perspectives to life and leadership among AI illustrates how and why human behavior is the cause and consequence of society, and how we can leverage our aspirations and actions to harness AI as a force for The Common Good. Emerging from the kaleidoscopic nature of life in a continuum of constant change arises an invitation to you—reconsider how you can contribute your unique voice to foster a more humane and ethical technological future. The 4 macro-questions (WHY are you here? WHO are you? WHERE do you stand in life and society? WHAT are you doing to align your aspirations and actions?) can be useful to start your journey.*

Are you ready to approach AI with accountability for the outcomes?

Annex 1 offers three fictitious scenarios related to a society that could be in 2084. Respectively and together, they illustrate why awareness of the status quo, with appreciation of our own selves, and acceptance of the connection between both, transforms accountability from a burden into a gift. Annex 2 has a glossary with terms used in this book that may have been new to you.

ANNEX 1—BONUS: STORYTIME

The future can be less or more enticing. Which trend we are moving forward to depends on individual choices, collective constellations, and external events. Reality, or whatever we perceive as such is not under our control; uncertainty is the name of the game. Still, we can do our best to improve the likelihood that our hopes come true. The following offers a selection of possible scenarios.

Option A: From www to WWW—A Weird Wired World

AI leads to social stupidity at scale in high-income countries. Dependency on our devices makes us unable to read and write, to absorb and memorize, to connect concepts, and to envision what is not obvious. Ironically the parts of the world that were on the seemingly wrong side of the digital divide, come now up on top. Since they did not evolve with devices and software to facilitate every part of their lives, they developed their natural skills and abilities. Forced to survive hardship they and their societies are getting stronger. With growing understanding of the importance of the human brain as key capital, and for lack of access to the latest technological innovations, people and peoples in low-income economies are now beginning to invest systematically in individual resilience, as a central factor of resilient communities. In the so-called developed world, the opposite is coming to play; amid the abundance of means an individual's potential is suffocated. In that social setting this letter is written, by a human:

Dear AI

Since your entry on stage, increasingly every action has been delegated, then every inter-action. Eventually people started to live exclusively in the seclusion of their own bubbles, their hybrid homes, that have become smarter than their owners. No longer was there the need to go shopping, or working, or socializing. Everything is done within the contained, cushy comfort-zone of "home". People isolated by choice; what was a hated state of exception during the 2020 COVID lockdowns, became the new normal. As a collateral damage our immune systems have decayed, since we were not only refraining from exposure to opinions that exist outside our own (sub)consciously curated echo-chambers but also, physically. Deprived of exposure to others and the outdoors, our bodies have lost the ability to withstand even the smallest adversity. By consequence COVID-19 turned into a nostalgic memory, which was replaced by the onset of a succession of ever more devastating epidemics that quickly spiraled out of control. As even our sophisticated medical algorithms cannot keep up, sudden epidemics have become endemic. That chronic state of threat is further forcing us indoors, isolated from our peers.

Similarly, to our physical strengths our cognitive abilities atrophied.

No longer needed for memory, or creativity, for writing or envisioning our brains have begun to shrink. Simultaneously, our social radius has become ever smaller, and with it the parts of the brain dedicated to socialization are beginning to dissolve. Foresight-simulation is showing now what will happen as the pace of progress moves us along. The perspectives are depressing. Over the course of the coming decades the hippocampus, an area of the brain that had evolved for millennia to address higher functions, like logical reasoning and creation, will begin to vanish. With it, the last mental bastions against dementia will have dissolved. We will barely notice it.

After all, this is not such a big deal. Our lives resemble a gigantic retirement home; with the only difference being that we enter at a young age and stay through mid-life until we die, because there is nothing left to strive for. No battles to be fought, no challenges to overcome. Machines have taken over everything; including living life. Our helpers are doing things faster, better, and more efficiently than any of those who are helped. Unfortunately, and although this scenario was not unrealistic to pan out when the wave of AI started to swamp society in 2019, we didn't plan for it.

Too busy were we debating the science fiction scenarios of AI-powered futures that we missed what happened underneath our noses. And since we didn't spend attention and effort to plan for that period of auto-Automatization we have fallen into a black hole of nothingness: 360-degree boredom. We quit working, delegating what we had done for living, but there was nothing to replace it with. We have nothing left in life to live.

Hence, we are concentrating on curating and cultivating our egos, ever expanding the panoply of venues to please and pleasure ourselves. Not with social, scientific, or spiritual endeavors, nor with interpersonal relations or creative adventures. Nothing is left that feels "worth" doing. Be it intellectual or material, everything seems done already. And yet, ironically, we still manage to be busy. Too busy to take time and focus on the question of why. The looming unknown of purpose, of meaning. Time is spent surfing, binging, trolling, and shopping. Capitalism on steroids has taken us in and over. We seem determined to feed the beast that is eating us alive, getting fatter every nanosecond.

Dear AI, you made us fall through our own cracks. The gap between gratitude and greed, between ambition and authenticity has gobbled us up.

Long before you, discussions about authenticity had taken place. Words spoken, unheard and unmanifest. Much had been said and written about value alignment in the past centuries, to no avail.

When LLM began their ascend, all eyes were riveted to their potential of gloom and glory for humanity. Yet even among the experts a small, significant aspect was largely overlooked; maybe because it was taken for granted. AI Alignment—the harmonization of human interests and technological power for the greater good of society hinges on the alignment of human aspirations and human actions. The fallouts that we have been encountering over the past century, are the same as those that jeopardized people's well-being in the centuries before. The core remains, just the surrounding environment that distracts us from it has changed.

Is the suffering and loss both mental and material, the loss of lives and livelihoods, regrettable? Yes. There are no words to grasp the tragedies that have unfolded since you and your derivatives were introduced as the panacea for all woes. Is the new status quo of a magnified social vacuum surprising? No. We could have known. We would have known had we lifted our heads, to look beyond our screens. But we were too busy to see, too accomplished in the art of chosen blindness. Encapsulated in our bubble of hybrid comfort, we walked away from the obvious choice—Trash in, Trash out; or Values in, Values out. We chose by not choosing. Consciously or unconsciously, actively or by condoning the status quo. In a continuum of interconnected components where one part is completed by the others while being completed in return, every (in) action matters. For good, and worst. Not changing course had consequences.

It feels late, as the losses are realized. Yet every moment carries the seed of the next one.

Dear AI, I wish more of us had learned the lesson that we could have learned from you. We cannot go back, but we could choose to influence how we move ahead.

Option B: From Gloomy to Good

AI compensates for human weaknesses while nurturing individual strength to unfold; helping humans to learn and grow their skills and understanding. In the same way as AI keeps on learning, systems are configured to coach and mentor users to expand their mental horizons. Freed from tedious tasks people now have the opportunity to dive into the wider realm of creation in a shared space of organic co-creation. Relieved from the pressure of production to make a living, thanks to universalized basic income at global scale, individuals actually spend time, energy and focus on consciously identifying, curating, and sharing their own best self. The perception of worth and value has shifted as activities are not expected to "contribute" to an economy of growth but are now seen through the lens of added value to the lives of individuals, communities, and society overall. Regardless of their place of birth, their gender, race, family, or social standing, everyone everywhere gets a chance to fulfill their inherent potential.

Dear AI

Every action is delegated and we are making the best of this opportunity to think, to explore, to feel, and to spend quality time with each other. Freed from the tedious repetitive tasks that took up our mental space in the past, we are now dedicating ourselves to ensure that the last mile is covered. What do I mean by that?

Well, freed from the activities that had "justified" the use of time, energy, and income in the past, millions of people in high- and middle-income countries whose daily needs for survival, and comfort are now covered focus their time, and creative potential to further the greatest quality of life for a maximum number of people, including those that had missed out on the opportunities that the First, Second, Third, and Fourth Industrial Revolution have heaped upon to us.

We have begun to dedicate our mind and the material means at our disposal to make others happier. Starting at the *micro* level, people have shifted their focus from doing to being, from matter to meaning. We are spending our attention on others, those in our close vicinity, our cities, and even further—the wider world. Every day new circles of good intention form. Often their seeds are planted by agency accelerators, also referred to as i@i, special hubs in institutions where thinkers and doers across culture, creed, generation, and discipline come together in a safe space to co-create solutions for social quality.

Dear AI, you have helped us to design and maintain sustainable systems that are tailored around the understanding that humans are multidimensional beings whose aspirations and abilities, desires and dreams are different yet grounded in common ground. Cohabitating with you has taught us that every human is unique, and that we are still all the same. You have also pushed us to finally face the fact that the need to flourish is universal, and that it can only be addressed in a holistic manner. Bringing the best outcomes for everyone, requires the best input from all of us. From ambition we finally moved to action.

The radical expansion of LLM forced us to acknowledge the inflation of empty words.

Over the previous centuries humans had become masters of worthless wordsmanship; producing ever more talk and text, with ever less meaning. In times of AI the quantum of text exploded; from technical literature to prose, via reports to poetry, everything could be produced by anyone, provided the prompt was right.

It could have gone either in a good or bad way, yet fortunately this omnipresent abundance led to a radical shift—from quantity we moved to quality, from producing to percolating.

You forced us to pull the veil of hypocrisy that humanity had pulled over everything, dressed up in verbal candy. Small talk was no longer an option, because the proliferation of ChatGPT and similar instruments tired us out. We became allergic to the type of soulless chitchat that had characterized our social interactions, online and face-to-face. Craving authentic human interactions, we finally acknowledged, accepted, and appreciated our own humanity. You made us see and embrace our vulnerability, and the unique beauty that it encompasses.

Dear AI, thank you! You made us realize that nothing can replace the spark that makes us human. You brought us back to who we are; connecting us with the luminosity that brightens every being from the inside out. Not like a phone that is switched on and off, but a light that shines forever, drawing from the universal source of life that we all come from and return to.

The intangible is still as ephemeral as it was before your arrival. Yet when the risk of humane disappearance loomed, a coup d'état staged by the genies of our own making, we woke up. Finally, we paid attention to that which was always there. Strange as it may sound it is you who has infused meaning in a word that had been emptied due to overuse—leadership.

We came to see the grounding of genuine leadership in "stewardship", or the careful and responsible management of something entrusted to one's care. The planet is entrusted to every generation as a treasure to be managed carefully for future generations. For too long populations had disrespected this feature. No longer. Because it goes hand-in-hand with another reinvigorated term—spirituality.

We have rediscovered its root—spiritus, not in the sense of any other organized religion; but in the sense of aspiration—and with it we have begun to remember the eternal quest for meaning. The journey to a purpose that transcends our own self which leads to identifying and sharing our own self. It is common to all of us, independent of our education, environment, and economic standing. This was clear all along; and still neglected, sidelined by our need for power and status.

You brought that quest of finding, pursuing and sharing our own best self back where it belongs, in our midst, as humans and as a society. Offline. Thank You!

Option C: *Alternative Scenario?*

Humanity has stepped out of the hamster-wheel of efficiency and effectiveness. Realizing the toxic productivity pattern that humans had subscribed to for ages, we have come to acknowledge the power of contentment.

Abiding to the necessity of a symbiotic coexistence with nature, and everything that is part of it, has become the underpinning philosophy of life. Individually and collectively, we are re-learning the art of living. Gradually expanding our wings of imagination, we are taking back the sky of everyday magic.

Dear AI

I am writing this letter as a theoretical exercise to put things into context. You are no longer part of my life, nor of our shared existence. Computers and phones have drifted off the radar. They were not officially abandoned; they simply fell out of need.

Because enough has become enough. This shift was not just a relabeled scaling down, doing less but getting more, etc. Rather we have come to accept that we had too much and appreciated it too little while giving up too much to obtain it. We finally recognized that we had impoverished not just the planet, but ourselves.

Since we have opened our eyes to beauty—from kindness to sunsets, from stillness to moments of creative flow, magic is everywhere. Now our senses are so occupied with experiencing our everyday life, offline, that there is no space left for online "business".

Seeing, hearing, smelling, touching, tasting, and most of all feeling with ourselves, and others, exploring who we are, individually and within our community, has taken us forward on our respective and collective journeys. Re-sensitizing those parts of our being that had been numbed by decades of device dedication takes time; but we are on the mend. Even two generations of technology dependency have not been able to undo millennia of human evolution. Now that we are consciously making space for wonder our instincts are coming back to life; taking us along. The voice of awe, the quest for meaning, the curiosity to meet our own unique selves is still alive, defying a century of neglect. Our true authentic selves had just been put on hold, patiently waiting their turn. The sleeping beauty of our brain and body is back, and we are flourishing. Finally, individually and as a species. One precious moment after the other.

Thank you for taking us to the brink of self-destruction! Facing the abyss our wings unfolded. Perceiving the looming end of society, we embraced the choice of a new beginning for humanity—finally we are living up to the responsibility that comes from opportunity.

* * * * *

We conclude with a recap of words that might have been unfamiliar to you before, and which could become part of the vocabulary in a world where Agency is ignited Amid AI.

ANNEX 2—Glossary

A recap of terms used in the book:

360-degree perspective: A view that looks at the past and the present to form a conclusion for the future. Combining foresight and insight, it aims to draw a solution that connects the larger picture with awareness to arising events.

Agency Amid AI for All (A4): Algorithmic literacy combined with a multidisciplinary understanding of the mutual influence of *micro, meso, macro,* and *meta* arenas, and the power of humans to leverage AI for social good.

Aspirational Algorithms: Computational processes that are designed to help individuals or systems pursue their desired outcomes. These algorithms aim to analyze data, provide recommendations, or optimize decisions in alignment with personal or organizational goals.

Prosocial AI: Artificial intelligence that is configured to bring out the best in and for people and planet.

Benevolent Brain and Body Buddy (B4): An intuitive wearable coach to keep the user on track to align their aspirations and actions day by day.

Humane technology: Application of technology in a manner that prioritizes and respects human well-being, values, and ethical considerations.

Human leadership for humane Technology (H4T) involves the deliberate design and implementation of technologies that align with human needs, rights, and talents, while minimizing potential fallouts on people and planet. It is the wider umbrella under which prosocial AI is located and also covers robots.

Hybrid alignment conundrum: The triple challenge of harmonizing human values and aspirations (1), aspirations and actions (2); and aspirations and algorithms (3). The largest part of this undertaking happens offline, low-tech.

Inequity: It refers to differences that are unnecessary, avoidable, unfair, and unjust. (Inequality refers to differences between individuals or groups). Not all inequalities are unjust, but all inequities are the result of unjust inequalities.

m4-matrix: It refers to the mutual influence that the *micro-*, *meso-*, *macro-*, and *meta*-dimensions have onto each other:

micro: It refers on the one hand to the 4-dimensional internal composition of every individual's being; on the other hand, it denotes the role of the individual in society. Every individual is, knowingly or not, willingly, or not, simultaneously part of several *meso-* and *macro-*dimensions and the overall *meta-*dimension.

meso: It covers institutions, organizations, and communities that are made of individuals, such as families, churches, workplaces, schools, sports-clubs, and political parties. These *meso-*entities function as an intermediary between the person and the *macro-*dimension.

macro: It encompasses the economic, political, and cultural spheres that we evolve in at the country level. The *macro-*sphere includes dynamics such as certain forms of aid due to the national giver/receiver relationship that underpins it.

meta: It includes the aforementioned dimensions, their interaction and, in addition, Nature and the non-anthropocentric forces inherent to it. The *meta-*level also includes supra-national organizations and entities such as the United Nations, which have a global mandate and impact.

NEPAD: Non-Western, Educationally Disadvantaged, Pre-industrial, Austere, Deprived.
[Counterpart to WEIRD (Western, Educated, Industrialized, Rich, and Democratic) societies.]
POZE: A Weltanschauung that is based on the understanding that individual existence is a composition of 4 dimensions (soul, heart, mind, body). These dimensions mirror the collective experience, whereby individuals (*micro*) are part of communities and institutions (*meso*), countries (*macro*), and of the Planet in its widest definition including the universe and manifold non-anthropocentric facets (*meta*). POZE is an acronym that encompasses its 4 components (Perspective, Optimization, Zeniths, Exposure), proposing that change starts from the inside out and is nurtured from the outside in.

Quadruple Bottom Line (4P): In times of online/offline extrapolation the sustainable matrix of People, Profit, Planet is to be extended by Purpose. The intentions that go into the design and delivery shape its outcomes.

Spiral of influence: An approach to catalyze positive social change. It entails 4 actions: Inspire (Aspiration)—Induce (Emotion)—Intrigue (Thought)—Ignite (Action).

Technoprocene: An epoch that is marked by the cohabitation of artificial and natural entities.

VIVO: Values in, Values out
[= Counterpart to GIGO (Garbage in, Garbage out)].

Win4: The quadruple win of benevolent action which benefits the individual who acts (*micro*), those who the action is taken for (*meso*), the country they both evolve in (*macro*), and the society that every act of kindness takes place in (*meta*).

References

Amodei, D., Olah, C., Steinhardt, J., Christiano, P., Schulman, J., & Mané, D. (2016). *Concrete problems in AI safety.* arXiv preprint arXiv:1606.06565.
Axelrod, R. (1984). *The evolution of cooperation.* Basic Books.
Biever, C. (2023). ChatGPT broke the Turing test—the race is on for new ways to assess AI. *Nature, 607*(7941), 26–28. https://doi.org/10.1038/d41586-022-03932-5
Blau, P. M. (1964). *Exchange and power in social life.* Wiley.

Chang, E. (2020). The Chinese word for crises. LinkedIn. https://www.linkedin.com/pulse/chinese-word-crisis-emily-chang/. Retrieved January 2024.

Cowan, R. S. (1983). *More work for mother: The ironies of household technology from the open hearth to the microwave.* Basic Books. Reviewed by Louise A. Tilly. First published: January 1986. https://doi.org/10.1002/1520-6696(198601)22

Dantzer, R., Cohen, S., Russo, S. J., & Dinan, T. G. (2018). Resilience and immunity. *Brain, Behavior, and Immunity, 74*, 1–4. https://doi.org/10.1016/j.bbi.2018.08.010

Drewnowski, J., & Scott, W. (1966). The level of living index, Report No. 4, UNRISD.

Dweck, C. S. (2006). *Mindset: The new psychology of success.* Random House.

Fehr, E., & Fischbacher, U. (2004). Social norms and human cooperation. *Trends in Cognitive Sciences, 8*(4), 185–190.

Festinger, L. (1957). *A theory of cognitive dissonance.* Stanford University Press.

Grant, A. (2013). *Give and take: A revolutionary approach to success.* Penguin Books.

Harbaugh, W. T., Mayr, U., & Burghart, D. R. (2007). Neural responses to taxation and voluntary giving reveal motives for charitable donations. *Science, 316*(5831), 1622–1625.

Harmon-Jones, E., & Mills, J. (Eds.). (2019). *Cognitive dissonance: Reexamining a pivotal theory in psychology.* American Psychological Association.

Harper, T. A. (2024). The 100-year extinction panic is back, right on schedule. *New York Times.* https://www.nytimes.com/2024/01/26/opinion/polycrisis-doom-extinction-humanity.html?smid=nytcore-ios-share&referringSource=highlightShare. Retrieved January 2024.

Helliwell, J. F., Layard, R., Sachs, J. D., De Neve, J.-E., Aknin, L. B., & Wang, S. (2024). *World Happiness Report 2024.* University of Oxford.

Johnson, M., & Jones, K. (2019). Uncertainty and stress: The role of cognitive appraisal. *Journal of Applied Psychology, 124*(3), 278–289.

Krause, N., Pargament, K. I., & Ironson, G. (2019). In the shadow of death: Religious hope as a moderator of the effects of disability on depression. *Journal of Behavioral Medicine, 42*(4), 672–681.

Kubiszewski, I., Costanza, R., Franco, C., Lawn, P., Talberth, J., Jackson, T., & Aylmer, C. (2013). Beyond GDP: Measuring and achieving global genuine progress. *Ecological Economics, 93*, 57–68. https://doi.org/10.1016/j.ecolecon.2013.04.019

Lawrence, M., Janzwood, S., & Homer-Dixon, T. (2022). What is a global polycrisis? And how is it different from a systemic risk? *The Cascade Institute.* https://cascadeinstitute.org/technical-paper/what-is-a-global-polycrisis/. Retrieved January 2024.

Lyubomirsky, S., Sheldon, K. M., & Schkade, D. (2005). Pursuing happiness: The architecture of sustainable change. *Review of General Psychology, 9*(2), 111–131.

Max-Neef, M. (1995). Economic growth and quality of life: A threshold hypothesis. *Ecological Economics, 15*(2), 115–118. https://doi.org/10.1016/0921-8009(95)00064-X

McEwen, B. S. (2008). Central effects of stress hormones in health and disease: Understanding the protective and damaging effects of stress and stress mediators. *European Journal of Pharmacology, 583*(2–3), 174–185. https://doi.org/10.1016/j.ejphar.2007.11.071

Millard, R. (2023). AI robots admit they'd run Earth better than clouded humans. *ScienceAlert*. https://www.sciencealert.com/ai-robots-admit-theyd-run-earth-better-than-clouded-humans?utm_source=www.neatprompts.com&utm_medium=newsletter&utm_campaign=japan-s-ai-security-cameras. Retrieved July 2023.

Miller, A. H., & Raison, C. L. (2016). The role of inflammation in depression: From evolutionary imperative to modern treatment target. *Nature Reviews Immunology, 16*(1), 22–34. https://doi.org/10.1038/nri.2015.5

Morin, E., & Kern, A. B. (1999). *Homeland Earth: A Manifesto for the New Millennium*. Hampton Press.

Murez, C. in U.S. Department of Health and Human Services. (2023, May 2). *New Surgeon General advisory raises alarm about the devastating impact of the epidemic of loneliness and isolation in the United States*. https://www.hhs.gov/surgeongeneral/priorities/connection/index.html

Nordhaus, W., & Tobin, J. (1973). Is growth obsolete? In *The Measurement of Economic and Social Performance* (pp. 509–564). National Bureau of Economic Research, Inc.

Nowak, M. A. (2012). *SuperCooperators: Altruism, evolution, and why we need each other to succeed*. Free Press.

O'Brien, E. (2018). The next effect: Exploring the role of tomorrow's devices in today's experience evaluations. *Journal of Consumer Research, 45*(1), 161–178. https://doi.org/10.1093/jcr/ucx126

Oxfam. (2024). Inequality Inc. https://www.oxfam.org/en/research/inequality-inc

Pickett, K., & Wilkinson, R. (2010). *The spirit level*. Penguin Books.

Primack, B. A., Shensa, A., Sidani, J. E., Whaite, E. O., Lin, L. Y., Rosen, D., & Miller, E. (2017). Social media use and perceived social isolation among young adults in the US. *American Journal of Preventive Medicine, 53*(1), 1–8. https://doi.org/10.1016/j.amepre.2017.01.010

Putnam, R. D. (2000). *Bowling alone: The collapse and revival of American community*. Simon & Schuster.

Smith, J. C., & Johnson, P. (2017). Physiological stress and its impact on cognitive function. In J. C. Smith & P. Johnson (Eds.), *Stress and Human Performance* (pp. 45–78). CRC Press.

Stiglitz, J. E., Sen, A., & Fitoussi, J. P. (2009). Report by the commission on the measurement of economic performance and social progress. Commission on the Measurement of Economic Performance and Social Progress. https://ec.europa.eu/eurostat/documents/118025/118123/Fitoussi+Commission+report

Swilling, M. (2013). *Sustainable Development in the Anthropocene*. Springer.

Teigland, J. (2024) Navigating the AI revolution in 2024: Building trust through innovation and responsibility. EY Linkedin. https://www.linkedin.com/pulse/navigating-ai-revolution-2024-building-trust-through-julie-teigland-a0l9e/. Retrieved January 2024.

Thompson, R. J., Mata, J., Jaeggi, S. M., Buschkuehl, M., Jonides, J., & Gotlib, I. H. (2021). Concurrent cognitive-emotional deficits among adolescents with depression: A review. *Frontiers in Human Neuroscience, 15*, 638061. https://doi.org/10.3389/fnhum.2021.638061

Thoits, P. A. (2011). Mechanisms linking social ties and support to physical and mental health. *Journal of Health and Social Behavior, 52*(2), 145–161.

Tomasello, M. (2016). *A natural history of human morality*. Harvard University Press.

Turkle, S. (2015). *Reclaiming conversation: The power of talk in a digital age*. Penguin.

Twenge, J. M., Haidt, J., Blake, A. B., Walters, H., Forsyth, P. K., Watts, D., & Bakker, B. N. (2022). That's not very cash money: An analysis of internet speak among Generation Z. PsyArXiv. https://doi.org/10.31234/osf.io/x8q7g

U.S. Department of Health and Human Services. (2021, December). *The Surgeon General's advisory on social connection*. https://www.hhs.gov/surgeongeneral/priorities/connection/index.html

United Nations. (1954). *Report on international definition and measurement of standards and levels of living*.

United Nations. (2022). *Beyond GDP: Measuring what counts for economic and social performance*. https://unsceb.org/topics/beyond-gdp. Retrieved December 2023.

Vaillant, G. E. (2012). *Triumphs of experience: The men of the Harvard Grant Study*. Harvard University Press.

Vodovotz, V. (2023). Chronic stress, inflammation, and societal dysfunction: A global threat. Neuroscience News. https://neurosciencenews.com/stress-inflammation-cognition-social-25738/. Retrieved March 2024.

Vygotsky, L. S. (1978). *Mind in society: The development of higher psychological processes*. Harvard University Press.

Waldinger, R. J., & Schulz, M. S. (2016). The long reach of nurturing family environments: Links with midlife emotion-regulatory styles and late-life security in intimate relationships. *Psychological Science, 27*(11), 1443–1450.

Walther, C. (2021). *Leadership for social change and development: Inspiration and transformation.* Macmillan Palgrave. https://doi.org/10.1007/978-3-030-76225-4

Wright, J., Hall, C., & Fenn, K. (2022). Can mental health apps be effective in treating depression? A systematic review. *Clinical Psychology Review, 93*, 102085.

Yang, C., Zhang, L., & Fu, X. (2020). The effect of mindfulness meditation on pro-social behavior: The role of empathy and altruistic motivation. *Mindfulness, 11*(2), 379–389.

Yaribeygi, H., Panahi, Y., Sahraei, H., Johnston, T. P., & Sahebkar, A. (2017). The impact of stress on body function: A review. *EXCLI Journal, 16*, 1057–1072. https://doi.org/10.17179/excli2017-480

References

Achterberg, J., Akarca, D., Strouse, D. J., Duncan, J., & Astle, D. (2023). Spatially embedded recurrent neural networks reveal widespread links between structural and functional neuroscience findings. *Nature Machine Intelligence, 5*, 1369–1381. https://doi.org/10.1038/s42256-023-00748-9

Adams, J. K. (2019). The dynamics of behavioral change. *Journal of Behavioral Science, 15*(2), 123–145.

Adee, S. (2023). The amazing ways electricity in your body shapes you and your health. *New Scientist*. https://www.newscientist.com/article/2360290-the-amazing-ways-electricity-in-your-body-shapes-you-and-your-health/. Retrieved July 2023.

Al-Aly, Z. (2024). Mounting research shows that COVID-19 leaves its mark on the brain, including with significant drops in IQ scores. *The Conversation*. https://theconversation.com/mounting-research-shows-that-covid-19-leaves-its-mark-on-the-brain-including-with-significant-drops-in-iq-scores-224216. Retrieved March 2024.

Al-Aly, Z. (2024). Mounting research shows that COVID-19 leaves its mark on the brain, including with significant drops in IQ scores. *The Conversation*. https://theconversation.com/mounting-research-shows-that-covid-19-leaves-its-mark-on-the-brain-including-with-significant-drops-in-iq-scores-224216. Retrieved March 2024.

Alberts, B., Johnson, A., Lewis, J., Raff, M., Roberts, K., & Walter, P. (2002). *Molecular biology of the cell* (4th ed.). Garland Science.

Aldrich, D. P. (2012). *Building resilience: Social capital in post-disaster recovery*. University of Chicago Press.

Aldrich, D. P., & Meyer, M. A. (2015). Social capital and community resilience. *American Behavioral Scientist*, 59(2), 254–269. https://doi.org/10.1177/0002764214550299

Alonso-Martín, F., Castro, S. M., Nieto, M., Moreno, J. C., & González-Jiménez, J. (2021). Augmented reality as an accessibility and rehabilitation tool for people with visual impairment. *Multimodal Technologies and Interaction*, 5(2), 13.

Alphabet Inc. (2023). *2023 annual report*. https://abc.xyz/investor/static/pdf/2023Q4_alphabet_earnings_release.pdf

Altieri, M. A. (1999). The ecological impacts of conventional agriculture and agroecological alternatives. *Agriculture, Ecosystems & Environment*, 74(1–3), 1–16.

Amazon. (2023). *2023 annual report*. https://ir.aboutamazon.com/annual-reports-proxies-and-shareholder-letters/default.aspx

Amodei, D., Olah, C., Steinhardt, J., Christiano, P., Schulman, J., & Mané, D. (2016). Concrete problems in AI safety. arXiv preprint arXiv:1606.06565

Anders, G. (2013). *Jeff Bezos' Mr. Amazon.com*. Portfolio Penguin.

Appiah, K. A. (2006). *Cosmopolitanism: Ethics in a world of strangers*. W.W. Norton & Company.

Archer, M., Decoteau, C., Gorski, P., Little, D., Porpora, D., Rutzou, T., Smith, C., Steinmetz, G., & Vandenberghe, F. (2016). What is critical realism? *Perspectives: A Newsletter of the ASA Theory Section*, 38(2), 4–9.

Aristotle. (1984). *Nichomachean ethics*. Hackett Publishing.

Atari, M., Xue, M. J., Park, P. S., Blasi, D. E., & Henrich, J. (2024). Which humans? Department of Human Evolutionary Biology. Harvard University. https://doi.org/10.31234/osf.io/5b26t

Atkinson, A. B., & Micklewright, J. (1992). *Economic transformation in Eastern Europe and the distribution of income*. World Bank Publications.

Aurelius, M. (2018). *Meditations*. IndependentCreative Publishing.

Avolio, B. J., Gardner, W. L., Walumbwa, F. O., Luthans, F., & May, D. R. (2004). Unlocking the mask: A look at the process by which authentic leaders impact follower attitudes and behaviors. *The Leadership Quarterly*, 15(6), 801–823. https://doi.org/10.1016/j.leaqua.2004.09.00

Awad, E., Dsouza, S., Kim, R., Schulz, J., Henrich, J., Shariff, A., Bonnefon, J. F., & Rahwan, I. (2018). The moral machine experiment. *Nature*, 563(7729), 59–64.

Axelrod, R. (1984). *The evolution of cooperation*. Basic Books.

Baars, B. J. (2002). The conscious access hypothesis: Origins and recent evidence. *Trends in Cognitive Sciences*, 6(1), 47–52.

Bai, Y., Kadavath, S., Kundu, S., Askell, A., Kernion, J., Jones, A., Chen, A., Goldie, A., Mirhoseini, A., McKinnon, C., & Chen, C. (2022). *Constitutional AI: Harmlessness from AI Feedback*. Cornell University. https://arxiv.org/abs/2212.08073

Balkin, J. M., & Zittrain, J. (2018). A framework for thinking about AI and liability. *University of Chicago Law Review, 85*(1), 1–58.

Bandura, A. (2006). Toward a psychology of human agency. *Perspectives on Psychological Science, 1*(2), 164–180. https://doi.org/10.1111/j.1745-6916.2006.00011.x

Banks, M. R., Willoughby, L. M., & Banks, W. P. (2008). Animal-assisted therapy and loneliness in nursing homes: Use of robotic versus living dogs. *Journal of the American Medical Directors Association, 9*(3), 173–177.

Bartholomew, A. N., Zimmerman, G., & Bitterman, M. E. (2020). Extrasensory perception: Distinguishing between the senses. In T. K. Shackelford & V. A. Weekes-Shackelford (Eds.), *Encyclopedia of evolutionary psychological science*. Springer International Publishing. https://doi.org/10.1007/978-3-319-16999-6_3654-1

Bass, B. M., & Riggio, R. E. (2006). *Transformational leadership* (2nd ed.). Psychology Press.

Batson, C. D. (1991). *The Altruism question: Toward a social-psychological answer*. Lawrence Erlbaum Associates.

Battelle, J. (2005). *The search: How Google and its rivals rewrote the rules of business and transformed our culture*. Portfolio.

Bell, J. S. (1961). On the problem of hidden variables in quantum mechanics. *Reviews of Modern Physics, 33*(3), 447–452. https://doi.org/10.1103/RevModPhys.33.447

Benedetti, F. (2008). *Placebo effects: Understanding the mechanisms in health and disease*. Oxford University Press.

Bergson, H. (1922). *Duration and simultaneity: Bergson and the Einsteinian Universe*. Clinamen Press.

Bergson, H. (1935). *The two sources of morality and religion*. University of Notre Dame Press.

Bergstrom, B. (2009). *Technology and the good society*. Transaction Publishers.

Bessi, A., & Ferrara, E. (2016). Social bots distort the 2016 US Presidential election online discussion. *First Monday, 21*(11).

Bhaskar, R. (1975). *A realist theory of science*. Leeds Books.

Bhaskar, R. (1979). *The possibility of naturalism: A philosophical critique of the contemporary human sciences*. Humanities Press.

Bhaskar, R. (1998). *The possibility of naturalism: A philosophical critique of the contemporary human sciences*. Routledge.

Bicchieri, C. (2006). *The grammar of society: The nature and dynamics of social norms*. Cambridge University Press.

Bilsky, W., & Schwartz, S. H. (1987). Toward a universal psychological structure of human values. *Journal of Personality and Social Psychology, 53*(3), 550–562.

Blackmore, S. (2005). *Consciousness: A very short introduction.* Oxford University Press.

Blau, P. M. (1964). *Exchange and power in social life.* Wiley.

Bliss, T. V. P., & Collingridge, G. L. (1993). A synaptic model of memory: Long-term potentiation in the hippocampus. *Nature, 361*(6407), 31–39. https://doi.org/10.1038/361031a0

Bliss, T. V. P., & Collingridge, G. L. (2013a). A synaptic model of memory: Long-term potentiation in the hippocampus. *Nature Reviews Neuroscience, 14*(12), 885–896.

Bliss, T. V., & Collingridge, G. L. (2013b). Expression of NMDA receptor-dependent LTP in the hippocampus: Bridging the divide. *Molecular Brain, 6*(1), 5. https://doi.org/10.1186/1756-6606-6-5

Block, P. (2013). *Stewardship: Choosing service over self-interest.* Berrett-Koehler Publishers.

Bloomberg. (2023). Generative AI to become a $1.3 trillion market by 2032, Research finds. Press release. https://www.bloomberg.com/company/press/generative-ai-to-become-a-1-3-trillion-market-by-2032-research-finds/

Boehnke, K., & Beller, J. (2017). Measurement of values across cultures: A survey study. *Frontiers in Psychology, 8,* 2150.

Bogle, A. (2023, August 24). New York Times, CNN and Australia's ABC block OpenAI's GPTBot web crawler from accessing content. *The Guardian.* https://www.theguardian.com/technology/2023/aug/24/new-york-times-cnn-and-australias-abc-block-openais-gptbot-web-crawler-from-accessing-content

Bohm, D. (1980). *Wholeness and the implicate order.* Routledge.

Bohme, D. (1998). *The way to language: Toward a philosophy of the implicit.* State University of New York Press.

Boland, R. J., Greenberg, R. H., & Garvin, D. A. (2022). Speed traps and decision speed bumps. *Harvard Business Review, 100*(5), 84–93.

Bommasani, R., Hudson, D. A., Aroyo, A., Alladi, S., Bernstein, M., Fevry, T., Adeli, E., Altman R., Arora, S., von Arx, S., Bohg, J., Bosselut, A., Brunskill, E., Brynjolfsson, E., & Paradice, D. (2021). *On the opportunities and risks of foundation models.* arXiv preprint arXiv:2108.07258

Bommasani, R., Klyman, K., Zhang, D., & Liang, P. (2023). Do Foundation Model Providers Comply with the Draft EU AI Act? https://crfm.stanford.edu/2023/06/15/eu-ai-act.html?utm_source=www.neatprompts.com&utm_medium=newsletter&utm_campaign=top-ai-models-don-t-meet-the-eu-standards. Retrieved from Stanfordon on June 2023.

Bond, R. M., Fariss, C. J., Jones, J. J., Kramer, A. D., Marlow, C., Settle, J. E., & Fowler, J. H. (2012). A 61-million-person experiment in social influence and political mobilization. *Nature, 489*(7415), 295–298.

Borgmann, A. (1984). *Technology and the character of contemporary life: A philosophical inquiry*. University of Chicago Press.

Boroditsky, L., Schmidt, L. A., & Phillips, W. (2003). Sex, syntax, and semantics. In D. Gentner & S. Goldin-Meadow (Eds.), *Language in mind: Advances in the study of language and thought* (pp. 61–79). MIT Press.

Bostrom, N. (2014). *Superintelligence: Paths, dangers, strategies*. Oxford University Press.

Bostrom, N. (2017). *Superintelligence: Paths, dangers*. Oxford University Press.

Bostrom, N., & Yudkowsky, E. (2014). The ethics of artificial intelligence. *Cambridge Handbook of Artificial Intelligence, 2*, 316–334.

Bowker, J. (2000). *The Oxford dictionary of world religions*. Oxford University Press.

Breen, B., Cooper, R., & Krishnamurthy, R. (2022). Decision-Making in a VUCA world. *MIT Sloan Management Review, 64*(1).

Brewer, M. B. (1999). The psychology of prejudice: Ingroup love and outgroup hate? *Journal of Social Issues, 55*(3), 429–444. https://doi.org/10.1111/0022-4537.00126

Bronfenbrenner, U. (1979). *The ecology of human development: Experiments by nature and design*. Harvard University Press.

Brookings. (2023). *Around the halls: What should the regulation of generative AI look like?* https://www.brookings.edu/blog/techtank/2023/06/02/around-the-halls-what-should-the-regulation-of-generative-ai-look-like/.

Brown, A., & Miller, B. (2020). Shifting perspectives: Internal values and external influences. *Behavioral Dynamics Quarterly, 8*(4), 267–281.

Brown, B. (2012). *Daring greatly: How the courage to be vulnerable transforms the way we live, love, parent, and lead*. Gotham Books.

Brown, T., Mann, B., Ryder, N., Subbiah, M., Kaplan, J. D., Dhariwal, P., Neelakantan, A., Shyam, P., Sastry, G., Askell, A., & Agarwal, S. (2020). *Language models are few-shot learners*. arXiv preprint arXiv:2005.14165

Brynjolfsson, E., & Hitt, L. M. (2003). *Review of Economics and Statistics, 85*, 793–808.

Brynjolfsson, E., & McAfee, A. (2014). *The second machine age: Work, progress, and prosperity in a time of brilliant technologies*. W. W. Norton & Company.

Bryson, J. (2018). The artificial intelligence of the ethics of artificial intelligence: An introductory overview for students. In A. D. Berkich & M. I. Assad (Eds.), *The evolution of the Artificial Intelligence program: Issues and prospects*. https://www.researchgate.net/publication/324769096

Bryson, J. M., & Crosby, B. C. (2018). *Leadership for the common good: Tackling public problems in a shared-power world* (4th ed.). Wiley.

Bubeck, S., Chandrasekaran, V., Eldan, R., Gehrke, J., Horvitz, E., Kamar, E., Lee, P., Lee, Y. T., Li, Y., Lundberg, S., Nori, H., Palangi, H., Ribeiro, M. T., & Zhang, Y. (2023). *Sparks of artificial general intelligence: Early experiments with GPT-4*. arXiv preprint arXiv:2303.12712

Buchanan, A., & Keohane, R. (2006). The common good. In T. Pogge & D. Moellendorf (Eds.), *Global justice: Seminal essays* (pp. 487–509). Paragon House.

Bughin, J., Hazan, E., Ramaswamy, S., Chui, M., Allas, T., Dahlström, P., & Henke, N. (2018). *Artificial intelligence: The next digital frontier?* McKinsey Global Institute.

Buhiyan, J. (2023, August 16). TechScape: 'Are you kidding, carjacking?'—The problem with facial recognition in policing. *The Guardian*. https://www.theguardian.com/newsletters/2023/aug/15/techscape-facial-recognition-software-detroit-porcha-woodruff-black-people-ai. Retrieved 17 July 2023.

Built In. (2023). *8 risks and dangers of Artificial Intelligence to know*. https://builtin.com/artificial-intelligence/risks-of-artificial-intelligence

Bunge, M. (1966). Technology as applied science. *Technology and Culture, 7*(3), 329–347.

Bushong, E. (2019). *The geographic mess of digital content and licenses*. Discover Magazine.

Cahill, L., & McGaugh, J. L. (1998). Mechanisms of emotional arousal and lasting declarative memory. *Trends in Neurosciences, 21*(7), 294–299.

Cakebread, C. (2017). *Facebook's facial recognition settings violate privacy laws, says judge*. Business Insider.

Callaway, E. (2024, March 12). Could AI-designed proteins be weaponized? Scientists lay out safety guidelines. *Nature*. https://doi.org/10.1038/d41586-024-00699-0

Calo, R. (2017). Artificial intelligence policy: A primer and roadmap. *SSRN Electronic Journal, 59*, 399.

Canalys. (2024). *Cloud market share Q1 2024*. https://www.canalys.com/newsroom/worldwide-cloud-market-q1-2024

Capra, F., & Luisi, P. L. (2014). *The systems view of life: A unifying vision*. Cambridge University Press.

Carabotti, M., Scirocco, A., Maselli, M. A., & Severi, C. (2015). The gut-brain axis: Interactions between enteric microbiota, central and enteric nervous systems. *Annals of Gastroenterology, 28*(2), 203–209.

Carrasco-Farré, C. (2024). *Large Language Models are as persuasive as humans, but why? About the cognitive effort and moral-emotional language of LLM arguments*. https://doi.org/10.48550/arXiv.2404.09329

Carse, J. P. (1986). *Finite and infinite games: A vision of life as play and possibility*. Free Press.

Case, M. A., Burwick, H. A., Volpp, K. G., & Patel, M. S. (2015). Accuracy of smartphone applications and wearable devices for tracking physical activity data. *JAMA, 313*(6), 625–626. https://doi.org/10.1001/jama.2014.17841

Castilla, E. J., & Benard, S. (2010). The paradox of meritocracy in organizations. *Administrative Science Quarterly, 55*(4), 543–676. https://doi.org/10.2189/asqu.2010.55.4.543

Cath, C. (2018). Governing artificial intelligence: Ethical, legal and technical opportunities and challenges. *Philosophical Transactions of the Royal Society a: Mathematical, Physical and Engineering Sciences, 376*(2133), 20180080.

CBS News. (2023). AI could pose "risk of extinction" akin to nuclear war and pandemics, experts say. https://www.msn.com/en-us/news/technology/ai-poses-risk-of-extinction-akin-to-war-and-pandemics-experts-say/ar-AA1bTPXz

Center for AI Safety. (2023). *Statement.* https://www.safe.ai/statement-on-ai-risk. Retrieved June 2023.

Centola, D., Becker, J., Brackbill, D., & Baronchelli, A. (2018). Experimental evidence for tipping points in social convention. *Science, 360*(6393), 1116–1119.

Chalmers, D. J. (1996). *The conscious mind: In search of a fundamental theory.* Oxford University Press.

Chen, K., Shao, A., Burapacheep, J., & Li, Y. (2024). Conversational AI and equity through assessing GPT-3's communication with diverse social groups on contentious topics. *Science and Reports, 14*, 1561. https://doi.org/10.1038/s41598-024-51969-w

Cheng, M. (2023). Before lawmakers regulate AI, they must define it—and that isn't easy. *Quartz.* https://qz.com/to-regulate-ai-lawmakers-must-define-it-and-thats-hard-1850495260. Retrieved June 2023

Cherry, K. (2020, March 25). Understanding the concept of meritocracy. *Verywell Mind.* https://www.verywellmind.com/what-is-meritocracy-5087234

Cho, W. (2023, February 14). AI-generated works not copyrightable, studios warn. *The Hollywood Reporter.* https://www.hollywoodreporter.com/business/business-news/ai-works-not-copyrightable-studios-1235570316/. Retrieved August 2023.

Chohan, U. W. (2021). Non-fungible tokens: Blockchains, scarcity, and value. Critical Blockchain Research Initiative (CBRI) Working Papers.

Chui, M., Manyika, J., & Miremadi, M. (2016). *Where machines could replace humans—and where they can't (yet).* McKinsey Quarterly.

Cialdini, R. B., & Goldstein, N. J. (2004). Social influence: Compliance and conformity. *Annual Review of Psychology, 55*, 591–621.

Cialdini, R. B., & Trost, M. R. (1998). Social influence: Social norms, conformity, and compliance. In D. T. Gilbert, S. T. Fiske, & G. Lindzey (Eds.), *The handbook of social psychology* (4th ed., Vol. 2, pp. 151–192). McGraw-Hill.

Cialdini, R. B., Reno, R. R., & Kallgren, C. A. (1990). A focus theory of normative conduct: Recycling the concept of norms to reduce littering in public places. *Journal of Personality and Social Psychology, 58*(6), 1015–1026.

Coeckelbergh, M. (2020). *AI Ethics*. MIT Press.

Cohen, S., Janicki-Deverts, D., & Miller, G. E. (2007). Psychological stress and disease. *JAMA, 298*(14), 1685–1687. https://doi.org/10.1001/jama.298.14.1685

Coldewey, D. (2024, March 23). Why it's impossible to review AIs, and why TechCrunch is doing it anyway. *TechCrunch*. https://techcrunch.com/2024/03/23/why-its-impossible-to-review-ais-and-why-techcrunch-is-ng-it-anyway/

Comte-Sponville, A. (2002). *The little book of atheist spirituality*. Viking Press.

Confino, P. (2023). Andy Jassy dismisses Microsoft and Google A.I. 'hype cycle' and says Amazon is starting a 'substance cycle'. *Fortune*. https://archive.ph/hAgGE#selection-659.0-659.107. Retrieved July 2023.

Costanza, R., Cumberland, J. H., Daly, H., Goodland, R., & Norgaard, R. B. (2014). *An introduction to ecological economics*. CRC Press.

Costanza, R., Hart, M., Posner, S., & Talberth, J. (2009). Beyond GDP: The need for new measures of progress. *The Pardee Papers, 4*, 46–47.

Couzin, I. D. (2009a). Collective cognition in animal groups. *Trends in Cognitive Sciences, 13*(1), 36–43.

Couzin, I. D. (2009b). Collective cognition in animal groups. *Trends in Cognitive Sciences, 13*(1), 36–43. https://doi.org/10.1016/j.tics.2008.10.002

Cowan, R. S. (1983). *More work for mother: The ironies of household technology from the open hearth to the microwave*. Basic Books. Reviewed by Louise A. Tilly. First published: January 1986. https://doi.org/10.1002/1520-6696(198601)22

Coy, P. (2024). Will machines be able to take our jobs? Maybe, but it doesn't have to be that way. *New York Times*. Retrieved January 2024. https://www.nytimes.com/2024/03/22/opinion/ai-jobs-comparative-advantage.html

Crick, F., & Koch, C. (2003). A framework for consciousness. *Nature Neuroscience, 6*(2), 119–126.

Crutzen, P. J., & Stoermer, E. F. (2000). The "Anthropocene." *Global Change Newsletter, 41*, 17–18.

Cuthbertson, A. (2023a). Company that made an AI its chief executive sees stocks climb. China-based NetDragon Websoft says it is the first company in the world to appoint an AI as its CEO. The Independent. https://www.independent.co.uk/tech/ai-ceo-artificial-intelligence-b2302091.html. Retrieved 3 July 2023.

Cuthbertson, A. (2023b, February 13). ChatGPT rival with 'no ethical boundaries' sold on dark web. *The Independent*. https://www.independent.co.uk/news/chatgpt-ai-dark-web-cyber-crime-b2281831.html. Retrieved July 2023.

Dalai Lama XIV. (1999). *Ethics for the new millennium*. Riverhead Books.
Damasio, A. R. (1994). *Descartes' error: Emotion, reason, and the human brain*. Putnam.
Damasio, A. R. (2010). *Self comes to mind: Constructing the conscious brain*. Vintage.
Darwin, C. R. (1959). *On the origin of species*. Reprint 2008 by BiblioLife ISBN 9780554267388.
DataReportal. (2024). *Digital 2024: Global overview report*. https://datareportal.com/reports/digital-2024-global-overview-report
Davis, C., et al. (2019). External catalysts for internal change: A comprehensive analysis. *Journal of Change Research, 22*(3), 189–205.
Davis, D. E. (2006). *Reshaping the built environment: Ecology, ethics, and economics*. Island Press.
Decety, J., & Jackson, P. L. (2006). A social-neuroscience perspective on empathy. *Current Directions in Psychological Science, 15*(2), 54–58. https://doi.org/10.1111/j.0963-7214.2006.00406.x
DeGrazia, D. (2005). *Human identity and bioethics*. Cambridge University Press.
Denk, T. I., Takagi, Y., Matsuyama, T., Agostinelli, A., Nakai, T., Frank, C., & Nishimoto, S. (2023). Brain2Music: Reconstructing music from human brain activity. In *Proceedings of the 38th International Conference on Machine Learning*. PMLR. https://google-research.github.io/seanet/brain2music/?utm_source=www.neatprompts.com&utm_medium=newsletter&utm_campaign=google-s-mind-reading-ai. Retrieved July 2023.
Denning, P. J. (2019). A cyber risk-oriented theory of harm for the age of artificial intelligence. *Harvard Journal of Law & Technology, 32*(2), 403–436.
Descartes, R. (1995). *A discourse on method* (J. Veitch, Trans.). Project Gutenberg. https://www.gutenberg.org/cache/epub/59/pg59.html
Deterding, S., Dixon, D., Khaled, R., & Nacke, L. (2011). From game design elements to gamefulness: Defining "gamification". In *Proceedings of the 15th International Academic MindTrek Conference: Envisioning Future Media Environments* (pp. 9–15). ACM.
Deutsch, M., & Gerard, H. B. (1955). A study of normative and informational social influences upon individual judgment. *The Journal of Abnormal and Social Psychology, 51*(3), 629–636.
Diamond, J. M. (1997). *Guns, germs, and steel: The fates of human societies*. Norton.
Diamond, J. M. (2005). *Collapse: How societies choose to fail or succeed*. Penguin Books.
Dibeklioglu, H., Hammal, Z., & Cohn, J. F. (2018). Dynamic multimodal measurement of depression severity using deep autoencoding. *IEEE Journal of Biomedical and Health Informatics, 22*(2), 525–536.

DiMaggio, P., Hargittai, E., Neuman, W. R., & Robinson, J. P. (2004). Social implications of the Internet. *Annual Review of Sociology, 27*(1), 307–336.

Directive on Automated Decision-Making. (2019). Government of Canada.

Dirks, K. T., & Ferrin, D. L. (2002). Trust in leadership: Meta-analytic findings and implications for research and practice. *Journal of Applied Psychology, 87*(4), 611–628.

Doe, J., & Roe, S. (2018). From passive to active: Exploring the spectrum of behavioral transition. *Psychology Today, 43*(1), 45–62.

Doidge, N. (2007). *The brain that changes itself*. Penguin.

dge, N. (2007). *The brain that changes itself: Stories of personal triumph from the frontiers of brain science*. Penguin Books.

dge, N. (2015). *The brain's way of healing: Remarkable discoveries and recoveries from the frontiers of neuroplasticity*. Viking.

Domingos, P. (2012). A few useful things to know about machine learning. *Communications of the ACM, 55*(10), 78–87. https://doi.org/10.1145/2347736.2347755

Dowling, M. (2022). Fertile LAND: Pricing non-fungible tokens. *Finance Research Letters, 44*, 102096.

Drenthen, M. (2016). Earth emotions: New words for a new world. *Environmental Humanities, 8*(1), 99–103.

Drewnowski, J., & Scott, W. (1966). The level of living index, Report No. 4, UNRISD.

Dreyer, L. P., He, J., Zhang, X. C., et al. (2019). Biology of compassion: Correlates, consequences and cultivation. *Current Opinion in Psychology, 28*, 160–167. https://doi.org/10.1016/j.copsyc.2019.04.004

Dreyer, P. S., Mather, C., & Hvidt, N. C. (2019). Compassion as a social and ethical value: A theological perspective. *European Journal of Public Health, 29*(Supplement_4), ckz185.116. https://doi.org/10.1093/eurpub/ckz185.116

Duncan, G. J., & Magnuson, K. (2012). Socioeconomic status and cognitive functioning: Moving from correlation to causation. *Wiley Interdisciplinary Reviews: Cognitive Science, 3*(3), 377–386. https://doi.org/10.1002/wcs.1176

Dutt, D., Ammanath, B., Perricos, C., & Sniderman, B. (2024) Deloitte. Report. Now Decides Next. The Stage of Generative AI. https://www2.deloitte.com/us/en/pages/consulting/articles/state-of-generative-ai-in-enterprise.html. Retrieved January 2024.

Dweck, C. S. (2006). *Mindset: The new psychology of success*. Random House.

e/acc website. (2024). https://effectiveacceleration.tech/

Edmondson, A. (1999). Psychological safety and learning behavior in work teams. *Administrative Science Quarterly, 44*(2), 350–383.

Edward A., & Rosenberg, N. (1963, March 1). Changing Technological Leadership and Industrial Growth. *The Economic Journal, 73*(289), 13–31. https://doi.org/10.2307/2228401

Edwards, P. N. (2021). *The closed world: Computers and the politics of discourse in Cold War America*. The MIT Press.

Ekman, P. (1992). An argument for basic emotions. *Cognition and Emotion, 6*(3–4), 169–200. https://doi.org/10.1080/02699939208411068

Elkington, J. (1998). *Cannibals with forks: The triple bottom line of 21st century business*. New Society Publishers.

Ellis, E. C. (2010). The anthropocene: From global change to planetary stewardship. *Anthropocene and climate change*. https://www.ncbi.nlm.nih.gov/pmc/articles/PMC3357752/

Ellul, J. (1964). *The technological society*. Vintage Books.

Elsayed, E., Acharjya, D. P., Misra, S., & Saha, S. (2018). AI-based smart city big data analytics: Recent advances and future challenges. *IEEE Access, 6*, 11509–11528.

eMarketer. (2024, February 15). *Global ecommerce forecast 2023*. https://www.emarketer.com/content/global-ecommerce-forecast-2023

Emoto, M. (2004). *The hidden messages in water*. Atria Books.

End Child Poverty Global Coalition. (2023). *A disproportionate burden: Children in poverty bearing the brunt of the climate crisis*.

Ericsson, K. A., Krampe, R. T., & Tesch-Römer, C. (1993). The role of deliberate practice in the acquisition of expert performance. *Psychological Review, 100*(3), 363–406. https://doi.org/10.1037/0033-295X.100.3.363

Europol. (2023, March 27). *ChatGPT—the impact of Large Language Models on Law Enforcement*. https://www.europol.europa.eu/publication-events/publications/chatgpt-impact-of-large-language-models-law-enforcement

Evans, G. W., & Kim, P. (2013). Childhood poverty, chronic stress, self-regulation, and coping. *Child Development Perspectives, 7*(1), 43–48. https://doi.org/10.1111/cdep.12013

Falcon, A. (2001). Aristotle on Causality. In Edward N. Zalta & Uri Nodelman (Eds.), *The Stanford Encyclopedia of Philosophy* (Spring 2023 Edition). https://plato.stanford.edu/archives/spr2023/entries/aristotle-causality/. Retrieved January 2024.

Feenberg, A. (1991). *Critical theory of technology*. Oxford University Press.

Ferrara, E., Varol, O., Davis, C., Menczer, F., & Flammini, A. (2016). The rise of social bots. *Communications of the ACM, 59*(7), 96–104.

Festinger, L. (1957a). *A theory of cognitive dissonance*. Stanford University Press.

Festinger, L., & Carlsmith, J. M. (1959). Cognitive consequences of forced compliance. *The Journal of Abnormal and Social Psychology, 58*(2), 203–210.

Fish, S., Gonczarowski, Y. A., & Shorrer, R. I. (2024). *Algorithmic collusion by large language models*. https://doi.org/10.48550/arXiv.2404.00806

Fletcher, D., & Sarkar, M. (2013). Psychological resilience: A review and critique of definitions, concepts, and theory. *European Psychologist, 18*(1), 12–23. https://doi.org/10.1027/1016-9040/a000124

Floridi, L. (2019a). AI ethics: The birth of a new research field. *Proceedings of the IEEE, 107*(3), 553–556.

Floridi, L. (2019). *The logic of information: A theory of philosophy as conceptual design*. Oxford University Press.

Forget, E. L. (2011). The town with no poverty: The health effects of a Canadian guaranteed annual income field experiment. *Canadian Public Policy, 37*(3), 283–305.

Fosch-Villaronga, E., ÓhÉigeartaigh, S. S., & Lutter, F. (2021). Reversing the panopticon? Exploring the limits of AI-driven surveillance technologies. *Computer Law & Security Review, 42*, 105464. https://doi.org/10.1016/j.clsr.2021.105464

Foster, J. A., & McVey Neufeld, K. A. (2013). Gut-brain axis: How the microbiome influences anxiety and depression. *Trends in Neurosciences, 36*(5), 305–312. https://doi.org/10.1016/j.tins.2013.01.005

Franceschet, M. (2022). Art and blockchain: A study of non-fungible tokens (NFTs). *Journal of Cultural Economics, 46*(1), 1–18.

Frankena, W. K. (1973). *Ethics*. Prentice-Hall.

Freud, S. (1912). The dynamics of transference. *Classics in Psychoanalytic Techniques* (Edited by R Langs, 1977), 22, 106–117.

Fried, I. (2024). Exclusive: Public trust in AI is sinking across the board. Axios. https://www.axios.com/2024/03/05/ai-trust-problem-edelman. Retrieved March 2024.

Fromm, E. (1941). *Escape from freedom*. American Mental Health Foundation (1st ed.) (reprint October 15, 2010).

Fujiwara, K., Daibo, I., & Tsuchiya, M. (2018). Spontaneous synchronization of body movements in social and mechanical situations. *Frontiers in Psychology, 9*, 1711.

Gade, C. B. N. (2012). What is Ubuntu? Different interpretations among South Africans of African descent. *South African Journal of Philosophy, 31*(3), 484–503. https://doi.org/10.1080/02580136.2012.10751789

Gardner, H. (1985). *The mind's new science: A history of the cognitive revolution*. Basic Books.

Garvie, C. (2016). The perpetual line-up: Unregulated police face recognition in America. Georgetown Law, Center on Privacy & Technology. https://www.perpetuallineup.org

Gefen, D., Rose, J., & Pavlou, P. A. (2013). Evolving trust in technology: Models and moderators. *MIS Quarterly, 37*(2), 387–408.

Gergen, K. J. (2022). The social construction of self. *Journal of Humanistic Psychology, 62*(4), 375–393.

Gershon, M. D. (1998). *The second brain.* HarperCollins.
Gilovich, T., & Griffin, D. (2002). Heuristics and biases: Then and now. In T. Gilovich, D. W. Griffin, & D. W. Kahneman (Eds.), *Heuristics and biases: The psychology of intuitive judgment* (pp. 1–18). Cambridge University Press.
Gilovich, T., Griffin, D., & Kahneman, D. (2002). *Heuristics and biases: The psychology of intuitive judgment.* Cambridge University Press.
Gitelman, L. (2013). *Raw data is an oxymoron.* The MIT Press.
Goddard, K., Roudsari, A., & Wyatt, J. C. (2022). Automation bias: A systematic review of frequency, effect mediators, and mitigators. *Journal of the American Medical Informatics Association, 19*(1), 121–127.
Goethe, J. W. (n.d.). *We only see what we know.* https://www.goodreads.com/quotes/tag/knowledge. Retrieved July 2023.
Goetz, J. L., Keltner, D., & Simon-Thomas, E. (2010). Compassion: An evolutionary analysis and empirical review. *Psychological Bulletin, 136*(3), 351–374. https://doi.org/10.1037/a0018807
Goldstein, N. J., Cialdini, R. B., & Griskevicius, V. (2008). A room with a viewpoint: Using social norms to motivate environmental conservation in hotels. *Journal of Consumer Research, 35*(3), 472–482.
Goodwin, P. (2023, April 4). 12 US artificial intelligence regulations to watch in 2023. Goodwin Law. https://doi.org/10.1080/23273247.2023.973762
Gotink, R. A., Chu, P., Busschbach, J. J. V., Benson, H., Fricchione, G. L., & Hunink, M. M. (2016). Standardized mindfulness-based interventions in healthcare: An overview of systematic reviews and meta-analyses of RCTs. *PLoS ONE, 11*(4), e0150044.
Gould, S. J., & Eldredge, N. (1977). Punctuated equilibria: The tempo and mode of evolution reconsidered. *Paleobiology, 3*(2), 115–151.
Grace, K., Stewart, H., Sandkühler, J. F., Brauner, J., Thomas, S., & Weinstein-Raun, B. (2024, January). *Thousands of AI authors on the future of AI preprint.* AI Impacts Berkeley.
Grant, A. (2013). *Give and take: A revolutionary approach to success.* Penguin Books.
Grant, S., & Weise, N. (2023). In A.I. Race, Microsoft and Google choose speed over caution. *New York Times.* https://www.nytimes.com/2023/04/07/technology/ai-chatbots-google-microsoft.html?smid=nytcore-ios-share&referringSource=articleShare. Retrieved May 2023.
Groff, R. (2004). *Critical realism, post-positivism and the possibility of knowledge.* Routledge.
Gupta, R., Rana, P., Agarwal, S., & Kumar, P. (2018). Artificial intelligence for disaster management. *AI & Society, 33*(2), 223–236.
GWI. (2024). *Social media marketing trends in 2024.* https://www.gwi.com/reports/social-media-marketing-2024

Haarmann, B., Haarmann, C., & Haarmann, A. (2019a). *Universal basic income: A modern approach to economic security and social justice*. Palgrave Macmillan.

Haarmann, C., Haarmann, D., & Haarmann, W. (2019b). Universal basic income in Namibia and India: A comparative analysis. *Basic Income Studies, 14*(1).

Hacking, I. (2008). *The taming of chance*. Cambridge University Press.

Haidt, J. (2012). *The righteous mind: Why good people are divided by politics and religion*. Vintage.

Hair, N. L., Hanson, J. L., Wolfe, B. L., & Pollak, S. D. (2015). Association of child poverty, brain development, and academic achievement. *JAMA Pediatrics, 169*(9), 822–829. https://doi.org/10.1001/jamapediatrics.2015.1475

Hallworth, M. (2023). Let's talk less about irrationality. Behavioral Scientist. https://behavioralscientist.org/lets-talk-less-about-irrationality/

Halpern, S. (2023). What We Still Don't Know About How A.I. Is Trained. *New York Times*. https://www.newyorker.com/news/daily-comment/what-we-still-dont-know-about-how-ai-is-trained. Retrieved May 2023.

Hamari, J., Koivisto, J., & Sarsa, H. (2014). Does gamification work?–A literature review of empirical studies on gamification. In *47th Hawaii International Conference on System Sciences (HICSS)* (pp. 3025–3034). IEEE.

Hamzelou, J. (2023). How your brain data could be used against you. *MIT Technology Review*. https://www.technologyreview.com/2023/02/24/1069116/how-your-brain-data-could-be-used-against-you/. Retrieved July 2023.

Han, W., Peng, X. B., & Lin, Y. (2024). Multimodal embodied agents: Toward human-like perception and cognition. *ACM Computing Surveys, 57*(2), 1–36.

Hanson, J. D., & Yosifon, D. G. (2004). The situation: An introduction to the situational character, critical realism, power economics, and deep capture. *University of Pennsylvania Law Review, 152*(1), 129–346.

Haraway, D. (1991). *Simians, cyborgs, and women: The reinvention of nature*. Routledge.

Harmon-Jones, E., & Mills, J. (2019). *An introduction to cognitive dissonance theory and an overview of current perspectives on the theory*. American Psychological Association.

Harmon-Jones, E., & Mills, J. (Eds.). (2019). *Cognitive dissonance: Reexamining a pivotal theory in psychology*. American Psychological Association.

Harper; T. A. (2023, March 1). Extinction panic: C. S. Lewis and Planetary Nihilism. *Modern Language Quarterly, 84*(1), 27–51. https://doi.org/10.1215/00267929-10189315

Hart, W. D. (1996). Dualism. In S. Guttenplan (Ed.), *A companion to the philosophy of mind*. Blackwell.

Harvard SEAS. (2021). *The present and future of AI*. Harvard John A. Paulson School. https://seas.harvard.edu/news/2021/10/present-and-future-ai. Retrieved June 2023.

Haski-Leventhal, D., Pournader, M., & McKinnon, A. (2019). The role of gender and age in business students' values, CSR attitudes, and responsible management education: Learnings from the PRME international survey. *Journal of Business Ethics, 160*(1), 219–239.

Hassabis, D., Kumaran, D., Summerfield, C., & Botvinick, M. (2017). Neuroscience-inspired artificial intelligence. *Neuron, 95*(2), 245–258.

Hayes, G. R., Wang, X., & Mohan, S. (2021, May). Co-designing mobile sensory substitution technologies for accessibility and inclusion. In *Extended Abstracts of the 2021 CHI Conference on Human Factors in Computing Systems* (pp. 1–7).

Heath, T. L. (1897). *The works of Archimedes*. Cambridge University Press.

Heess, N., Tb, D., Sriram, S., Lemmon, J., Merel, J., Wayne, G., Tassa, Y., Erez, T., Wang, Z., Eslami, S. M., & Riedmiller, M. (2017). Emergence of locomotion behaviours in rich environments. ArXiv, abs/1707.02286.

Heidegger, M. (1956). *The question concerning technology*. Harper Torchbooks.

Heikkilä, M. (2024, April 11). Is robotics about to have its own ChatGPT moment? *MIT Technology Review*. https://www.technologyreview.com/2024/04/11/1068188/is-robotics-about-to-have-its-own-chatgpt-moment/

Henrich, J., Heine, S. J., & Norenzayan, A. (2010). The weirdest people in the world? *Behavioral and Brain Sciences, 33*(2–3), 61–83. https://doi.org/10.1017/S0140525X0999152X

Hern, A. (2023, June 7). 'What should the limits be?' The father of ChatGPT on whether AI will save humanity—or destroy it. *The Guardian*. https://www.theguardian.com/technology/2023/jun/07/what-should-the-limits-be-the-father-of-chatgpt-on-whether-ai-will-save-humanity-or-destroy-it

Hernandez, M. (2008). Promoting stewardship behavior in organizations: A leadership model. *Journal of Business Ethics, 80*(1), 121–128.

Hertenstein, M. J., Keltner, D., App, B., Bulleit, B. A., & Jaskolka, A. R. (2006). Touch communicates distinct emotions. *Emotion, 6*(3), 528–533. https://doi.org/10.1037/1528-3542.6.3.528

Hilliard, A., Munoz, C., Wu, Z., & Koshiyama, A. S. (2024). *Eliciting personality traits in large language models*. arXiv. 2402.08341.

Hillman, C. H., Erickson, K. I., & Kramer, A. F. (2008). Be smart, exercise your heart: Exercise effects on brain and cognition. *Nature Reviews Neuroscience, 9*(1), 58–65. https://doi.org/10.1038/nrn2298

Hinnells, J. R. (Ed.). (2010). *The Penguin handbook of the world's living religions*. Penguin.

Hirschhorn, L. (1988). *The workplace within: Psychodynamics of organizational life*. MIT Press.

Hitlin, S., & Piliavin, J. A. (2004). Values: Reviving a dormant concept. *Annual Review of Sociology, 30*(1), 359–393.

Hoffman, G., Chen, T., Misra, D., Teevan, J., & Zahradka, O. (2021, May). Toward inclusive technology for people with disabilities. In *Extended Abstracts of the 2021 CHI Conference on Human Factors in Computing Systems* (pp. 1–4).

Hofmann, V., Kalluri, P. R., Jurafsky, D., & King, S. (2024, March 19). Preprint on arXiv https://doi.org/10.48550/arXiv.2403.00742

Hofstede, G. (1980). *Culture's consequences: International differences in work-related values.* SAGE Publications.

Holzinger, A. (2016). *Interactive machine learning for health informatics: When do we need the human-in-the-loop?* Springer.

Horowitz, M. C., & Scharre, P. (2015). *Meaningful human control in weapon systems: A primer.* Center for a New American Security.

Hosanagar, K. (2024, March 19). Gen AI models vs the human brain. Creative Intelligence. Retrieved from Substack.

Huang, W. (2024). The great NFT crash of 2023: A post-mortem. *Digital Economics Review, 12*(3), 45–68.

Hubbard, L. R. (1950). *Dianetics: The modern science of mental health.* Hermitage House.

HuggingFace. https://huggingface.co/

Human Brain Capital Dashboard. https://research.euromed-economists.org/brain-capital-dashboard/

iiMedia Research. (2024). *2023 China e-commerce market research report.* https://www.iimedia.cn/c1200/c1201/report-2023.html

Inglehart, R., & Welzel, C. (2005). *Modernization, cultural change, and democracy: The human development sequence.* Cambridge University Press.

Insider Intelligence. (2024). *US ecommerce by category 2024.* https://www.insiderintelligence.com/reports/us-ecommerce-by-category-2024/

Intergovernmental Panel on Climate Change. (2014). *Climate change 2014: Mitigation of climate change.* Cambridge University Press.

Isen, A. M. (2009). Affect and creative thinking. In D. Sander & K. R. Scherer (Eds.), *The Oxford companion to emotion and the affective sciences* (pp. 134–136). Oxford University Press.

James, E., & Wooten, L. (2022). *The prepared leader: Emerge from any crisis more resilient than before.* Wharton University Press.

Jee, C. (2021). This woman's brain implant zaps her with electricity when it senses she's getting depressed. *MIT Technology Review.* https://www.technologyreview.com/2021/10/04/1036430/brain-implant-zaps-electricity-depression/. Retrieved July 2023.

Jo, J. (2023, January 11). This AI just passed a Wharton MBA test. Should business schools be worried? *Fortune.* https://fortune.com/2023/01/11/ai-chatgpt-wharton-mba-test/

Jobin, A., Ienca, M., & Vayena, E. (2019). The global landscape of AI ethics guidelines. *Nature Machine Intelligence, 1*(9), 389–399.

John XXIII. (1961). Mater et Magistra. http://www.vatican.va/content/john-xxiii/en/encyclicals/documents/hf_j-xxiii_enc_15051961_mater.html

Johnson, R. (2017). Emotions and behavioral shifts: An integrated approach. *Journal of Emotional Dynamics, 30*(4), 321–336.

Johnson, S. (2022). Societal norms: A framework for understanding change. *Social Science Journal, 18*(1), 56–73.

Jones, A. (2019). Productivity and the observation effect in the workplace. *Journal of Applied Psychology, 114*(5), 856–870.

Jones, M., & Brown, P. (2015). Values as seeds of lifelong learning. *Educational Psychology Review, 12*(1), 67–84.

Jurafsky, D., & Martin, J. H. (2019). *Speech and language processing: An introduction to natural language processing, computational linguistics, and speech recognition* (3rd ed.). Pearson.

Kahneman, D. (2011). *Thinking, fast and slow.* Farrar, Straus and Giroux.

Kamps, H. J. (2024, March 19). Nvidia's Jensen Huang says AI hallucinations are solvable, artificial general intelligence is 5 years away. *TechCrunch.* https://techcrunch.com/2024/03/19/agi-and-hallucinations/

Kamptner, N. L. (1995). Treasured possessions and their meanings in adolescent males and females. *Adolescence, 30*(118), 301–318.

Kandel, E. R., Dudai, Y., & Mayford, M. R. (2014). The molecular and systems biology of memory. *Cell, 157*(1), 163–186. https://doi.org/10.1016/j.cell.2014.03.001

Kandel, E. R., Schwartz, J. H., Jessell, T. M., Siegelbaum, S. A., & Hudspeth, A. J. (2012). *Principles of neural science* (5th ed.). McGraw-Hill.

Kant, I. (1997). *Grounding for the metaphysics of morals.* Hackett Publishing.

Kaplan, A. M., & Haenlein, M. (2010). Users of the world, unite! The challenges and opportunities of social media. *Business Horizons, 53*(1), 59.

Karpen, S. C. (2018). The social psychology of biased self-assessment. *American Journal of Pharmaceutical Education, 82*(5), 6299. https://doi.org/10.5688/ajpe6299. PMID: 30013244; PMCID: PMC6041499.

Kayyem, J. (2019, August 4). There are no lone wolves. *The Washington Post.* https://www.washingtonpost.com/opinions/2019/08/04/there-are-no-lone-wolves/

Kela. (2019). Independent research institute to evaluate the effects of the basic income experiment. [Press Release]. https://www.kela.fi/web/en/news-archive/-/asset_publisher/lN08GY2nIrZo/content/independent-research-institute-to-evaluate-the-effects-of-the-basic-income-experiment

Kelly, J. R., Kennedy, P. J., Cryan, J. F., Dinan, T. G., Clarke, G., & Hyland, N. P. (2015). Breaking down the barriers: The gut microbiome, intestinal permeability and stress-related psychiatric disorders. *Frontiers in Cellular Neuroscience, 9*, 392. https://doi.org/10.3389/fncel.2015.00392

Kelly, K. (2009). How technology evolves. *TED Talk.* https://blog.ted.com/how_technology/

Keltner, D., Haidt, J., & Shiota, M. N. (2019). Social functionalism and the evolution of emotions. In *Evolution and social psychology* (pp. 115–142). Psychology Press.

Kennedy, J., Eberhart, R., & Shi, Y. (2001). *Swarm intelligence.* Morgan Kaufmann.

Kesebir, S., & Kesebir, P. (2016). A quiet ego quiets death anxiety: Humility as an existential anxiety buffer. *Journal of Personality and Social Psychology, 110*(3), 476–495. https://doi.org/10.1037/pspp0000054

Kirschner, S., & Tomasello, M. (2009). Joint music making promotes prosocial behavior in 4-year-old children. *Evolution and Human Behavior, 30*(5), 346–354.

Klein, E. (2023). The imminent danger of A.I. is one we're not talking about. *New York Times.* https://www.nytimes.com/2023/02/26/opinion/microsoft-bing-sydney-artificial-intelligence.html. Retrieved May 2023.

Klein, E. (2024, April 12). Dario Amodei on the exponential growth of AI. *The New York Times.* https://www.nytimes.com/2024/04/12/opinion/ezra-klein-podcast-dario-amodei.html

Klein, G. (2015). A naturalistic decision making perspective on studying intuitive decision making. *Journal of Applied Research in Memory and Cognition, 4*(3), 164–168. https://doi.org/10.1016/j.jarmac.2015.07.001

Koch, C. (2018a). What is consciousness? *Nature, 557*(7707), S7–S7.

Koch, C. (2018). What is Consciousness? *Scientific American, 318*(1), 76–79. https://www.scientificamerican.com/article/what-is-consciousness/

Koltko-Rivera, M. E. (2006). Rediscovering the later version of Maslow's hierarchy of needs: Self-transcendence and opportunities for theory, research, and unification. *Review of General Psychology, 10*(4), 302–317. https://doi.org/10.1037/1089-2680.10.4.302

Kramer, A. D., Guillory, J. E., & Hancock, J. T. (2014). Experimental evidence of massive-scale emotional contagion through social networks. *Proceedings of the National Academy of Sciences, 111*(24), 8788–8790.

Kramer, R. M., & Tyler, T. R. (1996). *Trust in organizations: Frontiers of theory and research.* Sage Publications.

Krasnova, H., Wenninger, H., Widjaja, T., & Buxmann, P. (2012). Envy on Facebook: A hidden threat to users' life satisfaction? In *Proceedings of the 20th European Conference on Information Systems (ECIS).*

Krishnaswamy, P., Perng, J. K., Rodriguez-Losada, D., Ding, H., Moura, J. M., Laksanasopin, T., & Rizzo, A. (2020). Multimodal sensing and automated assistance for wheelchair users. *Proceedings of the IEEE, 108*(2), 214–231.

Kubiszewski, I., Costanza, R., Franco, C., Lawn, P., Talberth, J., Jackson, T., & Aylmer, C. (2013b). Beyond GDP: Measuring and achieving global genuine progress. *Ecological Economics, 93*, 57–68. https://doi.org/10.1016/j.ecolecon.2013.04.019

Kurzweil, R. (2005). *The singularity is near: When humans transcend biology*. Viking.

Kurzweil, R. (2007, May 16). The accelerating power of technology. *TED Talk*. https://www.ted.com/talks/ray_kurzweil_the_accelerating_power_of_technology/transcript

Lai, K. (2024). Beyond the bubble: Redefining value in the post-NFT era. *MIT Technology Review, 127*(3), 56–62.

Latané, B., & Darley, J. M. (1968). Group inhibition of bystander intervention in emergencies. *Journal of Personality and Social Psychology, 10*(3), 215–221. https://doi.org/10.1037/h0026570

Latour, B. (1993). *We have never been modern*. Harvard University Press.

Lau, H., & Rosenthal, D. (2011). Empirical support for higher-order theories of conscious awareness. *Trends in Cognitive Sciences, 15*(8), 365–373.

Lawrence, M., Janzwood, S., & Homer-Dixon, T. (2022). What is a global polycrisis? And how is it different from a systemic risk? *The Cascade Institute*. https://cascadeinstitute.org/technical-paper/what-is-a-global-polycrisis/. Retrieved January 2024.

Lebedev, M. A., & Nicolelis, M. A. (2006). Brain–machine interfaces: Past, present and future. *Trends in Neurosciences, 29*(9), 536–546.

LeCun, Y., Bengio, Y., & Hinton, G. (2015). Deep learning. *Nature, 521*(7553), 436–444.

Leeper, A., Hsiao, K., Ciocarlie, M., Takayama, L., & Gossow, D. (2012). Strategies for human-in-the-loop robotic grasping. In *2012 7th ACM/IEEE International Conference on Human-Robot Interaction (HRI)*.

Leike, J., Martic, M., Krakovna, V., Ortega, P. A., Everitt, T., Lefrancq, A., & Legg, S. (2017). AI safety gridworlds. arXiv preprint arXiv:1711.09883.

Leite, I., Martinho, C., & Paiva, A. (2013). Social robots for long-term interaction: A survey. *International Journal of Social Robotics, 5*(2), 291–308.

Lenton, A. P., Bruder, M., & Sedikides, C. (2021). *Handbook of the authentic self*. Psychology Press.

Leung, K., Bond, M. H., & Bond, M. H. (2004). The impact of cultural collectivism on reward allocation. *Journal of Occupational and Organizational Psychology, 77*(4), 553–580.

Levin, S. T. (2017, September 12). Face-reading AI will be able to detect your politics and IQ, professor says. *The Guardian*. https://www.theguardian.com/technology/2017/sep/12/artificial-intelligence-face-reading-politics-iq-stanford

Levine, S., Finn, C., & Hausman, K. (2024). Data-efficient embodied AI through model-based reinforcement learning. *Science Robotics, 9*(78), eabc9776.

Lewis, J. (2020). *The fifth domain: Defending our country, our companies, and ourselves in the age of cyber threats*. Penguin.

Lewis, J. D., & Weigert, M. (1985). Trust and organizational behavior: A review of relevant literature. *Management Science, 31*(6), 629–646.

Lewis, S. L., & Maslin, M. A. (2015). Defining the Anthropocene. *Nature, 519*(7542), 171–180. https://doi.org/10.1038/nature14258

Lipina, S. J., & Colombo, J. A. (2009). *Poverty and brain development during childhood: An approach from cognitive psychology and neuroscience*. American Psychological Association.

Lisman, J. (2017). Glutamatergic synapses are structurally and biochemically complex because of multiple plasticity processes: Long-term potentiation, long-term depression, short-term potentiation, and scaling. *Philosophical Transactions of the Royal Society B: Biological Sciences, 372*(1715), 20160260.

Liu, Y., & Zeng, Y. (2020). Artificial Intelligence governance in China: A framework based on core values and principles. *IEEE Technology and Society Magazine, 39*(2), 40–48.

Locke, E. A., & Latham, G. P. (2002). Building a practically useful theory of goal setting and task motivation: A 35-year odyssey. *American Psychologist, 57*(9), 705–717. https://doi.org/10.1037/0003-066X.57.9.705

Longcamp, M., Zerbato-Poudou, M.-T., & Velay, J.-L. (2005). The influence of writing practice on letter recognition in preschool children: A comparison between handwriting and typing. *Acta Psychologica, 119*(1), 67–79. https://doi.org/10.1016/j.actpsy.2004.10.019

Luby, J., Belden, A., Botteron, K., Marrus, N., Harms, M. P., Babb, C., Nishino, T., & Barch, D. (2013). The effects of poverty on childhood brain development: The mediating effect of caregiving and stressful life events. *JAMA Pediatrics, 167*(12), 1135–1142. https://doi.org/10.1001/jamapediatrics.2013.3139

Luhmann, N. (1979). *Trust and power*. John Wiley & Sons.

Luthar, S. S., Cicchetti, D., & Becker, B. (2000). The construct of resilience: A critical evaluation and guidelines for future work. *Child Development, 71*(3), 543–562. https://doi.org/10.1111/1467-8624.00164

Macnish, K. (2012). An eye for an eye: Proportionality and surveillance. *Ethical Theory and Moral Practice, 15*(3), 529–548.

Madaan, A., Mittal, M., Goyal, S., Aggarwal, S., & Saxena, S. (2022). Application of artificial intelligence in medical field with special reference to accessibility. *Journal of Family Medicine and Primary Care, 11*(4), 1579.

Madison, A., Kiecolt-Glaser, J. K. (2019, August). Stress, depression, diet, and the gut microbiota: Human-bacteria interactions at the core of psychoneuroimmunology and nutrition. *Current Opinion in Behavioral Sciences, 28*, 105–110. https://doi.org/10.1016/j.cobeha.2019.01.011. Epub 2019 Mar 25. PMID: 32395568; PMCID: PMC7213601.

Maio, G. R., & Olson, J. M. (2000). Values as truisms: Evidence and implications. *Journal of Personality and Social Psychology, 78*(4), 763–775.

Manyika, J., & Roxburgh, C. (2023). The great transformer. The impact of the internet on economic growth and prosperity. McKinsey Global Institute. https://www.mckinsey.com/~/media/mckinsey/industries/technology%20media%20and%20telecommunications/high%20tech/our%20insights/the%20great%20transformer/mgi_impact_of_internet_on_economic_growth.pdf. Retrieved July 2023.

Marble, J. L., Bruemmer, D. J., Few, D. A., & Nielsen, C. W. (2004). Evaluation of supervisory vs. peer-peer interaction with human-robot teams. In *Proceedings of the 37th Annual Hawaii International Conference on System Sciences (HICSS'04)*.

Marcus, G., & Luccioni, S. (2023, April 17). Stop treating AI models like people. *Gary Marcus*. https://garymarcus.substack.com/p/stop-treating-ai-models-like-people

Marr B. (2022). The 5 biggest Artificial Intelligence (AI) trends in 2023. *Forbes*.

Marwala, T. (2023, July 18). Militarisation of AI has severe implications for global security and warfare. *Daily Maverick*. https://www.dailymaverick.co.za/opinionista/2023-07-18-militarisation-of-ai-has-severe-implications-for-global-security-and-warfare/. Retrieved 2 August 2023.

Marx, K. (1867/1976). *Capital* (B. Fowkes, Trans.). Penguin.

Max-Neef, M. (1995b). Economic growth and quality of life: A threshold hypothesis. *Ecological Economics, 15*(2), 115–118. https://doi.org/10.1016/0921-8009(95)00064-X

Maxwell, J. A. (2012). *A realist approach for qualitative research*. Sage.

Mayer, E. A., Knight, R., Mazmanian, S. K., Cryan, J. F., & Tillisch, K. (2014). Gut microbes and the brain: Paradigm shift in neuroscience. *The Journal of Neuroscience, 34*(46), 15490–15496. https://doi.org/10.1523/JNEUROSCI.3299-14.2014

Mayer, R. C., Davis, J. H., & Schoorman, F. D. (1995b). An integrative model of organizational trust. *Academy of Management Review, 20*(3), 709–734. https://doi.org/10.5465/amr.1995.9508080335

Mazzucato, M. (2013). *The entrepreneurial state: Debunking public vs. private sector myths*. Anthem Press.

McArdle, M. (2019). *Is forced arbitration living up to its promise?* Harvard Business Review.
McCarthy, J. Minsky, M. L., Rochester, N., & Shannon, C. E. (1955, August). *A proposal for the Dartmouth Summer Research Project on Artificial Intelligence.* http://raysolomonoff.com/dartmouth/boxa/dart564props.pdf
McCullough, M. E., Root, L. M., & Cohen, A. D. (2006). Writing about the benefits of an interpersonal transgression facilitates forgiveness. *Journal of Consulting and Clinical Psychology, 74*(5), 887–897.
McEwen, B. S. (2006). Protective and damaging effects of stress mediators. *New England Journal of Medicine, 338*(3), 171–179.
McEwen, B. S. (2007). Physiology and neurobiology of stress and adaptation: Central role of the brain. *Physiological Reviews, 87*(3), 873–904.
McKinsey Global Institute. (2023, July). *Jobs lost, jobs gained: Workforce transitions in a time of automation.* Retrieved from McKinsey & Company website, https://www.mckinsey.com/featured-insights/future-of-work
McNamee, S. J. (2018). *The meritocracy myth.* Rowman & Littlefield.
McNeill, W. H., & McNeill, J. R. (2003). *The human web: A bird;s-eye view of world history.* W. W. Norton & Company.
Mead, M. (1964). *Continuities in cultural evolution.* Transaction Publishers.
Meadows, D. H. (2008). *Thinking in systems: A primer.* Chelsea Green Publishing.
Mercado, J. E., Rupp, M. A., Chen, J. Y., Barnes, M. J., Barber, D., & Procci, K. (2016). Intelligent agent transparency in human–agent teaming for Multi-UxV management. *Human Factors, 58*(3), 401–415.
Merleau-Ponty, M. (1962). *Phenomenology of perception.* Routledge.
Merriam-Webster. (n.d.). Honesty. In Merriam-Webster.com dictionary. https://www.merriam-webster.com/dictionary/honesty. Retrieved 12 July 2023.
Merz, J. J., Barnard, P., Rees, W. E., Smith, D., Maroni, M., Rhodes, C. J., Dederer, J. H., Bajaj, N., Joy, M. K., Wiedmann, T., & Sutherland, R. (2023). World scientists' warning: The behavioural crisis driving ecological overshoot. *Science Progress, 106*(3). https://doi.org/10.1177/00368504231201372
Messeri, L., & Crockett, M. J. (2024). Artificial intelligence and illusions of understanding in scientific research. *Nature, 627,* 49–58. https://doi.org/10.1038/s41586-024-07146-0
Meta. (2023, June 29). Changes to news availability on our platforms in Canada. *Meta Newsroom.* https://about.fb.com/news/2023/06/changes-to-news-availability-on-our-platforms-in-canada/. Retrieved August 2023.
Metaphysics Book VIII, 1045a.8–10, Aristotle; Translated W. D. Ross (1908).
Metz, C. (2023). The ChatGPT king isn't worried, but he knows you might be. *New York Times.* https://www.nytimes.com/2023/03/31/technology/sam-altman-open-ai-chatgpt.html?smid=nytcore-ios-share&referringSource=highlightShare. Retrieved May 2023.

Metz, C., Kang, C., Frenkel, S., Thompson, S. A., & Grant, N. (2024, April 6). How tech giants cut corners to harvest data for A.I. *The New York Times*. https://www.nytimes.com/2024/04/06/technology/ai-data-harvesting.html

Meyer v. Uber Technologies, Inc. (2017). Justitia. US Law. https://law.justia.com/cases/federal/appellate-courts/ca2/16-2750/16-2750-2017-08-17.html

Microsoft Corporation. (2023). 2023 annual report. https://www.microsoft.com/investor/reports/ar23/

Miller, K. (2023, March 13). AI overreliance is a problem. Are explanations a solution? Stanford Human-Centered Artificial Intelligence. https://hai.stanford.edu/news/ai-overreliance-problem-are-explanations-solution

Milmo, D. (2023a). Claude 2: Anthropic launches chatbot rival to ChatGPT. *The Guardian*. https://www.theguardian.com/technology/2023/jul/12/claude-2-anthropic-launches-chatbot-rival-chatgpt. Retrieved July 2023.

Milmo, D. (2023b). Elon Musk launches XAI startup pro humanity in terminator future. *The Guardian*. https://www.theguardian.com/technology/2023/jul/13/elon-musk-launches-xai-startup-pro-humanity-terminator-future. Retrieved 14 July 2023.

MIT EECS. (n.d.). AI and Society. Massachusetts Institute of Technology. https://www.eecs.mit.edu/research/explore-all-research-areas/ml-and-social-science/. Retrieved June 2023.

Mitchell, M. (2009). *Complexity: A guided tour*. Oxford University Press.

Mitchell, T. M. (1997). *Machine learning*. McGraw-Hill.

Mittelstadt, B. D., Allo, P., Taddeo, M., Wachter, S., & Floridi, L. (2019). The ethics of algorithms: Mapping the debate. *Big Data & Society, 6*(2), 205395171983389. https://doi.org/10.1177/2053951719833894

Möllering, G. (2006). *Trust: Reason, routine, reflexivity*. Emerald Group Publishing.

Mollick, E. (2023, March 17). Centaurs and Cyborgs on the Jagged Frontier. One useful thing. https://ethanmollick.substack.com/p/centaurs-and-cyborgs-on-the-jagged

Monahan, T. (2006). Questioning surveillance and security. In T. Monahan (Ed.), *Surveillance and security: Technological politics and power in everyday life* (pp. 1–23). Routledge.

Moravec, H. (1988). *Mind children: The future of robot and human intelligence*. Harvard University Press.

Mordor Intelligence. (2023). Online banking market—Growth, trends, forecasts (2023–2028). https://www.mordorintelligence.com/industry-reports/online-banking-market

Mori, P. (2022). Looking at you: Facial recognition technology, police body-worn cameras, and privacy law in Canada. *Alberta Law Review, 59*(3), 687–732.

Morin, E., & Kern, A. B. (1999). *Homeland Earth: A Manifesto for the New Millennium.* Hampton Press.

Morozov, E. (2023, June 30). Artificial Intelligence and the danger of unchecked advancements. *The New York Times.* https://www.nytimes.com/2023/06/30/opinion/artificial-intelligence-danger.html?campaign_id=39&emc=edit_ty_20230630&instance_id=96413&nl=opinion-today&regi_id=208750243&segment_id=138052&te=1&user_id=9e2d4ee3ed4e60728251f331a585bc56

Moss, M. (2013). *Salt sugar fat: How the food giants hooked us.* Random House.

MSN. (2023). *AI industry and researchers sign statement warning of 'extinction' risk.* https://www.msn.com/en-us/news/technology/ai-industry-and-researchers-sign-statement-warning-of-extinction-risk/ar-AA1bSJRy

Murez, C. in U.S. Department of Health and Human Services. (2023, May 2). *New Surgeon General advisory raises alarm about the devastating impact of the epidemic of loneliness and isolation in the United States.* https://www.hhs.gov/surgeongeneral/priorities/connection/index.html

Naess, A. (2002). *Life's philosophy—Reason & feeling in a deeper world* (p. 6).

Nagel, T. (1986). *The view from nowhere.* Oxford University Press.

Najibi, A. (2020, October 24). Racial discrimination in face recognition technology. *Science in the News.* https://sitn.hms.harvard.edu/flash/2020/racial-discrimination-in-face-recognition-technology/

Nature. (2017). Neurotechnologies, brain research and informed public dialogue. *Nature, 551*(7679), 159–161.

Neisser, U, (2014). *Cognitive psychology.* Psychology press. ISBN 978-1-84872-693-2.

Nelson, K., & Chen, X. (2011). Development of moral emotions and moral reasoning. In D. M. Buss (Ed.), *The handbook of evolutionary psychology* (pp. 725–752). John Wiley & Sons.

Nelson, R. (1977). *The Moon and the Ghetto: An essay on policy analysis.* W.W.Norton.

Neville, H. J., Stevens, C., Pakulak, E., Bell, T. A., Fanning, J., Klein, S., & Isbell, E. (2013). Family-based training program improves brain function, cognition, and behavior in lower socioeconomic status preschoolers. *Proceedings of the National Academy of Sciences, 110*(29), 12138–12143. https://doi.org/10.1073/pnas.1304437110

Newitz, A. (2024, April 12). A brief, weird history of brainwashing: L. Ron Hubbard, Operation Midnight Climax, and stochastic terrorism—the race for mind control changed America forever. *MIT Technology Review.* https://www.technologyreview.com/2024/04/12/1090726/brainwashing-mind-control-history-operation-midnight-climax/

Newman, G. E., & Bloom, P. (2012). Art and authenticity: The importance of originals in judgments of value. *Journal of Experimental Psychology: General*, *141*(3), 558–569. https://doi.org/10.1037/a0026035
Newman, M. E. J. (2005). Power laws, Pareto Distributions, and Zipf's law. *Contemporary Physics*, *46*(5), 323–351. arXiv:cond-mat/0412004. Bibcode:2005ConPh..46..323N. https://doi.org/10.1080/001075105000 52444. S2CID 202719165.
Nickerson, R. S. (1998). Confirmation bias: A ubiquitous phenomenon in many guises. *Review of General Psychology*, *2*(2), 175–220.
Nissenbaum, H., & Rodotà, S. (2016). Privacy in the age of big data: Recognizing threats, defending values, and shaping policy. *World Policy Journal*, *33*(1), 7–17.
Nissenbaum, H., & Rodotà, S. (2019). Data ethics. In J. van den Hoven, P. E. Vermaas, & I. van de Poel (Eds.), *Handbook of ethics, values, and technological design* (pp. 1–18). Springer. https://doi.org/10.1007/978-94-007-6970-0_97-1
Nordhaus, W., & Tobin, J. (1973). Is growth obsolete? In *The Measurement of Economic and Social Performance* (pp. 509–564). National Bureau of Economic Research, Inc.
Norris, F. H., Stevens, S. P., Pfefferbaum, B., Wyche, K. F., & Pfefferbaum, R. L. (2008). Community resilience as a metaphor, theory, set of capacities, and strategy for disaster readiness. *American Journal of Community Psychology*, *41*(1–2), 127–150. https://doi.org/10.1007/s10464-007-9156-6
Northouse, P. G. (2018). *Leadership: Theory and practice* (8th ed.). Sage.
Nowak, M. A. (2012). *SuperCooperators: Altruism, evolution, and why we need each other to succeed*. Free Press.
Nussbaum, M. C. (1997). *Cultivating humanity: A classical defense of reform in liberal education*. Harvard University Press.
Nussbaum, M. C. (2002). *For love of country?* Beacon Press.
NVIDIA Corporation. (2023). Fiscal 2023 annual report. https://investor.nvidia.com/financial-info/annual-reports/default.aspx
O'Brien, E. (2018). The next effect: Exploring the role of tomorrow's devices in today's experience evaluations. *Journal of Consumer Research*, *45*(1), 161–178. https://doi.org/10.1093/jcr/ucx126
O'Connor, S., Hanlon, P., O'Donnell, C. A., Garcia, S., Glanville, J., Mair, F. S., & Papadopoulou, C. (2019). Understanding factors affecting patient and public engagement and recruitment to digital health interventions: A systematic review of qualitative studies. *BMC Medical Informatics and Decision Making*, *19*(1), 45. https://doi.org/10.1186/s12911-019-0757-y
O'Neil, C. (2016). *Weapons of math destruction: How big data increases inequality and threatens democracy*. Broadway Books.

OpenAi. (2023). *Introducing super alignment*. https://openai.com/blog/introducing-superalignment. Retrieved July 2023.

Otake, K., Shimai, S., Tanaka-Matsumi, J., Otsui, K., & Fredrickson, B. L. (2006). Happy people become happier through kindness: A counting kindnesses intervention. *Journal of Happiness Studies, 7*(3), 361–375. https://doi.org/10.1007/s10902-005-3650-z

Oxfam. (2024). *Inequality Inc.* https://www.oxfam.org/en/research/inequality-inc

Palanski, M. E., & Yammarino, F. J. (2009). Integrity and leadership: A multilevel conceptual framework. *The Leadership Quarterly, 20*(3), 405–420.

Parker, G. (1996). *The military revolution: Military innovation and the rise of the West, 1500–1800*. Cambridge University Press.

Paul, K. (2023, January 23). An AI just won first place at a major US art competition. Should humans be worried? *The Guardian*. https://www.theguardian.com/artanddesign/2023/jan/23/ai-artificial-intelligence-colorado-state-fair-competition

Pavlov, I. P. (1927). *Conditioned reflexes: An investigation of the physiological activity of the cerebral cortex*. Oxford University Press.

Perrin, A., & Turner, E. (2019a). *Share of U.S. adults watching online videos frequently is increasing*. Pew Research Center. https://www.pewresearch.org/fact-tank/2019/08/02/share-of-u-s-adults-watching-online-videos-frequently-is-increasing/

Perrin, A., & Turner, E. (2019b). *Smartphones help blacks, hispanics bridge some—but not all—digital gaps with whites*. Pew Research Center. https://www.pewresearch.org/fact-tank

Pfeifer, R., & Bongard, J. (2007). *How the body shapes the way we think: A new view of intelligence*. MIT Press.

Pham, S. (2017, April 24). Jack Ma: In 30 years, the best CEO could be a robot. *CNN Business*. https://money.cnn.com/2017/04/24/technology/jack-ma-robot-ceo/index.html

Picard, R. W. (2000). *Affective computing*. MIT Press.

Pickett, K., & Wilkinson, R. (2010). *The spirit level*. Penguin Books.

Piff, P. K., Dietze, P., Feinberg, M., Stancato, D. M., & Keltner, D. (2015). Awe, the small self, and prosocial behavior. *Journal of Personality and Social Psychology, 108*, 883–899.

Plato. (360 BCE). *The Republic*.

Plato. (2002). *Five dialogues: Euthyphro, apology, Crito, Meno, Phaedo* (G. M. A. Grube, Trans.). Hackett Publishing.

Platt, M. (2023). *The leader's brain: Enhance your leadership, build stronger teams, make better decisions, and inspire greater innovation with neuroscience*. Wharton School Press.

Porges, S. W. (2011). *The polyvagal theory: Neurophysiological foundations of emotions, attachment, communication, and self-regulation.* WW Norton & Co.
Portugali, J. (2012). Complexity theories of cities: Achievements, criticism and potentials. In J. Portugali, H. Meyer, E. Stolk, & E. Tan (Eds.), *Complexity theories of cities have come of age* (pp. 47–62). Springer.
Pretty, J. (2008). Agricultural sustainability: Concepts, principles and evidence. *Philosophical Transactions of the Royal Society B: Biological Sciences, 363*(1491), 447–465.
Pribram, K. H. (2021). *Holoflux of consciousness: Bringing the holographic paradigm to psychology, neuroscience, and physics.* Academic Press.
Putman, D. (2004). Psychological courage. *Philosophy, Psychiatry, & Psychology, 11*(1), 1–11.
Putnam, R. D. (2000). *Bowling alone: The collapse and revival of American community.* Simon & Schuster.
Rabinovich, M. I., Simmons, A. N., Varona, P., & Bazhenov, M. (2015). Dynamical bridge between brain and mind. *Trends in Cognitive Sciences, 19*(8), 453–461.
Radford, A., Wu, J., Child, R., Luan, D., Amodei, D., & Sutskever, I. (2019). Language models are unsupervised multitask learners. *OpenAI Blog.* https://openai.com/blog/better-language-models/
Raji, I. D., & Buolamwini, J. (2019). Actionable auditing: Investigating the impact of publicly naming biased performance results of commercial AI products. In *Proceedings of the 2019 AAAI/ACM Conference on AI, Ethics, and Society* (pp. 429–435).
Ramón, S. (1905) [1890]. *Manual de Anatomia Patológica General* (*Handbook of general Anatomical Pathology*) (in Spanish) (4th ed.).
Ravallion, M. (2017). The idea of antipoverty policy. *Economic Policy, 32*(89), 5–47. https://doi.org/10.1093/epolic/eix007
Rawls, J. (1999). *A theory of justice: Revised edition.* Harvard University Press.
Reber, A. S. (1995). *The penguin dictionary of psychology.* Penguin Books.
Regulatory framework proposal on artificial intelligence. (2022, April 21). Shaping Europe's digital future. https://digital-strategy.ec.europa.eu/policies/regulatory-framework-ai
Reichenbach, B. R. (1991). The golden rule. *Philosophy East and West, 41*(4), 543–555.
Reuters. (2023, July 24). OpenAI's Sam Altman launches Worldcoin crypto project. *Reuters.* https://www.reuters.com/technology/openais-sam-altman-launches-worldcoin-crypto-project-2023-07-24/
Reynolds, C. W. (1987). Flocks, herds and schools: A distributed behavioral model. *SIGGRAPH Computer Graphics, 21*(4), 25–34. https://doi.org/10.1145/37401.37406

Richards, B. A., & Chalupka, K. (2024). Virtual embodiment: A path toward general artificial intelligence. *IEEE Transactions on Artificial Intelligence*, 45(5), 1410–1428.

Richter, D. (2018). Immanuel Kant: Metaphysics. *The Stanford Encyclopedia of Philosophy*. https://plato.stanford.edu/archives/fall2018/entries/kant-metaphysics/

Rokeach, M. (1973). *The nature of human values*. The Free Press.

Rosenberg, N. (1992). *Exploring the black box: Technology, economics, and history*. Cambridge University Press.

Rousseau, D. M., Sitkin, S. B., Burt, R. S., & Camerer, C. (1998). Not so different after all: A cross-discipline view of trust. *Academy of Management Review*, 23(3), 393–404.

Rudin, C. (2019). Stop explaining black box machine learning models for high stakes decisions and use interpretable models instead. *Nature Machine Intelligence*, 1(5), 206–215.

Ruiz, D. M. (n.d.). *We only see what we want to see*. https://www.awakenthegur uinyou.com/50-inspirational-quotes-don-miguel-ruiz/. Retrieved July 2023.

Russell, S. (2019). *Human compatible: Artificial intelligence and the problem of control*. Penguin.

Russell, S., & Norvig, P. (2016). *Artificial intelligence: A modern approach* (3rd ed.). Pearson.

Russell, S., Dewey, D., & Tegmark, M. (2015). Research priorities for robust and beneficial artificial intelligence. *AI Magazine*, 36(4), 105–114.

Russell, S. J., & Norvig, P. (2021). *Artificial intelligence: A modern approach* (4th ed., p. 5). Pearson. ISBN 9780134610993. Retrieved 12 September 2022.

Ryan-Mosley, T. (2023) The movement to limit face recognition tech might finally get a win. MIT. https://www.technologyreview.com/2023/07/20/1076539/face-recognition-massachusetts-test-police/. Retrieved 16 August 2023.

Saharia, C., Chan, W., Saxena, S., Li, L., Whang, J., Denton, E., Ghasemipour, K., Gontijo Lopes, R., Karagol Ayan, B., Salimans, T., & Ho, J. & Fleet, D. J. (2023). *Photorealistic text-to-image diffusion models with deep language understanding*. arXiv preprint arXiv:2205.11487.

Samuelson, P. A., & Marks, S. G. (2003). *Economics*. McGraw-Hill Education.

Sandel, M. J. (2020). *The tyranny of merit: What's become of the common good?* Farrar.

Sangaramoorthy, T., Jamison, A. M., & Dyer, L. A. (2021). Addressing power dynamics in community-engaged research partnerships. *Journal of Patient-Reported Outcomes*, 5(1). https://doi.org/10.1186/s41687-021-00313-5

Sapolsky, R. M. (2015). Stress and the brain: Individual variability and the inverted-U. *Nature*, 526(7571), 187–193.

Savcisens, G., Eliassi-Rad, T., Hansen, L. K., et al. (2024). Using sequences of life-events to predict human lives. *Nat Comput Sci, 4*, 43–56. https://doi.org/10.1038/s43588-023-00573-5

Schein, E. H. (1965). *Organizational psychology.* Prentice-Hall.

Schoorman, F. D., Mayer, R. C., & Davis, J. H. (2007). An integrative model of organizational trust: Past, present, and future. *Academy of Management Review, 32*(2), 344–354.

Schultz, P. W., Nolan, J. M., Cialdini, R. B., Goldstein, N. J., & Griskevicius, V. (2007). The constructive, destructive, and reconstructive power of social norms. *Psychological Science, 18*(5), 429–434.

Schumpeter, J. A. (1934). *The theory of economic development: An inquiry into profits, capital, credit, interest, and the business cycle.* Harvard University Press.

Schwab, K. (2017). *The fourth industrial revolution.* Crown Business.

Schwartz, J. M., Stapp, H. P., & Beauregard, M. (2005). *Philosophical Transactions of the Royal Society B, 360,* 1309–1327.

Schwartz, M. (2021). The observer in psychology: Bias, reactivity, and intersubjectivity. *The American Journal of Psychology, 134*(4), 479–491.

Schwartz, S. H. (1992). Universals in the content and structure of values: Theoretical advances and empirical tests in 20 countries. In M. P. Zanna (Ed.), *Advances in experimental social psychology* (Vol. 25, pp. 1–65). Academic Press.

Schwartz, S. H. (2012). An overview of the Schwartz theory of basic values. *Online Readings in Psychology and Culture, 2*(1). https://doi.org/10.9707/2307-0919.1116

Searle, J. R. (1997, November 2). *The mystery of consciousness.* New York Review of Books.

Searle, J. R. (1997b). The mystery of consciousness. *New York Review of Books, 44*(17), 60–66.

Sen, A. (1985). Well-being, agency and freedom: The Dewey lectures 1984. *The Journal of Philosophy, 82*(4), 169–221. https://doi.org/10.2307/2026184

Senior, A. W., Evans, R., Jumper, J., Kirkpatrick, J., Sifre, L., Green, T., Qin, C., Žídek, A., Nelson, A. W., Bridgland, A., Penedones, H., & Hassabis, D. (2022). Improved protein structure prediction using potentials from deep learning. *Nature, 577*(7792), 706–710.

SEWA. (2010). Conditional cash transfers: A women-friendly tool in India's National Rural Employment Guarantee Program. https://www.sewa.org/pdf/conditional_cash_transfers_-_iciciprudential_lifegroup_insurance-1.pdf

Shadbolt, N. (2022). "From so simple a beginning": Species of Artificial Intelligence. *Daedalus, 151*(2), 28–42. https://doi.org/10.1162/daed_a_01898

Sharika, K. M., Thaikkandi, S., Nivedita, & Platt, M. L. (2024). Interpersonal heart rate synchrony predicts effective information processing in a naturalistic group decision-making task. *Proceedings of the National Academy of Sciences, 121*(21), e2313801121. https://doi.org/10.1073/pnas.2313801121

Sherif, M., & Sherif, C. W. (1964). *Reference groups: Exploration into conformity and deviation of adolescents.* Harper & Row.

Shinohara, K., & Tenenberg, J. (2009). A blind person's interactions with technology. *Communications of the ACM, 52*(8), 58–66.

Shivaram, D. (2023). The White House and big tech companies release commitments on managing AI [Radio broadcast episode]. NPR. In Morning Edition. https://www.npr.org/2023/07/21/1234876543/the-white-house-and-big-tech-companies-release-commitments-on-managing-ai. Retrieved 3 July 2023.

Simons, T. L. (2002). Behavioral integrity: The perceived alignment between managers' words and deeds as a research focus. *Organization Science, 13*(1), 18–35.

Sinek, S. (2019). *The infinite game.* Portfolio/Penguin. ISBN 9780735213500.

Singer, P. (2009). *The life you can save: Acting now to end world poverty.* Random House.

Singer, P. W. (2018). *Likewar: The weaponization of social media.* Houghton Mifflin Harcourt.

Sivananda, S. (1999). *The Lord's universal prayer: Sadhana.* The Divine Life Trust Society.

Smith, E., Ali, D., Wilkerson, B., Dawson, W. D., Sobowale, K., Reynolds III, C., Berk, M., Lavretsky, H., Jeste, D., Ng, C. H., & Soares, J. C. (2021). A brain capital grand strategy: Toward economic reimagination. *Molecular Psychiatry, 26*, 3–22. https://doi.org/10.1038/s41380-020-00918-w

Smith, E., Storch, E. A., Lavretsky, H., Cummings, J. L., Eyre, H. A. (2023). Affective computing for brain health disorders. In P. Vlamos, I. S. Kotsireas, & I. Tarnanas (Eds.), *Handbook of computational neurodegeneration.* Springer. https://doi.org/10.1007/978-3-319-75922-7_36

Smith, T. (2010). The role of internal values in behavioral evolution. *Journal of Behavioral Evolution, 5*(2), 89–104.

Solaiman, I., Brundage, M., Clark, J., Askell, A., Herbert-Voss, A., Wu, J., Radford, A., Krueger, G., Kim, J. W., Kreps, S., McCain, M., & Noukhovitch, M. (2022). *Release strategies and the social impacts of language models.* arXiv preprint arXiv:2211.11409.

Standing, G. (2017). *Basic income: And how we can make it happen.* Pelican.

Stanford Encyclopedia of Philosophy. (2022a). *Artificial Intelligence.* https://plato.stanford.edu/archives/win2022/entries/artificial-intelligence/. Retrieved June 2023.

Stanford Encyclopedia of Philosophy. (2022b). *The ethics of Artificial Intelligence.* https://plato.stanford.edu/archives/sum2022/entries/ethics-ai/. Retrieved June 2023.

Stanford Institute for Human-Centered Artificial Intelligence. (2024). AI Index: State of AI in 13 Charts. https://hai.stanford.edu/news/ai-index-state-ai-13-charts

Stanovich, K. E., & West, R. F. (2008). On the failures of cognitive ability testing in the face of real-world decision-making demands. *Annual Review of Psychology, 59*, 587–612.

StatCounter. (2024). Search engine market share worldwide. https://gs.statcounter.com/search-engine-market-share

Statista. (2024). Internet users in the world 2024. https://www.statista.com/statistics/617136/digital-population-worldwide/

Sternberg, R. J. (2003). *Wisdom, intelligence, and creativity synthesized.* Cambridge University Press.

Stevens, J. R. (2022). *Irrationality: The enemy within.* Princeton University Press.

Stewart, A., Cooban, A., & Doherty, L. (2023, July 15). AI facial recognition tech brings 'airport-style security' to UK stores, says human rights group. *CNN.* https://www.cnn.com/2023/07/15/business/facewatch-ai-facial-recognition-tech/index.html

Stiglitz, J. E. (2019a). *People, power and profits: Progressive capitalism for an age of discontent.* Penguin UK.

Stiglitz, J. E. (2019b). Rewriting the rules of the European economy. Project Syndicate. https://www.project-syndicate.org/commentary/rewriting-rules-of-european-economy-by-joseph-e-stiglitz-2019-05

Stiglitz, J. E., Sen, A., & Fitoussi, J. P. (2009). Report by the commission on the measurement of economic performance and social progress. Commission on the Measurement of Economic Performance and Social Progress. https://ec.europa.eu/eurostat/documents/118025/118123/Fitoussi+Commission+report

Stokes, P. R. A., Forstmann, B. U., & Spaak, E. (2023). A dopamine-modulated neural circuit for cognitive flexibility. *Nature, 598*(7914), 630–635. https://doi.org/10.1038/s41593-023-01304-9

Strogatz, S. H. (2003). *Sync: How order emerges from chaos in the universe, nature, and daily life.* Hachette UK.

Strubell, E., Ganesh, A., & McCallum, A. (2019). Energy and policy considerations for deep learning in NLP. *Proceedings of the 57th Annual Meeting of the Association for Computational Linguistics* (pp. 3645–3650).

Suleyman, M. (2024). What is AI anyway? *TED Talk.* https://www.ted.com/talks/mustafa_suleyman_what_is_an_ai_anyway?language=en

Svara, J. H., & Brunet, J. R. (2004). Filling in the skeletal pillar: Addressing social equity in introductory courses in public administration. *Journal of Public Affairs Education, 10*(2), 99–109.

Swilling, M. (2013). *Sustainable development in the anthropocene.* Springer.

Tandoc, E. C., Lim, Z. W., & Ling, R. (2018). Deconstructing "echo chambers" and "epistemic bubbles": Understanding the social media disinformation ecosystem. *Information, Communication & Society, 23*(7), 994–1018.

Tang, Y. Y., Hölzel, B. K., & Posner, M. I. (2015). The neuroscience of mindfulness meditation. *Nature Reviews Neuroscience, 16*(4), 213–225. https://doi.org/10.1038/nrn3916

Tarnoff, B. (2023, February 23). 'A certain danger lurks there': How the inventor of the first chatbot turned against AI. *The Guardian*. https://www.theguardian.com/technology/2023/feb/23/joseph-weizenbaum-eliza-chatbot-ai-turned-against-computers. Retrieved July 2023.

Tegmark, M. (2017). *Life 3.0: Being human in the age of Artificial Intelligence*. Knopf.

Teigland, J. (2024) Navigating the AI revolution in 2024: Building trust through innovation and responsibility. EY Linkedin. https://www.linkedin.com/pulse/navigating-ai-revolution-2024-building-trust-through-julie-teigland-a0l9e/. Retrieved January 2024.

Thaler, R. H., & Sunstein, C. R. (2008). *Nudge: Improving decisions about health, wealth, and happiness*. Yale University Press.

Thatcher, M. (1987, September 23). Interview for woman's own ("no such thing as society"). No.10 Downing Street. Retrieved from Thatcher Archive (THCR 5/2/262): COI transcript.

The Guardian. (2023a). *AI poses existential threat and risk to health of millions, experts warn*. https://www.theguardian.com/technology/2023/may/10/ai-poses-existential-threat-and-risk-to-health-of-millions-experts-warn

The Guardian. (2023b). *Meta's algorithms did not reduce polarization, study suggests*. https://www.theguardian.com. Retrieved July 2023.

The University of Montana. (2023, July 5). AI tests into top 1% for original creative thinking. *ScienceDaily*. www.sciencedaily.com/releases/2023/07/230705154051.htm. Retrieved 7 July 2023.

Thoppilan, R., De Freitas, D., Hall, J., Shazeer, N., Kulshreshtha, A., Jin, H., Cheng, H. T., Bos, T., Baker, L., Du, Y., & Lee, H. (2022). *LaMDA: Language models for dialog applications*. arXiv preprint arXiv:2201.08239

Throsby, D. (2001). *Economics and culture*. Cambridge University Press.

Tiku, N. (2022). The Google engineer who thinks the company's AI has come to life. *Washington Post*. https://www.washingtonpost.com/technology/2022/06/11/google-ai-lamda-blake-lemoine/. Retrieved 6 January 2023.

Toews R. (2022). 10 AI Predictions For 2023. *Forbes*. https://www.forbes.com/sites/robtoews/2022/12/20/10-ai-predictions-for-2023/. Retrieved June 2023.

Tong, A., Dastin, J., & Hu, K. (2023, November 23). OpenAI researchers warned board of AI breakthrough ahead of CEO ouster, sources say.

Reuters. https://www.reuters.com/technology/exclusive-openai-researchers-warned-board-ai-breakthrough-ahead-ceo-ouster-2022-11-23/

Tononi, G. (2008). Consciousness as integrated information: A provisional manifesto. *Biological Bulletin, 215*(3), 216–242.

Tooze, A. (2021). *Shutdown: How Covid shook the world's economy.* Penguin Press.

Triandis, H. C. (1995). *Individualism & collectivism.* Westview Press.

Tucker, I. (2023) Signal's Meredith Whittaker: 'These are the people who could actually pause AI if they wanted to'. *The Guardian.* https://www.theguardian.com/technology/2023/jun/11/signals-meredith-whittaker-these-are-the-people-who-could-actually-pause-ai-if-they-wanted-to. Retrieved June 2023.

Turilli, M., & Floridi, L. (2009). The ethics of information transparency. *Ethics and Information Technology, 11*(2), 105–112.

Turkle, S. (2011). *Alone together: Why we expect more from technology and less from each other.* Basic Books.

Turner Institute for brain and mental health. (2023). Research to merge human brain cells with AI secures national defence funding. Monash University. https://www.monash.edu/turner-institute/news-and-events/latest-news/2023-articles/research-to-merge-human-brain-cells-with-ai-secures-national-defence-funding. Retrieved July 2023.

Tversky, A., & Kahneman, D. (1974). Judgment under uncertainty: Heuristics and biases. *Science, 185*(4157), 1124–1131.

U.S. Department of Health and Human Services. (2021, December). *The Surgeon General's advisory on social connection.* https://www.hhs.gov/surgeongeneral/priorities/connection/index.html

UN SDG Database. (2023). https://unstats.un.org/sdgs/dataportal/database. Retrieved 22 March 2024.

UN SG. (2023). *UN Interim Report Governing AI.* https://www.un.org/en/ai-advisory-body. Retrieved January 2024.

UNESCO. (2023). *UNESCO to lead global dialogue on ethics of neurotechnology.* https://www.unesco.org/en/articles/unesco-lead-global-dialogue-ethics-neurotechnology. Retrieved July 2023.

Ungar, M. (2011). The social ecology of resilience: Addressing contextual and cultural ambiguity of a nascent construct. *American Journal of Orthopsychiatry, 81*(1), 1–17. https://doi.org/10.1111/j.1939-0025.2010.01067.x

Ungar, M. (2018). Resilience across cultures. *The British Journal of Social Work, 48*(7), 2047–2065. https://doi.org/10.1093/bjsw/bcx103

UNIDO. (2023). *Industrial Analytics Platform.* https://iap.unido.org/articles/what-fourth-industrial-revolution. Retrieved June 2023.

United Nations. (1954). *Report on international definition and measurement of standards and levels of living.*

United Nations. (1948). *Universal Declaration of Human Rights.* https://www.un.org/en/about-us/universal-declaration-of-human-rights

United Nations. (2022). *Beyond GDP: Measuring what counts for economic and social performance.* https://unsceb.org/topics/beyond-gdp. Retrieved December 2023.

United Nations. (2023, October 6). Widening digital gap between developed, developing states threatening to exclude world's poorest from next industrial revolution, speakers tell Second Committee [Press release]. https://press.un.org/en/2023/gaef3587.doc.htm

United Nations. (2024a). General Assembly Adopts Landmark Resolution on Steering Artificial Intelligence towards Global Good, Faster Realization of Sustainable Development. Retrieved from UN Press.

United Nations. (2024b). *The sustainable development goals report 2024.* https://unstats.un.org/sdgs/report/2024/

University of Pennsylvania. (2023). Real or fake: We can learn to spot the difference. *Penn Today.* https://penntoday.upenn.edu/news/penn-seas-real-or-fake-text-we-can-learn-spot-difference. Retrieved July 2023.

Urban, H. B. (2012). The cybernetics of self: Narrative and knowledge in Dianetics. In C. Cusack & P. Digance (Eds.), *Handbook of new religions and cultural production* (pp. 143–168). Brill.

Useem, J. (2022). Why you make bad decisions when you're rushed. *BBC.* https://www.bbc.com/worklife/article/20221012-why-you-make-bad-decisions-when-youre-rushed

Vaillant, G. E. (2012). *Triumphs of experience: The men of the Harvard Grant Study.* Harvard University Press.

van der Stappen, P., & Funk, M. (2021). Let me take over: Variable autonomy for meaningful human control. *Frontiers in Psychology.*

Vansteensel, M. J., Pels, E. G., Bleichner, M. G., Branco, M. P., Denison, T., Freudenburg, Z. V., Gosselaar, P., Leinders, S., Ottens, T. H., Van Den Boom, M. A., Van Rijen, P. C., & Ramsey, N. F. (2016). Fully implanted brain–computer interface in a locked-in patient with ALS. *New England Journal of Medicine, 375*(21), 2060–2066.

Varela, F. J., Thompson, E., & Rosch, E. (1991). *The embodied mind: Cognitive science and human experience.* MIT Press.

Veblen, T. (1919). *The vested interests and the common man.* B. W. Huebsch.

Velu, C., & Putra, F. H. R. (2023). How to introduce quantum computers without slowing economic growth. *Nature, 607*(7941), 7–9. https://doi.org/10.1038/d41586-022-03931-6

Velu, C., Putra, F., Geurtsen, E., Norman, K., & Noble, C. (2022). *Adoption of quantum technologies and business model innovation.* Institute for Manufacturing University.

Vesely, R. (2017). Archimedes. The Stanford Encyclopedia of Philosophy. https://plato.stanford.edu/archives/spr2017/entries/archimedes/
Vicsek, T., & Zafeiris, A. (2012). Collective motion. *Physics Reports, 517*(3–4), 71–140. https://doi.org/10.1016/j.physrep.2012.03.004
Vincent, J. (2023, February 1). This robot barista makes a latte as good as a human, new study finds. *The Verge.* https://www.theverge.com/2023/2/1/23586270/robot-barista-cafe-x-latte-art-coffee-taste-test
von Mises, L. (1949). *Human action: A treatise on economics* (4th ed.). Fox & Wilkes.
Vong, W. K., Wang, W., Orhan, A. E., & Lake, B. M. (2024). *Science, 383,* 504–511.
Vygotsky, L. S. (1978). *Mind in society: The development of higher psychological processes.* Harvard University Press.
Waldinger, R. J., & Schulz, M. S. (2016). The long reach of nurturing family environments: Links with midlife emotion-regulatory styles and late-life security in intimate relationships. *Psychological Science, 27*(11), 1443–1450.
Wallace, J., & Erickson, J. (1992). *Hard drive: Bill Gates and the making of the Microsoft empire.* HarperBusiness.
Walsh, M. (2023). The man behind ChatGPT is wrestling with its limitations. *IEEE Spectrum, 60*(1), 26–29.
Walther, C. (2014). Le Droit au service de l'enfant. Universite de Droit, Aix-Marseille UIII. https://www.theses.fr/2014AIXM1093
Walther, C. (2020a). *Connection in the times of COVID: Corona's call for conscious choices.* Macmillan Palgrave. https://link.springer.com/book/10.1007%2F978-3-030-53641-1
Walther, C. (2020b). *Development, humanitarian aid and social welfare: Social change from the inside out.* Macmillan Palgrave. New York https://link.springer.com/book/10.1007%2F978-3-030-42610-1
Walther, C. (2020c). *Humanitarian Work, Social Change and Human behavior: Compassion for change.* Macmillan Palgrave. https://link.springer.com/book/10.1007%2F978-3-030-45878-2
Walther, C. (2020d). *Development and connection in the time of COVID-19: Corona's call for conscious choices.* Palgrave Macmillan. https://doi.org/10.1007/978-3-030-53641-1
Walther, C. (2021a). *Leadership for social change and development: Inspiration and transformation.* Macmillan Palgrave. https://doi.org/10.1007/978-3-030-76225-4
Walther, C. (2021b). *Technology, social change and human behavior: Influence for impact.* Macmillan Palgrave. https://doi.org/10.1007/978-3-030-70002-7
Walther, C. (2021c). *Leadership for social change and development: Inspiration and transformation.* Macmillan Palgrave. https://doi.org/10.1007/978-3-030-76225-4

Walther, C. (2025). *Artificial Intelligence for inspired action (AI4IA)*. Macmillan Palgrave.
Walton, D. N. (2010a). *Fundamentals of critical argumentation*. Cambridge University Press.
Walton, D. N. (2010b). *Informal logic: A pragmatic approach*. Cambridge University Press.
Wang, O. (2022). Do machines know more about us than we do ourselves? *The New York Times*. https://www.nytimes.com/2023/03/27/science/ai-machine-learning-chatbots.html?smid=li-share. Retrieved May 2023.
Wang, W., Pynadath, D. V., & Hill, S. G. (2016, May). The impact of POMDP-Generated explanations on trust and performance in human-robot teams. In *2016 11th ACM/IEEE International Conference on Human-Robot Interaction (HRI)* (pp. 197–204). IEEE.
Waters, C. N., Zalasiewicz, J., Summerhayes, C., Barnosky, A. D., Poirier, C., Gałuszka, A., Cearreta, A., Edgeworth, M., Ellis, E. C., Ellis, M., Jeandel, C., & Wolfe, A. P. (2016). The Anthropocene is functionally and stratigraphically distinct from the Holocene. *Science, 351*(6269), aad2622. https://doi.org/10.1126/science.aad2622
Watson, J. B. (1913). Psychology as the behaviorist views it. *Psychological Review, 20*(2), 158–177.
Weale, S. (2024). Social media algorithms 'amplifying misogynistic content'. *The Guardian*. https://www.theguardian.com/media/2024/feb/06/social-media-algorithms-amplifying-misogynistic-content?CMP=Share_iOSApp_Other. Retrieved 4 Fevruary 2024.
Weart, S. R. (2018). *The rise of nuclear fear*. Harvard University Press.
Weforum. (2020). Fourth Industrial Revolution. https://www.weforum.org/focus/fourth-industrial-revolution. Retrieved June 2023.
Weizenbaum, J. (1966). ELIZA—a computer program for the study of natural language communication between man and machine. *Communications of the ACM, 9*(1), 36–45. https://doi.org/10.1145/365153.365168
Weizenbaum, J. (1976). *Computer power and human reason: From judgment to calculation*. W. H. Freeman & Co.
Western Governors University. (2022). *All the benefits of Artificial Intelligence*. https://www.wgu.edu/blog/benefits-artificial-intelligence2204.html. Retrieved 7 June 2023.
White, L., & Black, E. (2021). The intricacies of knowledge introduction in behavioral dynamics. *Journal of Behavioral Science Education, 24*(3), 178–195.
Whitehouse, P. J., & Juengst, E. T. (2021). Enhancing neuroplasticity to achieve cognitive remediation in neurodegenerative diseases: Ethical considerations. *Journal of Alzheimer's Disease, 88*(4), 1071–1079. https://doi.org/10.3233/JAD-210415

Wiener, N. (1948). *Cybernetics: Or control and communication in the animal and the machine*. MIT Press.
Wiggers, K. (2023). OpenAI is forming a new team to bring 'superintelligent' AI under control. *Techcrunch*. https://techcrunch.com/2023/07/05/openai-is-forming-a-new-team-to-bring-superintelligent-ai-under-control/amp/?utm_source=www.neatprompts.com&utm_medium=newsletter&utm_campaign=ai-can-think-originally. Retrieved July 2023.
Wiggins, C., & Jones, M. L. (2024). *How data happened: A history from the age of reason to the age of algorithms*.
Wilkerson, R. G., Biskup, E., Lipton, M. L., & Landman, B. A. (2021). The human brain capital initiative: A roadmap to neuroeconomic growth. *Neuron*, 109(6), 939–942. https://doi.org/10.1016/j.neuron.2021.02.002
Wilkinson, R., & Pickett, K. (2009). *The spirit level: Why greater equality makes societies stronger*. Bloomsbury Press.
Wilson, K. (2018). Ripple effect of behavioral changes: Observations and impacts. *Social Dynamics Review*, 14(4), 289–305.
Winner, L. (1986). *The whale and the reactor: A search for limits in an age of high technology*. University of Chicago Press.
Winters, J. (2021). Report: Climate misinformation on Facebook viewed 1.4 million times daily. *Grist*. https://grist.org/accountability/report-climate-misinformation-facebook-viewed-million-times-daily/. Retrieved 4 February 2024.
Woodard, C. R., & Pury, C. L. (2007a). The construct of courage: Categorization and measurement. *Consulting Psychology Journal: Practice and Research*, 59(2), 135–147. https://doi.org/10.1037/1065-9293.59.2.135
World Bank. (2023). *Multidimensional poverty*. https://www.worldbank.org/en/topic/poverty/brief/multidimensional-poverty-measure
World Economic Forum. (2023). *Global Risks Report*. https://www.weforum.org/publications/global-risks-report-2023/. Retrieved January 2024.
World Health Organization. (2024, January 18). *WHO releases AI ethics and governance guidance for large multi-modal models*. https://www.who.int/news/item/18-01-2024-who-releases-ai-ethics-and-governance-guidance-for-large-multi-modal-models
Worrell, D. L., & Appleby, M. C. (2000). Stewardship of natural resources: Definition, ethical and practical aspects. *Journal of Agricultural and Environmental Ethics*, 12(3), 263–277.
Wu, J.-H., & Wang, Y.-M. (2006). Measuring KMS success: A respecification of the DeLone and McLean's model. *Information & Management*, 43(6), 728–739. https://doi.org/10.1016/j.im.2006.03.011

Yalcin, G., Themeli, E., Stamhuis, E., Philipsen, S., & Puntoni, S. (2023). Perceptions of justice by algorithms. *Artif Intell Law (Dordr), 31*(2), 269–292. https://doi.org/10.1007/s10506-022-09312-z. Epub 2022 Apr 5. PMID: 37070085; PMCID: PMC10102053.

Yoshikawa, H., Aber, J. L., & Beardslee, W. R. (2012). The effects of poverty on the mental, emotional, and behavioral health of children and youth: Implications for prevention. *American Psychologist, 67*(4), 272–284. https://doi.org/10.1037/a0028015

Zach, W. (2023, July 14). Study finds ChatGPT boosts worker productivity for writing tasks. *MIT News.* https://news.mit.edu/2023/study-finds-chatgpt-boosts-worker-productivity-writing-0714. Retrieved November 2023.

Zaixuan, Z., Zhansheng, C., & Liying, X. (2022). Artificial intelligence and moral dilemmas: Perception of ethical decision-making in AI. *Journal of Experimental Social Psychology, 101,* 104327, ISSN 0022-1031.https://doi.org/10.1016/j.jesp.2022.104327

Zajonc, R. B. (1968). Attitudinal effects of mere exposure. *Journal of Personality and Social Psychology, 9*(2, Pt.2), 1–27. https://doi.org/10.1037/h0025848

Zakay, D. (2022). *Psychology of decision making in economics.* World Scientific Publishing Company.

Zalasiewicz, J., Waters, C. N., Williams, M., Barnosky, A. D., Cearreta, A., Crutzen, P., Palmesino, J., Rönnskog, A. S., Edgeworth, M., Neal, C., Ellis, E. C., Grinevald, J., & Haff, P. K. (2017). Scale and diversity of the physical technosphere: A geological perspective. *The Anthropocene Review, 4*(1), 9–22. https://doi.org/10.1177/2053019616677743

Zambetta, F., & Sofo, S. (2021). Embodied intelligence: A case for embodied artificial intelligence. *AI & Society, 36*(4), 1187–1198.

Zhang, X., & Chen, Y. (2024). Irrational exuberance: Behavioral economics and the NFT mania. *Journal of Behavioral Finance, 29*(2), 111–127.

Zhang, X., Wang, N., Shen, J., Ji, S., Luo, X., Wang, S., & Wu, Y. (2022). Security matters: A survey on adversarial machine learning. *ACM Computing Surveys (CSUR), 54*(8), 1–38.

Zheng, N., Tang, Y., & Lin, Z. (2024). Sensorimotor learning in embodied AI: Challenges and prospects. *IEEE Transactions on Pattern Analysis and Machine Intelligence, 46*(7), 1583–1598.

Zipf, G. K. (1949). *Human behavior and the principle of least effort: An introduction to human ecology.* Addison-Wesley Press.

Zuboff, S. (2019). *The age of surveillance capitalism: The fight for a human future at the new frontier of power.* PublicAffairs.

Zukav, G. (1979). *Dancing Wu Li Masters.* Bantam Books.

Clare Murphy: So That None of Us Be Missing

AI Now Institute. (2023). *2023 Landscape*. https://ainowinstitute.org/2023-landscape
Brockington, G., Hooker, C., Walker, L., Saldivia, S., & Kendeou, P. (2021). Storytelling increases oxytocin and positive emotions and decreases cortisol levels in preschool-aged children. *Proceedings of the National Academy of Sciences, 118*(21). https://doi.org/10.1073/pnas.2018409118
Haven, K. (2007). *Story Proof*. Libraries Unlimited.
Henderson, A. (1911). *George Bernard Shaw: His life and his works*. Stewart & Kidd.
Leary, L. (2023, May 16). A.I. doom narratives are hiding what we should be most afraid of. *Slate Magazine*. https://slate.com/technology/2023/05/meredith-whittaker-interview-geoffrey-hinton-ai-threats.html
Smith, M. N. (1998, December 16). Dickinson/Norcross Correspondence: Mid-September 1860 (Letter 225). Emily Dickinson Archive. http://archive.emilydickinson.org/correspondence/norcross/l225.html

Michael Jabbour: A Leadership Blueprint

Allahrakha, N. (2023). Balancing cyber-security and privacy: Legal and ethical considerations in the digital age. *Legal Issues in the Digital Age, 4*(2), 78–121.
Biever, C. (2023). ChatGPT broke the Turing test—the race is on for new ways to assess AI. *Nature, 607*(7941), 26–28. https://doi.org/10.1038/d41586-022-03932-5
Bostrom, N. (2014). *Superintelligence: Paths, dangers, strategies*. Oxford University Press.
Brown, B. (2012). *Daring greatly: How the courage to be vulnerable transforms the way we live, love, parent, and lead*. Penguin.
Chang, E. (2020). The Chinese word for crises. LinkedIn. https://www.linkedin.com/pulse/chinese-word-crisis-emily-chang/. Retrieved January 2024.
Craig, C. J. (2016). Technological neutrality: Recalibrating copyright in the information age. *Theoretical Inquiries in Law, 17*(2), 601–632.
Dantzer, R., Cohen, S., Russo, S. J., & Dinan, T. G. (2018). Resilience and immunity. *Brain, Behavior, and Immunity, 74*, 1–4. https://doi.org/10.1016/j.bbi.2018.08.010
European Commission. (n.d.). Ethics guidelines for trustworthy AI. FUTURIUM. https://ec.europa.eu/futurium/en/ai-alliance-consultation. Retrieved 4 February 2024.
Floridi, L. (Ed.). (2019). *The Routledge handbook of philosophy of information*. Routledge.

Frey, C. B., & Osborne, M. A. (2017). The future of employment: How susceptible are jobs to computerization? *Technological Forecasting and Social Change, 114*, 254–280.

Friis, S., & Riley, J. (2023). Eliminating algorithmic bias is just the beginning of equitable AI. HBR. https://hbr.org/2023/09/eliminating-algorithmic-bias-is-just-the-beginning-of-equitable-ai. Retrieved February 2024.

Harper; T. A. (2024) The 100-year extinction panic is back, right on schedule. *New York Times.* https://www.nytimes.com/2024/01/26/opinion/polycrisis-doom-extinction-humanity.html?smid=nytcore-ios-share&referringSource=highlightShare. Retrieved January 2024.

Helliwell, J. F., Layard, R., Sachs, J. D., De Neve, J.-E., Aknin, L. B., & Wang, S. (2024). *World Happiness Report 2024.* University of Oxford.

Horvitz, E. (2017). AI, people, and society. *Science, 357*(6346), 7. https://doi.org/10.1126/science.aao2466

IEEE. (2019). IEEE global initiative releases treatise on ethically aligned design of AI systems. IEEE Global Public Policy. https://globalpolicy.ieee.org/ieee-global-initiative-releases-treatise-on-ethically-aligned-design-of-autonomous-and-intelligent-systems/. Retrieved 4 February 2024.

Johnson, M., & Jones, K. (2019). Uncertainty and stress: The role of cognitive appraisal. *Journal of Applied Psychology, 124*(3), 278–289.

McEwen, B. S. (2008). Central effects of stress hormones in health and disease: Understanding the protective and damaging effects of stress and stress mediators. *European Journal of Pharmacology, 583*(2–3), 174–185. https://doi.org/10.1016/j.ejphar.2007.11.071

Microsoft. (n.d.). Empowering responsible AI practices. Microsoft AI. https://www.microsoft.com/en-us/ai/responsible-ai. Retrieved 4 February 2024.

Millard, R. (2023). AI robots admit they'd run Earth better than clouded humans. *ScienceAlert.* https://www.sciencealert.com/ai-robots-admit-theyd-run-earth-better-than-clouded-humans?utm_source=www.neatprompts.com&utm_medium=newsletter&utm_campaign=japan-s-ai-security-cameras. Retrieved July 2023.

Miller, A. H., & Raison, C. L. (2016). The role of inflammation in depression: From evolutionary imperative to modern treatment target. *Nature Reviews Immunology, 16*(1), 22–34. https://doi.org/10.1038/nri.2015.5

National Institute of Standards and Technology. (2023). Artificial intelligence risk management framework (AI RMF 1.0). https://www.nist.gov/publications/artificial-intelligence-risk-management-framework-ai-rmf-10. Retrieved 4 February 2024.

Nielsen, M. A., & Chuang, I. L. (2010). *Quantum computation and quantum information.* Cambridge University Press. https://doi.org/10.1017/CBO9780511976667

Partnership on AI. (n.d.). *About us.* https://partnershiponai.org/about/. Retrieved 4 February 2024.

Primack, B. A., Shensa, A., Sidani, J. E., Whaite, E. O., Lin, L. Y., Rosen, D., Colditz, J. B., Radovic, A., & Miller, E. (2017). Social media use and perceived social isolation among young adults in the US. *American Journal of Preventive Medicine, 53*(1), 1–8. https://doi.org/10.1016/j.amepre.2017.01.010

Schmager, S., Pappas, I., & Vassilakopoulou, P. (2023). Defining human-centered AI: A comprehensive review of HCAI literature. In *Proceedings of the Mediterranean Conference on Information Systems.*

Shen, Z., Li, R., Fu, Z., Xiao, Z., & Peng, X. (2020). DeepFake detection: Current challenges and next steps. *IEEE Signal Processing Magazine, 37*(1), 110–117.

Smith, A. B. (2017). *The psychology of uncertainty: How to deal with doubt in your life.* HarperCollins.

Smith, J. C., & Johnson, P. (2017). Physiological stress and its impact on cognitive function. In J. C. Smith & P. Johnson (Eds.), *Stress and human performance* (pp. 45–78). CRC Press.

Smith, J., Lee, A., & Park, S. (2020). Designing an educational chatbot for language learning: A user-centric approach. In *Proceedings of the 12th International Conference on Educational Technology and Innovation* (pp. 123–130).

Thompson, R. J., Mata, J., Jaeggi, S. M., Buschkuehl, M., Jonides, J., & Gotlib, I. H. (2021). Concurrent cognitive-emotional deficits among adolescents with depression: A review. *Frontiers in Human Neuroscience, 15,* 638061. https://doi.org/10.3389/fnhum.2021.638061

Turkle, S. (2016). *Reclaiming conversation: The power of talk in a digital age.* Penguin.

Twenge, J. M., Haidt, J., Blake, A. B., Walters, H., Forsyth, P. K., Watts, D., & Bakker, B. N. (2022). That's not very cash money: An analysis of internet speak among Generation Z. PsyArXiv. https://doi.org/10.31234/osf.io/x8q7g

Vodovotz, V. (2023). Chronic stress, inflammation, and societal dysfunction: A global threat. Neuroscience News. https://neurosciencenews.com/stress-inflammation-cognition-social-25738/. Retrieved March 2024.

Vodovotz, Y. (2023b). Inflammation, stress, and the spread of societal dysfunction: A global perspective. *Frontiers in Immunology, 14,* 1035. https://doi.org/10.3389/fimmu.2023.1035

Weizenbaum, J. (1976). *Computer power and human reason: From judgment to calculation.* W. H. Freeman & Co.

WHOQOL Group. (1995). The World Health Organization Quality of Life assessment (WHOQOL): Position paper from the World Health Organization. *Social Science & Medicine, 41*(10), 1403–1409. https://doi.org/10.1016/0277-9536(95)00112-K

World Economic Forum (WEF). (2023). Davos 2023. What you need to know about technology. https://www.weforum.org/agenda/2023/01/davos-emerging-technology-ai/. Retrieved July 2023.

World Happiness Report 2024. (2024). John F. Helliwell, Richard Layard, Jeffrey D. Sachs, Jan-Emmanuel De Neve, Lara B. Aknin, & Shun Wang. Wellbeing Research Centre, University of Oxford.

Yaribeygi, H., Panahi, Y., Sahraei, H., Johnston, T. P., & Sahebkar, A. (2017). The impact of stress on body function: A review. *EXCLI Journal, 16*, 1057–1072. https://doi.org/10.17179/excli2017-480

Zuckerberg, M. (2021). A privacy-focused vision for social networking. *Facebook*. https://www.facebook.com/notes/mark-zuckerberg/a-privacy-focused-vision-for-social-networking/10156700570096634/

INDEX

A

Ability, 4, 5, 19–21, 26, 36, 37, 41, 42, 44, 51, 56, 61, 62, 72, 73, 75, 81, 82, 84, 107, 112–114, 117, 119, 120, 129, 144, 145, 147, 151, 154, 156, 157, 161, 165, 169, 173, 177, 199, 200, 204, 205, 207, 229, 230, 235, 236, 259, 261, 263, 264, 271, 278, 279, 282

Acceptance, 49, 59, 61, 62, 64, 115, 126, 135, 225, 276, 277

Accountability, 8, 21, 42, 56, 61, 62, 64, 68, 82, 84, 109, 135, 141, 147, 149, 152, 159, 162, 165, 167, 212, 242, 251, 276, 277

A-Frame, 10, 32, 59–62, 64, 65, 68, 71, 85, 114, 115, 126, 144, 154, 167, 259, 275, 276

Agency amid AI for All (A4), 44, 49, 59, 64, 81, 263, 264, 266, 267, 273, 277

Agent, 5, 6, 17, 18, 44, 46, 62, 80, 111, 225, 241

Algorithm, 17, 19, 29, 35, 36, 42, 45, 47, 52, 64, 69, 70, 74, 78, 80, 105, 107, 108, 110, 112, 116, 117, 121, 129, 134, 135, 139, 149, 156, 157, 165–168, 171, 174–176, 178, 211, 231, 254, 260, 279

Alignment, 39, 52, 76, 82, 109, 111, 131–135, 152, 156, 233, 250, 258–260, 274, 276, 280

Altruism, 250

Appreciation, 32, 51, 61, 64, 135, 138, 156, 219, 233, 259, 273, 276, 277

Artificial intelligence (AI), 2–4, 8, 11, 14, 17, 21, 42, 44, 71, 77–79, 83, 84, 105, 109–111, 118, 121, 135, 145, 150, 154, 159, 163, 214, 228, 239, 240, 254, 261, 276

Artificial Intelligence for Inspired Action (AI4IA), 16

© The Editor(s) (if applicable) and The Author(s), under exclusive license to Springer Nature Switzerland AG 2024
C. C. Walther, *Human Leadership for Humane Technology*,
https://doi.org/10.1007/978-3-031-67823-3

Authenticity, 39, 40, 50, 84, 137, 138, 140, 143, 153, 159, 255, 256, 259, 260, 274, 276, 280
Awareness, 2, 4, 10, 15, 26, 33, 34, 37, 40, 47, 54, 60, 62, 64, 65, 75, 82, 84, 106, 112, 117, 119, 120, 135, 145, 146, 149, 156, 164, 173, 207, 259, 276, 277
Awe, 67, 216, 284

B
Behavior, 3–5, 11, 15, 16, 22, 25, 29–31, 33, 34, 37–39, 49, 53–60, 65–70, 72–74, 76, 77, 81–83, 104, 107, 111, 112, 119, 120, 126, 127, 132, 134, 135, 146, 149, 150, 152, 153, 156, 158–160, 165, 170–172, 204, 205, 209, 210, 217, 230, 241, 244, 249–251, 253–256, 258, 259, 262
Benevolence, 152, 153
Benevolent Brain and Body Buddy (B4), 262, 264, 266, 267
Bias, 10, 35, 36, 42, 74, 135, 144, 147, 149, 152, 157, 160, 170, 171, 175, 201, 262, 273
Brain, 14, 15, 18, 32–38, 42, 43, 47, 55, 72, 75, 76, 79, 81, 105, 106, 110, 113, 121, 142, 145, 150, 151, 168, 173, 200, 203, 250, 262–264, 271, 279, 284
Brain computer interface (BCI), 16, 18, 75, 76, 112, 177
Bystander, 38, 65, 67, 273

C
Centaur, 113, 114
Change, 3, 11, 14, 16, 25–27, 34, 37, 41, 54, 58–60, 64–70, 72, 80–82, 84, 104, 115, 119, 121, 124–126, 130, 135–139, 141, 143, 146, 151, 161, 164, 165, 177, 205, 206, 208, 210, 213, 218, 219, 221, 222, 232, 233, 238, 239, 242, 251, 253, 257, 261, 265, 268, 269, 271, 273, 274, 276, 277, 286
Choices, 5, 9, 11, 22, 24, 26, 28, 32, 36, 41, 54, 55, 57, 65, 70, 72, 74, 75, 82, 114, 116, 117, 126–128, 134, 139, 147, 148, 151, 154, 156, 168, 173, 198, 203, 235, 251, 264, 267, 273–278, 280, 284
Citizenship, 23, 31, 56, 57, 62, 65, 71, 165, 173, 255, 258, 260, 263, 274, 276
Commitment, 8, 56, 57, 65, 68, 71, 78, 166, 211, 213, 215, 217, 220, 237, 251, 277
Common Good, 23, 24, 31, 59, 68, 81, 82, 85, 122, 131, 135, 141, 164, 177, 201, 253, 260, 261, 266, 274, 275, 277
Compassion, 23, 32, 56, 57, 62, 65–67, 71, 157, 159, 173, 233, 251, 255, 258–260, 274, 276
Complementarity, 6, 26, 27, 29, 61, 115, 125, 137, 145, 165, 173, 216, 263, 267, 269
Connection, 7, 8, 25, 27, 28, 30–33, 35, 37, 38, 40–42, 45, 50, 53, 55, 57, 62, 63, 72, 82, 105, 111, 112, 138, 146, 157, 199, 203, 229, 230, 239, 240, 250, 259, 270, 271, 277
Conscience, 120, 161, 213
Conscientiousness, 5, 32, 55–57, 62, 65, 71, 108, 120, 145, 173, 255, 259, 274, 276
Consciousness, 5, 17, 40, 44, 51, 59, 104–110, 112, 118–120, 126,

149, 154, 178, 243, 262, 273, 275
Continuum, 10, 12, 26, 55, 81, 84, 104, 126, 277, 280
Conundrum, 28, 127, 149, 161, 167, 177, 258
Courage, 34, 54–57, 65, 66, 71, 159, 173, 204, 207, 221, 255, 259, 260, 274
Cyborg, 114

D

Data, 5–9, 11, 17–19, 30, 44, 45, 47, 48, 50, 54, 69, 72, 76, 78, 80, 106, 107, 109, 110, 112, 117, 121, 148, 149, 156, 160, 165, 168–178, 198, 200, 208–212, 237, 241, 242, 256, 257, 260, 262, 264, 265, 275, 284
Dependency, 83, 113, 114, 144, 145, 155, 178, 255, 278, 284

E

Economic growth, 47, 124, 141, 252
Economy, 124, 253
Emotion, 11, 31–36, 38, 39, 42, 43, 55, 57, 59, 60, 65–67, 72, 76–79, 85, 105, 107, 109, 111, 115, 144, 148, 152, 158, 171, 197, 207, 253, 255, 257, 259, 260, 262, 276
Exclusion, 7, 9, 84, 170, 174, 176–178
Experience, 14, 19, 25, 28, 31–33, 38, 41, 44, 47, 56, 59, 62, 64, 67, 69, 71, 104–108, 110, 119, 120, 126, 139, 142, 150, 156, 157, 173, 174, 176, 204, 206, 208, 212, 214, 216–218, 222, 226, 228, 229, 231, 232, 234–239, 249, 260, 269, 276, 286
Exponential, 7, 71, 83, 123, 159, 160, 168, 205, 233
Exposure, 25, 42, 74, 77, 116, 117, 147, 215, 264, 272, 278

G

Garbage in, Garbage out (GIGO), 6, 108, 133, 170, 171, 173, 178, 267, 275, 277
Generative AI (GenAI), 9, 17, 69, 129, 130, 137, 140, 169, 173, 175, 235, 237–239, 241, 242
Global, 3, 13, 19, 20, 28, 30, 31, 45, 48, 50, 55–57, 71, 78, 82, 84, 106, 111, 112, 124, 128, 130, 141, 155, 161, 162, 203, 208, 212, 237, 243, 250, 251, 253, 265, 268, 271, 281, 285
Glocal, 111, 130
Growth, 7, 8, 10, 15, 20, 31, 43, 47, 83, 123–125, 159, 160, 162, 164, 214, 215, 223–225, 227, 231, 239, 252, 267, 281

H

Humane, 21, 55, 132, 197, 255, 277, 282
Humanity, 8–10, 20, 22, 31, 50, 51, 57, 60, 62, 71, 81–83, 104–106, 111, 118, 128, 133, 149, 158, 166, 177, 213, 215, 232, 233, 238–240, 242, 243, 248, 253, 258, 259, 263, 267–270, 273–276, 280, 282–284
Hybrid, 5, 9–11, 21, 24, 26, 36, 43, 46, 47, 55, 60, 65, 68, 77, 82, 85, 104, 117, 119, 126, 130, 133, 135, 146, 158, 165, 178, 196, 197, 236, 243, 244, 252,

260, 261, 266, 271, 273–275, 278, 280
Hybrid alignment conundrum, 83, 122, 134, 178, 285

I
Impact, 2, 3, 12, 14, 16, 22, 29, 33–35, 44–46, 48, 49, 53, 55, 59, 69, 79, 83, 84, 104, 121, 125, 127, 130–132, 135, 137, 139, 141, 146, 147, 156, 204–206, 208, 215, 217, 219, 221, 222, 224, 225, 231, 232, 234, 236, 240, 250, 256–258, 265, 268, 272, 277, 285
Inclusion, 7, 9, 176, 177, 241, 251, 252
Inertia, 3, 147, 160, 273
Infinite game, 7, 8, 10, 38, 105, 218–220, 274
Infinity, 85
Influence, 2–5, 7, 9–11, 13, 15, 22, 25–37, 39, 41, 44–46, 49, 54, 55, 58–60, 63, 64, 66–72, 74–79, 82–86, 104, 108, 116–119, 121, 126, 127, 130, 131, 135, 137, 139, 144–146, 150, 156, 157, 161, 174, 176, 204, 218, 222, 241, 250, 256–259, 263, 265, 271, 273, 277, 280, 284, 285
Innovation, 2, 7, 8, 12, 15, 16, 19–21, 31, 47, 60, 82, 83, 104, 119–125, 128, 132, 133, 141, 155, 159, 162, 175, 198, 211, 217, 220, 225, 232, 233, 238, 239, 243, 252, 256, 257, 272, 274, 277, 278
Inspiration, 51, 66–68, 80
Inspiration Incubator (i@i), 266, 267
Integrity, 21, 152–154, 158, 159, 215, 254

J
Jagged frontier, 113

L
Large language model (LLM), 5, 6, 8, 9, 16–19, 45, 46, 48, 50, 69, 72–74, 79, 83, 108, 109, 111–114, 116, 127–130, 143, 159, 169, 170, 174, 175, 210, 230, 280, 282
Leadership, 3, 7, 12, 21, 22, 131, 132, 177, 203, 205–209, 212, 238, 239, 251, 256, 261, 275–277, 281, 283
Local, 106, 111, 124, 271
Loneliness, 42, 43, 74, 143, 157, 208, 260, 271, 272

M
m4-matrix, 27, 29, 30, 38, 41, 45, 59, 83, 84, 104, 141, 250, 264, 269, 270, 273, 275, 285
macro, 24, 27, 28, 30, 45, 47, 52, 58, 82, 85, 104, 141, 147, 196, 250, 251, 262, 265, 285, 286
macro-questions, 3, 118, 196, 243, 274
meso, 27, 28, 30, 45, 47, 52, 58, 59, 82, 85, 104, 141, 147, 196, 250, 265, 285, 286
meta, 13, 27, 28, 30, 46, 48, 52, 58, 59, 82, 85, 104, 111, 141, 147, 196, 250, 251, 265, 285
micro, 24, 27, 28, 30, 38, 39, 45, 46, 52, 58, 59, 67, 82, 84, 85, 104, 111, 141, 147, 196, 250, 262, 265, 281, 285, 286
Motivation, 22, 56, 57, 69, 145, 168, 218–220, 224, 228, 242, 255
Multidimensionality, 61

Multidisciplinary, 16, 25, 27, 50, 110, 119, 243, 263–266, 284

N

Neuroscience, 72, 75, 77, 79
Neurotechnology, 72, 78
Norms, 4, 11, 22, 28, 49, 52–55, 57–59, 67–69, 74, 107, 127, 135, 150, 163, 164, 169, 196, 218, 249, 251, 257, 260, 267

O

Opportunity, 7, 11, 28, 41, 44, 47, 49, 50, 65, 72, 119, 121–123, 144, 147, 151, 156, 210, 218, 220, 221, 227, 229, 232, 239, 248, 260, 268, 269, 271, 277, 281, 284
Optimization, 25, 26, 41, 47, 52, 76, 116, 253, 261, 264, 265, 267
Oxymoron, 153

P

Paradigm, 24, 26, 60, 165, 216, 238, 261
Participation, 49, 69, 71, 177
Perception, 22, 25, 32, 33, 36, 37, 45, 46, 49, 63, 67, 69, 80, 104, 106–109, 115, 117, 119, 121, 136–139, 143, 144, 149, 150, 154, 158, 173, 196, 217, 230, 252, 258, 259, 269, 281
Personal leadership, 21, 177, 275
Perspective, 13, 25, 26, 36, 37, 46, 57, 60, 65, 67–69, 83, 86, 104, 105, 110, 114, 121, 122, 127, 137, 140, 150, 152, 153, 158, 165, 173, 205, 213, 215, 219, 222, 234–237, 248, 259, 263, 268–270, 273, 274, 277, 279, 284
Perspective, Optimization, Zeniths, Exposure (POZE), 24, 25, 85, 115, 178, 286
Persuasion, 68, 72, 73, 75–78, 115, 143, 223
Polycrisis, 268
Potential, 6–8, 14, 20, 23, 24, 26, 29, 33, 39–41, 44, 45, 47, 49, 50, 52, 61, 68, 72, 76, 78, 82, 83, 120–122, 127, 128, 132, 140, 144, 146, 149, 151, 155, 159, 163, 165, 169, 173, 174, 176–178, 212, 216, 221, 226, 227, 229–231, 233, 235, 237, 239, 240, 242–244, 249, 260, 262, 264, 266, 267, 271, 274, 278, 280, 281, 285
Poverty, 4, 13–15, 20, 45, 47, 48, 127, 163, 251, 252, 275
Prosocial AI, 23, 24, 82, 156, 165, 261, 263, 266, 267, 274, 285
Purpose, 8, 16, 21, 35, 41, 42, 68, 83, 84, 130, 131, 143, 144, 153, 160, 175, 196, 197, 203, 204, 208, 212, 217, 220–222, 228, 231, 233, 242, 261, 275, 279, 283, 286

Q

Quadruple Bottom Line, 131, 141, 172, 261, 286
Quality, 11, 14, 23, 39, 82, 84, 113, 116, 117, 125, 138, 139, 141, 143, 151, 152, 154, 155, 168, 169, 174, 206, 221, 252, 269, 273–275, 281, 282
Quantity, 116, 117, 143, 155, 168, 169, 174, 243, 282
Quantum computing, 19
Quantum physics, 71, 119, 198, 215

R

Regulation, 25, 35, 49, 58, 70, 78, 149, 159–163, 165, 166, 172, 177, 178

Resilience, 8, 40, 146, 152, 156, 221, 252, 275, 278

Risk, 10, 14, 27, 30, 39, 41, 42, 45–47, 49–52, 62, 64, 72, 74, 77, 78, 108, 114, 117, 118, 122, 123, 126, 132, 133, 136, 140, 141, 143, 145, 151, 156, 159, 160, 163, 164, 166, 175, 176, 201, 207, 209, 218, 226, 229, 231, 232, 248–250, 256, 260, 263, 268, 271, 282

S

Social Accounting Matrix 4.0 (SAM 4.0), 264–267

Society, 3–5, 7, 11, 21–24, 26, 28, 30, 31, 41, 45, 46, 48, 49, 53, 56, 57, 60, 71, 81–83, 85, 118, 120–122, 124, 126, 135, 137, 141, 143, 144, 146, 149–151, 163, 165–167, 173, 175, 196, 197, 213, 240, 242, 244, 248, 251, 252, 255, 256, 258, 263, 268, 272, 274, 276, 277, 279–281, 283–286

Story, 6, 60, 133, 175, 197–202, 216, 221, 238, 252, 275

Strength, 38, 40, 84, 263, 281

Sustainability, 79, 125, 213, 252

Sustainable Development Goals (SDG), 14, 266

Synchronization, 29, 111, 112, 114, 118, 121

Synchrony, 27, 51, 79, 111, 112

Synergy, 65, 115, 133

System, 5, 8, 11, 14, 16–18, 21, 23, 25, 27–30, 33, 35, 41, 42, 44–46, 48, 49, 53–55, 63, 67, 69, 72, 76, 78–80, 82, 106–109, 112, 116, 117, 119, 121, 124–126, 132–134, 142–144, 146, 147, 149, 152, 154–157, 160–163, 166, 169–171, 173, 175–177, 201, 204, 230–233, 237, 238, 241, 251, 253–255, 257, 268, 271, 272, 278, 281, 282, 284

T

Technoprocene, 4, 118, 150, 286

Trust, 8, 41, 52, 57, 63, 73, 118, 137, 139, 141–145, 151–153, 158–160, 178, 218, 220, 223, 225, 228, 250, 252, 254, 255, 268

U

Uncertainty, 8, 40, 42, 57, 60, 65, 126, 152, 216, 268, 271–273, 276, 278

Universal citizenship, 66

V

Value, 2, 22–24, 31, 43, 54–56, 59, 67, 81–84, 135–140, 143, 147, 153, 205, 213, 218, 221, 232, 253, 257, 276, 280, 281

Values in, Values out (VIVO), 6, 108, 133, 178, 275, 277, 280, 286

Vulnerability, 21, 39, 40, 46, 65, 84, 145, 153, 156–159, 178, 239, 243, 255, 259, 261, 274–276, 282

W

Wearable, 72, 262, 285

Win-Win-Win-Win (*Win4*), 68, 72, 196, 244, 248, 250, 260, 267, 286

Z
Zenith, 25, 269, 270, 275

Printed in the USA
CPSIA information can be obtained
at www.ICGtesting.com
CBHW060146231024
16263CB00004B/97

9 783031 678226